Crafting and Implementing Strategy
What Every Manager Should Know

Crafting and Implementing Strategy
What Every Manager Should Know

Arthur A. Thompson, Jr.

A. J. Strickland III

IRWIN

Chicago • Bogotá • Boston • Buenos Aires • Caracas

London • Madrid • Mexico City • Sydney • Toronto

IRWIN
Concerned About Our Environment

In recognition of the fact that our company is a large end-user of fragile yet replenishable resources, we at IRWIN can assure you that every effort is made to meet or exceed Environmental Protection Agency (EPA) recommendations and requirements for a "greener" workplace.

To preserve these natural assets, a number of environmental policies, both companywide and department-specific, have been implemented. From the use of 50% recycled paper in our textbooks to the printing of promotional materials with recycled stock and soy inks to our office paper recycling program, we are committed to reducing waste and replacing environmentally unsafe products with safer alternatives.

Senior sponsoring editor:	*Kurt L. Strand*
Senior developmental editor:	*Libby Rubenstein*
Senior marketing manager:	*Kurt Messersmith*
Project editor:	*Mary Conzachi*
Production manager:	*Laurie Kersch*
Interior designer:	*Annette Spadoni*
Cover designer:	*Steven Vena*
Art coordinator:	*Mark Malloy*
Compositor:	*The Clarinda Co.*
Typeface:	*10/12 Times Roman*
Printer:	*R. R. Donnelley & Sons Company*

Library of Congress Cataloging-in-Publication Data

Thompson, Arthur A., 1940–
    Crafting and implementing strategy : what every manager
should know / Arthur A. Thompson, A. J. Strickland.
       p. cm.
    Includes index.
    ISBN 0-256-16329-4
    1. Strategic planning. 2. Corporate planning. I. Strickland, A.
J. (Alonzo J.) II. Title.
HD30.28.T527   1995
658.4′012—dc20   94–14310

Printed in the United States of America
1 2 3 4 5 6 7 8 9 0 DO 1 0 9 8 7 6 5 4

To Hasseline and Kitty

CONTENTS

What Is Strategy and Who Is Responsible for Devising It?

A strategy is a commitment to undertake one set of actions rather than another.

Sharon M. Oster
Professor, Yale University

This book is about the managerial tasks of crafting, implementing, and executing company strategies. A company's strategy consists of the array of competitive moves and business approaches managers employ to produce successful company performance. Strategy, in effect, is management's game plan for strengthening the organization's market position, pleasing customers, and achieving performance targets. Managers devise strategies because of a compelling need to shape how the company's business is conducted and to provide a basis for uniting actions and decision making in various parts of the organization. The strategy managers decide on indicates that "among all the paths and actions we could have chosen, we have decided to follow this route and rely upon these business approaches." Without a strategy, a manager has no thought-out course to follow, no road map to manage by, no unified action program to produce the intended results.

Management's game plan for running the company successfully involves every major function and department—purchasing, production, finance, marketing, human resources, R & D. Each has a role in the strategy. The strategy-making challenge is to mold all of a company's decisions and actions into a cohesive *pattern*. Current strategy is indicated by the prevailing pattern of competitive moves and business approaches; any new moves and approaches being considered signal how the current strategy may be embellished or recast.

Crafting and implementing strategy are core management functions. Among all the things managers do, few functions affect company performance more fundamentally than how well its management team charts the company's long-term direction, develops competitively effective strategic moves and business approaches, and then executes the chosen strategy in ways that produce the targeted results. Indeed, *good strategy and good strategy execution are the most trustworthy signs of good management*. Managers don't deserve a gold-star for designing shrewd strategies but failing to carry them out well—weak implementation opens the door for company performance to fall short of

Powerful execution of a powerful strategy is not only a proven recipe for business success but also the best test of excellent management.

1

full potential. Competent execution of a mediocre strategy scarcely qualifies managers for a gold-star award either. Only when managers combine good strategy-making with good strategy execution will actual results closely approach maximum potential.

Granted, good strategy combined with good strategy execution provides no *guarantee* that a company will avoid periods of weak performance. Sometimes it takes several years for management's efforts to show good results; sometimes well-managed organizations have performance problems because of adverse conditions beyond management's ability to foresee or react to. But neither the "we need more time" reason nor the bad luck of adverse events excuses weak performance year after year. Management has the responsibility to adjust to unexpectedly tough conditions by undertaking strategic defenses and business approaches that can overcome adversity. Indeed, the essence of good strategy-making is to build a market position strong enough and an organization capable enough to produce successful performance despite unforeseeable events, potent competition, and internal problems. The rationale for applying the twin standards of good strategy-making and good strategy execution to determine whether a company is well managed is therefore compelling: The better conceived a company's strategy and the more proficient its execution, the greater the chance the company will be a solid performer.

▶ WHO IS RESPONSIBLE FOR CRAFTING AND IMPLEMENTING A COMPANY'S STRATEGY?

A company's chief executive officer (CEO), as captain of the ship, has the heaviest burden for crafting and implementing company strategy. The title of CEO carries with it the mantles of chief direction-setter, chief objective-setter, chief strategy-maker, and chief strategy-implementer for the total enterprise. Primary responsibility for leading the tasks of formulating and implementing a strategic plan for the whole organization necessarily rests with the CEO, even though many other managers normally have a hand in the process. What the CEO views as strategically important usually is reflected in the company's strategy, and the CEO customarily puts a personal stamp of approval on big strategic decisions and actions.

Vice presidents (VPs) for production, marketing, finance, human resources, and other functional departments have important strategy-making and strategy-implementing responsibilities as well. Normally, the production VP has a lead role in developing the company's production strategy, the marketing VP oversees the marketing strategy effort, the financial VP is in charge of devising an appropriate financial strategy, and so on. Usually, functional vice presidents also help devise key elements of the overall company strategy and develop major new strategic initiatives, working closely with the CEO to hammer out a consensus and to coordinate various pieces of the strategy more effectively. Only in the smallest, owner-managed companies is the strategy-making, strategy-implementing task small enough for a single manager to craft and direct implementation of *all* the key elements of a company's strategy.

However, managerial positions with strategy-making and strategy-implementing responsibility are by no means restricted to CEOs, vice presidents, and owner–entrepreneurs. Every major organizational unit in a company—business unit, division, staff support group, plant, or district office—has either a leading or supporting role in the company's strategic game plan. And the manager in charge of that organizational unit, with guidance from superiors, usually ends up crafting some or most of the unit's business plan and directing implementation of the unit's designated strategic role in the company's overall strategic plan. While managers farther down in the managerial hierarchy obviously have a narrower, more specific strategy-making/strategy-implementing role than managers closer to the top, every manager, to one extent or another, is a strategy-maker and strategy-implementer for the area he or she has authority over and supervises.

> **Every company manager has a strategy-making, strategy-implementing role — it is flawed thinking to view strategy as solely a top-management responsibility.**

Involving middle- and lower-echelon managers as integral members of a company's strategy-making/strategy-implementing team is a necessity as a company's operations become more geographically scattered and diversified. The bigger a company's operations, the more infeasible and unwieldy it is for a few senior executives to personally craft or decide how to implement all the actions and programs that round out the total strategy. Managers in the corporate office seldom know enough about the situational specifics in all geographical areas and operating units to wisely prescribe or direct every move made in the field. This is why top-level managers commonly push some strategy-making responsibility down to managerial subordinates who head the organizational subunits where specific strategic results must be achieved. Delegating a strategy-making role to on-the-scene managers charged with implementing whatever strategic moves are made in their areas fixes accountability for strategic success or failure. When the managers who implement the strategy are also its architects, it is hard for them to shift the blame or make excuses if they don't achieve the target results. And, having participated in developing the strategy they are responsible for implementing and executing, they usually have stronger buy-in and support for the strategy, an essential condition for effective strategy execution.

In diversified companies where the strategies of several different businesses have to be managed, there are usually four distinct levels of strategy managers:

- The chief executive officer and other senior corporation-level executives who have primary responsibility and personal authority for strategic decisions affecting the total enterprise and the collection of individual businesses the enterprise may have diversified into.

- Managers who have profit-and-loss responsibility for one specific business unit and who have been delegated a major leadership role in formulating and implementing strategy for that unit.

- Functional area managers within a given business unit who have direct authority over a major piece of the business (manufacturing, marketing and sales, finance, R&D, personnel) and whose role is to support the business unit's overall strategy with strategic actions in their own areas.

- Managers of major operating units (plants, sales districts, local offices) who have on-the-scene responsibility for developing the details of strategic efforts in their areas and for implementing and executing their designated piece of the overall strategic plan at the grassroots level.

Single-business enterprises need no more than three of these levels (business-level strategy managers, functional area strategy managers, and operating-level strategy managers). In a large single-business company, the team of strategy managers consists of the chief executive, who functions as chief strategist with final authority over both strategy and its implementation; the vice presidents in charge of key functions (R&D, production, marketing, finance, human resources, etc.); plus as many operating-unit managers of the various plants, sales offices, distribution centers, and staff support departments as it takes to handle the company's scope of operations. Proprietorships, partnerships, and owner-managed enterprises, however, typically have only one or two key strategists since in small-scale enterprises the whole strategy-making/strategy-implementing function can be handled by a few people.

Managerial jobs involving strategy formulation and implementation abound in not-for-profit organizations as well. In federal and state government, heads of local, district, and regional offices function as strategy-makers and strategy-implementers in their efforts to respond to the needs and situations of the areas they serve (a district manager in Portland may need a slightly different strategy than a district manager in Orlando). In municipal government, the heads of various departments (fire, police, water and sewer, parks and recreation, health, etc.) have primary strategy-making/strategy-implementing roles because they have line authority for the operations of their departments and thus can influence departmental objectives, the formation of a strategy to achieve these objectives, and how the strategy is implemented.

Managerial jobs with strategy-making/strategy-implementing roles are thus the norm rather than the exception. The job of crafting and implementing strategy touches virtually every managerial job in one way or another, at one time or another. Crafting and implementing strategy is basic to the task of managing; it is not something just top-level managers deal with.

■ ROLE AND TASKS OF STRATEGIC PLANNERS

If senior and middle managers have the lead roles in strategy-making and strategy-implementing in their areas of responsibility, what's left for strategic planners to do? Is there a legitimate place in big companies for a strategic planning department staffed with specialists in planning and strategic analysis? The answer is yes. But the planning department's role should consist chiefly of collecting information that strategy-makers need, doing background analyses, establishing and administering an annual strategy review cycle whereby managers reconsider and refine their strategic plans, and coordinating the review and approval of the strategic plans developed for all the various parts of the company. Strategic planners can help managers at all levels crystallize strategic issues that need to be addressed; they can provide useful data, help analyze industry and competitive conditions, and develop assessments of the company's strategic performance. But strategic planners should not be used to relieve line managers of the responsibility to make strategic plans for their own operating units.

When strategic planners are asked to go beyond providing staff assistance and actually prepare a strategic plan for management's consideration, any of three adverse consequences may occur. One, weak managers will gladly avoid dealing with the tough strategic problems in their areas and let strategic planners do their strategic thinking for them. But planners, however expert they may be in strategic analysis and the mechanics of crafting strategy, can't be expected to know as much about all the ins and outs of the situation as on-the-scene managers who are responsible for staying on top of

It is a mistake to have professional strategic planners prepare strategies for someone else to implement.

things in their assigned area on a daily basis. This puts them at a disadvantage not only in devising sound action recommendations but also in considering the difficulties of competently implementing what they recommend. A company that allows managers to shift strategic problems in their areas onto someone else's desk deludes its managers into thinking they shouldn't be held responsible for crafting a strategy for their own organizational unit or for devising solutions to strategic problems in their area of responsibility. Two, giving planners responsibility for strategy-making and line managers responsibility for implementing someone else's recommended actions makes it hard to fix accountability for poor results. Planners can place the blame for poor performance on weak implementation; implementers can claim the problem rests with bad strategy.

Three, when line managers lack an ownership stake in or strong personal commitment to the strategic plan developed by company planners, they are prone to consider it as just a paper document, give it lip service, and then let most of the planners' recommendations die through inaction. The hard truth is that when the strategy-making function is handed off to a strategic planning staff (or to a task force of lower-level managers), the door is opened for senior managers to have little buy-in to what is proposed. Skepticism or disagreement over planners' recommendations breeds inaction. Implementation never becomes a priority and strategic planning starts to be seen as a useless bureaucratic exercise. All three conse-

Lukewarm buy-in to the strategy proposals of strategic planners is a guaranteed plan-killer.

quences are unacceptable: Formal efforts to develop company strategies get a bum rap as ineffective, company managers don't develop the skills or the discipline to think strategically about the business, and there's much bigger risk of organizational drift and a strategy-making vacuum.

On the other hand, when line managers are expected to be the chief strategy-makers and strategy-implementers for the areas they head, their own strategy and their own implementation approach are put to the test of workability. Consequently, their buy-in to proposed strategic moves and business approaches in their area of responsibility and how to implement them becomes a given. There's good reason to expect them to commit the time and resources needed to making their strategies work. (Their annual performance reviews and perhaps even their future careers with the organization are at risk if their strategies often fail or if target results in their area are frequently not achieved!) When those who craft strategy must also implement that strategy, there's no question who is accountable for results. Furthermore, delegating authority for crafting and implementing the strategy of an organizational unit to the unit manager pushes strategic decisions down to the manager closest to the scene of the action who *should* know best what to do. Unit managers who consistently prove incapable of crafting and implementing good strategies and achieving target results have to be moved to less responsible positions.

∎ THE STRATEGIC ROLE OF THE BOARD OF DIRECTORS

Since lead responsibility for crafting and implementing strategy falls to key managers, the chief strategic role of an organization's board of directors is to see that the overall managerial task of crafting and implementing strategy is competently done. Boards of directors normally review important strategic moves and officially approve the strategic plans submitted by senior management—a procedure that makes the board ultimately responsible for the strategic actions taken. But directors rarely can or should play a hands-on role in developing competitive moves and business approaches. The immediate task of directors in ratifying strategy and new direction-setting moves is to ensure that the proposed strategic actions have been adequately analyzed and are superior to available alternatives; flawed proposals are customarily withdrawn for revision by management.

> The role of the board of directors is to critically appraise and ultimately approve strategic action plans but rarely, if ever, to develop the details.

The longer-range task of directors is to evaluate the caliber of senior executives' strategy-making/strategy-implementing skills. The board must determine whether the current CEO is doing a good job as chief strategist and organizational leader (as a basis for awarding salary increases and bonuses and deciding on retention or removal) and must evaluate the strategic skills of other senior executives in line to succeed the current CEO. In recent years at General Motors, IBM, American Express, Goodyear, and Compaq Computer, company directors concluded that executives were not adapting their company's strategy fast enough and fully enough to the changes sweeping their markets, pressured the CEO to resign, and installed new leadership to provide the impetus for strategic renewal. Board members who fail to do their job of reviewing the strategy-making/strategy-implementing skills of senior executives face embarrassment or even lawsuits when an outdated strategy causes company performance to sour and management fails to come up with a promising turnaround strategy.

▶ WHY THIS BOOK HAS RELEVANCE FOR EVERY MANAGER

If every manager in a company has a strategy-making/strategy-implementing role, then every manager needs to understand basic strategic concepts and principles, have a working acquaintance with the tools of strategic analysis, and be familiar with the fundamentals of crafting and implementing strategic initiatives and business approaches. The more managers know about the whys and hows of good strategy making and good strategy implementation, the better equipped they will be to perform their strategy-related tasks and the more they can contribute to developing and executing a winning company strategy.

This book strives to provide managers with what they need to know to do a first-rate job of crafting and implementing strategies in their areas of authority and responsibility. The content is suitable for a wide spectrum of managers—from experienced practitioners who want to refresh or sharpen their strategy-making and strategy-implementing skills to managers who have had no systematic training in the rigors of strategic thinking. In our experience, many managers have only a dim idea of what crafting and implementing strategy involve. This is not so much their fault or shortcoming as it is that their college degrees were in, say, engineering or liberal arts rather than in business, and because scarcely any corporate training programs focus on the concepts and techniques of crafting and implementing strategy. Even managers who've been to business school may lack strong backgrounds in the concepts and techniques of strategic thinking and strategic management. This is because the subject matter of crafting and implementing strategy is predominantly of post-1980 vintage. Strategic management is the youngest management discipline, and business school courses in the subject have undergone wholesale revolution in the last 10 years. While many managers have gained a nodding acquaintance with strategy concepts from reading articles in the business press, such fragmented and sporadic glimpses into this or that aspect of strategic management are not an effective substitute for a comprehensive, current, mainstream treatment like we provide here.

▶ THE CONTENT AND ORGANIZATION OF THIS BOOK

This book examines every key element of crafting, implementing, and executing company strategies. There's coverage of defining the business, developing missions and strategic visions, setting strategic and financial objectives, conducting industry and competitive analysis, doing company situation analysis, benchmarking, activity-based costing, the basic types of competitive strategies, ways to create sustainable competitive advantage, evaluating business diversification, building core competencies, reengineering core business processes, the strategy-related pros and cons of various organization designs, creating a strategy-supportive budget, devising strategy-supportive policies and operating procedures, instituting best practices and total quality management programs, reshaping corporate cultures, and tying incentives and rewards to achieving strategic performance targets.

In the first two chapters we present an overview of the strategic management process and examine the tasks of developing a strategic vision, setting objectives, and actually crafting a strategy. We'll also discuss ethical as well as market-related and company-related concerns that shape company strategy. In Chapters 3 and 4 we cover the techniques of industry and competitive analysis and company situation analysis. Chapter 5 describes the importance of sustainable competitive advantage and how the various types of competitive strategies rely on offensive moves to build competitive advantage and on defensive moves to protect competitive advantage. Chapter 6 discusses the complexities of matching a company's strategy to its circumstances, both external and internal. In Chapter 7 we survey the generic types of corporate diversification strategies and explain how a company can diversify in ways that create or compound competitive advantage for its core business units. Chapter 8 focuses on the techniques and procedures for assessing the strategic attractiveness of a diversified company's business portfolio.

The last three chapters spotlight strategy implementation and execution—what managers have to do to convert strategic plans into actions and good results. Chapter 9 deals with building a capable organization—selecting able people for key positions, creating core competencies and unique organizational capabilities, reengineering business processes, and developing an organization structure conducive to effective strategy execution. Chapter 10 looks at the roles of budget allocations, policies, best practices, internal support systems, and strategically appropriate reward systems in the strategy implementation process. Chapter 11 covers building a strategy-supportive corporate culture and exerting the internal leadership needed to drive implementation forward and improve strategy execution.

Throughout the chapters, we've included a series of "margin notes" highlighting basic concepts, important points, and core truths about crafting and implementing strategy in competitive markets. You'll also find an array of boxed-off illustrations and examples describing how companies have put strategic concepts and analysis techniques into practice.

All told, we think you'll find the chapter discussions serious, substantive, and thorough. The book's subtitle— "What Every Manager Should Know" — is an accurate reflection of the contents. Conscientious readers will come away better prepared to think in strategic terms, craft good strategies, and implement them in creditable fashion. Casual readers, at the very least, will understand why and how to make decisions from a total company perspective and should be more perceptive students of their company's business.

The Five Strategy-Related Tasks That Managers Have to Do

> "Cheshire Puss," she [Alice] began . . . "would you please tell me which way I ought to go from here?"
> "That depends on where you want to get to," said the cat.
>
> **Lewis Carroll**

> My job is to make sure the company has a strategy and that everybody follows it.
>
> **Kenneth H. Olsen**
> **Former CEO, Digital Equipment Corp.**

The strategy-making/strategy-implementing process consists of five interrelated managerial tasks:

1. Deciding what business the company will be in and forming a strategic vision of where the organization needs to be headed—in effect, infusing the organization with a sense of purpose, providing long-term direction, and establishing a clear mission to be accomplished.

2. Converting the strategic vision and mission into measurable objectives and performance targets.

3. Crafting a strategy to achieve the desired results.

4. Implementing and executing the chosen strategy efficiently and effectively.

5. Evaluating performance, reviewing new developments, and adjusting the long-term direction, objectives, strategy, or implementation to incorporate actual experience, changing conditions, new ideas, and new opportunities.

Figure 1–1 displays the process. Together, these five components define what we mean by the term *strategic management* and form the core of all that follows.

▶ DEVELOPING A STRATEGIC VISION AND BUSINESS MISSION

The foremost direction-setting question senior managers of any enterprise need to ask is, "What is our vision for the company—what are we trying to do and to become?" Developing a carefully reasoned answer to this question pushes managers to consider what the company's business character is and should be, as well as helping develop a sense of where the company needs to be headed over the next 5 to 10 years. Management's answer

FIGURE 1-1   *The Five Tasks of Strategic Management*

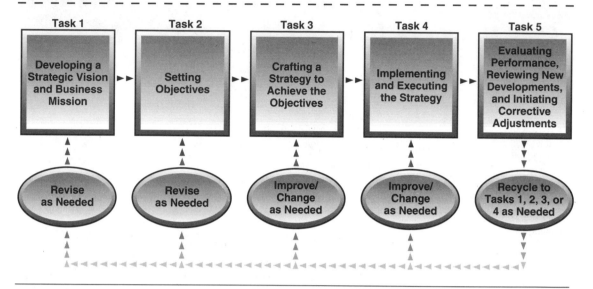

to "who we are, what we do, and where we're headed" charts a course for the organization and helps establish a strong organizational identity. What a company seeks to do and to become is commonly called the company's mission.

Visionless companies are unsure about what business position they are trying to stake out.

A mission statement defines a company's business succinctly, providing a clear view of what the company is trying to accomplish for its customers. Managers also have to think strategically about where they are trying to take the company. Management's view of what kind of company it is trying to create and the kind of business position it wants to stake out represents a *strategic vision* for the company. By developing and communicating a business mission and strategic vision, management provides the organization's stakeholders with a sense of purpose and a persuasive rationale for the company's future direction. Some examples of company mission and vision statements are presented in Illustration 1.

SETTING OBJECTIVES

The purpose of setting objectives is to convert the general statement of business mission and company direction into specific performance targets, something by which the organization's progress can be measured. Objective setting implies challenge, establishing performance targets that require stretch and disciplined effort. The challenge of trying to close the gap between actual and desired performance pushes an organization to be more inventive, to exhibit some urgency in improving its financial performance and its

---

ILLUSTRATION 1   *Examples of Company Mission and Vision Statements*

Otis Elevator
Our mission is to provide any customer a means of moving people and things up, down, and sideways over short distances with higher reliability than any similar enterprise in the world.

Avis Rent-a-Car
Our business is renting cars. Our mission is total customer satisfaction.

McCormick & Company
The primary mission of McCormick & Company is to expand our worldwide leadership position in the spice, seasoning, and flavoring markets.

The Saturn Division of General Motors
To market vehicles developed and manufactured in the United States that are world leaders in quality, cost, and customer satisfaction through the integration of people, technology, and business systems and to transfer knowledge, technology, and experience throughout General Motors.

Public Service Company of New Mexico
Our mission is to work for the success of people we serve by providing our customers reliable electric service, energy information, and energy options that best satisfy their needs.

American Red Cross
The mission of the American Red Cross is to improve the quality of human life; to enhance self-reliance and concern for others; and to help people avoid, prepare for, and cope with emergencies.

Eastman Kodak
To be the world's best in chemical and electronic imaging.

McCaw Cellular Communications
Develop a reliable wireless network that empowers people with the freedom to travel anywhere—across the hall or across the continent—and communicate effortlessly.

Compaq Computer
To be the leading supplier of PCs and PC servers in all customer segments.

Long John Silver's
To be America's best quick-service restaurant chain. We will provide each guest great-tasting, healthful, reasonably priced fish, seafood, and chicken in a fast, friendly manner on every visit.

---

business position, and to be more intentional and focused in its actions. Setting challenging but achievable objectives thus helps guard against complacency, drift, internal confusion over what to accomplish, and status quo organizational performance. As Mitchell Leibovitz, CEO of Pep Boys—Manny, Moe and Jack, puts it, "If you want to have ho-hum results, have ho-hum objectives."

Objectives are yardsticks for tracking performance.

The objectives managers establish should include both short-range and long-range performance targets. Short-range objectives spell out the immediate improvements and outcomes management desires. Long-range objectives prompt managers to consider what to do *now* to position the company to perform well over the longer term. Rarely is there much strategic value in striving to hit near-term targets that could sap the company's long-term competitive strength and performance capabilities.

Objective setting is required of *all* managers. Every organizational unit in a company needs concrete, measurable performance targets that contribute meaningfully toward achieving company objectives. When companywide objectives are broken down into specific targets for each organizational unit and when lower-level managers are held accountable for achieving them, a results-oriented climate builds throughout the enterprise. The ideal condition is a team effort where each organizational unit is striving for results in its area of responsibility that will help the company reach its performance targets and achieve its strategic objectives.

From a companywide perspective, two types of performance yardsticks are called for: financial objectives and strategic objectives. *Financial objectives* are important because acceptable financial performance is critical to preserving an organization's vitality and securing the resources it needs to grow and prosper. *Strategic objectives* serve to prompt managerial efforts to strengthen a company's overall business and competitive position.

Companies need strategic objectives as well as financial objectives.

Financial objectives typically relate to such measures as earnings growth, return on investment, borrowing power, cash flow, and shareholder returns. Strategic objectives, however, concern a company's competitiveness and long-term business prospects: growing faster than the industry average, overtaking key competitors on product quality or customer service or market share, achieving lower overall costs than rivals, boosting the company's reputation with customers, winning a stronger foothold in international markets, exercising technological leadership, gaining a sustainable competitive advantage, and capturing attractive growth opportunities. Strategic objectives serve notice that management not only intends to deliver a good financial performance but also intends to improve the company's competitive strength and business position.

Examples of the kinds of strategic and financial objectives companies set are shown in Illustration 2.

▶ CRAFTING A STRATEGY

Strategy-making brings into play the critical managerial issue of *how* to achieve the targeted results in light of the organization's circumstances. Objectives are the ends, and strategy is management's means of achieving them. In effect, strategy is the pattern of actions and business approaches managers employ to achieve company performance targets. The task of crafting a strategy starts with solid diagnosis of the company's internal

Strategy consists of the actions and business approaches management is employing to achieve company performance targets.

and external situation. Only when armed with hard analysis of the big picture are managers prepared to devise a sound strategy to achieve targeted strategic and financial results. Why? Because misdiagnosis of the situation greatly raises the risk of pursuing ill-conceived strategic actions.

A company's strategy is typically a blend of (1) deliberate and purposeful actions and (2) as needed reactions to unanticipated developments and fresh competitive pressures. As

---

ILLUSTRATION 2   *Strategic and Financial Objectives of Well-Known Corporations*

NationsBank
To build the premier financial services company in the United States.

Ford Motor Company
To satisfy our customers by providing quality cars and trucks, developing new products, reducing the time it takes to bring new vehicles to market, improving the efficiency of all our plants and processes, and building on our teamwork with employees, unions, dealers, and suppliers.

Exxon
Provide shareholders a secure investment with a superior return.

Alcan Aluminum
To be the lowest-cost producer of aluminum and to outperform the average return on equity of the Standard & Poor's industrial stock index.

General Electric
To become the most competitive enterprise in the world

by being No. 1 or No. 2 in market share in every business the company is in.

Apple Computer
To offer the best possible personal computing technology, and to put that technology in the hands of as many people as possible.

Atlas Corporation
To become a low-cost, medium-size gold producer, producing in excess of 125,000 ounces of gold a year and building gold reserves of 1,500,000 ounces.

Quaker Oats Company
To achieve return on equity at 20 percent or above, real earnings growth averaging 5 percent or better over time, be a leading marketer of strong consumer brands, and improve the profitability of low-return businesses or divest them.

Source: Company annual reports.

---

illustrated in Figure 1–2, strategy is more than what managers have carefully planned and *intend* to do as part of some grand strategic design. New circumstances are forever emerging, whether they be important technological developments, new product introductions by rivals that catch on quickly with buyers, newly enacted government regulations and policies, or widening consumer interest in different kinds of performance features. The future contains enough uncertainty that managers cannot plan every strategic action in advance and pursue their *intended strategy* without any need for alteration. Consequently, company strategies end up being a composite of planned actions (intended strategy) and as-needed reactions to unforeseen conditions (unplanned strategic responses). Thus, *strategy is best*

Strategy is both proactive (intended) and reactive (adaptive).

conceived as a combination of planned actions and on-the-spot adaptive reactions to fresh-developing industry and competitive events. The strategy-making task involves developing a game plan, or intended strategy, and then adapting it as events unfold. A company's actual strategy is thus something managers must continue to craft as events transpire outside and inside the company.

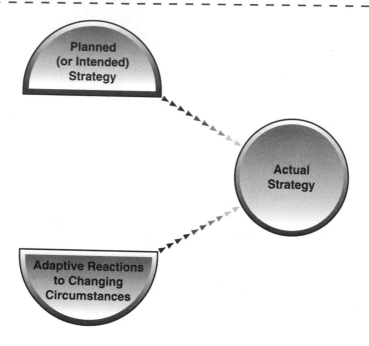

FIGURE 1–2   *A Company's Actual Strategy Is Partly Planned and Partly Reactive to Changing Circumstances*

■ STRATEGY AND ENTREPRENEURSHIP

Crafting strategy is an exercise in entrepreneurship and outside-in strategic thinking. The challenge is for company managers to keep their strategies closely matched to such outside drivers as changing buyer preferences, the latest actions of rivals, market opportunities and threats, and newly appearing business conditions. Company strategies can't be kept responsive to changes in the business environment unless managers exhibit entrepreneurship in studying market trends, listening to customers, enhancing the company's competitiveness, and steering company activities in new directions in a timely manner. Good strategy making is therefore inseparable from good business entrepreneurship. One cannot exist without the other.

Strategy making is fundamentally a market-driven entrepreneurial activity

A company encounters two dangers when its managers fail to exercise strategy-making entrepreneurship. One is a stale strategy. The faster a company's business environment is changing, the more critical it becomes for its managers to be good entrepreneurs in diagnosing shifting conditions and instituting strategic adjustments. Coasting with a status quo strategy tends to be riskier than modifying strategy to match changing circumstances. Strategies that are increasingly out of touch with market realities make a company a good candidate for a performance crisis.

The second danger is inside-out strategic thinking. Managers with weak entrepreneurial skills are usually risk-averse and hesitant to embark on a new strategic course so long as the present strategy is producing acceptable results. They have an observable propensity to pay perfunctory attention to market trends and to listen to customers infrequently. Often, they either dismiss new outside developments as unimportant (''We don't think it will really affect us'') or else study them to death before any actions are taken. Comfortable with their current strategy, they focus energy and attention inward on internal problem

Good strategy making is more outside-in than inside-out.

solving, organizational processes and procedures, reports and deadlines, company politics, and the administrative demands of their job. Consequently, the strategic actions they initiate tend to be inside-out, governed by the company's traditional approaches, what is acceptable to various internal political coalitions, what is philosophically comfortable, and what is safe organizationally and for their careers. Inside-out strategies, while not disconnected from industry and competitive conditions, stop short of being market-driven and customer-driven in a true sense. Rather, outside considerations end up being compromised to accommodate internal considerations. The weaker a manager's entrepreneurial instincts and capabilities, the greater a manager's propensity to engage in inside-out strategizing, an outcome which raises the potential for reduced competitiveness and weakened organizational commitment to customer satisfaction.

Good barometers of managers' entrepreneurial spirit are how boldly or cautiously they embrace strategic opportunities, the emphasis they place on competitive innovation, and whether they consistently initiate ideas for improving organizational performance. Entrepreneurial strategy-makers are inclined to be first-movers, responding quickly and opportunistically to new developments. They are willing to take prudent risks and initiate trailblazing strategies. In contrast, reluctant entrepreneurs are risk-averse; they tend to be late-movers, hopeful about their chances of soon catching up and concerned about avoiding the first-mover's mistakes. Reluctant entrepreneurs prefer incremental strategic change over bold or sweeping strategic moves.

All managers, not just senior executives, are called upon to take prudent risks and exercise entrepreneurship in strategy-making. Entrepreneurship is involved when a district customer service manager, as part of a company's commitment to better customer service, crafts a strategy to speed the response time on service calls by 25 percent and commits $15,000 to equip all service trucks with mobile telephones. Entrepreneurship is involved when a warehousing manager contributes to a company's strategic emphasis on total quality by figuring how to reduce the error frequency on filling customer orders from one error per every hundred orders to one error per every hundred thousand orders. A sales manager exercises strategic entrepreneurship in deciding to run a special advertising promotion and cut sales prices by 5 percent to wrest market share from rivals. A manufacturing manager exercises strategic entrepreneurship in deciding, as part of a companywide emphasis on greater cost competitiveness, to source an important component from a lower-priced South Korean supplier instead of making it in-house. Company strategies can't be truly market-

and customer-driven unless the strategy-related activities of managers across the company have an outside-in entrepreneurial character and contribute to boosting customer satisfaction and achieving sustainable competitive advantage.

■ WHY COMPANY STRATEGIES EVOLVE

Frequent fine-tuning and tweaking of a company's strategy, first in one department or functional area and then in another, are a normal part of the strategy-making process. On occasion, quantum changes in strategy are called for—when a competitor makes a dramatic move, when technological breakthroughs occur, or when crisis strikes and managers are forced to make radical strategy alterations quickly. Because strategic moves and new action approaches are ongoing here and there across the business, an organization's strategy forms over a period of time and then reforms as the number of changes begin to mount. The current version of strategy typically stands as a blend of holdover approaches, fresh actions and reactions in process, and potential moves in the planning stage. Except for crises (where many strategic moves are often made quickly to produce a substantially new strategy almost overnight) and new company start-ups (where strategy exists mostly in the form of plans and intended actions), key elements of a company's strategy commonly emerge in bits and pieces as the business develops.

A company's strategy is dynamic, emerging in bits and pieces as the enterprise develops and responds to changing conditions.

Rarely is a company's strategy so well conceived and durable that it can withstand the test of time virtually unchanged. Even the best-laid business plans must be adapted to shifting market conditions, altered customer needs and preferences, strategic maneuvering of rival firms, experience of what is working and what isn't, emerging opportunities and threats, unforeseen events, and fresh thinking about how to improve the strategy. This is why strategy-making is a dynamic process and why a manager is obligated to reevaluate strategy regularly, refining and recasting it as needed.

However, when strategy is changing so fast and so fundamentally that the game plan is undergoing major overhaul every few months, the managers in charge are almost certainly guilty of poor strategic analysis, erratic decision making, and weak strategizing. Quantum changes in strategy are needed occasionally, especially in crises, but they cannot be made too often without creating undue organizational confusion and disrupting performance. Well-crafted strategies normally have a life of at least several years, requiring only minor "tweaking" to keep them in tune with changing circumstances.

■ WHAT DOES A COMPANY'S STRATEGY CONSIST OF?

Company strategies concern *how:* how to grow the business, how to satisfy customers, how to outcompete rivals, how to respond to changing market conditions, how to manage each functional piece of the business, how to achieve strategic and financial objectives. The hows of strategy tend to be company-specific, customized to a company's own situation and performance objectives. In the business world, companies have great strategic freedom. They can diversify broadly or narrowly, into related or unrelated industries, via acquisition, joint venture, strategic alliances, or internal startup. Even when a company elects to concentrate on a single business, prevailing market conditions usually offer enough strategy-making latitude that close competitors can easily avoid pursuing carbon copy strategies. Some may pursue low-cost leadership, while others seek to differentiate themselves by stressing one or another combination of product/service attributes, and still others cater to the specialized needs of narrowly targeted buyer segments. Hence, generic descriptions of what company strategy includes necessarily have to be nonspecific.

Figure 1–3 depicts the kinds of actions and approaches that make up a company's overall strategy. Many, if not most, of the pieces of a company's strategy are visible to outside observers,

Company strategies are partly visible and partly hidden to outside view.

thus allowing the greatest part of a company's strategy to be deduced from its actions and public pronouncements. Yet, outsiders can only speculate about one portion of the strategy —the actions and moves company managers are considering. Managers often, for good reason, choose not to reveal certain elements of their strategy until the time is right.

To get a better understanding of the content of company strategies, see the overview of McDonald's strategy in Illustration 3.

FIGURE 1–3   *Understanding a Company's Strategy — What to Look For*

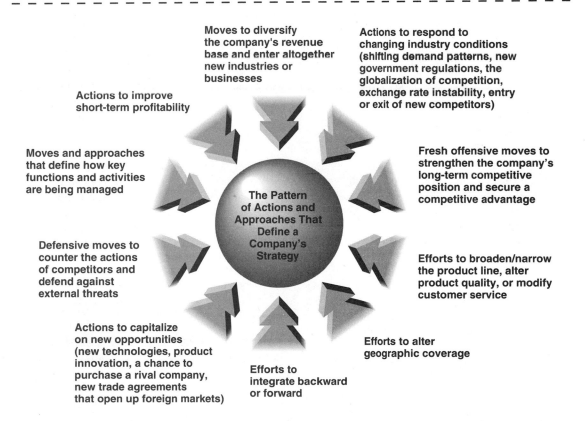

Moves to diversify the company's revenue base and enter altogether new industries or businesses

Actions to respond to changing industry conditions (shifting demand patterns, new government regulations, the globalization of competition, exchange rate instability, entry or exit of new competitors)

Actions to improve short-term profitability

Moves and approaches that define how key functions and activities are being managed

Fresh offensive moves to strengthen the company's long-term competitive position and secure a competitive advantage

The Pattern of Actions and Approaches That Define a Company's Strategy

Defensive moves to counter the actions of competitors and defend against external threats

Efforts to broaden/narrow the product line, alter product quality, or modify customer service

Actions to capitalize on new opportunities (new technologies, product innovation, a chance to purchase a rival company, new trade agreements that open up foreign markets)

Efforts to integrate backward or forward

Efforts to alter geographic coverage

ILLUSTRATION 3   *A Strategy Example: McDonald's*

Going into 1994 McDonald's was the leading food service retailer in the global consumer marketplace, with a strong brand name and systemwide restaurant sales exceeding $23 billion. Sales had tripled since 1983, when McDonald's served 28 million customers in 70 countries daily. Two-thirds of its 14,000 restaurants were franchised to 4,000 owner/operators around the world. The company had pioneered food quality specifications, equipment technology, marketing and training programs, operating systems, and supply systems that were considered the standards of the industry throughout the world. The company's strategic priorities were continued growth, providing exceptional customer care, remaining an efficient and quality producer, offering high value, and effectively marketing McDonald's brand on a global scale. McDonald's strategy had the following core elements:

Growth Strategy

- Add 700–900 restaurants annually, some company owned and some franchised, with about two-thirds being outside the United States.
- Promote more frequent customer visits via the addition of breakfast and dinner menu items, low price specials, and Extra Value Meals.

Franchising Strategy

- Be highly selective in granting franchises. (McDonald's approach was to recruit only highly motivated, talented entrepreneurs with integrity and business experience and train them to become active, on-premises owners of McDonald's; no franchises were granted to corporations, partnerships, or passive investors.)

Store Location and Construction Strategy

- Locate restaurants only on sites that offer convenience to customers and afford long-term sales growth potential. (The company utilized sophisticated site selection techniques to obtain premier locations. In the United States, the company was supplementing its traditional suburban and urban locations with openings in food courts, major airports, hospitals, and universities; outside the United States, the strategy was to establish an initial presence in center cities, then open freestanding units with drive-thrus outside of center cities. Where site ownership was impractical, McDonald's secured long-term leases.)
- Reduce site costs and building costs by using standardized, cost-efficient store designs and consolidating purchases of equipment and materials via a global sourcing system. (One of the company's four approved designs was half the size of a traditional restaurant, required a smaller parcel of land, was about 25 percent cheaper, and could accommodate nearly the same volume.)
- Utilize store and site designs that are attractive and pleasing inside and out, and where feasible provide drive-thru service and play areas for children.

Product Line Strategy

- A limited menu.
- Expand product offerings into new categories of fast food (chicken, Mexican, pizza, etc.) and include more items for health-conscious customers.
- Do extensive testing to ensure consistent, high quality and ample customer appeal before rolling out new menu items systemwide.

Store Operations

- Establish stringent product standards, strictly enforce restaurant operating procedures (especially concerning food preparation, store cleanliness and friendly, courteous counter service), and build close working relationships with suppliers to assure that food is safe and of the highest quality. (Generally, McDonald's did not supply food, paper products, or equipment to restaurants; instead, it approved suppliers from whom these items could be purchased.)
- Develop new equipment and production systems that improve the ability to serve hotter, better-tasting food faster and with greater accuracy.

Sales Promotion, Marketing, and Merchandising

- Enhance the McDonald's image of quality, service, cleanliness, and value globally via heavy media advertising and in-store merchandise promotions funded with fees tied to a percentage of sales revenues at each restaurant.

- Continue to use value pricing and Extra Value Meals to build customer traffic.
- Use Ronald McDonald to create greater brand awareness among children and the *Mc* prefix to reinforce the connection of menu items and McDonald's.

Human Resources and Training

- Offer wage rates that are equitable and nondiscriminatory in every location; teach job skills; reward both individual accomplishments and teamwork; offer career opportunities.
- Hire restaurant crews with good work habits and courteous attitudes and train them to act in ways that will impress customers.
- Provide proper training on delivering customer satisfaction and running a fast-food business to franchisees, restaurant managers, and assistant managers. (Instructors at five Hamburger University campuses,

in Illinois, Germany, England, Australia and Japan, in 1993 trained over 3,000 students in 22 languages.)

Social Responsibility

- Operate in a socially responsible manner by supporting educational programs for student employees, Ronald McDonald Houses (at year-end 1993, there were 157 houses in ten countries providing a home-away-from-home for families of seriously ill children receiving treatment at nearby hospitals), workforce diversity and voluntary affirmative action, minority-owned franchises (McDonald's franchises included the largest and most successful group of minority entrepreneurs in the United States), recycling (McDonald's McRecycle USA program has won national awards), and providing nutritional information on McDonald's products to customers.

Source: Company annual reports.

■ STRATEGY AND STRATEGIC PLANS

Developing a strategic vision and mission, establishing objectives, and deciding on a strategy are basic direction-setting tasks. They map out where the organization is headed, its short-range and long-range performance targets, and the competitive moves and internal action approaches to be used in achieving the targeted results. Together, they constitute a *strategic plan*. In some companies, especially large corporations committed to regular strategy reviews and formal strategic planning, a document describing the upcoming year's strategic plan is prepared and circulated to managers and employees (although parts of the plan may be omitted or expressed in general terms for reasons of competitive security). In other companies, the strategic plan is not written for widespread distribution but rather exists as an unwritten consensus and commitment among managers about where to head, what to accomplish, and how to proceed. Organizational objectives are the part of the strategic plan that are most often spelled out explicitly and communicated to managers and employees.

However, annual strategic plans seldom anticipate all the strategically relevant situations that will transpire in the next 12 months. Unforeseen events, unexpected opportunities or threats, even new proposals often warrant modifying planned actions. Postponing the recrafting of strategy until it's time to work on next year's strategic plan is both foolish and unnecessary. Managers who confine their strategizing to the regularly scheduled time in the company's annual planning cycle (when they can't avoid turning something in) have a wrongheaded concept about their strategy-making responsibilities and why having a good strategy contributes to better organizational performance.

Once-a-year strategizing under ''have-to'' conditions is not a prescription for managerial success.

▶ STRATEGY IMPLEMENTATION AND EXECUTION

The strategy-implementing function consists of seeing what it will take to make the strategy work and to reach the targeted performance on schedule. The skill here is being good at figuring out what must be done to put the strategy in place, execute it proficiently, and produce good results. Implementing strategy is primarily a hands-on, close-to-the-scene administrative task that includes the following principal aspects:

* Building an organization capable of carrying out the strategy successfully.
* Developing budgets that steer resources into the internal activities that are critical to strategic success.
* Establishing strategy-supportive policies.
* Motivating people to pursue the target objectives energetically and, if need be, modifying their duties and job behavior to better fit the requirements of successful strategy execution.
* Tying the reward structure tightly to the achievement of the targeted results.
* Creating a corporate culture and work climate conducive to successful strategy implementation.
* Installing a variety of internal support systems that enable company personnel to carry out their strategic roles effectively day in and day out.
* Instituting best practices and programs for continuous improvement.
* Exerting the internal leadership needed to drive implementation forward and to keep improving the way strategy is being executed.

The administrative aim is to create fits between the way things are done and what it takes for effective strategy execution. The stronger the fits, the better the execution of strategy. The most important fits are between strategy and organizational capabilities, between strategy and reward structure, between strategy and internal support systems, and between strategy and the organization's culture (the latter emerges from the values and beliefs shared by organizational members, the company's approaches to managing their employees, ingrained behaviors, work practices, and ways of thinking). Fitting the ways the organization does things internally to what it takes for effective strategy execution serves to unite the organization firmly behind the accomplishment of strategy.

The strategy-implementing task is easily the most complicated and time-consuming part of strategic management. It cuts across virtually all facets of managing and must be initiated from many points inside the organization. The strategy-implementer's agenda for action emerges from careful assessment of what the organization must do differently and better to carry out the strategic plan proficiently. Each manager has to think through the answer to, ''What has to be done in my area of responsibility to carry out my piece of the overall strategic plan and how can I best get it done?'' How much internal change is needed to implement a strategy depends on the degree to which internal practices deviate from what the strategy requires, and how well strategy and organizational culture match.

As changes and actions are identified, management must supervise the details of implementation and apply enough pressure on the organization to convert objectives into actual results. Depending on the amount of internal change involved, full implementation can take several months to several years.

> **Strategy implementation is fundamentally an action-oriented, make-it-happen activity.**

▶ EVALUATING PERFORMANCE, REVIEWING NEW DEVELOPMENTS, AND INITIATING CORRECTIVE ADJUSTMENTS

None of the previous four tasks are one-time exercises. New circumstances always crop up that make corrective adjustments desirable. Long-term direction may need to be altered, the business redefined, and management's vision of the organization's future course narrowed or broadened. Performance targets may need raising or lowering in light of past experience and future prospects. Strategy may need to be modified because of shifts in long-term direction, because new objectives have been set, or because of changing conditions in the environment.

The search for ways to improve strategy execution is continuous. Sometimes an aspect of implementation does not go as well as intended and changes have to be made. Progress, typically, is uneven—some tasks get done easily; others prove nettlesome. Implementation is a process, not an event. It occurs through the pooling effect of many administrative decisions about how to do things and how to create stronger fits between strategy and internal operating practices

> **A company's mission, objectives, strategy, and approach to implementation are never final; adjustments are normal and necessary.**

and many incremental actions on the part of work groups and individuals across the organization. Budget revisions, policy changes, reorganization, reengineered activities and work processes, personnel changes, benchmarking, continuous improvement programs (like total quality management), and revised compensation practices are typical ways of trying to make the chosen strategy work better.

▶ WHY STRATEGIC MANAGEMENT IS AN ONGOING PROCESS

Because each one of the five tasks of strategic management requires constant evaluation and a decision whether to continue with things as they are or to make changes, a manager cannot afford to divert attention to other matters for long. Nothing about the strategic management process is final—all prior actions are subject to modification as conditions in the surrounding environment change and ideas for improvement emerge. Strategic management is a process filled with motion. Changes in the organization's situation, either from the inside or outside or both, fuel the need for strategic adjustments. This is why, in Figure 1–1, we highlight the recycling feature inherent in the strategic management process. While strategic adjustments sometimes involve sharp breaks and radical transformations, more usually it entails a steady stream of incremental changes that mean a company is never quite the same from one year to the next.

The task of evaluating performance and initiating corrective adjustments is both the end and the beginning of the strategic management cycle. External and internal events guarantee revision in mission, objectives, strategy, and implementation will be needed sooner or later. It is incumbent on management to push for better performance—to find ways to improve the existing strategy and how it is being executed. Changing external conditions add further impetus to the need for periodic revisions in a company's mission, performance objectives, strategy, and approaches to strategy execution. Adjustments usually involve fine-tuning, but occasions for a major strategic reorientation do arise—sometimes prompted by significant external developments and sometimes by sharply sliding financial performance. Managers must stay close enough to the situation to detect when changing conditions require a strategic response and when they don't. Their job is to read the market, recognize significant changes early, and initiate adjustments as needed to capitalize on events as they unfold.

■ CHARACTERISTICS OF THE PROCESS

Although strategic management involves developing a mission, setting objectives, forming a strategy, implementing and executing the strategic plan, and evaluating performance, actually carrying out these five tasks is not so cleanly divided into separate, neatly sequenced compartments. There is much interplay among the five tasks. For example, considering what strategic actions to take raises issues about whether and how the strategy can be satisfactorily implemented. Deciding on a company mission shades into setting objectives for the organization—both involve directional priorities. To set challenging but achievable objectives, managers must consider both current performance and the strategy options available to improve performance. Deciding on a strategy is entangled with decisions about long-term direction and whether objectives have been set too high or too low. A strong case can be made that the direction-setting tasks of developing a mission, setting objectives, and crafting strategy need to be integrated, not done individually.

Strategic management is a process; the boundaries between the five tasks are conceptual, not real.

Second, the five strategic management tasks are not performed in isolation from the other responsibilities a manager has—supervising day-to-day operations, dealing with crises, going to meetings, preparing reports, handling people problems, and taking on special assignments and civic duties. Thus, although strategic management activities are the most important managerial functions related to organizational success or failure, they are not all managers must do or be concerned about.

Third, crafting and implementing strategy can make erratic demands on a manager's time. An organization's situation does not change in an orderly or predictable way. The events that prompt reconsideration of strategy can build quickly or gradually, they can emerge singly or all at once, and the implications they have for strategic change can be easy or hard to diagnose. Hence, the task of reviewing and adjusting the strategic game plan can take up big chunks of management time some months and little in other months. As a practical matter, there is as much skill in knowing *when* to institute strategic changes as there is in knowing *what* to do.

Last, the most time-consuming aspect of strategic management is trying to get the best strategy-supportive performance out of every individual and trying to perfect the current strategy by refining its content and execution. Managing strategy consists mostly of improving bits and pieces of the strategy that are already in place, not developing and instituting radical strategic changes. In fact, excessive changes in strategy can be disruptive to employees and confusing to customers, and they are usually unnecessary. Most of the time, there's more to be gained from improving execution of the present strategy. Persistence in trying to make a sound strategy work better is often the key to success.

▶ THE BENEFITS OF A STRATEGIC APPROACH TO MANAGING

The message of this book is that doing a good job of managing inherently requires good strategic thinking and good strategic management. Today's managers have to think strategically about their company's position and about the impact of changing conditions. They have to monitor the external situation closely enough to know when to institute strategic change. They have to know the business well enough to know what kind of strategic changes to initiate. Simply said, the fundamentals of strategic management need to drive the whole approach to managing organizations. The chief executive officer of one successful company put it well:

> In the main, our competitors are acquainted with the same fundamental concepts and techniques and approaches that we follow, and they are as free to pursue them as we are. More often than not, the difference between their level of success and ours lies in the relative thoroughness and self-discipline with which we and they develop and execute our strategies for the future.

The advantages of first-rate strategic thinking and conscious strategy management (as opposed to freewheeling improvisation, gut feel, and drifting along) include (1) providing better guidance to the entire organization on the crucial point of "what we are trying to do and to achieve"; (2) making managers more alert to the winds of change, new opportunities, and threatening developments; (3) providing managers with a rationale to evaluate competing budget requests for investment capital and new staff, a rationale that argues strongly for steering resources into strategy-supportive, results-producing areas; (4) helping to unify the numerous strategy-related decisions by managers across the organization; and (5) creating a more proactive management posture and counteracting tendencies for reactive and defensive decisions.

The advantage of being proactive as opposed to reactive is that trail-blazing strategies can be key to better long-term performance. Business history shows that high-performing enterprises often initiate and lead, instead of just reacting and defending. They launch strategic offensives to outinnovate and outmaneuver rivals and to secure sustainable competitive advantage, then they use their market edge to achieve superior financial performance. Aggressive pursuit of a creative, opportunistic strategy can propel a firm into a leadership position, paving the way for its products/services to become the industry standard.

On the following pages, we will probe the strategy-related tasks of managers and the methods of strategic analysis much more intensively. When you get to the end of the book, we think you will see that two factors separate the best-managed organizations from the rest: (1) superior strategy making and entrepreneurship, and (2) competent implementation and execution of the chosen strategy. There's no escaping the fact that the quality of managerial strategy making and strategy implementation has a significant impact on organization performance. A company that lacks clear-cut direction, has vague or undemanding objectives, has a muddled or flawed strategy, or can't seem to execute its plans competently is a company whose performance is probably suffering, whose business is at long-term risk, and whose management is less than capable.

▶ **TERMS TO REMEMBER**

In the chapters to come, we'll be using some key phases and terms over and over again. You'll find the following definitional listing helpful.

- *Strategic vision*—a view of an organization's future direction and business course; a guiding concept for what the organization is trying to do and to become.

- *Organization mission*—management's customized answer to the question, "What is our business and what are we trying to accomplish on behalf of our customers?" A mission statement broadly outlines the organization's activities and business makeup.

- *Performance objectives*—the organization's targets for achievement.

- *Financial objectives*—the targets management has established for the organization's financial performance.

- *Strategic objectives*—the targets management has established for strengthening the organization's overall position and competitive vitality.

- *Long-range objectives*—the results to be achieved either within the next three to five years or else on an ongoing basis year after year.

- *Short-range objectives*—the organization's near-term performance targets; the amount of short-term improvement signals how fast management is trying to achieve the long-range objectives.

- *Strategy*—the pattern of actions and business approaches managers employ to achieve organizational objectives. A company's actual strategy is partly planned and partly reactive to changing circumstances.

- *Strategic plan*—a statement outlining an organization's mission and future direction, near-term and long-term performance targets, and strategy.

- *Strategy formulation*—the entire direction-setting management function of conceptualizing an organization's mission, setting performance objectives, and crafting a strategy. The end product of strategy formulation is a strategic plan.

- *Strategy implementation*—the full range of managerial activities associated with putting the chosen strategy into place, supervising its pursuit, and achieving the targeted results.

The Three Strategy-Making Tasks: Developing a Strategic Vision, Setting Objectives, and Crafting a Strategy

CHAPTER

TWO

In this chapter, we provide an in-depth look at each of the three strategy-making tasks: developing a strategic vision and business mission, setting performance objectives, and crafting a strategy to produce the desired results. We also examine the kinds of strategic decisions made at each management level, the major determinants of a company's strategy, and four frequently used managerial approaches to forming a strategic plan.

▶ DEVELOPING A STRATEGIC VISION AND MISSION: THE FIRST DIRECTION-SETTING TASK

Management's view of what kind of company it is trying to create and its intent to stake out specific business positions represent a *strategic vision* for the company. A strategic vision provides a big picture perspective of "who *we* are, what *we* do, and where *we* are headed." It leaves no doubt about the organization's long-term direction and where management intends to take the company. A well-conceived strategic vision is a prerequisite to effective strategic leadership. A manager cannot function effectively as an organization leader or a strategy-maker without a sound concept of the business, of what activities to pursue and not to pursue, and of the kind of long-term competitive position to try to build in relation to both customers and competitors. We will use the terms *strategic vision* and *strategic mission* or *business mission* interchangeably despite a preference for *strategic vision* because of its inherent emphasis on "what we are about and where we are headed."

Strategic visions and company mission statements are always highly personalized. Generic statements, applicable to any company or to any industry, have no managerial

---

ILLUSTRATION 4   *Delta Airlines Strategic Vision*

In late 1993, Ronald W. Allen, Delta's chief executive officer, described the company's vision and business mission in the following way:

We want Delta to be the **Worldwide Airline of Choice.**

Worldwide, because we are and intend to remain an innovative, aggressive, ethical, and successful competitor that offers access to the world at the highest standards of customer service. We will continue to look for opportunities to extend our reach through new routes and creative global alliances.

Airline, because we intend to stay in the business we know best—air transportation and related services. We won't stray from our roots. We believe in the long-term prospects for profitable growth in the airline industry, and we will continue to focus time, attention, and investment on enhancing our place in that business environment.

Of Choice, because we value the loyalty of our customers, employees, and investors. For passengers and shippers, we will continue to provide the best service and value. For our personnel, we will continue to offer an ever more challenging, rewarding, and result-oriented workplace that recognizes and appreciates their contributions. For our shareholders, we will earn a consistent, superior financial return.

Source: *Sky Magazine,* December 1993, p. 10.

---

value. The purpose of a strategic vision/mission statement is to set an organization apart from others in its industry and to establish its own special identity, business emphasis, and path for development. For example, the mission of a globally active New York bank like Citicorp has little in common with that of a locally owned small-town bank, even though both are in the banking industry. Compaq Computer is not on the same strategic path as IBM, even though both sell personal computers. General Electric is not on the same long-term strategic course as Whirlpool Corp., even though both are leaders in the major home appliance business. Similarly, there are important differences between the long-term strategic direction of such fierce business rivals as Intel and Motorola, Philips and Matsushita, Eastman Kodak and Fuji Photo Film Co., Michelin and Bridgestone/Firestone, Procter & Gamble and Unilever, and British Telecom and AT&T.

Effective strategy making begins with a concept of what the organization should and should not do and a vision of where the organization needs to be headed.

Sometimes companies mistakenly couch their mission in terms of making a profit. However, profit is more correctly an *objective* and a *result* of what the company does. Mission statements based on making a profit say nothing about the business arena in which profits are to be sought; they are incapable of distinguishing one type of profit-seeking enterprise from another—and yet the business and long-term direction of Sears is plainly different from the business and long-term direction of Toyota Motor Corp., even though both endeavor to earn a profit. The answer to the question of "What will we do to make a profit and for whom?" reveals a company's true business mission.

Forming a well-conceived strategic vision and expressing it in the form of a company mission statement has three distinct aspects:

- Understanding what business a company is really in.
- Communicating the vision and mission in ways that are clear, exciting, and inspiring.

- Deciding when to alter the company's strategic course and change its business mission.

■ UNDERSTANDING AND DEFINING THE BUSINESS

Specifying an organization's business is neither obvious nor easy. Is IBM in the computer business (a product-oriented definition) or the information and data processing business (a customer service or customer needs type of definition) or the advanced electronics business (a technology-based definition)? Is Coca-Cola in the soft-drink business (in which case its strategic vision can be trained narrowly on the actions of its competitors, namely, Pepsi, 7Up, Dr Pepper, Canada Dry, and Schweppes)? Or is it in the beverage industry (in which case management must think strategically about positioning Coca-Cola products in a market that includes fruit juices, alcoholic drinks, milk, bottled water, coffee, and tea)? This is not a trivial question for Coca-Cola. Many young adults get their morning caffeine fix by drinking cola instead of coffee; with a beverage industry perspective as opposed to a soft-drink industry perspective, Coca-Cola management is more likely to perceive a long-term growth opportunity in winning youthful coffee drinkers over to its colas.

> A company's business is defined by what is being satisfied, who is being satisfied, and how the satisfaction is being achieved.

Arriving at a good business definition usually requires taking three factors into account:[1]

1. Customer needs, or *what* is being satisfied.
2. Customer groups, or *who* is being satisfied.
3. The technologies used and functions performed, or *how* customers needs are satisfied.

Defining a business in terms of what to satisfy, whom to satisfy, and how the organization will go about producing the satisfaction makes a complete definition. It takes all three to pin down what business a company is really in. Just knowing what products or services a firm provides is never enough. Products or services per se are not important to customers; what turns a product or service into a business is satisfying a need or want. Customer groups are relevant because they indicate the market to be served — the geographic domain to be covered and the types of buyers the firm is going after.

Technology and functions performed are important because they indicate *how* the company will satisfy the customers' needs and how much of the industry's production chain its own activities will span. For instance, a firm's business can be *specialized,* concentrated in just one stage of an industry's total production-distribution chain, or *fully integrated,* spanning all parts of the industry chain. Wal-Mart, Home Depot, Toys "R" Us, and The Limited are essentially one-stage firms, with operations focused in the retail end of the consumer goods industry; they don't manufacture the items they sell. Delta Airlines is a one-stage enterprise; it doesn't manufacture the airplanes it flies and it doesn't operate the airports at which it lands. Delta has made a conscious decision to limit its business mission to moving travelers from one location to another via commercial jet aircraft. Major international oil companies like Exxon, Mobil, and Chevron, however, are fully integrated; they lease drilling sites, drill wells, pump oil, transport crude oil in their own ships, refine it in their own refineries, and sell gasoline and other petroleum products through their own networks of branded distributors and service station outlets. Because of the disparity in functions performed and technology employed, the business of a retailer like Lands' End or Wal-Mart is much narrower and quite different from a fully integrated enterprise like Exxon.

Between these two extremes, firms can stake out *partially integrated* positions, participating only in selected stages of the industry. Goodyear, for instance, manufactures tires and operates a chain of company-owned retail tire stores, but it has not integrated backward into rubber plantations and other components needed in tire making. General Motors (GM) is the world's most integrated manufacturer of cars and trucks, making in-house some 60–70 percent of the parts and components used in assembling GM vehicles. But it is moving to outsource a growing fraction of its parts and systems components, and it relies totally on a network of independent, franchised dealers to handle sales and service functions. Thus, one way of distinguishing a firm's business, especially among firms in the same industry, is by looking at which functions it performs in the production-distribution chain and how far its scope of operation extends across all the business activities required to get products to end-users.

A good example of a business mission statement that incorporates needs served, the target market, and functions performed is Polaroid's business definition during the early 1970s: "Perfecting and marketing instant photography to satisfy the needs of more affluent U.S. and West European families for affection, friendship, fond memories, and humor." McDonald's mission is focused on "serving a limited menu of hot, tasty food quickly in a clean, friendly restaurant for a good value" to a broad base of fast-food customers worldwide (McDonald's serves approximately 28 million customers daily at some 14,000 restaurants in over 70 countries). Trying to identify the needs served, the target market, and the functions performed in a single, incisive sentence is a challenge, and many firms have a mission statement that fails to explicitly cover all three bases.

A BROAD OR NARROW BUSINESS DEFINITION?

A small Hong Kong printing company that defines its business broadly as "Asian-language communications" gains no practical guidance in making direction-setting decisions; with such a definition the company could pursue limitless courses, many well beyond its scope and capability. To have managerial value, strategic visions, business definitions, and mission statements must be narrow enough to pin down the real arena of business interest. Otherwise, they cannot serve as boundaries for what to do and not do and as beacons of where managers intend to take the company. Consider the following definitions based on broad-narrow scope:

Broad Definition	Narrow Definition
• Beverages	• Soft drinks
• Footwear	• Athletic footwear
• Furniture	• Wrought iron lawn furniture
• Global mail delivery	• Overnight package delivery
• Travel and tourism	• Ship cruises in the Caribbean

Broad-narrow definitions are relative, of course. Being in "the furniture business" is probably too broad a concept for a company intent on being the largest manufacturer of wrought iron lawn furniture in North America. On the other hand, soft drinks has proved too narrow a scope for a growth-oriented company like Coca-Cola which, with its beverage industry perspective, acquired Minute-Maid and Hi-C (to capitalize on growing consumer interest in fruit juice products) and Taylor Wine Company (using the California Cellars brand to establish a foothold in wines).[2]The U.S. Postal Service operates with a broad definition, providing global mail delivery services to all types of senders. Federal Express, however, operates with a narrow business definition based on handling overnight package delivery for customers who have unplanned emergencies and tight deadlines.

Diversified firms have more sweeping business definitions than do single-business enterprises. Their mission statements typically are phrased narrowly enough to pinpoint their current customer-market-technology arenas but are open-ended and adaptable enough to incorporate expansion into new businesses. Alcan, Canada's leading aluminum company, used broad, inclusive words in expressing its strategic vision and mission:

> Diversified companies have broader missions and business definitions than single-business enterprises.

> Alcan is determined to be the most innovative diversified aluminum company in the world. To achieve this position, Alcan will be one, global, customer-oriented enterprise committed to excellence and lowest cost in its chosen aluminum businesses, with significant resources devoted to building an array of new businesses with superior growth and profit potential.

Thermo Electron Corp., a substantially more diversified enterprise, used simultaneous broad-narrow terms to define its arenas of business interest:

> Thermo Electron Corporation develops, manufactures, and markets environmental, analytical, and test instruments, alternative-energy power plants, low-emission combustion systems, paper- and waste-cycling equipment, and biomedical products. The company also operates power plants and provides services in environmental sciences and analysis, thermal waste treatment, and specialty metals fabrication and processing, as well as research and product development in unconventional imaging, laser technology, and direct-energy conversion.

Times Mirror Corp., also a diversified enterprise, describes its business scope in broad but still fairly explicit terminology:

> Times Mirror is a media and information company principally engaged in newspaper publishing; book, magazine and other publishing; and cable and broadcast television.

John Hancock's mission statement communicates a shift from its long-standing base in insurance to a broader mission in insurance, banking, and diversified financial services:

> At John Hancock, we are determined not just to compete but to advance, building our market share by offering individuals and institutions the broadest possible range of products and services. Apart from insurance, John Hancock encompasses banking products, full brokerage services, and institutional investment, to cite only a few of our diversified activities. We believe these new directions constitute the right moves . . . [and are] the steps that will drive our growth throughout the remainder of this century.

MISSION STATEMENTS FOR FUNCTIONAL DEPARTMENTS

There is also a place for mission statements for key functions (R&D, marketing, finance) and support units (human resources, training, information systems). Every department within an enterprise can benefit from a consensus statement that spells out its contribution to the company mission, what its principal role and activities are, and the direction in which it needs to be moving. The more that functional and departmental managers have thought through and debated with subordinates and higher ups what their unit needs to focus on and accomplish, the clearer their view should be of how to lead the unit. Three examples from actual companies indicate how a functional mission statement puts the spotlight on a unit's organizational *role* and *scope:*

- The mission of the human resources department is to contribute to organizational success by developing effective leaders, creating high-performance teams, and maximizing the potential of individuals.

- The mission of the corporate claims department is to minimize the overall cost of liability, workers compensation, and property damage claims through competitive cost containment techniques and loss prevention and control programs.

- The mission of corporate security is to provide services for the protection of corporate personnel and assets, through preventive measures and investigations.

■ COMMUNICATING THE STRATEGIC VISION

How to describe the strategic vision, word it in the form of a mission statement, and communicate it down the line to lower-level managers and employees is almost as important as the strategic soundness of the organization's business concept and long-term direction. A mission statement that inspires and challenges can help build committed effort from employees, thus serving as a powerful motivational tool.[3] Bland language, platitudes, and motherhood-and-apple-pie-style verbiage should be scrupulously avoided. Managers need to communicate the vision in words that arouse a strong sense of organizational purpose and that induce employee buy-in. In organizations with freshly changed missions, executives need to provide a convincing rationale for the new direction especially if it requires significant changes within the company. Otherwise the revised mission does little to win employee's commitment and may provoke employee suspicion and mistrust of management's intent—outcomes which make it that much harder to move the organization down a newly chosen path.

A well-worded mission statement generates enthusiasm for the future course that management has charted—people like to be part of a worthwhile cause.

The best-worded mission statements are simple and concise; they speak loudly and clearly, generate enthusiasm for the firm's or unit's future course, and elicit personal effort and dedication from everyone in the organization. They have to be presented and then repeated over and over as a worthy organizational challenge, one capable of benefiting customers in a valuable and meaningful way. It is crucial that the mission stress the payoff for customers and not the payoff for stockholders—it goes without saying that the company intends to profit shareholders from its efforts to provide real customer value. Illustration 5 is a good example of an inspiration-oriented company vision and mission.

ILLUSTRATION 5   *Novacare's Business Mission and Vision*

NovaCare is a fast-growing health care company specializing in providing patient rehabilitation services on a contract basis to nursing homes. Rehabilitation therapy is a $10 billion industry, of which 35% is provided contractually; the contract segment is highly fragmented with over 1,000 competitors. In 1990 NovaCare was a $100 million company, with a goal of being a $275 million business by 1993. The company stated its business mission and vision as follows:

> NovaCare is people committed to making a difference . . . enhancing the future of all patients . . . breaking new ground in our professions . . . achieving excellence . . . advancing human capability . . . changing the world in which we live.
>
> We lead the way with our enthusiasm, optimism, patience, drive and commitment.
>
> We work together to enhance the quality of our patients' lives by reshaping lost abilities and teaching new skills. We heighten expectations for the patient and family. We rebuild hope, confidence, self-respect and a desire to continue.
>
> We apply our clinical expertise to benefit our patients through creative and progressive techniques. Our ethical and performance standards require us to expend every effort to achieve the best possible results.

> Our customers are national and local health care providers who share our goal of enhancing the patients' quality of life. In each community, our customers consider us a partner in providing the best possible care. Our reputation is based on our responsiveness, high standards and effective systems of quality assurance. Our relationship is open and proactive.
>
> We are advocates of our professions and patients through active participation in the professional, regulatory, educational, and research communities at national, state, and local levels.
>
> Our approach to health care fulfills our responsibility to provide investors with a high rate of return through consistent growth and profitability.
>
> Our people are our most valuable asset. We are committed to the personal, professional, and career development of each individual employee. We are proud of what we do and dedicated to our Company. We foster teamwork and create an environment conducive to productive communication among all disciplines.
>
> NovaCare is a company of people in pursuit of this Vision.

Source: Company annual report.

■ WHEN TO CHANGE THE MISSION—WHERE ENTREPRENEURSHIP COMES IN

A member of Maytag's board of directors summed it up well when commenting on why the company acquired a European appliance-maker and expanded its arena of business interest to include international markets as well as domestic markets: "Times change, conditions change." New events and altered circumstances make it incumbent on managers to continually reassess their company's position and prospects, always checking for *when* it's time to steer a new course and adjust the mission. The key strategic question here is, "What new directions should we be moving in *now* to get ready for the changes we see coming in our business?"

> The entrepreneurial challenge in developing a mission is to recognize when market conditions make a new long-term direction desirable.

Repositioning an enterprise in light of emerging developments and changes on the horizon lessens the chances of getting trapped in a stagnant or declining core business or allowing attractive new growth opportunities to slip away because of inaction. Good entrepreneurs have a sharp eye for shifting customer wants and needs, emerging technological capabilities, changing international trade conditions, and other important signs of growing or shrinking business opportunity. They attend quickly to the problems and complaints that users have with the industry's current products and services. When a customer says, "If only . . . ," they listen carefully and try to respond. Such clues and information stimulate them to think creatively and strategically about ways to break new ground. Appraising new customer-market-technology opportunities ultimately leads to entrepreneurial judgments about which fork in the road to take. A strategy leader must evaluate the risks and prospects of each path, and make direction-setting decisions to position the enterprise for success in the years ahead. *A well-chosen mission prepares a company for the future*.

Many companies in consumer electronics and telecommunications, believing that their future products will incorporate microprocessors and other elements of computer technology, are broadening their vision about industry boundaries and establishing new business positions through acquisitions, alliances, and joint ventures that will give them better access to cutting-edge technology. Cable TV companies and telephone companies are in a strategic race to install fiber optics technology and to position themselves to market a whole new vista of services to households and businesses—pay-per-view TV, home shopping, electronic mail, electronic banking, home security systems, energy management systems, information services, and high-speed data transfer. Numerous companies in manufacturing, seeing the collapse of trade barriers and the swing to a world economy, have broadened their strategic vision from serving domestic markets to serving global markets. Coca-Cola, Kentucky Fried Chicken, and McDonald's are pursuing market opportunities in China, Europe, Japan, and the Soviet Union. Japanese automobile companies are fighting for a share of the European car market. CNN, Turner Broadcasting's very successful all-news cable channel, is solidifying its position as the first global all-news channel, a major shift from 10 years ago when its mission was to build a loyal U.S. audience. Hence a company's mission has a finite life, one subject to change whenever top management concludes that the present mission is no longer adequate.

A well-conceived, well-worded mission statement has real managerial value:

1. It crystalizes senior executives' own views about the firm's long-term direction and business make-up.

2. It reduces the risk of visionless management and rudderless decision making.

3. It conveys an organizational purpose and identity that motivates employees to go all out and do their very best work.

4. It provides a beacon lower-level managers can use to form departmental missions, set departmental objectives, and craft functional and departmental strategies that are in sync with the company's direction and strategy.

5. It helps an organization prepare for the future.

▶ SETTING OBJECTIVES: THE SECOND DIRECTION-SETTING TASK

Setting objectives converts the strategic vision and directional course into target outcomes and performance milestones. Objectives represent a managerial commitment to produce specified results in a specified time frame. They spell out *how much* of *what kind* of performance *by when*. They direct attention and energy to what needs to be accomplished.

Objectives represent a managerial commitment to achieve specific performance targets by a certain time.

■ THE MANAGERIAL VALUE OF SETTING OBJECTIVES

Unless an organization's long-term direction and business mission are translated into *measurable* performance targets and managers are pressured to show progress in reaching these targets, organizational statements about direction and mission will end up as window dressing and unrealized dreams of accomplishment. Experience teaches that *companies whose managers set objectives for each key result area and then aggressively pursue actions calculated to achieve their performance targets typically outperform companies whose managers have good intentions, try hard, and hope for success.*

For performance objectives to have value as a management tool, they must be stated in *quantifiable* (measurable) terms and they must contain a *deadline for achievement*. This especially means avoiding generalities like "maximize profits," "reduce costs," "become more efficient," or "increase sales" which specify neither how much or when. The whole idea behind objective setting is to sound a call for action—what to achieve, when to achieve it, and who is to be responsible. Spelling out organization objectives in measurable terms and then holding managers accountable for reaching their assigned targets within a specified time frame (1) substitutes purposeful strategic decision making for aimless actions and confusion over what to accomplish and (2) provides a set of benchmarks for judging the organization's performance.

■ THE KINDS OF OBJECTIVES TO SET

Objectives are needed for each *key result* that managers deem important to success.[4] Two types of key result areas stand out: those relating to *financial performance* and those relating to *strategic performance*. Achieving acceptable financial performance is a must; otherwise the organization's survival is at risk. Achieving acceptable strategic performance is essential to sustaining and improving the company's long-term market position and competitiveness. Specific kinds of financial and strategic performance objectives are shown below:

> Strategic objectives need to be competitor-focused, usually aimed at unseating whoever is the industry's best in a particular category.

Financial Objectives	**Strategic Objectives**
• Faster revenue growth	• A bigger market share
• Faster earnings growth	• A higher, more secure industry rank
• Higher dividends	• Higher product quality
• Wider profit margins	• Lower costs relative to key competitors
• Higher returns on invested capital	• Broader or more attractive product line
• Stronger bond and credit ratings	• A stronger reputation with customers
• Bigger cash flows	• Superior customer service
• A rising stock price	• Recognition as a technology leader and/or product innovator

- Recognition as a blue-chip company
- A more diversified revenue base
- Stable earnings during recessionary periods

- Increased ability to compete in international markets
- Expanded growth opportunities
- Total customer satisfaction

Illustration 6 provides a sampling of the strategic and financial objectives three well-known enterprises have set for themselves.

■ STRATEGIC OBJECTIVES VERSUS FINANCIAL OBJECTIVES: WHICH TAKE PRECEDENCE?

Although both financial and strategic objectives carry top priority, there are times when improving near-term financial performance requires killing or postponing strategic moves that hold promise for strengthening the enterprise's business and competitive position for the long haul. The pressures on managers to opt for better near-term financial performance and sacrifice strategic moves aimed at building a stronger competitive position are especially pronounced when (1) an enterprise is struggling financially, (2) the resource commitments for strategically beneficial moves will materially detract from the bottom-line for several years, and (3) the proposed strategic moves are risky and have an uncertain market and competitive payoff.

Yet, there are dangers that management will succumb to the lure of immediate gains in margins and return on investment when it means paring or forgoing strategic moves that would build a stronger business position. A company that consistently passes up opportunities to strengthen its long-term competitive position for near-term gains in financial performance risks diluting its competitiveness, losing momentum in its markets,

---

ILLUSTRATION 6   *Examples of Corporate Objectives: McDonald's, Rubbermaid, and McCormick & Co.*

McDonald's

- To achieve 100 percent total customer satisfaction . . . everyday . . . in every restaurant . . . for every customer.

Rubbermaid

- To increase annual sales from $1 billion to $2 billion in five years.
- To enter a new market every 18 to 24 months.
- To have 30% of sales each year come from products not in the company's product line five years earlier.
- To be the lowest-cost, highest-quality producer in the household products industry.
- To achieve a 15% average annual growth in sales, profits, and earnings per share.

McCormick & Co.

- Achieve a 20% return on equity.
- Achieve a net sales growth rate of 10% per year.
- Maintain an average earnings per share growth rate of 15% per year.
- Maintain total debt to total capital at 40% or less.
- Pay out 25% to 35% of net income in dividends.
- Make selective acquisitions which complement our current businesses and can enhance our overall returns.
- Dispose of those parts of our business which do not or cannot generate adequate returns or do not fit our business strategy.

Source: Company annual reports.

and impairing its ability to stave off market challenges from ambitious rivals. The business landscape is littered with ex-market leaders who put more emphasis on the financial objective of boosting next quarter's profit than on the strategic objective of strengthening long-term market position. The danger of trading off long-term gains in market position for near-term gains in bottom-line

> **Building a stronger, long-term competitive position benefits shareholders more lastingly than improving short-term profitability.**

performance is greatest when a profit-conscious market leader has competitors who invest relentlessly in gaining market share in preparation for the time when they will be big enough and strong enough to outcompete the leader in a head-to-head market battle. The surest path to protecting and sustaining a company's profitability quarter after quarter and year after year is to pursue strategic actions that strengthen its competitiveness and business position.

THE CONCEPT OF STRATEGIC INTENT

A company's strategic objectives are important for another reason—they indicate *strategic intent* to stake out a particular business position.[5] The strategic intent of a large company may be industry leadership on a national or global scale. The strategic intent of a small company may be to dominate a market niche. The strategic intent of an up-and-coming enterprise may be to overtake the market leaders. The strategic intent of a technologically innovative company may be to pioneer a promising discovery and open a whole new vista of products and market opportunities—as did Xerox, Apple Computer, Microsoft, Merck, and Sony.

> **A company exhibits *strategic intent* when it relentlessly pursues a specific long-term strategic objective.**

The time horizon underlying a company's strategic intent is long-term. Companies that rise to prominence in their markets almost invariably begin with strategic intents that are out of proportion to their immediate capabilities and market positions. They set ambitious long-term strategic objectives and then pursue them relentlessly, sometimes even obsessively, over a 10- to 20-year period. In the 1960s, Komatsu, Japan's leading earth-moving equipment company, was less than one-third the size of Caterpillar, had little market presence outside Japan, and depended on its small bulldozers for most of its revenue. Komatsu's strategic intent was to "encircle Caterpillar" with a broader product line and then compete globally against Caterpillar. By the late 1980s, Komatsu was the industry's second-ranking company, with a strong sales presence in North America, Europe, and Asia plus a product line that included industrial robots and semiconductors as well as a broad array of earth-moving equipment.

Often, a company's strategic intent takes on a heroic character, serving as a rallying cry for managers and employees alike to go all out and do their very best. Canon's strategic intent in copying equipment was to "beat Xerox." The strategic intent of the U.S. government's Apollo space program was to land a person on the moon ahead of the Soviet Union. Throughout the 1980s, Wal-Mart's strategic intent was to "overtake Sears" as the largest U.S. retailer (a feat accomplished in 1991). In such instances, strategic intent signals a deep-seated commitment to winning—unseating the industry leader, remaining the industry leader (and becoming more dominant in the process), or otherwise beating long odds to gain a significantly stronger business position. A capably managed enterprise whose strategic objectives go well beyond its present reach and resources is potentially a more formidable competitor than a company with modest strategic intent.

LONG-RANGE VERSUS SHORT-RANGE OBJECTIVES

An organization needs both long-range and short-range objectives. Long-range objectives serve two purposes. First, setting performance targets five or more years ahead pushes managers to take actions *now* in order to achieve the targeted long-range performance *later* (a company that has an objective of doubling its sales within five years can't wait until the third or fourth year of its five-year strategic plan to begin growing its sales and customer base). Second, having explicit long-range objectives prompts managers to weigh the impact of today's decisions on longer-range performance. Without the pressure to meet long-range performance targets, it is human nature to base decisions on what is most expedient at the moment and to worry about the future later; such shortsightedness jeopardizes a company's long-term business position.

Short-range objectives spell out the immediate and near-term results to be achieved. They indicate the *speed* at which management wants the organization to progress as well as the *level of performance* being aimed for over the next two or three periods. Short-range objectives can be identical with long-range objectives anytime an organization is already performing at the targeted long-term level. For instance, if a company has an ongoing objective of 15 percent profit growth every year and is currently achieving this objective, then the company's long-range and short-range profit objectives coincide. The most important situation where short-range objectives differ from long-range objectives occurs when managers are trying to elevate organizational performance and cannot reach the long-range/ongoing target in just one year. Short-range objectives then serve as stairsteps or milestones for reaching the ultimate target.

■ THE "CHALLENGING BUT ACHIEVABLE" TEST

Objectives should not represent whatever levels of achievement management decides would be nice. Wishful thinking has no place in objective setting. For objectives to serve as a tool for *stretching* an organization to reach its full potential, they must meet the criterion of being *challenging but achievable*. Satisfying this criterion means setting objectives in the light of several important inside-outside considerations:

Company performance targets should be challenging but achievable.

- What performance levels will industry and competitive conditions realistically allow?
- What results will it take for the organization to be a successful performer?
- What performance is the organization capable of *when pushed?*

To set challenging but achievable objectives, managers must judge what performance is possible in light of external conditions against what performance the organization is capable of achieving. The tasks of objective-setting and strategy-making often become intertwined at this point. Strategic choices, for example, cannot be made in a financial vacuum; the money has to be there to execute the chosen strategy. Consequently, decisions about strategy are contingent on setting the organization's financial performance objectives high enough (1) to execute the chosen strategy, (2) to fund other needed actions, and (3) to please investors and the financial community. Objectives and strategy also intertwine when it comes to matching the means (strategy) with the ends (objectives). If a company's strategy is not capable of achieving established objectives (because the objectives are set unrealistically high or because the present strategy can't deliver the desired performance), the objectives or the strategy need adjustment to produce a better fit.

■ THE NEED FOR OBJECTIVES AT ALL MANAGEMENT LEVELS

For strategic thinking and strategy-driven decision making to permeate organization behavior, performance targets must be established not only for the organization as a whole but also for each of the organization's distinct businesses and product lines down to each functional area and department within the business-unit/product-line structure.[6] Only when every manager, from the chief executive officer down to the lowest level manager, is held accountable for achieving specific results in the units they head and each unit's objectives support achievement of company objectives is the objective-setting process complete enough to ensure that the whole organization is headed down the chosen path and that each part of the organization knows what it needs to accomplish.

The objective-setting process is more top-down than it is bottom-up. To see why strategic objectives at one managerial level tend to drive objectives and strategies at the next level down, consider the following example. Senior executives of a diversified corporation establish a corporate profit objective of $5 million for next year. After discussion between corporate management and the general managers of the firm's five different businesses, each business is given the challenging but achievable profit objective of $1 million by year-end. A concrete result has thus been agreed on and translated into measurable commitments at two levels in the managerial hierarchy. The general manager of business unit X, after some analysis and discussion with functional area managers, concludes that reaching the $1 million profit objective will require selling 100,000 units at an average price of $50 and producing them at an average cost of $40 (a $10 profit margin times 100,000 units equals $1 million profit). Consequently, the general manager and the manufacturing manager decide on a production objective of 100,000 units at a unit cost of $40, and the general manager and the marketing manager agree to a sales objective of 100,000 units at a target selling price of $50. In turn, the marketing manager breaks the sales objective of 100,000 units down into unit sales targets for each sales territory, each item in the product line, and each salesperson.

A top-down process of establishing performance targets for strategy-critical activities, processes, and departmental units is a rational and systematic way of breaking companywide targets down into pieces that lower-level units and managers are responsible for achieving. Such an approach also provides a valuable degree of *unity* and *cohesion* to the objective-setting and strategy-making taking place in different parts of the organization. Generally, organizationwide objectives and strategy need to be established first so they can *guide* objective-setting and strategy-making at lower levels. Top-down

> Objective setting needs to be more of a top-down process than a bottom-up process.

objective-setting and strategizing direct lower-level units toward objectives and strategies that support the total enterprise. When objective-setting and strategy-making begin at the bottom levels of an organization and organizationwide objectives and strategies reflect the aggregate of what has bubbled up from below, there's no reason to expect the resulting strategic action plan to be consistent, cohesive, or coordinated. Bottom-up objective-setting, with no guidance from above, nearly always signals an absence of strategic leadership on the part of senior executives.

▶ CRAFTING A STRATEGY: THE THIRD DIRECTION-SETTING TASK

Organizations need strategies to guide how to achieve objectives and how to pursue the organization's mission. Strategy-making is all about *how*—how to reach performance targets, how to outcompete rivals, how to achieve sustainable competitive advantage, how to strengthen the enterprise's long-term business position, how to make management's strategic vision for the company a reality. A strategy is needed for the company as a whole, for each business the company is in, and for

---
An organization's strategy is all about *how*—how to achieve performance targets and how to compete successfully.
---

each functional piece of each business—R&D, purchasing, production, sales and marketing, finance, human resources, and so on. An organization's overall strategy and managerial game plan emerges from the *pattern* of actions already initiated and the plans managers have for fresh moves. In forming a strategy out of the many feasible options, a manager forges a response to market change, seeks new opportunities, and synthesizes the different moves and approaches taken at various times in various parts of the organization.[7]

The strategy-making spotlight, however, needs to stay on the important facets of management's game plan for running the enterprise—those action elements that determine what market position the company is trying to stake out and that underpin whether the company will be successful or not. Low-priority issues (whether to increase the advertising budget, whether to raise the dividend, whether to locate a new plant in state X or state Y) and routine managerial housekeeping (whether to own or lease company vehicles, how to reduce sales force turnover) are not basic to the strategy, even though they must be decided. Moreover, strategy is inherently action-oriented; it concerns what to do, when to do it, and who should be involved in the effort. Unless there is action, unless something happens, unless somebody does something, strategic thinking and planning simply go to waste and, in the end, amount to nothing.

An organization's strategy evolves over time. It's seldom possible to plan all the bits and pieces of a company's strategy in advance and then go for long periods without encountering any need for changes. Reacting and responding to happenings either inside the company or in the surrounding environment are a normal part of the strategy-making process. The dynamic character of competition, changing buyer needs and expectations, fluctuations in costs, mergers and acquisitions among major industry players, new regulations, the raising or lowering of trade barriers, and countless other events can make certain pieces of the intended strategy obsolete. There is always something new to react to and some new strategic window opening up. This is why the task of crafting strategy is unending, involving diligent monitoring of the situation to make adjustments as they are needed. And that is why a company's actual strategy turns out to be a blend of its intended strategy and its unplanned reactions to fresh developments.

■ THE STRATEGY-MAKING PYRAMID

Strategy making is not just a task for senior executives. In very large enterprises, decisions about what approaches to take and what new moves to initiate involve senior executives in the corporate office, heads of business units and product divisions as well as major functional areas within a business or division (i.e. manufacturing, marketing and sales, finance, and human resources), plant managers, product managers, district and regional sales managers, and lower-level supervisors. In diversified enterprises, strategies are initiated at four distinct organization levels:

*   *Corporate strategy*—for the company as a whole and all of its businesses.
*   *Business strategy*—for each separate business the company has diversified into.
*   *Functional strategy*—for specific functional units within a business. Each business usually has a production strategy, a marketing strategy, a finance strategy, and so on.
*   *Operating strategy*—still narrower strategies for basic operating units, such as plants, sales districts and regions, and departments within functional areas.

Figure 2–1 shows the strategy-making pyramid for a diversified company. In single-business enterprises, there are only three levels of strategy-making (business strategy, functional strategy, and operating strategy) unless diversification into other businesses becomes an active consideration.

■ CORPORATE STRATEGY

Corporate strategy is the overall managerial game plan for a diversified company. Corporate strategy extends companywide—an umbrella over all its businesses. It consists of the moves made to establish business positions in different industries and the approaches used to manage the company's group of businesses. Figure 2–2 depicts the core elements that identify a diversified company's corporate strategy. Crafting corporate strategy for a diversified company involves four kinds of initiatives:

Corporate strategy concerns itself with how to build business positions in different industries and how to improve the performance of the group of businesses the company has diversified into.

1. *Making the moves to accomplish diversification.* The first concern in diversification is what the company's portfolio of businesses should include—specifically, what industries to diversify into, and whether to enter the chosen industries by starting a new business from scratch, or acquiring a company already in business (an established leader, an up-and-coming company, or a troubled company with turnaround potential). This decision establishes whether diversification is based narrowly in a few industries or broadly in many industries, and it shapes how the company will be positioned in each of the target industries.

2. *Initiating actions to boost the combined performance of the businesses into which the firm has diversified.* As positions are created in the chosen industries, corporate strategy making concentrates on ways to get better performance out of the

FIGURE 2–1   *The Strategy-Making Pyramid*

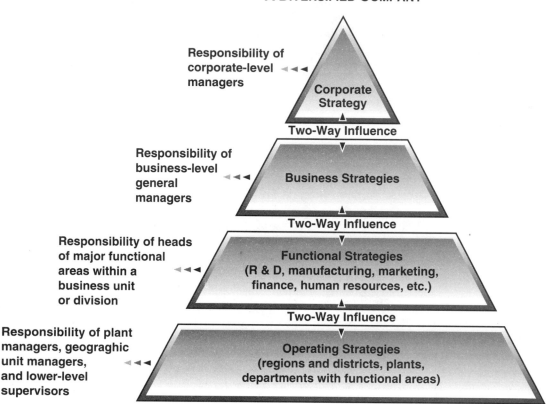

A DIVERSIFIED COMPANY

Responsibility of corporate-level managers ◄◄◄

Corporate Strategy

Two-Way Influence

Responsibility of business-level general managers ◄◄◄

Business Strategies

Two-Way Influence

Responsibility of heads of major functional areas within a business unit or division ◄◄◄

Functional Strategies
(R & D, manufacturing, marketing, finance, human resources, etc.)

Two-Way Influence

Responsibility of plant managers, geograghic unit managers, and lower-level supervisors ◄◄◄

Operating Strategies
(regions and districts, plants, departments with functional areas)

A SINGLE BUSINESS COMPANY

Responsibility of executive-level managers ◄◄◄

Business Strategy

Two-Way Influence

Responsibility of heads of major functional areas within a business ◄◄◄

Functional Strategies
(R & D, manufacturing, marketing, finance, human resources, etc.)

Two-Way Influence

Responsibility of plant managers, geograghic unit managers, and lower-level supervisors ◄◄◄

Operating Strategies
(regions and districts, plants, departments with functional areas)

FIGURE 2–2   *Identifying the Corporate Strategy of a Diversified Company*

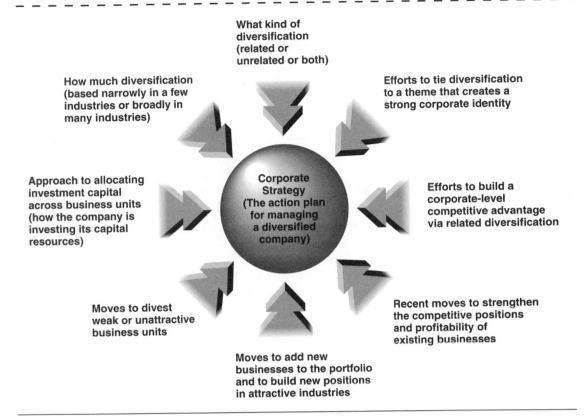

business-unit portfolio. Decisions must be reached about how to strengthen the long-term competitive positions and profitabilities of the businesses in which the firm has invested. Corporate parents can help their business subsidiaries be more successful by financing additional capacity and efficiency improvements, by supplying missing skills and managerial know-how, by acquiring another company in the same industry and merging the two operations into a stronger business, and/or by acquiring new businesses that strongly complement existing businesses. The overall plan for managing a group of diversified businesses usually involves pursuing rapid-growth strategies in the most promising businesses, keeping the other core businesses healthy, initiating turnaround efforts in weak-performing businesses with potential, and divesting businesses that are no longer attractive or that don't fit into management's long-range plans.

3. *Finding ways to capture the synergy among related business units and turn it into competitive advantage.* When a company diversifies into businesses having related technologies, similar operating characteristics, the same distribution channels,

common customers, or some other synergistic relationship, it gains competitive advantage potential not open to a company that has diversified into totally unrelated businesses. With related diversification there are usually opportunities to transfer skills, share expertise, or share facilities, thereby reducing overall costs, strengthening the competitiveness of some of the company's products, or enhancing the capabilities of particular business units—any of which can represent a significant source of competitive advantage. The greater the relatedness among the businesses of a diversified company, the greater the opportunities for skills transfer and/or sharing across businesses, and the bigger the window for creating competitive advantage. Indeed, what makes related diversification so attractive is the synergistic *strategic fit* across related business units that allows company resources to be leveraged into a combined performance *greater* than the units could achieve operating independently. The 2 + 2 = 5 aspect of strategic fit makes related diversification a very appealing strategy for boosting corporate performance and shareholder value.

4. *Establishing investment priorities and steering corporate resources into the most attractive business units.* A diversified company's businesses are usually not equally attractive from the standpoint of investing additional funds. This facet of corporate strategy making requires setting priorities to guide capital investment in the businesses and channeling resources into areas where earnings potentials are higher and away from areas where they are lower. Corporate strategy may include divesting business units that are chronically poor performers or those in an increasingly unattractive industry. Divestiture frees up unproductive investments for redeployment to promising business units or for financing attractive new acquisitions.

Corporate strategy is crafted at the highest levels of management. Senior corporate executives normally have lead responsibility for devising corporate strategy and for choosing among whatever recommended actions bubble up from lower-level managers. Key business-unit heads may also be influential, especially in strategic decisions affecting the businesses they head. Major strategic decisions are usually reviewed and approved by the company's board of directors.

■ BUSINESS STRATEGY

Business strategy (or *business-level strategy*) *is the overall game plan for a single business.* It is mirrored in the pattern of approaches and moves crafted by management to produce successful performance in *one specific line of business.* The core elements of business strategy are illustrated in Figure 2–3. For a stand-alone single-business company, corporate strategy and business strategy are one and the same since there is only one business; the distinction between corporate strategy and business strategy is relevant only when the firm has diversified.

The central thrust of business strategy is how to build and strengthen the company's long-term competitive position in the marketplace. Towards this end, business strategy is concerned principally with (1) forming responses to emerging buyer needs and preferences and changes underway in the industry, the economy at large, the regulatory and political arena, and other relevant areas; (2) crafting competitive moves and market approaches that can lead to

The central business strategy issue is *how* to build a stronger long-term competitive position.

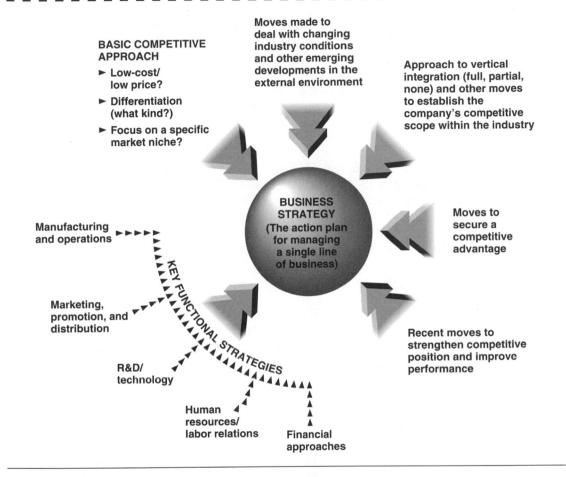

FIGURE 2-3   *Identifying Strategy for a Single-Business Company*

BASIC COMPETITIVE APPROACH
► Low-cost/low price?
► Differentiation (what kind?)
► Focus on a specific market niche?

Moves made to deal with changing industry conditions and other emerging developments in the external environment

Approach to vertical integration (full, partial, none) and other moves to establish the company's competitive scope within the industry

BUSINESS STRATEGY (The action plan for managing a single line of business)

Moves to secure a competitive advantage

Manufacturing and operations

KEY FUNCTIONAL STRATEGIES

Marketing, promotion, and distribution

R&D/technology

Human resources/labor relations

Financial approaches

Recent moves to strengthen competitive position and improve performance

sustainable competitive advantage; (3) uniting the strategic initiatives of functional departments; and (4) addressing specific strategic issues facing the company's business.

Clearly, business strategy encompasses whatever moves and new approaches managers deem prudent in response to market forces, economic trends and developments, buyer needs and demographics, new legislation and regulatory requirements, and other external factors. A good strategy is well matched to the external circumstance; as it changes in significant ways, then needed adjustments in strategy are made. Whether a company's response to external change is quick or slow tends to be a function of how long events must unfold before managers can assess any implications for the business and how much longer it then takes to form a strategic response. Some external changes, of course, require little or no response, while others call for significant strategy alterations. On occasions, external factors change in ways that pose a formidable strategic hurdle—for example, cigarette manufacturers face a tough challenge holding their own against the mounting antismoking campaign.

What separates a powerful business strategy from a weak one is the strategist's ability *to forge a series of moves and approaches capable of producing sustainable competitive advantage*. With a competitive advantage, a company has good prospects for above-average profitability and success in the industry. Without competitive advantage, a company risks being locked into mediocre performance by stronger rivals. Crafting a business strategy that yields sustainable competitive advantage has three facets: (1) deciding where a firm has the best chance to win a competitive edge, (2) developing product/service attributes that have strong buyer appeal and set the company apart from rivals, and (3) neutralizing the competitive moves of rival companies.

A business strategy is powerful if it produces a sizable and sustainable competitive advantage; it is weak if it results in competitive disadvantage.

A company's competitive strategy is typically both offensive and defensive—some of its actions are aggressive, directly challenging the market position held by competitors; others are to counter moves made by rivals. The three most popular competitive approaches are (1) striving to be the industry's low-cost producer (thereby aiming for a low-cost/low-priced competitive advantage over rivals); (2) pursuing differentiation based on such advantages as quality, performance, service, styling, technological superiority, or unusually good value; and (3) focusing on a narrow market niche and winning a competitive edge by doing a better job than rivals of serving the special needs and tastes of buyers in that niche.

Internally, business strategy involves developing the skills and capabilities necessary to achieve competitive advantage. Successful companies usually aim at building competencies in one or more core activities crucial to strategic success and then use these core competencies to get outcompete rivals. A *core competence* is something a firm does especially well in comparison to rival companies. It thus represents a source of competitive strength. Core competencies can relate to R&D, mastery of a technological process, manufacturing capability, sales and distribution, customer service, or anything that is a competitively significant aspect of creating, producing, or marketing the company's product or service. A core competence is a basis for competitive advantage because it represents specialized expertise that rivals don't have and cannot readily match.

A successful business strategy must also aim at uniting strategic initiatives among the various functional areas such as purchasing, production, R&D, finance, human resources, sales and marketing, and distribution. Strategic actions are needed in each functional area to *support* the company's competitive approach and overall business strategy. Strategic unity and coordination across the various functional areas add power to the business strategy.

Business strategy also incorporates action plans for addressing any special strategy-related issues unique to the company's competitive position and internal situation, such as whether to add new capacity, replace an obsolete plant, increase R&D funding for a promising technology, or reduce burdensome interest expenses. Such custom-tailoring of strategy to fit a company's specific situation is one of the reasons why every company in an industry has a different business strategy.

Lead responsibility for business strategy belongs to the manager in charge of the business. Even if the manager does not personally direct the business's strategy-making process, preferring instead to delegate the task to others, he or she is still accountable to the company for the strategy and its results. The business head, as chief strategist for the business, has at least two other responsibilities. The first is seeing that supporting strategies in each of the major functional areas of the business are well conceived and consistent with each other. The second is getting major strategic moves approved by higher authority (i.e., the board of directors and/or corporate-level officers) if necessary, and keeping them informed of important new developments, deviations from plan, and potential strategy revisions. In diversified companies, business-unit heads may have the additional obligation of making sure business-level objectives and strategy conform to corporate-level objectives and strategy themes.

■ FUNCTIONAL STRATEGY

Functional strategy concerns the managerial game plan for a particular department or key functional activity within a business. A company's marketing strategy, for example, represents the managerial plan for running its marketing-related activities. A company needs a functional strategy for every major departmental unit and aspect of the business. Functional strategies, while narrower in scope than business strategy, add relevant detail to the overall business plan by establishing the actions, approaches, and practices for operating a particular department or business function. The primary role of a functional

> *Functional strategy* is concerned with the managerial game plan for running a major functional activity within a business. A business needs as many functional strategies as it has major functional activities.

strategy is to *support* the company's overall business strategy and competitive approach. A second objective of a functional strategy is to describe how the functional area will achieve its established objectives and mission. Thus, functional strategy in the production/manufacturing area represents the plan for *how* manufacturing activities will be managed to support business strategy and achieve the manufacturing department's objectives and mission. Functional strategy in the finance area consists of *how* financial activities will be managed in supporting business strategy and achieving the finance department's objectives and mission.

Lead responsibility for strategy-making in the functional areas of a business is normally delegated to the respective functional department heads unless the business-unit head decides to exert a strong influence. In crafting strategy, a functional department head ideally works closely with key subordinates and touches base with the heads of other functional areas and the business head often. There's nothing to be said for functional managers who plot strategy independently of each other or the business manager—this simply fosters disconnected or conflicting strategies. Coordinated and mutually supportive functional strategies are essential if the overall business strategy is to have maximum impact. Without coordination among a business's marketing strategy, production strategy, finance strategy, and human resources strategy, functional areas risk working at cross purposes and undermining the company's potential for success. Coordination across functional area strategies is best accomplished during the deliberation stage. If inconsistent functional strategies are sent up the line for final approval, it is up to the business head to spot the conflicts and get them resolved.

■ OPERATING STRATEGY

Operating strategies concern even narrower strategic initiatives and approaches for managing key operating units (plants, sales districts, distribution centers) and for handling

---

Operating strategies outline how to manage key organizational units within a business and how to perform strategically significant activities.

---

daily operating tasks that have strategic significance (advertising campaigns, materials purchasing, inventory control, maintenance, shipping). Operating strategies, while of lesser scope, add further detail and completeness to functional strategies and the overall business plan. Lead responsibility for operating strategies is usually delegated to front-line managers, subject to review and approval by their bosses.

Even though operating strategies are at the bottom of the strategy-making pyramid, their importance should not be downplayed. For example, a major plant that fails in its strategy to achieve production volume, unit cost, and quality targets can undermine the achievement of company sales and profit objectives and undercut the whole company's strategic efforts to build a quality image with customers. One cannot reliably judge the importance of a given strategic move by the managerial or organizational level where it is initiated.

Front-line managers are part of an organization's strategy-making team because operating units have strategy-critical performance targets and need to have strategic action plans in place to guide their actions and ensure a proper allocation of resources. A regional manager needs a strategy customized to the region's particular situation and objectives. A plant manager needs a strategy for accomplishing the plant's objectives, carrying out the plant's part of the company's overall manufacturing plan, and responding to any strategy-related problems at the plant. A company's advertising manager needs a strategy for getting maximum audience exposure and sales impact from the ad budget. The following two examples illustrate how operating strategy supports higher-level strategies:

- A company with a low-price, high-volume business strategy and a need to achieve low manufacturing costs launches a companywide effort to boost worker productivity by 10 percent. To contribute to the productivity-boosting objective: (1) the manager of employee recruiting develops a strategy for interviewing and testing job applicants that is thorough enough to weed out all but the most highly motivated, best-qualified candidates; (2) the manager of information systems devises a way to use office technology to boost the productivity of office workers; (3) the employee benefits manager devises an improved incentive-compensation plan to reward increased output by manufacturing employees; and (4) the purchasing manager launches a program to obtain new efficiency-increasing tools and equipment more quickly and at a lower cost.

- A distributor of plumbing equipment emphasizes quick delivery and accurate order filling as keystones of its customer service approach. To support this strategy, the warehouse manager (1) develops an inventory-stocking strategy that allows 99 percent of all orders to be completely filled without back ordering any item and (2) institutes a warehouse staffing strategy that allows any order to be shipped within 24 hours.

■ UNITING THE STRATEGY-MAKING EFFORT

The previous discussion underscores that a company's *strategic plan is a collection of strategies* devised by different managers at different levels in the organizational hierarchy. The larger the enterprise, the more points of strategic initiative it must have. Management's direction-setting effort is not complete until the separate layers of strategy are unified into a coherent, supportive pattern. Ideally the pieces and layers of strategy should fit together like the pieces of a puzzle. Unified objectives and strategies don't emerge from an undirected process where managers at each level set objectives and craft strategies independently. Indeed, functional and operating-level managers have a duty to set performance targets and develop strategic actions that will help achieve business objectives and make business strategy more effec-tive.

Harmonizing objectives and strategies piece by piece and level by level can be tedious and frustrating, requiring numerous consultations and meetings, annual strategy reviews and approvals, and months (sometimes years) of building consen-sus.

> Objectives and strategies that are unified from top to bottom do not come from an undirected process where managers at each level have objective-setting and strategy-making autonomy.

The work of gaining strategic consensus while trying to keep all managers and departments focused on what's best for the total enterprise, as opposed to what's best for their department or their career, is often a big obstacle in unifying the layers of objectives and strategies.[8] Gaining broad consensus is particularly difficult when there is ample room for opposing views and disagreement. It is not unusual for managerial discussions about an organization's mission and basic direction, what objectives to set, and what strategies to use to provoke heated debates and strong differences of opinion.

Figure 2–4 portrays the networking of objectives and strategies down through the managerial hierarchy. The two-way arrows indicate that there are simultaneous bottom-up and top-down influences on missions, objectives, and strategies at each level. These vertical linkages, if managed in a way that promotes coordination, can help unify the direction-setting and strategy-making activities of many managers into a mutually reinforcing pattern. The tighter the coordination, the tighter the linkages in the missions, objectives, and strategies of the various organizational units. Tight linkages keep organizational units from straying from the company's charted strategic course.

As a practical matter, however, corporate and business missions, objectives, and strategies need to be clearly outlined and communicated down the line before much progress can be made in direction setting and strategy making at the functional and operating levels. Direction and guidance needs to flow from the corporate level to the business level and from the business level to the functional and operating levels of the managerial hierarchy. The strategic disarray that occurs in an organization when senior managers don't exercise strong direction-setting and strategic leadership is akin to what would happen to a football team's offensive performance if the quarterback decided

> Functional and operating-level managers have a duty to set performance targets and invent strategic actions that will help achieve business objectives and improve the execution of business strategy.

not to call a play for the team but, instead, gave each player the latitude to pick whatever play he thought would work best at his respective position. Similarly, if the quarterback

FIGURE 2–4   *The Networking of Missions, Objectives, and Strategies through the Managerial Hierarchy*

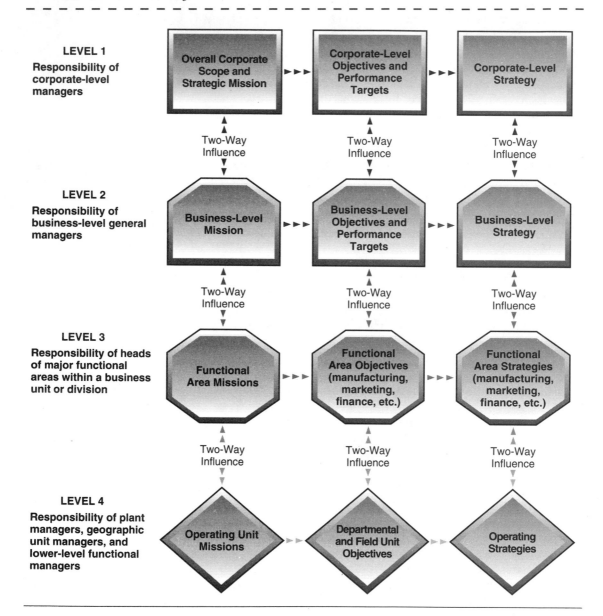

insisted on calling plays which his teammates could not execute, he would be instigating strategic mayhem. In business, as in sports, all of the strategy-makers in a company are on the same team. They are obligated to perform their strategy-making tasks in a manner that benefits the overall company, not in a manner that suits personal or departmental interests. A company's strategy is at full power only when its many pieces are united. Strategic unity is more likely when the strategizing process proceeds more from the top downward than from the bottom upward. Lower-level managers cannot do unified strategy making without understanding the company's direction and higher-level strategies.

▶ THE FACTORS THAT SHAPE A COMPANY'S STRATEGY

Many situational considerations enter into crafting strategy. Figure 2–5 depicts the primary factors that shape a company's strategic approaches. The interplay of these factors and the influence that each has on the strategy-making process varies from company to company. No two strategic choices are made in exactly the same context; even in the same industry situational factors differ enough from company to company that each company ends up pursuing a customized strategy. This is why carefully sizing up all the various situational factors, both external and internal, is the starting point in crafting strategy.

■ SOCIETAL, POLITICAL, REGULATORY, AND CITIZENSHIP CONSIDERATIONS

An enterprise's activities are always constrained by law, by government policies and regulatory requirements, by social convention, and by community citizenship ideas. Outside pressures also come from other sources—special interest groups, the glare of investigative reporting, a fear of unwanted political action, and the stigma of negative opinion. Societal concerns over health and nutrition, alcohol and drug abuse, hazardous waste disposal, sexual harassment, and the effect of plant closings on local communities have impacted the strategies of many companies. American concerns over the magnitude of foreign imports and political debate over whether to impose tariffs to cure the chronic U.S. trade deficit have been driving forces in the strategic decisions of Japanese and European companies to locate plants in the United States.

> Societal, political, regulatory, and citizenship concerns put boundaries on what strategic actions a company cannot or should not take.

Factoring in societal values and priorities, community concerns, and the potential for onerous legislation and regulatory requirements to situation analysis has become a regular procedure at more and more companies. Intense public pressure and adverse media coverage have made such practices prudent. The task of making an organization's strategy socially responsible means (1) conducting organizational activities ethically and in the general public interest, (2) responding positively to emerging societal priorities and expectations, (3) demonstrating a willingness to take action ahead of regulatory confrontation, (4) balancing stockholder interests against the larger interests of society as a whole, and (5) being a good citizen in the community.

FIGURE 2–5   *Factors Shaping the Choice of Company Strategy*

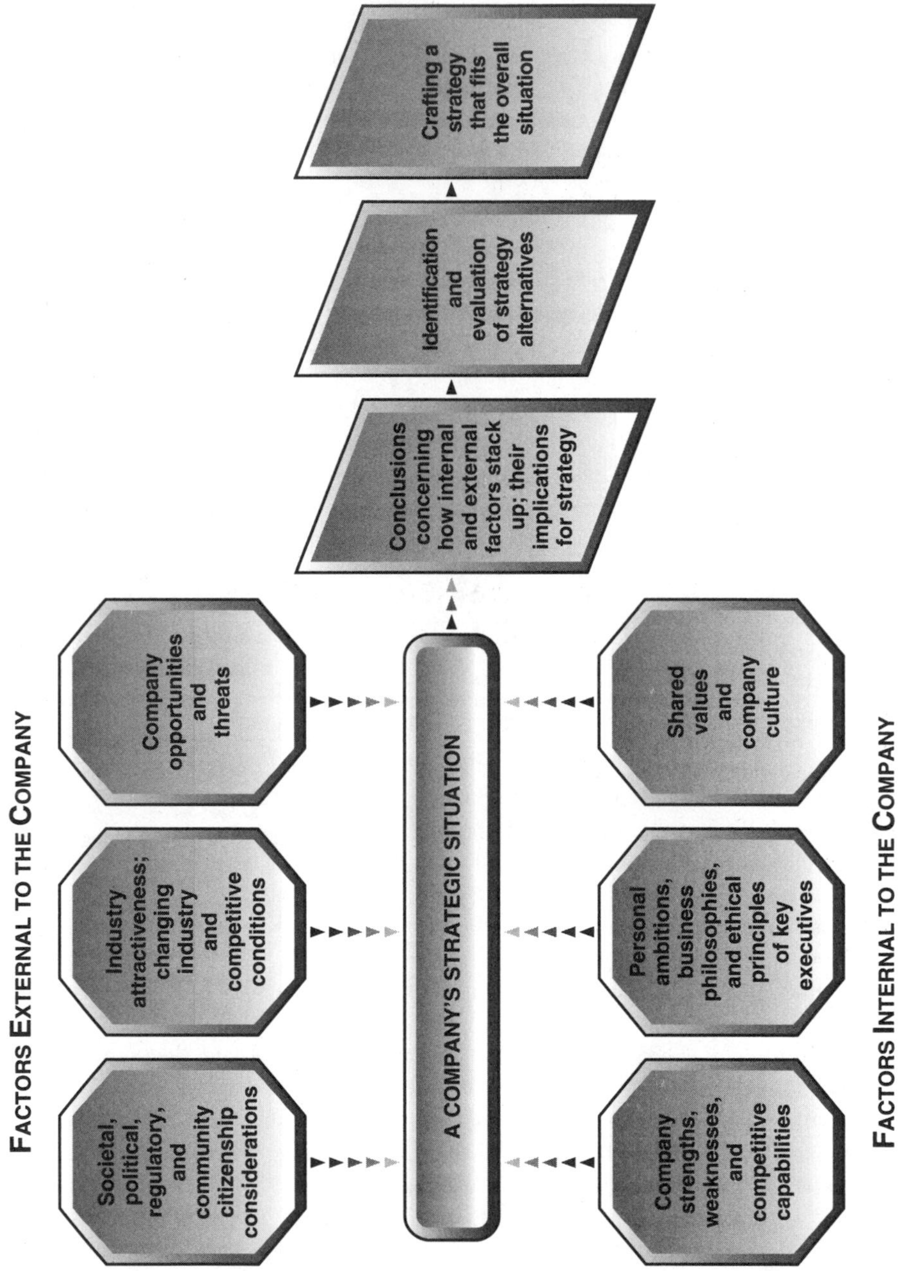

FACTORS EXTERNAL TO THE COMPANY

Societal, political, regulatory, and community citizenship considerations

Industry attractiveness; changing industry and competitive conditions

Company opportunities and threats

A COMPANY'S STRATEGIC SITUATION

Conclusions concerning how internal and external factors stack up; their implications for strategy

Identification and evaluation of strategy alternatives

Crafting a strategy that fits the overall situation

Company strengths, weaknesses, and competitive capabilities

Personal ambitions, business philosophies, and ethical principles of key executives

Shared values and company culture

FACTORS INTERNAL TO THE COMPANY

Acknowledgement of the role of corporate social responsibility is showing up in company mission statements. John Hancock, for example, concludes its mission statement with the following sentence:

> In pursuit of this mission, we will strive to exemplify the highest standards of business ethics and personal integrity, and shall recognize our corporate obligation to the social and economic well-being of our community.

At Union Electric, a St. Louis-based utility company, the following statement is official corporate policy:

> As a private enterprise entrusted with an essential public service, we recognize our civic responsibility in the communities we serve. We shall strive to advance the growth and welfare of these communities and shall participate in civic activities which fulfill that goal . . . for we believe this is both good citizenship and good business.

■ INDUSTRY ATTRACTIVENESS AND COMPETITIVE CONDITIONS

Industry attractiveness and competitive conditions are also significant factors in determining strategy. A company's assessment of the industry and competitive environment has a direct bearing on how it should try to position itself in the industry and on its basic competitive strategy approach. When competitive conditions intensify significantly, a company must respond with strategic actions to protect its position. Fresh moves on the part of rival companies, changes in the industry's price-cost-profit economics, and new technological developments can alter the requirements for competitive success and mandate reconsideration of strategy. When a firm concludes that its

> A company's strategy ought to closely match industry and competitive conditions.

industry environment has grown unattractive and it is better off investing company resources elsewhere, it may begin a strategy of disinvestment and eventual abandonment. A strategist, therefore, has to be a student of industry and competitive conditions.

■ SPECIFIC MARKET OPPORTUNITIES AND THREATS

Particular business opportunities and external threats are key influences on company strategy that point to the need for strategic action. A company's strategy needs to be deliberately aimed at capturing its best growth opportunities, especially the ones that hold the most promise for building sustainable competitive advantage and enhancing profitability. Likewise, strategy should be geared to providing a defense against external threats to the company's well-being and

> A well-conceived strategy aims at capturing a company's best growth opportunities and defending against external threats to future performance.

future performance. For strategy to be successful, it has to be well matched to market opportunities and threatening external developments; this usually means crafting offensive moves to capitalize on the company's most promising market opportunities and crafting defensive moves to protect the company's competitive position and long-term profitability.

■ ORGANIZATIONAL STRENGTHS, WEAKNESSES, AND COMPETITIVE CAPABILITIES

Experience shows that in matching strategy to a firm's internal situation, management should build strategy around what the company does well and avoid strategies whose success depends on something the company does poorly or has never done at all. In short, *strategy must be well matched to company strengths, weaknesses, and competitive capabilities*. Pursuing an opportunity without the organizational competences and resources to capture it is foolish. An organization's strengths make some opportunities and strategies attractive; likewise its internal weaknesses and its present competitive market position make certain strategies risky or impossible.

One of the most pivotal strategy-shaping internal considerations is whether a company has or can build the core strengths or competences needed to execute a strategy proficiently. An organization's core strengths — the things it does especially well — are an important strategic consideration because of (1) the skills and capabilities they provide in capitalizing on a particular opportunity, (2) the competitive edge they may give a firm in the marketplace, and (3) the potential they have for becoming a cornerstone of strategy.

A company's strategy ought to be grounded in what it is good at doing and it ought to avoid what it is not so good at doing.

The best path to competitive advantage is found when a firm has core strengths in one or more of the key requirements for market success, and rivals not only do not have matching or offsetting competences but also can't develop comparable strengths except at high cost and/or over an extended period of time.[9]

Even if an organization has no outstanding core competences (and many do not), it still must shape its strategy to suit its particular skills and available resources. It never makes sense to develop a strategic plan that cannot be executed with the skills and resources a firm is able to muster.

■ THE PERSONAL AMBITIONS, BUSINESS PHILOSOPHIES, AND ETHICAL BELIEFS OF MANAGERS

Managers do not dispassionately assess what strategic course to steer. Their choices are often influenced by their vision of how to compete and how to position the enterprise and by what image and standing they want the company to have. Both casual observation and formal studies indicate that managers' ambitions, values, business philosophies, attitudes toward risk, and ethical beliefs have important influences on strategy.[10] Sometimes the influence of a manager's personal values, experiences, and emotions is conscious and deliberate; at other times it may be unconscious. As one expert has noted in explaining the relevance of personal factors to strategy, "People have to have their hearts in it."[11]

The personal ambitions, business philosophies, and ethical beliefs of managers are usually stamped on the strategies they craft.

Several examples of how business philosophies and personal values enter into strategy formation are particularly noteworthy. Japanese managers are strong proponents of strategies that take a long-term view and that aim at building market share and competitive position. In contrast, some corporate executives and Wall Street financiers have been criticized for overemphasizing short-term profits at the expense of long-term competitive positioning and for being more attracted to strategies involving a financial play on assets (leveraged buyouts and stock buybacks) than to using corporate resources for long-term strategic investments. Japanese companies also display a quite different philosophy regarding the role of suppliers. Their preferred supplier strategy is to enter into long-term partnership arrangements with key suppliers because they believe that working closely with the same supplier year after year improves the quality and reliability of component parts, permits just-in-time delivery, and reduces inventory carrying costs. In the West, the traditional strategic approach has been to play suppliers off against one another, doing business on a short-term basis with whoever offers the best price and promises acceptable quality.

Attitudes toward risk also have a big influence on strategy. Risk-avoiders are inclined toward conservative strategies that have a quick payback and produce sure, short-term profits. Risk-takers lean more toward opportunistic strategies where visionary moves can produce a big payoff over the long term. Risk-takers prefer innovation to imitation and bold strategic offensives to defensive moves to protect the status quo.

Managerial values also shape the ethical quality of a firm's strategy. Managers with strong ethical convictions require their companies to observe a strict code of ethics in all aspects of the business; they expressly forbid such practices as accepting or giving kickbacks, badmouthing rivals' products, and buying political influence with political contributions. Further examples of unethical company practices include charging excessive interest rates on credit card balances, employing bait-and-switch sales tactics, marketing products suspected of having safety problems, and using ingredients that are known health hazards.

■ THE INFLUENCE OF SHARED VALUES AND COMPANY CULTURE ON STRATEGY

An organization's policies, practices, traditions, and philosophical beliefs combine to give it a distinct culture. A company's strategic actions reflect this culture and its managerial values. In some cases a company's core beliefs and culture even dominate the choice of strategic moves. This is because culture-related values and beliefs become so embedded in management's strategic thinking and strategic actions that they shape how the company responds. Such firms have a culture-driven bias about how to handle strategic issues and what kinds of strategic moves it will consider or reject. Strong cultural influences partly account for why companies gain reputations for such strategic traits as technological leadership, product innovation, dedication to superior craftsmanship, a proclivity for financial wheeling and dealing, a desire to grow rapidly by

A company's values and culture can dominate the kinds of strategic moves it considers or rejects.

acquiring other companies, a strong people-orientation, or unusual emphasis on customer service and total customer satisfaction.

In recent years, more companies have begun to articulate the core beliefs and values underlying their business approaches. One company expressed its core beliefs and values this way:

> We are market-driven. We believe that functional excellence, combined with teamwork across functions and profit centers, is essential to achieving superb execution. We believe that people

are central to everything we will accomplish. We believe that honesty, integrity, and fairness should be the cornerstone of our relationships with consumers, customers, suppliers, stockholders, and employees.

Wal-Mart's founder, Sam Walton, was a fervent believer in frugality, hard work, constant improvement, dedication to customers, and genuine care for employees. The company's commitment to these values is deeply ingrained in its strategy of low prices, good values, friendly service, productivity through the intelligent use of technology, and hard-nosed bargaining with suppliers.[12] At Hewlett-Packard, the company's basic values, known internally as "the HP Way," include sharing the company's success with employees, showing trust and respect for employees, providing customers with products and services of the greatest value, being genuinely interested in providing customers with effective solutions to their problems, making profit a high stockholder priority, avoiding the use of long-term debt to finance growth, individual initiative and creativity, teamwork, and being a good corporate citizen.[13] At both Wal-Mart and Hewlett-Packard, the value systems are deeply ingrained and widely shared by managers and employees. Whenever this happens, values and beliefs are more than platitudes; they become a way of life within the company.[14]

► LINKING STRATEGY WITH ETHICS

Strategy ought to be ethical. It should involve rightful actions, not wrongful ones; otherwise, it won't pass the test of moral scrutiny. This means more than conforming to what is legal. Ethical and moral standards go beyond the prohibitions of law and "thou shalt not" to the issues of *duty*. Ethics concerns human duty and the principles on which these responsibilities rest.[15]

Every business has an ethical responsibility to each of five constituencies: owners/ shareholders, employees, customers, suppliers, and the community at large. Each of these constituencies affects the organization and is affected by it. Each is a stakeholder in the enterprise, with certain expectations as to what the enterprise should do and how it should do it.[16] Owners/shareholders, for instance, expect a return on their investment. Business executives have a moral duty to pursue profitable management of the owners' investment and to protect the company's financial well-being.

Every strategic action a company takes should be ethical.

A company's duty to employees arises out of respect for the worth and dignity of individuals who devote their energies to the business and who depend on the business for their economic well-being. Principled strategy-making requires that employee-related decisions be made equitably and compassionately, with concern for due process and for the impact that strategic change has on employees' lives. At best, the chosen strategy should promote employee interests in wage and salary levels, career opportunities, job security, and overall working conditions. At worst, the chosen strategy should not disadvantage employees. Even in crises where adverse employee impact cannot be avoided, businesses have an ethical duty to minimize whatever the hardships imposed by workforce reductions, plant closings, job transfers, relocations, retraining, and loss of income.

The duty to the customer arises out of expectations that attend the purchase of a good or service. Inadequate appreciation of this duty has led to product liability laws and a host of regulatory agencies to protect consumers. All kinds of strategy-related ethical issues still abound here, however: Should a seller inform consumers *fully* about the contents of its product, especially if it contains ingredients that, though officially approved for use, are suspected of having potentially harmful

> **A company has ethical duties to owners, employees, customers, suppliers, the communities where it operates, and the public at large.**

effects? Is it ethical for the makers of alcoholic beverages to sponsor college events, given that many college students are under 21? Is it ethical for cigarette manufacturers to advertise at all (even though it is legal)? Is it ethical for manufacturers to produce and sell products they know have faulty parts or defective designs that may not become apparent until after the warranty expires?

A company's ethical duty to its suppliers arises out of the market relationship that exists between them. They are both partners and adversaries. They are partners in the sense that the quality of suppliers' parts affects the quality of a firm's own product. They are adversaries in the sense that the supplier wants the highest price and profit it can get, while the buyer wants a cheaper price, better quality, and speedier service. A company confronts several ethical issues in its supplier relationships: Is it ethical to threaten to cease doing business with a supplier unless the supplier agrees not to do business with key competitors? Is it ethical to reveal one supplier's price quote to a rival supplier? Is it ethical to accept gifts from suppliers? Is it ethical to pay a supplier in cash?

A company's ethical duty to the community at large stems from its status as a citizen of the community and as a social institution. It is reasonable to expect businesses to be good citizens—to pay their fair share of taxes for fire and police protection, waste removal, streets and highways and to exercise care in the impact their activities have on the environment and on the communities in which they operate. The community and public interest should be accorded the same recognition and attention as the interests of the other four constituencies. Whether a company is a good citizen is demonstrated ultimately by the way it supports community activities, encourages employees to participate in community affairs, handles the health and safety aspects of its operations, accepts responsibility for handling environmental pollution, relates to regulatory bodies and employee unions, and otherwise exhibits high ethical standards.

CARRYING OUT ETHICAL RESPONSIBILITIES

Management, not constituent groups, is responsible for managing the enterprise. Thus, management's perception of its ethical duties and of constituents' claims drives whether and how its strategy is linked to ethical behavior. Ideally, managers weigh strategic decisions from each constituent's point of view and, where conflicts arise, strike a rational, objective, equitable balance among the interests of all five constituencies. If any constituencies conclude that management is not doing its duty, they have their own avenues for recourse: Concerned investors can take action at the annual shareholders' meeting, appeal to the board of directors, or sell their stock. Concerned employees can unionize and bargain collectively or they can seek employment elsewhere. Customers can buy from the company's competitors. Suppliers can find other buyers or pursue other market alternatives. The community can do anything from staging protest marches to bringing about political and governmental action.[17]

A management that truly cares about business ethics and corporate social responsibility is proactive, rather than reactive, in linking strategic action and ethics. It steers away from ethically or morally questionable business opportunities. It won't do business with suppliers that engage in activities the company does not condone. It produces products that are safe for its customers to use. It operates a workplace environment that is safe for employees. It recruits and hires employees whose values and behavior are in keeping with the company's principles and ethical standards. It acts to reduce any environmental pollution it causes. It cares about *how* it does business and whether its actions reflect integrity and high ethical standards. Illustration 7 describes Harris Corporation's ethical commitments to its stakeholders.

■ TESTS OF A WINNING STRATEGY

What are the criteria for weeding out candidate strategies? How can a manager judge which strategic option is best for the company? What are the standards for determining whether a strategy is successful or not? Three tests can be used to evaluate the merits of one strategy versus another and to gauge how good a strategy is:

A winning strategy exhibits a good fit with the situation, builds sustainable competitive advantage, and improves company performance.

- *The goodness of fit test.* A good strategy is well-matched to a company's external market circumstances and to its internal strengths, weaknesses, and competitive capabilities.
- *The competitive advantage test.* A good strategy leads to sustainable competitive advantage. The bigger the competitive edge a strategy helps build, the more powerful and effective it is.
- *The performance test.* A good strategy boosts company performance. Two kinds of performance improvements are the most telling: gains in profitability and gains in the company's long-term business strength and competitive position.

Strategic options judged to have low potential on one or more of these criteria are candidates for being screened from further consideration. The strategic option judged to have the highest potential on all three counts can be regarded as the best or most attractive strategic alternative. Once a strategic commitment has been made and enough time has elapsed to see some actual results, these same tests can be used to assess how well a company's current strategy is performing. The bigger the margins by which a strategy satisfies all three criteria when put to test in the marketplace, the more it qualifies as a winning strategy.

There are, of course, some additional criteria for judging the merits of a particular strategy: clarity, internal consistency among all the pieces of strategy, timeliness, match to the personal values and ambitions of key executives, the degree of risk involved, and flexibility. These can be used to supplement the three tests posed above whenever it seems appropriate.

| ILLUSTRATION 7 | *Harris Corporation's Commitments to Its Stakeholders* |

Harris Corp. is a major supplier of information, communication, and semiconductor products, systems, and services to commercial and governmental customers throughout the world. The company utilizes advanced technologies to provide innovative and cost-effective solutions for processing and communicating data, voice, text, and video information. The company's sales exceed $2 billion, and it employs nearly 23,000 people. In a recent annual report, the company set forth its commitment to satisfying the expectations of its stakeholders:

Customers—For customers, our objective is to achieve ever-increasing levels of satisfaction by providing quality products and services with distinctive benefits on a timely and continuing basis worldwide. Our relationships with customers will be forthright and ethical, and will be conducted in a manner to build trust and confidence.

Shareholders—For shareholders, the owners of our company, our objective is to achieve sustained growth in earnings per share. The resulting stockprice appreciation combined with dividends should provide our shareholders with a total return on investment that is competitive with similar investment opportunities.

Employees—The people of Harris are our company's most valuable asset, and our objective is for every employee to be personally involved in and share the success of the business. The company is committed to providing an environment which encourages all employees to make full use of their creativity and unique talents; to providing equitable compensation, good working conditions, and the opportunity for personal development and growth which is limited only by individual ability and desire.

Suppliers—Suppliers are a vital part of our resources. Our objective is to develop and maintain mutually beneficial partnerships with suppliers who share our commitment to achieving increasing levels of customer satisfaction through continuing improvements in quality, service, timeliness, and cost. Our relationships with suppliers will be sincere, ethical, and will embrace the highest principles of purchasing practice.

Communities—Our objective is to be a responsible corporate citizen. This includes support of appropriate civic, educational, and business activities, respect for the environment, and the encouragement of Harris employees to practice good citizenship and support community programs. Our greatest contribution to our communities is to be successful so that we can maintain stable employment and create new jobs.

Source: 1988 Annual Report.

▶ APPROACHES TO PERFORMING THE STRATEGY-MAKING TASK

Companies and managers perform the strategy-making task differently. In small, owner-managed companies strategy-making is developed informally. Often the strategy is never reduced to writing but exists mainly in the entrepreneur's own mind and in verbal understandings with key subordinates. Large companies, however, tend to develop their plans via an annual strategic planning cycle (complete with prescribed procedures, forms, and timetables) that includes broad management participation, lots of studies, and many meetings to probe and question. The larger and more diverse an enterprise, the more managers feel it is better to have a structured annual process with written plans, management scrutiny, and official approval at each level.

Along with variations in the organizational process of formulating strategy are variations in how managers personally participate in analyzing the company's situation and deliberating what strategy to pursue. The four basic strategy-making styles managers use are:[18]

The master strategist approach—Here the manager personally functions as chief strategist and chief entrepreneur, exercising *strong* influence over assessments of the situation, over the strategy alternatives that are explored, and over the details of strategy. This does not mean that the manager personally does all the work; it means that the manager personally becomes the chief architect of strategy, shaping some or all of the major pieces of strategy. The manager acts as strategy commander and has a large ownership stake in the chosen strategy.

The delegate-it-to-others approach—Here the manager in charge delegates the exercise of strategy making to others, perhaps a strategic planning staff or a task force of trusted subordinates. The manager then personally stays off to the side, keeps in touch with how things are progressing via reports and conversations, offers guidance if need be, responds to trial balloons, and then approves the strategic plan after it has been formally presented and discussed and a consensus emerges. A manager that delegates the strategy-making task to others rarely has much ownership in the recommendations and, privately, may not see much urgency in pushing *truly hard* to implement some or much of what has been stated in writing in the company's official strategic plan. Also, it is generally understood that ''of course, we may have to proceed a bit differently if conditions change''—which gives the manager flexibility to go slow or ignore those approaches that ''on further reflection may not be the thing to do at this time.'' This approach has the advantage of letting the manager pick and chose from the strategic ideas that have been presented, and it allows room for broad participation and input from many managers and areas. The weakness is that a manager can end up so detached from the process that no real strategic leadership is exercised—indeed, subordinates are likely to conclude that strategic planning isn't very important to the boss. The stage is then set for rudderless direction setting. Often any strategy-making that does occur is short-term and reactive—addressing today's problems rather than positioning the enterprise to capture tomorrow's opportunities.

The collaborative approach—This is a middle approach where the manager enlists the help of key subordinates in hammering out a consensus strategy that all the key players will back and do their best to implement successfully. The biggest strength of this approach is that those charged with crafting the strategy also are charged with implementing it. Giving subordinate managers implementation responsibilities enhances their commitment to forming the strategy. And when subordinates have had a hand in proposing their part of the overall strategy, they can be held accountable for making it work—the ''I told you it was a bad idea'' alibi won't fly.

The champion approach—In this style of presiding over strategy formulation, the manager doesn't have a big personal stake in the details of strategy or in the time-consuming task of leading others through the strategy-making exercises. Rather, the idea is to encourage subordinate managers to develop, champion, and implement sound strategies on their own. Here strategy moves upward from the ''doers'' and the ''fast-trackers.'' Executives serve as judges, evaluating the strategy proposals reaching their desk. This approach works best in large diversified corporations where the CEO cannot personally orchestrate strategy in each of the many business divisions. Headquarters executives must delegate the initiative for strategy making to managers at the business-unit level in order to capitalize on having people in the enterprise who can see strategic opportunities that they cannot. Corporate executives may well articulate general strategic themes as guidelines for strategic thinking, but the key to developing good strategy is stimulating and rewarding strategic initiatives conceived by champion managers. With this approach, the total strategy ends up being the sum of the championed initiatives that get approved.

These four managerial approaches to forming strategy illuminate several aspects about how strategy emerges. In situations where the manager in charge personally functions as the chief architect of strategy, the choice of what strategic course to steer is a product of his or her own vision about how to position the enterprise and of his or her own ambitions, values, business philosophies. Highly centralized strategy making works well when the manager in charge has a powerful, insightful vision of what needs to be done and how to do it. The primary weakness of the master strategist approach is that the caliber of the strategy depends so heavily on one person's strategy-making skills. It also breaks down in large enterprises where many strategic initiatives are needed and the strategy-making task is too complex for any one person to handle alone.

On the other hand, the group approach to strategy making has its risks too. Sometimes, the strategy that emerges is a middle-of-the-road compromise, void of bold, creative initiative. At other times, it represents political consensus, with the outcome shaped by influential subordinates, by powerful functional departments, or by majority coalitions that have a common interest in promoting their particular version of what the strategy ought to be. Politics and the exercise of power are most likely to come into play when there is no strong consensus about what strategy to adopt; this opens the door for a political solution. The collaborative approach is also conducive to political strategic choices since powerful departments and individuals have ample opportunity to try to build a consensus for their favored strategic approach. However, the big danger of a delegate-it-to-others approach is a serious lack of top-down direction and strategic leadership.

The strength of the champion approach is also its weakness. The value of championing is that it encourages people at lower organizational levels to make suggestions and propose innovative ideas. Individuals with attractive strategic proposals are given the latitude and resources to try them out, thus helping keep strategy fresh and renewing an organization's capacity for innovation. On the other hand, the championed actions, because they come from many places in the organization, are not likely to form a coherent pattern or promote clear strategic direction. With championing, the chief executive has to work at ensuring that what is championed adds power to the overall organization strategy; otherwise, strategic initiatives may be launched in directions that have no integrating links or overarching rationale.

Of the four basic approaches managers can use in crafting strategy, none stands out as inherently superior—each has strengths and weaknesses.

All four styles of crafting strategy thus have strengths and weaknesses. All four can succeed or fail depending on how well the approach is managed and depending on the strategy-making skills and judgments of the individuals involved.

Thinking Strategically about Industry and Competitive Conditions

Analysis is the critical starting point of strategic thinking.

Kenichi Ohmae

Awareness of the environment is not a special project to be undertaken only when warning of change becomes deafening . . .

Kenneth R. Andrews

Crafting strategy is an exercise that requires strategic thinking and analysis; it's not an activity where managers can succeed through good intentions, sheer effort, or creativity. Judgments about what strategy to pursue have to be grounded in a probing assessment of a company's external environment and internal situation. Unless a company's strategy is well matched to both external and internal circumstances, its suitability is suspect. The two biggest situational considerations are (1) industry and competitive conditions (the heart of a single-business company's external environment) and (2) a company's internal capabilities, weaknesses, and competitive position. This chapter examines the techniques of *industry and competitive analysis,* the term commonly used to refer to external-situation analysis of a single-business company. In the next chapter, we'll cover the tools of *company situation analysis.* Industry and competitive analysis look broadly at a company's external *macroenvironment;* company situation analysis looks at a firm's immediate *microenvironment.*

Figure 3–1 illustrates the kinds of strategic thinking managers need to do to diagnose a company's situation. Note the logical flow from scrutinizing the company's external and internal situation to evaluating alternatives to selecting a strategy. Managers must have a keen grasp of the strategic aspects of a company's macro- and microenvironments to arrive at a sound strategic vision, set realistic objectives, and craft a winning strategy. Absent such understanding the door is wide open for managers to be seduced into a strategic game plan that doesn't fit their company's situation, that holds little prospect for building competitive advantage, and that is unlikely to boost company performance.

▶ THE FRAMEWORK OF INDUSTRY AND COMPETITIVE ANALYSIS

Industries differ in their economic characteristics, competitive status, and future outlooks. The pace of technological change can range from fast to slow. Capital requirements can vary from big to small. The market can extend from local to worldwide. Products can be standardized or highly differentiated. Competition can be strong or weak and can reflect

FIGURE 3–1   *How Strategic Thinking and Strategic Analysis Lead to Good Strategic Choices*

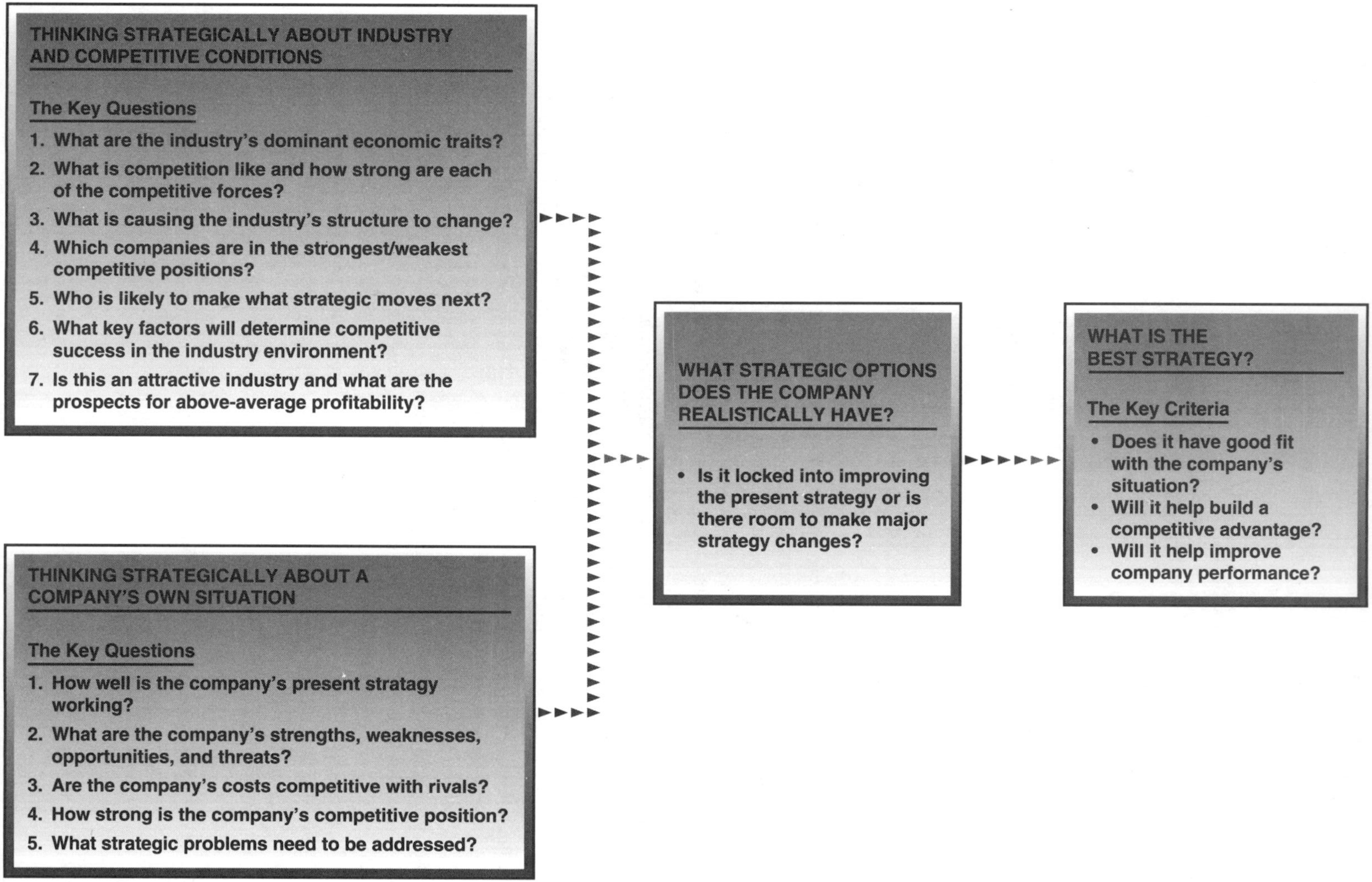

WHAT IS THE BEST STRATEGY?

The Key Criteria

- Does it have good fit with the company's situation?
- Will it help build a competitive advantage?
- Will it help improve company performance?

WHAT STRATEGIC OPTIONS DOES THE COMPANY REALISTICALLY HAVE?

- Is it locked into improving the present strategy or is there room to make major strategy changes?

THINKING STRATEGICALLY ABOUT INDUSTRY AND COMPETITIVE CONDITIONS

The Key Questions

1. What are the industry's dominant economic traits?
2. What is competition like and how strong are each of the competitive forces?
3. What is causing the industry's structure to change?
4. Which companies are in the strongest/weakest competitive positions?
5. Who is likely to make what strategic moves next?
6. What key factors will determine competitive success in the industry environment?
7. Is this an attractive industry and what are the prospects for above-average profitability?

THINKING STRATEGICALLY ABOUT A COMPANY'S OWN SITUATION

The Key Questions

1. How well is the company's present strategy working?
2. What are the company's strengths, weaknesses, opportunities, and threats?
3. Are the company's costs competitive with rivals?
4. How strong is the company's competitive position?
5. What strategic problems need to be addressed?

varying degrees of emphasis on price, quality, promotion, service, and other competitive variables. Industry conditions vary so much that leading companies in unattractive industries can find it hard to earn respectable profits, while weak companies in attractive industries can turn in good performances. Moreover, industry conditions shift and evolve as various defining aspects of the business environment grow or diminish in influence.

> Wise strategy-making begins with understanding a company's present situation—what external conditions it faces and what its capabilities are.

Industry and competitive analysis uses a tool kit of concepts and techniques to get a fix on changing industry conditions and on the nature and strength of competitive forces. It's a way of thinking strategically about any industry's overall situation and drawing conclusions about whether the industry would make an attractive investment for company funds. The objective of industry and competitive analysis is to obtain penetrating answers to the following seven questions:

1. What are the industry's dominant economic traits?
2. What is competition like and how strong are each of the competitive forces?
3. What is causing the industry's competitive structure to change?
4. Which companies are in the strongest/weakest competitive positions?
5. Who's likely to make what competitive moves next?
6. What key factors will determine competitive success or failure?
7. How attractive is the industry in terms of its prospects for above-average profitability?

The answers to these questions build understanding of a firm's surrounding environment and, collectively, form the basis for matching company strategy to changing industry conditions.

► QUESTION 1: WHAT ARE THE INDUSTRY'S DOMINANT ECONOMIC TRAITS?

Because industries differ significantly in their basic character and structure, industry and competitive analysis begins with an overview of the industry's dominant economic traits. As a working definition, we use the word *industry* to mean a group of firms whose products have so many of the same attributes that they compete for the same buyers. The factors to consider in profiling an industry's economic features are fairly standard:

- Market size.
- Scope of competition (local, regional, national, international, or global).
- Market growth rate and location of the industry in the growth cycle (early development, rapid growth and takeoff, early maturity, late maturity and saturation, stagnant and aging, decline and decay).
- Number of rivals and their relative sizes—is the industry fragmented with many small companies or concentrated and dominated by a few large companies?
- The number of buyers and their relative sizes.

- The prevalence of backward and forward integration.

- Ease of entry and exit.

- The pace of technological change in both production process innovation and new product introductions.

- Whether the product(s)/service(s) of rival firms are highly differentiated, weakly differentiated, or essentially identical.

- Whether companies can realize scale economies in purchasing, manufacturing, transportation, marketing, or advertising.

- Whether high rates of capacity utilization are crucial to achieving low-cost production efficiency.

- Whether the industry has a strong learning and experience curve such that average unit cost declines as *cumulative* output (and thus the experience of ''learning by doing'') builds up.

- Capital requirements.

- Whether industry profitability is above/below par.

Table 3–1 provides a sample business profile of the sulfuric acid industry.

TABLE 3–1   *A Sample Profile of an Industry's Dominant Economic Characteristics*

Market size: $400–$500 million annual revenues; total volume of 4 million tons.

Scope of competitive rivalry: Primarily regional; producers rarely sell outside a 250-mile radius of plant due to high cost of shipping long distances.

Market growth rate: 2% to 3% annually.

Stage in life cycle: Mature.

Number of companies in industry: About 30 companies with 110 plant locations and capacity of 4.5 million tons. Market shares range from a low of 3% to a high of 21%.

Customers: About 2,000 buyers; most are industrial chemical firms.

Degree of vertical integration: Mixed; 5 of the 10 largest companies are integrated backward into mining operations and also forward in that sister industrial chemical divisions buy over 50% of the output of their plants; all other companies are engaged solely in manufacturing.

Ease of entry/exit: Moderate entry barriers exist in the form of capital requirements to construct a new plant of minimum efficient size (cost equals $10 million) and ability to build a customer base inside a 250-mile radius of plant.

Technology/innovation: Production technology is standard and changes have been slow; biggest changes are occurring in products—about 1–2 newly formulated specialty chemicals products containing sulfuric acid are being introduced annually, accounting for nearly all of industry growth.

Product characteristics: Highly standardized; the brands of different producers are essentially identical (buyers perceive little real difference from seller to seller and regard the product as a commodity).

Scale economies: Moderate; all companies have virtually equal manufacturing costs but scale economies exist in shipping in multiple carloads to same customer and in purchasing large quantities of raw materials.

Experience curve effects: Not a factor in this industry.

Capacity utilization: Manufacturing efficiency is highest between 90% to 100% of rated capacity; below 90% utilization, unit costs run significantly higher.

Industry profitability: Subpar to average; the commodity nature of the industry's product results in intense price cutting when demand slackens, but prices firm up during periods of strong demand. Profits track the strength of demand for the industry's products.

An industry's economic characteristics are important because of the implications they have for strategy. For example, in capital-intensive industries where investment in a single plant can run several hundred million dollars, a firm can spread the burden of high fixed costs by pursuing a strategy that promotes high utilization of fixed assets and generates more revenue per dollar of fixed-asset investment. Thus, commercial airlines devise strategies to boost the revenue productivity of their multimillion dollar jets by cutting ground time at airport gates (to get in more flights per day with the same plane) and by using multi-tiered price discounts to fill up otherwise empty seats. In industries characterized by one product advance after another, companies must spend enough time and money on R&D to keep their technical prowess and innovative capability abreast of competitors—a strategy of continuous product innovation becomes a condition of survival.

> Industry characteristics impose boundaries on the strategies a company can pursue.

In industries like semiconductors, the presence of a *learning/experience* curve effect in manufacturing causes unit costs to decline about 20 percent each time *cumulative* production volume doubles. With a 20 percent experience curve effect, if the first 1 million chips cost $100 each, by a production volume of 2 million the unit cost would be $80 (80 percent of $100), by a production volume of 4 million the unit cost would be $64 (80 percent of $80), and so on. When an industry is characterized by a strong experience curve effect in its manufacturing operations, the company that moves first to produce a new product and develops a strategy to capture the largest market share can win the competitive advantage of being the low-cost producer. The bigger the experience curve effect, the larger the cost advantage of the company with the largest *cumulative* production volume, as shown in Figure 3–2.

> When unit costs decline substantially as cumulative production volume builds, becoming the largest volume manufacturer can mean becoming the industry's lowest-cost producer.

FIGURE 3–2   *Comparison of Experience Curve Effects for 10%, 20% , and 30% Cost Reductions for Each Doubling of Cumulative Production Volume*

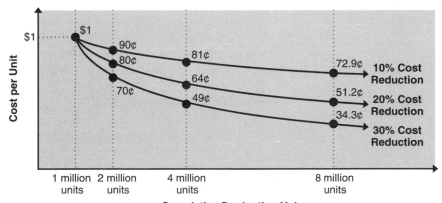

| TABLE 3-2 | *Examples of the Strategic Importance of an Industry's Key Economic Characteristics* |

Factor/Characteristic	Strategic Importance
• Market size	• Tiny markets don't tend to attract big/new competitors; big markets often draw the interest of large, cash-rich corporations looking to acquire companies with good earnings growth potential.
• Market growth rate	• Fast growth breeds new entry; growth slowdowns spawn increased rivalry and a shakeout of weak competitors.
• Capacity surpluses or shortages	• Surpluses push prices and profit margins down; shortages pull them up.
• Industry profitability	• High-profit industries attract new entrants; depressed conditions encourage exit.
• Entry/exit barriers	• High barriers protect positions and profits of existing firms; low barriers make existing firms vulnerable to entry.
• Product is a big-ticket item for buyers.	• More buyers will shop for lowest price.
• Standardized products	• Buyers have more power because it is easier to switch from seller to seller.
• Rapid technological change	• Raises risk factor; investments in technology facilities/equipment may become obsolete before they wear out.
• Capital requirements	• Big requirements make investment decisions critical; timing becomes important; creates a barrier to entry and exit.
• Vertical integration	• Raises capital requirements; often creates competitive differences and cost differences among fully versus partially versus nonintegrated firms.
• Economies of scale	• Increases volume and market share needed to be cost competitive.
• Rapid product innovation	• Shortens product life cycle; increases risk because of opportunities for leapfrogging.

Table 3–2 presents some additional examples of how an industry's economic traits are relevant to managerial strategy-making.

▶ QUESTION 2: WHAT IS COMPETITION LIKE AND HOW STRONG ARE EACH OF THE COMPETITIVE FORCES?

Industry and competitive analysis requires managers to dig deeply into the industry's competitive process in order to discover the main sources and strength of competitive pressure. This analytical step is essential because managers cannot devise a successful strategy without understanding the industry's competitive character.

■ THE FIVE COMPETITIVE FORCES

Even though competitive pressures are not identical from one industry to another, the competitive process works similarly enough from industry to industry to use a common analytical framework to gauge the nature and intensity of competitive forces. As Professor Michael Porter of the Harvard Business School has convincingly demonstrated, *the state of competition in an industry is a composite of five competitive forces:*[1]

1. The rivalry among competing sellers in the industry.

2. The market attempts of companies in other industries to win customers over to their own *substitute* products.

3. The potential entry of new competitors.

4. The bargaining power and leverage exercisable by suppliers of inputs.

5. The bargaining power and leverage exercisable by buyers of the product.

Porter's *five-forces model,* as depicted in Figure 3–3, is a powerful tool for systematically diagnosing the principal competitive pressures in a market and assessing how strong and important is each one. Not only is Porter's the most widely used technique for analyzing competition, but it is also relatively easy to use.

THE RIVALRY AMONG COMPETING SELLERS

The strongest of the five competitive forces is usually the jockeying for position and buyer favor that goes on among rival firms. Rivalry emerges between competitors when one or another sees an opportunity to better meet customer needs or is under pressure to improve its performance. The intensity of the rivalry reflects how vigorously the competitors use tactics such as lower prices, snazzier features, increased customer services, longer warranties, special promotions, and new product introductions. Rivalry can range from friendly to cutthroat, depending on how frequently and how aggressively companies undertake actions that threaten rivals' profitability. Ordinarily, rivals are clever at enhancing buyer appeal through a variety of means, and they persist in trying to exploit weaknesses in each other's market approaches.

Regardless of the intensity of industry rivalry, every company needs a successful strategy for competing—ideally, one that *produces a competitive edge* and strengthens the company's position with its customers. The big complication in most industries is that the success of any one firm's strategy hinges on the strategies its rivals develop and how those strategies are implemented. The best strategy for one firm depends, in other words, on the competitive capabilities and strategies of rival companies. Such interdependence means that whenever one firm makes a strategic move, its rivals will often retaliate.

> Competitive jockeying among rival firms is a dynamic process in which firms initiate new offensive and defensive moves and emphasis swings from one mix of competitive weapons to another.

This pattern of action and reaction makes competitive rivalry a war games type of contest conducted, one hopes, according to the rules of fair competition. Indeed, from a strategy-making perspective, *competitive markets are economic battlefields.*

Not only do competitive contests among rival sellers assume different intensities but so do the mixes of competitive tactics they employ. The relative emphasis that rival companies put on price, quality, performance features, customer service, warranties, advertising, and product innovation shifts as they maneuver to catch buyers' attention. Rivalry is thus dynamic; the current competitive scene is always changing as companies act and react, sometimes quickly and sometimes methodically, and as their strategic emphasis swings from one mix of competitive tactics to another.

Two principles of competitive rivalry stand out: (1) the launch of a powerful competitive strategy by one company intensifies the competitive pressures on the remaining companies, and (2) the rules of competition which determine the requirements

FIGURE 3–3   *The Five-Forces Model of Competition: A Key Analytical Tool*

FIRMS IN OTHER INDUSTRIES OFFERING SUBSTITUTE PRODUCTS

Competitive pressures coming from the market attempts of outsiders to win buyers over to their products

Competitive pressures coming from suppliers' exercise of bargaining power and leverage

SUPPLIERS OF KEY INPUTS

RIVALRY AMONG COMPETING SELLERS

Competitive forces arising from rivals' jockeying for a better market position and a competitive advantage

Competitive pressures coming from buyers' exercise of bargaining power and leverage

BUYERS

Competitive pressures coming from the threat of entry of new rivals

POTENTIAL NEW ENTRANTS

Source: Adapted from Michael E Porter, "How Competitive Forces Shape Strategy," *Harvard Business Review* 57, no. 2 (March–April 1979), pp. 137–45.

for market success are shaped by how rivals maneuver and deploy different competitive weapons. Once an industry's prevailing rules of competitive rivalry are understood, managers can determine the strength of the rivalry, and whether it is likely to increase or diminish in intensity.

In industry after industry, several factors seem to influence the tempo of rivalry among competing sellers:[2]

1. *Rivalry increases as the number of competitors increases and as they become more equal in size and capability*. Up to a point, the greater the number of competitors, the greater the probability of fresh, creative strategic initiatives. In addition, when rivals are more equal in size and capability, they can usually compete on a fairly even footing, making it harder for one or two firms to win the competitive battle and dominate the market.

2. *Rivalry is usually stronger when demand for the product is growing slowly*. In a rapidly expanding market, there tends to be enough business for everybody to grow. Indeed, it may take all of a firm's financial and managerial resources just to keep abreast of the growth in buyer demand. But when growth slows or when market demand drops unexpectedly, expansion-minded firms and/or firms with excess capacity often cut prices and use other sales-increasing tactics, thereby igniting a battle for market share that can result in a shakeout of the weak and less-efficient firms. The industry then consolidates into a smaller, but individually stronger, number of sellers.

3. *Rivalry is more intense when industry conditions tempt competitors to use price cuts or other competitive weapons to boost unit volume*. Whenever fixed costs account for a large fraction of total cost, unit costs tend to be lowest at or near full capacity since fixed costs can be spread over more units of production. Unused capacity imposes a significant cost-increasing penalty because fewer units are carrying the fixed cost burden. In such cases, if market demand weakens and capacity utilization begins to fall off, the pressure of rising unit costs pushes rival firms into secret price concessions, special discounts, rebates, and other tactics to increase sales, thus heightening competition. Likewise, when a product is perishable, seasonal, or costly to hold in inventory, competitive pressures build quickly anytime a firm decides to dump its excess supplies on the market.

4. *Rivalry is stronger when the costs incurred by customers in switching from one brand to another are low*. The lower the costs of switching, the easier it is for rival sellers to raid each another's customers. High switching costs will give a seller some protection against the efforts of rivals to raid its customers.

5. *Rivalry is stronger when any competitor becomes dissatisfied with its market position and attempts to bolster its standing at the expense of rivals*. Firms that are losing ground or find themselves in financial trouble often react aggressively by acquiring smaller rivals, introducing new products, boosting advertising, discounting prices, and so on. Such actions can trigger a new round of competitive maneuvering and a hotly contested battle for market share.

6. *Rivalry increases in proportion to the size of the payoff from a successful strategic move*. The more rewarding an opportunity, the more likely some firm will

aggressively pursue it. The payoff, however, varies in part with the speed of retaliation. When competitors respond slowly (or not at all), the initiator of a fresh competitive strategy can reap benefits in the intervening period and perhaps gain a first-mover advantage that is not easily surmounted. The greater the benefits of moving first, the more likely some firm will accept the risk and try it.

7. *Rivalry tends to be more vigorous when it costs more to get out of a business than to stay in and compete.* The higher the exit barriers (and thus the more costly it is to abandon a market), the stronger the incentive for firms to remain and compete as best they can, even though they may be earning low profits or even incurring a loss.

8. *Rivalry becomes more volatile and unpredictable the more diverse competitors are in terms of their strategies, personalities, corporate priorities, resources, and countries of origin.* A diverse group of sellers often contains one or more mavericks willing to employ unconventional approaches, thus generating a livelier and less predictable competitive environment. Attempts by cross-border rivals to gain stronger footholds in each other's domestic markets will always boost the intensity of rivalry, especially when foreign rivals with lower costs are involved.

9. *Rivalry increases when strong companies outside the industry acquire weak firms in the industry and launch aggressive, well-funded moves to transform their new acquisitions into major market contenders.* A classic example of this occurred when Philip Morris (PM), a leading cigarette firm with excellent marketing abilities, shook up the U.S. beer industry's approach to marketing by acquiring stodgy Miller Brewing Company in the late 1960s. In short order, Philip Morris revamped the marketing of Miller High Life and pushed it to the Number 2 selling brand. PM also pioneered low-calorie beers with the introduction of Miller Lite—a move that made light beer the fastest-growing segment in the beer industry.

In sizing up the competitive pressures created by rivalry among existing competitors, the strategist's job is to identify what weapons are currently being used, to stay on top of the game, and to judge how much pressure on profitability will come from cross-company rivalry. Competitive rivalry is intense when competitors are driving down industry profits; rivalry is moderate when most companies can earn acceptable profits; and weak when most companies in the industry can earn above-average returns on investment. Chronic outbreaks of cutthroat competition among rival sellers make an industry brutally competitive.

THE COMPETITIVE FORCE OF POTENTIAL ENTRY

New entrants to a market bring new production capacity, the desire to establish a secure place in the market, and sometimes substantial resources with which to compete.[3] Just how serious a competitive threat a new entrant poses depends on two major factors: *barriers to entry* and *the expected reaction of incumbent firms to new entry*. A barrier to entry exists whenever it is hard for a newcomer to break into the market and/or economic factors put a potential entrant at a disadvantage relative to its competitors. There are several types of entry barriers:[4]

• *Economies of scale*—Scale economies deter entry because they force potential competitors either to enter on a large-scale basis (a costly and perhaps risky move) or to accept a cost disadvantage (and consequently lower profitability). Large-scale entry is a difficult barrier to hurdle because it can create chronic industrywide overcapacity problems and because it can so threaten the market shares of existing firms that they retaliate aggressively to maintain their position. Either way, a potential entrant is often discouraged by the prospect of lower profits. Entrants may encounter scale-related barriers throughout their business, from production to advertising, marketing and distribution, financing, after-sale customer service, raw materials purchasing, and R&D.

- *Inability to gain access to technology and specialized knowledge*—Many industries require technological capability and skills not readily available to a new entrant. Key patents can effectively bar entry, as can lack of technically skilled personnel and an inability to execute complicated manufacturing techniques. Existing firms often carefully guard technology that gives them an edge in manufacturing capability.

- *The existence of learning and experience curve effects*— When lower unit costs are partly or mostly a result of experience in production and other learning curve benefits, a new entrant has a cost disadvantage competing against firms with greater accumulated experience.

- *Brand preferences and customer loyalty*—Buyers are often attached to established brands. European consumers, for example, are fiercely loyal to their national brands of major household appliances. High brand loyalty means that a potential entrant must be prepared to spend enough money on advertising and sales promotion to overcome customer loyalties and build its own clientele. Substantial time and money can be involved. In addition, if it is difficult or costly for a customer to switch to a new brand, a new entrant must persuade buyers that its brand is worth the switching costs. To overcome the barrier of switching costs, new entrants may have to offer buyers a discounted price or an extra margin of quality or service. All this can mean lower profit margins for new entrants—and an increased risk to start-up companies dependent on sizable, early profits to support their new investment.

- *Capital requirements*—The larger the total dollar investment needed to enter the market successfully, the more limited the pool of potential entrants. The most obvious capital requirements are associated with manufacturing plant and equipment, working capital to finance inventories and customer credit, introductory advertising and sales promotion to establish a clientele, and cash reserves to cover startup losses.

- *Cost disadvantages independent of size*—Existing firms may have cost advantages not available to potential entrants regardless of the entrant's size. These advantages can include access to the best and cheapest raw materials, possession of patents and proprietary technology, the benefits of learning and experience curve effects, existing plants built and equipped years earlier at lower costs, favorable locations, and lower borrowing costs.

- *Access to distribution channels*—In the case of consumer goods, a potential entrant may face the barrier of gaining adequate access to distribution channels. Wholesale distributors may be reluctant to take on a product that lacks buyer recognition. A network of retail dealers may have to be set up from scratch. Retailers have to be convinced to give a new brand ample display space and an adequate trial period. The more distribution channels have been tied up by existing producers, the tougher will be the entry. To overcome this barrier, potential entrants may have to offer better margins to dealers and distributors or give advertising allowances and other promotional incentives. As a consequence, a potential entrant's profits may be squeezed unless and until its product gains enough acceptance so that distributors and retailers want to carry it.

- *Regulatory policies*—Government agencies can limit or even bar entry by requiring licenses and permits. Regulated industries like electric and gas utilities, radio and television broadcasting, liquor retailing, and railroads feature government-controlled entry. In international markets, host governments commonly limit foreign entry and must approve all foreign investment applications. Stringent government-mandated safety regulations and environmental pollution standards can also raise entry costs.

- *Tariffs and international trade restrictions*—National governments commonly use tariffs and trade restrictions (antidumping rules, local content requirements, and quotas) to raise entry barriers for foreign firms. For example, tariffs imposed by the South Korean government have resulted in a Ford Taurus costing South Korean car buyers over $40,000. European governments have required that certain Asian products, from electronic typewriters to copying machines, contain European-made parts and labor equal to 40 percent of selling price. To protect European chipmakers from low-cost Asian competition, European governments instituted a rigid formula for calculating floor prices for computer memory chips.

Even if a potential entrant is willing to tackle the problems of entry barriers, it still faces the issue of how existing firms will react.[5] Will incumbent firms offer only passive resistance or will they aggressively defend their market positions using price cuts, increased advertising, new product improvements, and other tactics to challenge a new entrant? A potential entrant can have second thoughts when financially strong incumbent firms send clear signals that they will stoutly defend their market positions. A potential entrant may also be turned away when incumbent firms can use leverage with distributors and customers to keep their business.

The best test of whether potential entry is a strong or weak competitive force is to ask if the industry's growth and profit prospects are attractive enough to induce additional entry. When the answer is no, potential entry is not a source of competitive pressure. When the answer is yes (as in industries where lower-cost foreign competitors are busily entering new markets), then potential entry is a strong force. The stronger the threat of entry, the greater the motivation of incumbent firms to fortify their positions against newcomers to make entry more costly or difficult.

The competitive threat of potential entry is stronger when entry barriers are low and a newcomer can expect to earn attractive profits.

One additional point: the threat of entry changes as the industry's profit prospects grow brighter or dimmer and as entry barriers rise or fall. For example, the expiration of a key patent can greatly increase the threat of entry. A technological discovery can create an economy-of-scale advantage where none existed before. New actions by incumbent firms to increase advertising, strengthen distributor-dealer relations, step up R&D, or improve product quality can raise the barriers to entry. In international markets, entry barriers for foreign-based firms fall as tariffs are lowered, as domestic wholesalers and dealers seek out lower-cost foreign-made goods, and as domestic buyers become more willing to purchase foreign brands.

COMPETITIVE PRESSURES FROM SUBSTITUTE PRODUCTS

Firms in one industry are, quite often, in close competition with firms in another industry because their respective products are good substitutes. The producers of eyeglasses compete with the makers of contact lens. The producers of wood stoves compete against producers of kerosene heaters and portable electric heaters. The sugar industry is in competition with companies that produce artificial sweeteners. The container market is fiercely competitive with producers of plastic containers vying for customers from the glass bottles and jars sector, manufacturers of paperboard cartons, and tin and aluminum can producers. Aspirin manufacturers must stay aware of how their product compares with other pain relievers.

Competitive pressures from substitute products operate in several ways. First, the presence of readily available and competitively priced substitutes places a ceiling on the prices a company can afford to charge for its own product without giving customers an incentive to switch to substitutes.[6] This price ceiling, at the same time, puts a lid on the profits that industry members can earn unless they find ways to cut costs. When substitutes are cheaper than an industry's product, industry members come under heavy competitive pressure to reduce their prices and find ways to absorb the price cuts with cost reductions. Second, the availability of substitutes inevitably invites customers to compare quality and performance as well as price. For example, firms that buy glass bottles and jars from glassware manufacturers monitor whether they can just as effectively package their products in plastic containers, paper cartons, or tin cans. Competitive pressures from substitute products push industry participants to convince customers their company's product is more advantageous than the substitute product. Usually this requires a competitive strategy that differentiates the company's product from substitute products through some combination of lower price, better quality, or better service and performance features.

> Competition from substitute products is strongest when the prices of substitutes are attractive, buyers' switching costs are low, and buyers believe substitutes have equal or better features.

Another determinant of whether substitutes are a strong or weak competitive force is how difficult or costly it is for customers to switch to substitute products.[7] Typical switching costs include employee retraining, additional equipment purchases, payments for expert technical help, quality testing, and the wrenching costs of severing old relationships to establish new ones. If switching costs are high, sellers of substitutes must offer a major cost or performance benefit in order to entice the industry's customers away. When switching costs are low, it's much easier for sellers of substitutes to convince buyers to change over to their product.

As a rule, then, the lower the price of substitutes, the higher their quality and performance, and the lower the user's switching costs, the more intense are the competitive pressures posed by substitute products. The best indicators of the competitive strength of substitute products are the rate at which their sales are growing, their market inroads, their plans for expanding production capacity, and the size of their profits.

THE POWER OF SUPPLIERS

Whether the suppliers to an industry are a weak or strong competitive force depends on market conditions in the supplier industry and the significance of the item they supply.[8]

Industry suppliers are a strong competitive force whenever their actions can put certain rivals at a competitive disadvantage.

The competitive force of suppliers is greatly diminished when they supply a standard commodity available on the open market from a large number of suppliers with ample capability to fill orders. Then it is relatively simple to choose which supplier offers the best deal. In such cases, suppliers have market power only when supplies become tight and users, anxious to secure what they need, agree to terms more favorable to suppliers. Suppliers are likewise in a weak bargaining position whenever there are good substitute inputs and switching is neither costly nor difficult. For example, soft drink bottlers can effectively check the power of aluminum can suppliers by using more plastic containers and glass bottles.

Suppliers also have less leverage when the industry they are supplying is a *major* customer. In this case, the well-being of suppliers becomes closely tied to the well-being of their major customers. Suppliers then have a big incentive to protect the customer industry via reasonable prices, improved quality, and the development of new products and services that might enhance their customers' competitive positions, sales, and profits. Sometimes forming close working relationships with major suppliers allows companies to gain substantial benefits in the form of better quality components, just-in-time deliveries, and reduced inventory costs.

On the other hand, powerful suppliers can put an industry in a profit squeeze with price increases that cannot be fully passed on to the industry's own customers. Suppliers become a strong competitive force when the item they provide makes up a sizable fraction of the costs of an industry's product, is crucial to the industry's production process, and/or significantly affects the quality of the industry's product. Likewise, a supplier (or group of suppliers) gains bargaining leverage the more difficult or costly it is for users to switch to alternate suppliers. Big suppliers with good reputations and growing demand for their output are harder to wring concessions from than struggling suppliers striving to broaden their customer base or more fully utilize their production capacity.

Suppliers are also more powerful when they can offer a component cheaper than industry members can make it themselves. For instance, most producers of outdoor power

---
Powerful suppliers can affect a company's competitiveness based on the prices they can command, the quality of what they supply, and the treatment they give preferred customers.

---

equipment (lawnmowers, rotary tillers, snowblowers, etc.) find it cheaper to source the small engines they need from outside manufacturers, rather than make their own, because the quantity they need is too little to justify investing in and mastering the process. Specialists in small engine manufacture, by supplying many kinds of engines to the whole power equipment industry, obtain a big enough sales volume to capture scale economies, become proficient in all the manufacturing techniques, and keep costs well below what power equipment firms could achieve on their own. Small engine suppliers can price their engines below what it would cost their customers to make them, and high enough over their own costs to generate an attractive profit margin. In such situations, the supplier's bargaining position is strong *until* the volume a customer needs becomes large enough to justify backward integration. Then the balance of power shifts away from the supplier. The more credible the threat of backward integration into the supplier's business, the more leverage companies have in negotiating favorable terms with their suppliers.

Finally, suppliers play an important competitive role when they, for one reason or another, do not have the incentive or the capability to provide items of adequate quality. For example, if auto parts suppliers provide lower-quality components to the U.S. automobile manufacturers, they can so increase the warranty and defective goods costs of the U.S. auto firms that the latter's profits, reputation, and competitive position in the world automobile market are seriously impaired.

THE POWER OF BUYERS

Just as with suppliers, the competitive strength of buyers ranges from strong to weak. Buyers have substantial bargaining leverage in a number of situations.[9] The most obvious is when buyers are large and purchase a sizable percentage of the industry's output. The bigger the buyers and the larger the quantities they purchase, the better position they have in negotiating with sellers. Often, purchasing in large quantities gives a buyer enough leverage to obtain price concessions and other favorable terms. Buyers are also in a good negotiating position when the costs of switching to competing brands or substitutes are relatively low. When buyers have the flexibility to source from among several sellers, they have added room to negotiate with sellers. When sellers' products are virtually identical, it is relatively easy for buyers to switch from seller to seller at little or no cost. However, when sellers' products are strongly differentiated, buyers are usually less able to switch without incurring sizable changeover costs, which weakens their negotiating power.

> **Buyers are a strong competitive force when they have bargaining leverage over price, quality, service, or other terms of sale.**

One last point: All buyers in an industry are not likely to possess equal degrees of bargaining power with sellers, and some may be less sensitive than others to price, quality, or service. For example, in the apparel industry, major manufacturers confront significant customer power when selling to retail chains like Wal-Mart or Sears. But they can get much better prices selling to small owner-managed apparel boutiques.

STRATEGIC IMPLICATIONS OF THE FIVE COMPETITIVE FORCES

The five-forces model helps expose the composition of competitive forces. *Analysis of the competitive environment requires an assessment of the strength of each one of the five competitive forces.* The collective impact of these forces determines the nature of competition in a given industry. As a rule, the stronger competitive forces are, the lower is the collective profitability of participant firms. The most brutal competition occurs when the five forces create market conditions tough enough to impose prolonged subpar profitability or even losses on most or all firms. The competitive structure of an industry is clearly unattractive from a profit-making standpoint if rivalry among sellers is

> **Good competitive strategies provide good defenses against the five competitive forces.**

very strong, entry barriers are low, competition from substitutes is strong, and both suppliers and customers are able to exercise considerable bargaining leverage. On the other hand, when competitive forces are not collectively strong, the competitive structure of the industry is favorable or attractive from the standpoint of earning superior profits. The ideal competitive environment from a profit-making perspective is where both suppliers and customers are in a weak bargaining position, there are no good substitutes, entry barriers are relatively high, and rivalry among present sellers is only moderate. However, even when only some of the five competitive forces are strong, an industry can be competitively attractive to those firms whose market position and strategy provide a good enough defense against competitive pressures so it can earn above-average profits.

▶ QUESTION 3: WHAT IS CAUSING THE INDUSTRY'S COMPETITIVE STRUCTURE TO CHANGE?

An industry's economic features and competitive structure say a lot about the basic nature of the industry environment but very little about the ways in which the environment may be changing. All industries are characterized by trends and new developments that, either gradually or speedily, produce changes important enough to require a strategic response from participating firms. The popular hypothesis about industries' passage through evolutionary phases or life cycle stages helps explain industry change but is incomplete.[10] Life cycle stages are keyed to the overall industry growth rate, which is why concepts like rapid growth, early maturity, saturation, and decline are used to describe the stages. However, there's more to what causes an industry to change than just its position on the growth curve.

■ THE CONCEPT OF DRIVING FORCES

Industry and competitive conditions change *because forces are in motion that create incentives or pressures for change.*[11] The most dominant forces are called *driving forces* because they have the biggest influences on what kinds of changes will take place in the industry's structure and competitive environment. Managers do not really understand industry and competitive conditions until they understand the fundamental drivers of change. Driving force analysis has two steps: identifying the driving forces and assessing their impact on the industry.

Industry conditions change because certain forces are at work that cause industry participants (competitors, customers, suppliers) to alter their actions.

■ THE MOST COMMON DRIVING FORCES

Many events can affect an industry powerfully enough to qualify as driving forces. Some are one of a kind, but most fall into one of the following basic categories.[12]

• *Changes in the long-term industry growth rate*—Shifts in industry growth affect the balance between industry supply and buyer demand, entry and exit, and how hard it will be for a firm to capture additional sales. An increase in long-term demand can attract new entrants to the market and encourage established firms to invest in additional capacity. A shrinking market can cause some companies to exit the industry and induce those remaining to close plants and retrench.

- *Changes in who buys the product and how they use it*—Shifts in buyer composition and new ways of using the product can force adjustments in customer service (credit, technical assistance, maintenance, and repair), change the way the industry's product is marketed through a different mix of dealers and retail outlets, prompt producers to broaden/narrow their product lines, increase/decrease capital requirements, and change sales and promotion approaches. As an example, the development of new cable converter boxes now allows home-computer service firms like Prodigy, CompuServe, and America Online to sign up cable companies to deliver their games, bulletin boards, and data and electronic shopping services to home subscribers via cable television.

- *Product innovation*—Product innovation can broaden an industry's customer base, rejuvenate industry growth, and widen the degree of product differentiation among rival sellers. Successful new product introductions strengthen the market position of the innovating companies, usually at the expense of companies who don't change products or are slow to follow the new product introductions of rivals. Industries where product innovation has been a significant driving force include copying equipment, cameras and photographic equipment, computers, electronic video games, toys, prescription drugs and medical technology, frozen foods, and personal computer software.

- *Process innovation*—Advances in processing capability can dramatically alter an industry's landscape, making it possible to produce at lower cost and dramatically changing how manufacturing activities are performed. Developments in process technology can also generate changes in capital requirements, minimum efficient plant sizes, the pros and cons of vertical integration, and learning or experience curve effects.

- *Marketing innovation*—When firms are successful in introducing new ways to market their products, they can spark a burst of buyer interest, widen industry demand, increase product differentiation, and/or lower unit costs—any or all of which can alter the competitive positions of rival firms and force revisions in strategy.

- *Entry or exit of major firms*—The entry of one or more foreign companies into what was a largely domestic market nearly always shakes up competition. Similarly, when an established domestic firm from another industry attempts to enter either by acquisition or by launching its own start-up venture, it usually intends to apply its skills and resources in some innovative fashion, thus introducing a new competitive element. Just as a major firm's entry changes the competitive structure, so also does the exit of a major firm. By reducing the number of market leaders, perhaps increasing the dominance of the leaders who remain, the exiting firm causes a rush to capture its customers. Entry or exit of a major firm often produces a ''new ballgame'' not only with different key players but also with different rules for competing.

- *Diffusion of technical know-how*—As knowledge about how to perform a particular activity or to execute a new manufacturing technology spreads, any technically based competitive advantage held by firms originally possessing this knowledge erodes.

This diffusion can occur through scientific journals, trade publications, on-site plant tours, word of mouth among suppliers and customers, and former employees. It can also occur when the owners of technological expertise license others to use it or form a partnership with a company interested in turning the technology into a new business venture. Quite often, needed technological know-how can be acquired by simply buying a company that has the desired skills, patents, or manufacturing capabilities. Technology transfer across national boundaries has emerged as one of the most important driving forces in globalizing markets and competition. Examples of technology transfers that have turned largely domestic industries into increasingly global ones include automobiles, tires, consumer electronics, telecommunications, and computers.

- *Increasing globalization of the industry*—Industries move toward globalization for any of several reasons. One or more nationally prominent firms may launch aggressive long-term strategies to win a globally dominant market position. Demand for the industry's product may pop out in more and more countries. Trade barriers may drop. Technology transfer may open the door for more companies in more countries to enter the industry arena on a major scale. Significant labor cost differences among countries may create a strong reason to locate plants for labor-intensive products in low-wage countries. Significant cost economies may accrue to firms with world-scale volumes as opposed to national-scale volumes. Globalization is most likely to be a driving force in industries *(a)* where natural resources are geographically scattered all over the globe, *(b)* where low-cost production is critical, and *(c)* where one or more growth-oriented, market-seeking companies are pushing hard to gain a significant competitive position in as many attractive country markets as they can.

- *Changes in cost and efficiency*—In industries where economies of scale are emerging or where strong learning curves enable firms with the most production experience to undercut rivals' prices, large market share becomes such an advantage that firms adopt volume-building strategies and a race for growth dominates the industry. Sharply increasing costs for a key input (either raw materials or labor) can precipitate a scramble either *(a)* to line up reliable supplies of the input at affordable prices or *(b)* to search out lower-cost substitutes. Whenever important changes in cost or efficiency take place in an industry, there can be big swings in the cost competitiveness of key rivals as cost differences widen or shrink.

- *Emerging buyer preferences for a differentiated product instead of a commodity product (or for a more standardized product instead of strongly differentiated products)*—Sometimes growing numbers of buyers move toward a standard "one size fits all" bargain-priced product and away from the premium brands with snappy features and options. Such a development can so dominate the market that it limits the strategic freedom of industry producers to doing little more than competing hard on price. A shift away from standardized products occurs when sellers are able to win buyers by introducing new features, making style changes, offering options and accessories, and creating image differences via advertising and packaging. Then the driver of change is the contest among rivals to outdifferentiate one another. Industries evolve depending on whether the market forces in motion are acting to increase or decrease the emphasis on product differentiation.

- *Regulatory influences and government policy changes*—Regulatory and governmental actions can force significant changes in industry practices and strategic approaches. Deregulation has been a driving force in the airline, banking, natural gas, and telecommunications industries. In international markets, newly enacted policies of host governments to open their domestic markets to foreign participation or to close markets to protect domestic companies are a major factor in shaping whether the competitive struggle between foreign and domestic companies occurs on a level playing field or whether it is tilted toward domestic firms (owing to host government protectionism).

- *Changing societal concerns, attitudes, and lifestyles*—Emerging social issues and changing attitudes and lifestyles can be powerful instigators of industry change. Consumer concerns about salt, sugar, chemical additives, cholesterol, and nutrition have resulted in the food industry's reformulation of food processing techniques; there's a growing trend toward using healthier ingredients and researching ways to produce healthier products that also taste good. Safety concerns and regulations have been major drivers of change in the automobile, toy, and outdoor power equipment industries, to mention a few. Increased interest in physical fitness has produced whole new industries to supply exercise equipment, jogging clothes and shoes, and medically supervised diet programs. Societal concerns about air and water pollution have been major forces in industries that discharge waste products. Growing antismoking sentiment is posing a major long-term threat to the cigarette industry's sales.

- *Reductions in uncertainty and business risk*—A young industry is typically characterized by an unproven cost structure and much uncertainty over potential market size, how much time and money will be needed to surmount technological problems, and what distribution channels to emphasize in accessing potential buyers. Emerging industries tend to attract only risk-taking entrepreneurial companies. Over time, however, if pioneering firms become successful and uncertainty about the industry's viability fades, more conservative firms will usually enter the industry. Often, the late-arriving firms are larger, financially strong firms looking to invest in attractive growth industries. In international markets, conservatism is prevalent in the early stages of globalization. Firms desiring a foothold in foreign markets guard against risk by relying initially on exporting, licensing, and joint ventures to enter the international arena. Then, as experience in making a success out of foreign operations accumulates and as perceived risk levels decline, companies move more quickly and aggressively to form wholly-owned subsidiaries and to pursue full-scale, multicountry competitive strategies.

The foregoing list of *potential* driving forces in an industry indicates why it is too simplistic to view industry change only in terms of the growth stages model and why it is essential to probe for the *causes* underlying the emergence of new competitive conditions.

However, while *many* changes may be occurring in a given industry, no more than three or four are likely to qualify as *driving* forces in the sense that they act as *the major determinants* of how the industry evolves and operates. Thus, strategic analysts must resist the temptation to label every change they see as a driving force. The analytical task is to evaluate the forces of industry and competitive change carefully enough to separate major factors from minor ones.

The task of driving forces analysis is to separate the major causes of industry change from the minor ones.

Sound analysis of an industry's driving forces is a prerequisite to sound strategy-making. Without keen awareness of what external factors will have the greatest effect on the company's business over the next one to three years, managers are ill-prepared to craft a strategy to match changing external conditions. Moreover, when management's views about the implications of each driving force are fuzzy or off-base, managers are ill-prepared to craft a strategy that can respond to those forces and their consequences for the industry. So driving forces analysis is not something company managers can take lightly; it has practical strategy-making value and is basic to the task of thinking strategically about the business.

■ ENVIRONMENTAL SCANNING TECHNIQUES

One way to predict the driving forces that may emerge is to use environmental scanning techniques. *Environmental scanning* involves studying and interpreting the sweep of social, political, economic, ecological, and technological events in an effort to spot new events and budding trends that have potential to impact the industry. Environmental scanning looks well beyond the next one to three years. For example, environmental scanning could be used to make judgments about the demand for energy in the year 2010, what kinds of household appliances will be in the house of the future, what people will be doing with computers 20 years from now, or what will happen to our forests in the 21st century if the demand for paper grows at present rates. Environmental scanning thus attempts to ferret out "first of a kind" happenings and new ideas and approaches that are catching on and to extrapolate their possible implications 5 to 20 years into the future.

Environmental scanning raises management's awareness about potential developments that could impact industry conditions or pose new opportunities and threats.

Managers can use *environmental scanning* to spot budding trends and clues of change that may develop into new driving forces.

Environmental scanning can be accomplished by systematically monitoring and studying current events, constructing scenarios, and employing the Delphi method (a technique for finding consensus among a group of knowledgeable experts). Environmental scanning methods are highly qualitative and subjective. The appeal of environmental scanning, notwithstanding its speculative nature, is that it helps managers lengthen their planning horizon, translate vague inklings of future opportunities or threats into clearer strategic issues (for which they can begin to develop strategic answers), and think strategically about future developments in the surrounding environment.[13] Companies that undertake formal environmental scanning on a fairly continuous and comprehensive level include General Electric, AT&T, Coca-Cola, Ford, General Motors, Du Pont, and Shell Oil.

▶ ## QUESTION 4: WHICH COMPANIES ARE IN THE STRONGEST/WEAKEST POSITIONS?

The next step in examining the industry's competitive structure is to study the market positions of rival companies. One technique for revealing the competitive positions of industry participants is *strategic group mapping*.[14] This analytical tool is a bridge between looking at the industry as a whole and at each company individually; it is most useful when an industry has so many competitors that it is impractical to examine each one in depth.

■ USING STRATEGIC GROUP MAPS TO ASSESS THE COMPETITIVE POSITION OF RIVAL FIRMS

A strategic group consists of those rival firms with similar competitive approaches and positions in the industry.[15] Companies in the same strategic group can resemble one another in any of several ways: They may have comparable product line breadth, use the same kinds of distribution channels, be vertically integrated to much the same degree, offer buyers similar services and technical assistance, use essentially the same product attributes to appeal to similar types of buyers, emphasize the same distribution channels, depend on identical technological approaches, and/or sell in the same price/quality range. An industry contains only one strategic group when all sellers approach the market with essentially identical strategies. At the other extreme, there are as many strategic groups as there are competitors when each rival pursues a distinctively different competitive approach and occupies a substantially different competitive position in the marketplace.

> Strategic group maps help managers understand the different competitive positions that rival firms occupy.

The procedure for constructing a strategic group map and deciding which firms belong in which strategic group is straightforward:

- Identify the competitive characteristics that differentiate firms in the industry—typical variables are price/quality range (high, medium, low), geographic coverage (local, regional, national, global), degree of vertical integration (none, partial, full), product line breadth (wide, narrow), use of distribution channels (one, some, all), and degree of service offered (no frills, limited, full service).

- Plot the firms on a two-variable map using pairs of these differentiating characteristics.

- Assign firms that fall in about the same strategy space to the same strategic group.

- Draw circles around each strategic group, making the circles proportional to the size of the group's respective share of total industry sales revenues.

This produces a two-dimensional *strategic group map* such as the one for the retail jewelry industry portrayed in Illustration 8.

To map the positions of strategic groups accurately within the industry, several guidelines need to be observed.[16]

1. *The two variables selected as axes for the map should not be highly correlated;* if they are, the circles on the map will fall along a diagonal and strategy-makers will learn

ILLUSTRATION 8   *Strategic Group Map of Competitors in the Retail Jewelry Industry*

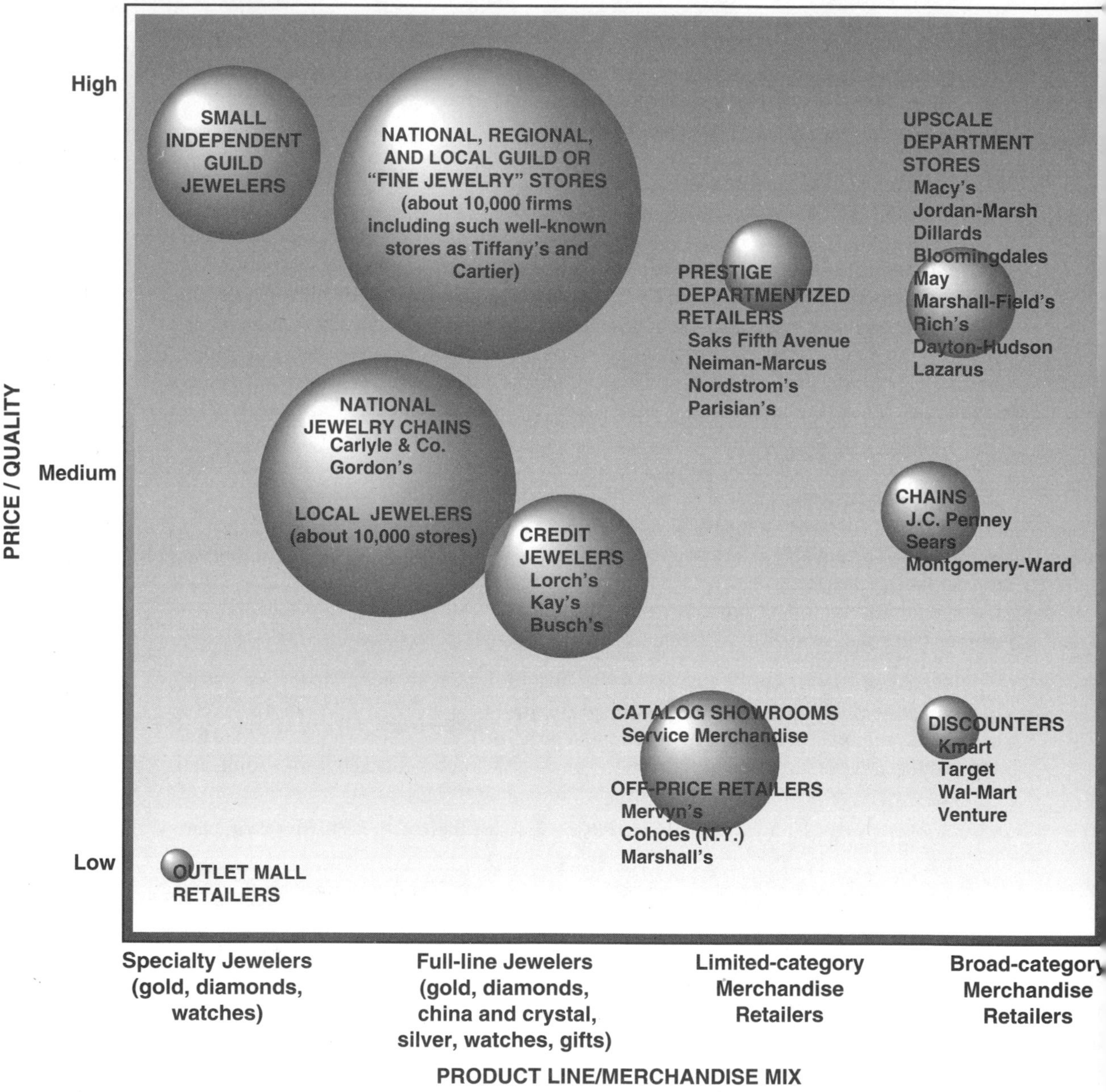

High

SMALL INDEPENDENT GUILD JEWELERS

NATIONAL, REGIONAL, AND LOCAL GUILD OR "FINE JEWELRY" STORES (about 10,000 firms including such well-known stores as Tiffany's and Cartier)

PRESTIGE DEPARTMENTIZED RETAILERS
Saks Fifth Avenue
Neiman-Marcus
Nordstrom's
Parisian's

UPSCALE DEPARTMENT STORES
Macy's
Jordan-Marsh
Dillards
Bloomingdales
May
Marshall-Field's
Rich's
Dayton-Hudson
Lazarus

PRICE / QUALITY

Medium

NATIONAL JEWELRY CHAINS
Carlyle & Co.
Gordon's

LOCAL JEWELERS (about 10,000 stores)

CREDIT JEWELERS
Lorch's
Kay's
Busch's

CHAINS
J.C. Penney
Sears
Montgomery-Ward

CATALOG SHOWROOMS
Service Merchandise

OFF-PRICE RETAILERS
Mervyn's
Cohoes (N.Y.)
Marshall's

DISCOUNTERS
Kmart
Target
Wal-Mart
Venture

Low

OUTLET MALL RETAILERS

Specialty Jewelers (gold, diamonds, watches)

Full-line Jewelers (gold, diamonds, china and crystal, silver, watches, gifts)

Limited-category Merchandise Retailers

Broad-category Merchandise Retailers

PRODUCT LINE/MERCHANDISE MIX

Note: The sizes of the circles are roughly proportional to the market shares of each group of competitors.

nothing more about the relative positions of competitors than they would by considering just one of the variables. For instance, if companies with broad product lines use multiple distribution channels while companies with narrow lines use a single distribution channel, then one of the variables is redundant. Looking at broad versus narrow product lines reveals just as much about who is positioned where as is learned by adding in consideration of single versus multiple distribution channels.

2. *The variables chosen as axes for the map should expose big differences in how rivals have positioned themselves to compete in the marketplace.* This, of course, means analysts must identify the characteristics that differentiate rival firms and use these differences as variables for the axes and as the basis for deciding which firm belongs in which strategic group.

3. *The variables used as axes don't have to be either quantitative or continuous;* rather, they can be discrete variables or defined in terms of distinct classes and combinations.

4. *Drawing the circles on the map in proportion to the combined sales of the firms in each strategic group allows the map to reflect the relative sizes of each strategic group.*

5. *If more than two good competitive variables can be used as axes for the map, several maps can be drawn to give different exposures to the competitive positioning relationships present in the industry's structure.* Because there is not necessarily one best map for portraying how competing firms are positioned in the market, it is advisable to experiment with different pairs of competitive variables.

Strategic group analysis helps deepen management understanding of competitive rivalry.[17] To begin with, *driving forces and competitive pressures often favor some strategic groups and hurt others.* Firms in adversely affected strategic groups may try to shift to a more favorably situated group; how hard such a move is depends on whether entry barriers into the target strategic group are high or low. Attempts by rival firms to enter a new strategic group nearly always increase competitive pressures. If certain firms are known to be trying to change their competitive positions on the map, then attaching arrows to the circles showing the targeted direction helps clarify the picture of competitive jockeying among rivals.

Driving forces and competitive pressures affect different strategic groups differently and cause profit prospects to vary from group to group.

A second indicator of competitive intensity is whether *the profit potential of strategic groups varies due to the strengths and weaknesses in each group's market position.* Differences in profitability can occur because of differing degrees of bargaining leverage with suppliers or customers and differing degrees of exposure to competition from substitute products outside the industry. Firms in low-profit strategic groups may try to switch to high-profit strategic groups.

Generally speaking, *the closer strategic groups are to each other on the map, the stronger competitive rivalry among member firms.* While firms within a strategic group are the closest rivals, their next closest rivals are found in the immediately adjacent groups. Firms in strategic groups that are *far apart* on the map hardly compete at all. For instance, Tiffany's and Wal-Mart both sell gold and silver jewelry, but the prices and perceived qualities of their products are much too different to generate any real competition between them. For the same reason, Timex is not a meaningful competitive rival of Rolex, and Subaru is not a close competitor of Lincoln or Mercedes-Benz.

▶ QUESTION 5: WHAT STRATEGIC MOVES ARE RIVALS LIKELY TO MAKE NEXT?

Studying the actions and behavior of one's closest competitors is essential. A company can't expect to outmaneuver its rivals without monitoring their actions and anticipating what moves they are likely to make next. As in sports, a good scouting report is invaluable. The strategies rivals are using and the actions they are likely to take next usually have a direct bearing on what a company's own best strategic moves are—whether it will need to defend against specific actions taken by rivals or whether rivals' moves provide an opening for a new offensive thrust.

IDENTIFYING COMPETITORS' STRATEGIES

A quick profile of key competitors can be drawn by studying how they are positioned in the marketplace, their strategic objectives as revealed by actions recently taken, and their basic competitive approaches. Table 3–3 provides an outline for categorizing the objectives and strategies of rival companies. Using this summary to profile a competitor's strategy, along with drawing a strategic group map, usually suffices to diagnose the competitive intent and market position of rivals.

EVALUATING WHO THE INDUSTRY'S MAJOR PLAYERS ARE GOING TO BE

It's usually obvious who the *current* major contenders are, but these same firms may not necessarily be the industry's future leaders. Some may be losing ground or be ill-equipped to cope with emerging competitive pressures and market trends. Smaller companies may emerge as up-and-coming contenders against larger-but-vulnerable rivals. Long-standing market leaders sometimes slide quickly down the industry's ranks; others end up being acquired. Today's industry leaders aren't automatically tomorrow's.

In deciding whether a competitor is favorably or unfavorably positioned to gain market ground, managers need to ascertain what potential exists for the competitor to do better or worse than other rivals. Usually, how securely a company holds its present market share is a function of its vulnerability to driving forces and competitive pressures. Pinpointing which rivals stand to gain market position and which rivals seem destined to lose market share helps a strategist anticipate a rival's next moves.

Successful strategists scout their competitors to understand their strategies, size up their strengths and weaknesses, and anticipate their next moves.

■ PREDICTING COMPETITORS' NEXT MOVES

This is the hardest, yet most useful, part of competitor analysis. Good clues about what moves a specific competitor may make next come from finding out how much pressure the rival is under to improve its financial performance. Aggressive rivals on the move are strong candidates for some type of new strategic initiative. Content rivals are likely to continue their present strategy with only minor fine-tuning. Ailing rivals can be performing so poorly that fresh strategic moves, either offensive or defensive, are

TABLE 3-3	*Categorizing the Objectives and Strategies of Competitors*				
Competitive Scope	**Strategic Intent**	**Market Share Objective**	**Competitive Position/Situation**	**Strategic Posture**	**Competitive Strategy***

• Local
• Regional
• National
• Multicountry
• Global
	• Be the dominant leader
	• Overtake the present industry leader
	• Be among the industry leaders (top five)
	• Move into the top 10
	• Move up a notch or two in the industry rankings
	• Overtake a particular rival (not necessarily the leader)
	• Maintain position
	• Just survive
		• Aggressive expansion via both acquisition and internal growth
		• Expansion via internal growth (boost market share at the expense of rival firms)
		• Expansion via acquisition
		• Hold on to present share (by growing at a rate equal to the industry average)
		• Give up share if necessary to achieve short-term profit objectives (stress profitability, not volume)
			• Getting stronger; on the move
			• Well-entrenched; able to maintain its present position
			• Stuck in the middle of the pack
			• Going after a different market position (trying to move from a weaker to a stronger position)
			• Struggling; losing ground
			• Retrenching to a position that can be defended
				• Mostly offensive
				• Mostly defensive
				• A combination of offense and defense
				• Aggressive risk-taker
				• Conservative follower
					• Striving for low-cost leadership
					• Mostly focusing on a market niche:
					  –High end
					  –Low end
					  –Geographic
					  –Buyers with special needs
					  –Other
					• Pursuing differentiation based on:
					  –Quality
					  –Service
					  –Technological superiority
					  –Breadth of product line
					  –Image and reputation
					  –Other attributes

*Note: Since a focus strategy can be aimed at any of several market niches and a differentiation strategy can be keyed to any of several attributes, it is best to be explicit about what kind of focus strategy or differentiation strategy a given firm is pursuing. All focusers do not pursue the same market niche, and all differentiators do not pursue the same differentiating attributes.

virtually certain. Since managers generally operate from assumptions about the industry's future and beliefs about their own firm's situation, insights into their strategic thinking come from examining their public pronouncements about where the industry is headed and what it will take to be successful, listening to what they are saying about their firm's situation, gathering information from the grapevine about what they are doing, and studying their past actions and leadership styles. Another thing to consider is whether a rival has the flexibility to make major strategic changes or whether it is locked into pursuing its same basic strategy with minor adjustments.

To succeed in predicting a competitor's next moves, one has to have a good feel for the rival's situation, how its managers think, and what its options are. Doing the necessary detective work can be tedious and time-consuming since the information comes in bits and pieces from many sources. But scouting competitors well enough to anticipate their next moves allows

Managers who fail to study competitors closely risk being blindsided by surprise actions on the part of rivals.

managers to prepare effective countermoves (perhaps even beat a rival to the punch!) and to take rivals' probable actions into account in designing their own company's best course of action.

QUESTION 6: WHAT ARE THE KEY FACTORS FOR COMPETITIVE SUCCESS?

An industry's *key success factors* (KSFs) are the strategy-related action approaches, competitive capabilities, and business outcomes which every firm must be competent at doing or concentrate on achieving in order to be competitively and financially successful. In other words, KSFs are business aspects all firms in the industry must pay close attention to—the specific outcomes crucial to market success (or failure) and the competences and competitive capabilities with the most direct bearing on company profitability. In the beer industry, the KSFs are full utilization of brewing capacity (to keep manufacturing costs low), a strong network of wholesale distributors (to gain access to as many retail outlets as possible), and clever advertising (to induce beer drinkers to buy a particular brand and thereby pull beer sales through the established wholesale/retail channels). In apparel manufacturing, the KSFs are appealing designs and color combinations (to create buyer interest), and low-cost manufacturing efficiency (to permit attractive retail pricing and ample profit margins). In tin and aluminum cans, where the cost of shipping empty cans is substantial, one of the keys is having plants located close to end-use customers so that the plant's output can be marketed within economical shipping distances (regional market share is far more crucial than national share).

> An industry's *key success factors* spell the difference between profit and loss and, ultimately, between competitive success and failure.

Determining the industry's key success factors, in light of prevailing and anticipated industry and competitive conditions, is a top-priority analytical consideration. At the very least, managers need to know the industry well enough to conclude what is more important to competitive success and what is less important. Company managers who misdiagnose what factors are truly crucial to long-term competitive success are prone to employ ill-conceived strategies or pursue less-important competitive targets. Frequently, a company with perceptive understanding of industry KSFs can gain sustainable competitive advantage by training its strategy on industry KSF's and devoting its energies to being distinctively better than rivals at succeeding on these factors. Indeed, using one or more of the industry's KSFs as *cornerstones* for the company's strategy is usually a necessary aspect of any winning managerial game plan.

> A sound strategy entails excelling in one or more industry key success factors.

Key success factors vary from industry to industry and even over time within the same industry as driving forces and competitive conditions change. Table 3–4 provides a shopping list of the most common types of key success factors. Only rarely does an industry have more than three or four key success factors at any one time. And even among these three or four, one or two usually outrank the others in importance. Managers, therefore, have to resist the temptation to include factors that have only minor importance

---

TABLE 3–4	*Types of Key Success Factors*

Technology-related KSFs

- Scientific research expertise (important in pharmaceuticals, medicine, space exploration, other high-tech industries).
- Production process innovation capability.
- Product innovation capability.
- Expertise in a given technology.

Manufacturing-related KSFs

- Low-cost production efficiency (achieve scale economies, capture experience curve effects).
- Quality of manufacture (fewer defects, less need for repairs).
- High utilization of fixed assets (important in capital intensive/high-fixed-cost industries).
- Low-cost plant locations.
- Access to adequate supplies of skilled labor.
- High labor productivity (important for items with high labor content).
- Low-cost product design and engineering (reduces manufacturing costs).
- Flexibility to manufacture a range of models and sizes/take care of custom orders.

Distribution-related KSFs

- A strong network of wholesale distributors/dealers.
- Gaining ample space on retailer shelves.
- Having company-owned retail outlets.
- Low distribution costs.
- Fast delivery.

Marketing-related KSFs

- A well-trained, effective sales force.
- Available, dependable service and technical assistance.
- Accurate filling of buyer orders (few back orders or mistakes).
- Breadth of product line and product selection.
- Merchandising skills.
- Attractive styling/packaging.
- Customer guarantees and warranties (important in mail-order retailing, big ticket purchases, new product introductions).

Skills-related KSFs

- Superior talent (important in professional services).
- Quality control know-how.
- Design expertise (important in fashion and apparel industries).
- Expertise in a particular technology.
- Ability to come up with clever, catchy ads.
- Ability to get newly developed products out of the R&D phase and into the market very quickly.

Organizational Capability

- Superior information systems (important in airline travel, car rental, credit card, and lodging industries).
- Ability to respond quickly to shifting market conditions (streamlined decision making, short lead times to bring new products to market).
- More experience and managerial know-how.

Other Types of KSFs

- Favorable image/reputation with buyers.
- Overall low cost (not just in manufacturing).
- Convenient locations (important in many retailing businesses).
- Pleasant, courteous employees.
- Access to financial capital (important in newly emerging industries with high degrees of business risk and in capital-intensive industries).
- Patent protection.

on their list of key success factors—the purpose of identifying KSFs is to make judgments about what things are more important to competitive success and what things are less important. To compile a list of every factor that matters even a little bit defeats the purpose of concentrating management attention on those factors truly crucial to long-term competitive success.

▶ QUESTION 7: IS THE INDUSTRY ATTRACTIVE AND WHAT ARE ITS PROSPECTS FOR ABOVE-AVERAGE PROFITABILITY?

The final step of industry and competitive analysis is to review the overall industry situation and develop reasoned conclusions about the relative attractiveness or unattractiveness of the industry, both near-term and long-term. An assessment that the industry is fundamentally attractive typically calls for an aggressive grow-and-build strategy, expanding sales efforts and investing in additional facilities and equipment as needed to strengthen the firm's long-term competitive position in the business. If the industry and competitive situation is judged to be relatively unattractive, more successful industry participants may choose to invest cautiously, look for ways to protect their long-term competitiveness and profitability, perhaps acquire smaller firms if the price is right, or consider diversification into more attractive businesses. Weaker companies may consider leaving the industry or merging with a rival. Outsiders considering entry may decide against investing in the business and look elsewhere for opportunities.

Important factors to consider in drawing conclusions about industry attractiveness include:

- The industry's growth potential.

- Whether the industry will be favorably or unfavorably impacted by the prevailing driving forces.

- The potential for the entry/exit of major firms (probable entry reduces attractiveness to existing firms; the exit of a major firm or several weak firms opens up market share growth opportunities for the remaining firms).

- The stability/dependability of demand (as affected by seasonality, the business cycle, the volatility of consumer preferences, inroads from substitutes, etc.).

- Whether competitive forces will become stronger or weaker.

- The severity of problems/issues confronting the industry as a whole.

- The degrees of risk and uncertainty in the industry's future.

- Whether competitive conditions and driving forces are conducive to rising or falling industry profitability.

As a general proposition, if an industry's overall profit prospects are above average, the industry can be considered attractive. If its profit prospects are below average, it is unattractive. However, it is a mistake to think of industries as being attractive or unattractive in an absolute sense. Attractiveness is relative, not absolute, and conclusions one way or the other are in the eye of the beholder. Companies on the outside may

> A well-situated company can still earn unusually good profits in an otherwise unattractive industry.

look at an industry's environment and conclude that it is an unattractive business for them to get into; they may see more profitable opportunities elsewhere. But a favorably positioned company already in the industry may survey the very same business environment and conclude that the industry is attractive because it has the resources and competitive capabilities to exploit the vulnerabilities of its weaker rivals, gain market share, build a strong leadership position, and grow its revenues and profits at a rapid clip. Hence, industry attractiveness *always* has to be appraised from the standpoint of a particular company. Industries unattractive to outsiders may be attractive to insiders. Industry environments unattractive to weak competitors may be attractive to strong competitors.

While companies contemplating entry into an industry can rely on the above list of factors, along with the answers to the first six questions, to draw conclusions about industry attractiveness, companies already in the industry need to consider the following additional aspects:

- The company's competitive position in the industry and whether its position is likely to grow stronger or weaker (being a well-entrenched leader in an otherwise lackluster industry can still produce good profitability).

- The company's potential to capitalize on the vulnerabilities of weaker rivals (thereby converting an unattractive *industry* situation into a potentially rewarding *company* opportunity).

- Whether the company is insulated from, or able to defend against, the factors that make the industry unattractive.

- Whether continued participation in this industry adds importantly to the firm's ability to be successful in other industries in which it has business interests.

▶ ACTUALLY DOING AN INDUSTRY AND COMPETITIVE ANALYSIS

Table 3–5 provides a worksheet for reporting the pertinent facts and conclusions of industry and competitive analysis. It pulls the relevant concepts and considerations together in systematic fashion and makes it easier to do a concise, understandable analysis of the industry and competitive environment.

TABLE 3–5 *Industry and Competitive Analysis Summary Profile*

1. Dominant Economic Characteristics of the Industry Environment

- Market growth.

- Geographic scope.

- Industry structure.

- Scale economies.

- Experience curve effects.

- Capital requirements.

2. Competition Analysis

- Rivalry among competing sellers (a strong, moderate, or weak force/weapons of competiton).

- Threat of potential entry (a strong, moderate, or weak force/ assessment of entry barriers).

- Competition from substitutes (a strong, moderate, or weak force and why).

- Power of suppliers (a strong, moderate, or weak force and why).

- Power of customers (a strong, moderate, or weak force and why).

3. Driving Forces

4. Competitive Position of Major Companies/Strategic Groups

- Favorably positioned and why.

- Unfavorably positioned and why.

5. Competitor Analysis

- Strategic approaches/predicted moves of key competitors.

- Who to watch and why.

6. Key Success Factors

7. Industry Prospects and Overall Attractiveness

- Factors making the industry attractive.

- Factors making the industry unattractive.

- Special industry issues/problems.

- Profit outlook (favorable/unfavorable).

Two things should be kept in mind in doing industry and competitive analysis. One, the task of analyzing a company's external situation cannot be reduced to a mechanical, formula-like exercise in which facts and data are plugged in and definitive conclusions come pouring out. There can be several appealing scenarios about how an industry will evolve and what future competitive conditions will be like. For this reason, strategic analysis always leaves room for differences of opinion about how all the factors add up and how industry and competitive conditions will change. However, while no strategy analysis methodology can guarantee a single conclusive diagnosis, it doesn't make sense to shortcut strategic analysis and rely on opinion and casual observation. Managers become better strategists when they know what analytical questions to pose, can use situation analysis techniques to find answers, and have the skills to read clues about which way the winds of industry and competitive change are blowing.

Two, sweeping industry and competitive analyses need to be done every one to three years; in the interim, managers are obliged to continually update and reexamine their thinking as events unfold. There's no substitute for being a good student of industry and competitive conditions and staying on top of what's happening in the industry. Anything else leaves a manager unprepared to initiate shrewd and timely strategic adjustments.

Thinking Strategically about a Company's Situation

CHAPTER
FOUR

Understand what really makes a company "tick."

Charles R. Scott
CEO, Intermark Corp.

The secret of success is to be ready for opportunity when it comes.

Disraeli

If a company is not "best in world" at a critical activity, it is sacrificing competitive advantage by performing that activity with its existing technique.

James Brian Quinn

In the previous chapter we described how to use the tools of industry and competitive analysis to think strategically about a company's external situation. In this chapter we discuss how to size up a company's strategic position in that environment. Company situation analysis centers on a consideration of the following five questions:

1.   How well is the present strategy working?
2.   What are the company's strengths, weaknesses, opportunities, and threats?
3.   Are the company's prices and costs competitive?
4.   How strong is the company's competitive position?
5.   What strategic issues does the company face?

To explore these questions, four new analytical techniques are used: SWOT analysis, value chain analysis, strategic cost analysis, and competitive strength assessment. These techniques are basic strategic management tools because they expose the relative attractiveness of a company's industry position and whether the present strategy needs to be modified.

▶ QUESTION 1: HOW WELL IS THE PRESENT STRATEGY WORKING?

Evaluating how well a company's present strategy is working starts with a clearheaded view of what the strategy is and what the company's strategic and financial objectives are. The first thing to establish is the company's basic competitive approach—whether it is (1) striving to be a low-cost leader or (2) stressing ways to differentiate its product offering from rivals or (3) concentrating its efforts on a narrow market niche. Another strategy-defining consideration is the company's competitive scope within the industry— how many stages of the industry's production-distribution chains it operates in (one, several, or all), the extent of its geographic market coverage, and the size and diversity of its customer base. The company's functional strategies in production, marketing, finance, human resources, and so on, further illuminate the picture of company strategy. In addition, the company may have initiated some recent strategic moves (e.g., a price cut, stepped-up advertising, entry into a new geographic area, or merger with a competitor) that aim at securing a particular competitive advantage and/or improved competitive position. Reviewing the rationale for each piece of the strategy—for each competitive move and each functional approach—should clarify the present strategy.

While there's merit in evaluating the strategy from a qualitative standpoint (as concerns its completeness, internal consistency, rationale, and suitability to the situation), the best evidence of how well a company's strategy is working comes from studying the company's recent strategic and financial performance and seeing what story the numbers tell about the results the strategy is producing. The most obvious indicators of strategic and financial performance include (1) the firm's market share ranking in the industry, (2) whether the firm's profit margins are increasing or decreasing and how large they are relative to rival firms, (3) trends in the firm's net profits and return on investment, (4) the company's credit rating, (5) whether the firm's sales are growing faster or slower than the market as a whole, (6) the firm's image and reputation with its customers, and (7) whether the company is regarded as a leader in technology, product innovation, product quality, or customer service. The stronger a company's current overall performance, the less likely the need for radical changes in strategy. The weaker a company's strategic and financial performance, the more its current strategy must be questioned. Weak performance is usually a sign of weak strategy or weak execution or both.

> *The stronger a company's strategic and financial performance, the more likely it has a well-conceived, well-executed strategy.*

▶ QUESTION 2: WHAT ARE THE COMPANY'S STRENGTHS, WEAKNESSES, OPPORTUNITIES, AND THREATS?

Sizing up a firm's internal strengths and weaknesses and its external opportunities and threats is commonly termed SWOT analysis. It is an easy-to-use technique for getting a quick *overview* of a firm's strategic situation. SWOT analysis underscores the basic principle that strategy must produce a good fit between a company's internal capability (its strengths and weaknesses) and its external circumstances (reflected in part by its opportunities and threats).

■ IDENTIFYING STRENGTHS AND WEAKNESSES

A *strength* is something a company is good at doing or a characteristic that gives it an important capability. A strength can be a skill, important expertise, a valuable organizational resource or competitive capability, or an achievement that puts the company in a position of market advantage (like having a better product, stronger name recognition, superior technology, or better customer service). A strength can also result from alliances or cooperative ventures with a partner having expertise or capabilities that enhance a company's competitiveness.

A *weakness* is something a company lacks or does poorly (in comparison to others) or a condition that puts it at a disadvantage. A weakness may not necessarily make a company vulnerable competitively, depending on how much it matters in the marketplace. Table 4–1 indicates the kinds of things managers should consider in determining a company's internal strengths and weaknesses.

Once managers identify a company's internal strengths and weaknesses, the two lists need to be evaluated from a strategy-making perspective. Some strengths are more important than others because they matter more in determining performance, in competing successfully, and in forming a powerful strategy. Likewise, some internal weaknesses can prove fatal, while others are either not significant or can be easily remedied. Sizing up a company's strengths and weaknesses is akin to constructing a *strategic balance sheet*—strengths are *competitive assets* and weaknesses are *competitive liabilities*. The

---

| **TABLE 4–1** | *SWOT Analysis — What to Look for in Sizing up a Company's Strengths, Weaknesses, Opportunities, and Threats* |

Potential Internal Strengths

- Core competences in key areas
- Adequate financial resources
- Well thought of by buyers
- An acknowledged market leader
- Well-conceived functional area strategies
- Access to economies of scale
- Insulated (at least somewhat) from strong competitive pressures
- Proprietary technology
- Cost advantages
- Better advertising campaigns
- Product innovation skills
- Proven management
- Ahead on experience curve
- Better manufacturing capability
- Superior technological skills
- Other?

Potential Internal Weaknesses

- No clear strategic direction
- Obsolete facilities
- Subpar profitability because . . .
- Lack of managerial depth and talent
- Missing some key skills or competences
- Poor track record in implementing strategy
- Plagued with internal operating problems
- Falling behind in R&D
- Too narrow a product line
- Weak market image
- Weak distribution network
- Below-average marketing skills
- Unable to finance needed changes in strategy
- Higher overall unit costs relative to key competitors
- Other?

Potential External Opportunities

- Serve additional customer groups
- Enter new markets or segments
- Expand product line to meet broader range of customer needs
- Diversify into related products
- Vertical integration (forward or backward)
- Falling trade barriers in attractive foreign markets
- Complacency among rival firms
- Faster market growth
- Other?

Potential External Threats

- Entry of lower-cost foreign competitors
- Rising sales of substitute products
- Slower market growth
- Adverse shifts in foreign exchange rates and trade policies of foreign governments
- Costly regulatory requirements
- Vulnerability to recession and business cycle
- Growing bargaining power of customers or suppliers
- Changing buyer needs and tastes
- Adverse demographic changes
- Other?

issues are whether a company's strengths/assets adequately overcome its weaknesses/liabilities (50–50 balance is definitely not the desired condition!), how to meld strengths into an attractive strategy, and whether internal changes are needed to tilt the balance more toward the assets and away from the liabilities.

> A company's internal strengths usually represent competitive assets; its internal weaknesses usually represent competitive liabilities.

From a strategy-making perspective, a company's strengths are significant because they can form the foundation for strategy and the basis for gaining competitive advantage. If a company doesn't have strong competencies and competitive assets upon which to craft an attractive strategy, managers need to take decisive remedial action to develop organizational strengths and capabilities that can underpin a sound strategy. At the same time, managers have to correct weaknesses that make the company vulnerable, hurt its strategic performance, or disqualify it from pursuing an attractive opportunity. The strategy-making principle here is simple: *A company's strategy should be well-suited to its strengths, weaknesses, and competitive capabilities.* It is foolhardy to pursue a strategic plan that cannot be competently executed with the skills and resources a company can marshal or that can be undermined by company weaknesses. As a rule, managers should build their strategy around what the company does best and avoid strategies that place heavy demands on areas where the company is weakest or has unproven ability.

CORE COMPETENCIES

One of the trade secrets of first-rate strategic management is consolidating a company's technological, production, and marketing know-how into core competencies that enhance its competitiveness. *A core competence is something a company does especially well in comparison to its competitors.*[1] In practice, there are many possible types of core competencies: excellent skills in manufacturing a high-quality product, know-how in creating an operating system to fill customer orders accurately and quickly, the ability to provide better after-sale service, more expertise and proven experience in achieving high operating efficiency with low operating costs, a unique formula for selecting good retail locations, unusual innovativeness in developing new products, skillful merchandising and product display, mastery of an important technology, an efficient and accurate system for researching customer tastes and spotting new market trends, superior employee training programs, outstanding skills in working with customers on new applications and uses of the product, and expertise in integrating multiple technologies to create whole families of new products. Typically, a core competence relates to a set of skills, expertise in performing particular activities, or a company's scope and depth of technological know-how; it resides in a company's people, not in assets appearing on the balance sheet.

> Successful strategists seek to capitalize on what a company does best—its expertise, strengths, core competences, and strongest competitive capabilities.

The importance of a core competence to strategy-making rests with (1) the added capability it gives a company in going after a particular market opportunity, (2) the competitive edge it can yield in the marketplace, and (3) its potential for being a cornerstone of strategy. It is always easier to build competitive advantage when a firm has a core competence in activities important to market success, when rival companies do not have offsetting competencies, and when it is costly and time-consuming for rivals to match the competence. Core competencies are thus valuable competitive assets, capable of being the mainsprings of a company's success.

Core competencies empower a company to build competitive advantage.

■ IDENTIFYING EXTERNAL OPPORTUNITIES AND THREATS

Market opportunity is a big factor in shaping a company's strategy. Indeed, managers can't match strategy to the company's situation without first identifying each industry opportunity and appraising the growth and profit potential each one holds. Depending on industry conditions, opportunities can be plentiful or scarce and can range from wildly attractive (an absolute must to pursue) to marginally interesting (low on the company's list of strategic priorities).

In appraising industry opportunities and ranking their attractiveness, managers have to guard against equating industry opportunities with company opportunities. Not every company in an industry is well positioned to pursue each opportunity that exists in the industry. A company's strengths and weaknesses make it better suited to pursuing some industry opportunities than others. *The industry opportunities most relevant to a particular company are those that offer important avenues for profitable growth, those where a company has the most potential for competitive advantage, and those which the company has the financial resources to pursue.* An industry opportunity that a company doesn't have the capability to capture is an illusion.

Often, certain factors in a company's external environment pose *threats* to its well-being. Threats can stem from the emergence of cheaper technologies, rivals' introduction of new or better products, the entry of low-cost foreign competitors into a company's market stronghold, new regulations that are more burdensome to a company than to its competitors, vulnerability to a rise in interest rates, the potential of a hostile takeover, unfavorable demographic shifts, adverse changes in foreign exchange rates, political upheaval in a foreign country where the company has facilities, and the like. Table 4–1 also presents a checklist to aid in identifying a company's external opportunities and threats.

Successful strategists aim at capturing a company's best growth opportunities and creating strong defenses against external threats.

Opportunities and threats not only affect the attractiveness of a company's situation but point to the need for strategic action. To be adequately matched to a company's circumstances, strategy must (1) be aimed at pursuing opportunities well suited to the company's capabilities and (2) provide a defense against external threats. SWOT analysis is therefore more than an exercise in making four lists. The important part of SWOT analysis involves evaluating strengths, weaknesses, opportunities, and threats and drawing conclusions about the attractiveness of the company's situation and the possible need for strategic action. Some of the pertinent strategy-making questions to consider, once the SWOT listings have been compiled, are:

- Does the company have any internal strengths or core competencies around which an attractive strategy can be built?

- Do the company's weaknesses make it competitively vulnerable and/or do they disqualify the company from pursuing certain industry opportunities? Which weaknesses does strategy need to correct?

- Which industry opportunities does the company have the skills and resources to pursue with a real chance of success? Which industry opportunities are best from the company's standpoint? (*Remember:* Opportunity without the means to capture it is an illusion.)

- What external threats should management be worried most about and what strategic moves should be considered in crafting a good defense?

Unless company managers are acutely aware of the company's internal strengths and weaknesses and its external opportunities and threats, they are ill-prepared to craft a strategy tightly matched to the company's circumstances. SWOT analysis is therefore an essential component of thinking strategically about a company's situation.

▶ QUESTION 3: ARE THE COMPANY'S PRICES AND COSTS COMPETITIVE?

Company managers are often stunned when a competitor cuts prices to "unbelievably low" levels or when a new market entrant comes on strong with a very low price. The competitor may not, however, be dumping, buying market share, or waging a desperate move to gain sales; it may simply have substantially lower costs. One of the most telling signs of whether a company's market position is strong or precarious is whether its prices and costs are competitive with industry rivals. Price-cost comparisons are especially critical in a commodity-product industry where there are essentially no value-added differences among the products of rival sellers, price competition is typically the ruling market force, and lower-cost companies have the upper hand. But even in industries where products are differentiated and competition swirls around the different value-creating attributes of competing brands as much as around price, rival companies have to keep their costs *in line* and make sure that any added costs and price premiums are justified by the extra value buyers perceive they get.

Assessing whether a company's costs are competitive with those of its rivals is a crucial part of company situation analysis.

Competitors quite frequently don't incur the same costs in supplying their products to end-users. The differences can range from trivial to competitively significant. Disparities in costs among competitors can stem from:

- Differences in the prices paid for raw materials, components parts, energy, and other items purchased from suppliers.

- Differences in basic technology and the age of plants and equipment. (Because rival companies usually invest in plants and key pieces of equipment at different times, their facilities can have somewhat different technological efficiencies and different fixed costs. Older facilities are typically less efficient, but if they were less expensive to construct or acquired at bargain prices, they *may* still be reasonably cost competitive with modern facilities.)

- Differences in internal operating costs due to economies of scale associated with plant size and learning and experience curves, as well as differences in wage rates, productivity levels, operating practices, organization structures and staffing levels, tax rates, and the like.

- Differences in rival firms' exposure to inflation rates and changes in foreign exchange rates (as can occur in global industries where competitors' plants are located in different countries).

- Differences in marketing costs, sales and promotion expenditures, and advertising expenses.

- Differences in inbound transportation costs and outbound shipping costs.

- Differences in forward channel distribution costs (the costs and markups of distributors, wholesalers, and retailers associated with getting the product from the point of manufacture into the hands of end-users).

For a company to be competitively successful, its costs must be in line with those of its rivals. While some cost disparity is justified so long as the products or services of competing companies are sufficiently differentiated, a high-cost firm's market position becomes increasingly vulnerable the more its costs exceed those of its rivals.

> The higher a company's costs are above those of close rivals, the more competitively vulnerable it becomes.

■ STRATEGIC COST ANALYSIS AND VALUE CHAINS

Given the numerous opportunities for cost disparities, a company must be alert to how its costs compare with rivals' costs. This is where *strategic cost analysis* comes in. *Strategic cost analysis focuses on a firm's cost position relative to its rivals.*

THE VALUE CHAIN CONCEPT

The primary analytical tool of strategic cost analysis is a *value chain* identifying the activities, functions, and business processes that have to be performed in designing, producing, marketing, delivering, and supporting a product or service.[2] The chain of value-creating activities starts with raw materials supply and continues on through parts and components production, manufacturing and assembly, wholesale distribution, and retailing to the ultimate end-user of the product or service.

> Strategic cost analysis involves comparing a company's cost position relative to key competitors activity by activity.

A *company's* value chain shows the linked set of activities and functions it performs internally; a representative company value chain is shown in Figure 4–1. The chain includes a profit margin because a markup over the cost of performing the firm's value-creating activities is customarily part of the price (or total cost) born by buyers—creating value for buyers greater than the costs of production is a fundamental objective of business enterprise.

By disaggregating a company's operations into strategically relevant activities and business processes, it is possible to better understand the

> Value chains are a tool for thinking strategically about the relationship among activities performed inside and outside the firm—which ones are strategy-critical and how core competencies can be developed.

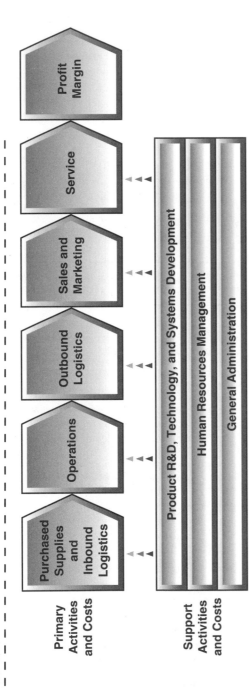

FIGURE 4—1 *Representative Company Value Chain*

Primary Activities and Costs

Purchased Supplies and Inbound Logistics → Operations → Outbound Logistics → Sales and Marketing → Service → Profit Margin

Support Activities and Costs

Product R&D, Technology, and Systems Development

Human Resources Management

General Administration

Primary Activities

- **Purchased supplies and inbound logistics**—Activities, costs, and assets associated with purchasing fuel, energy, raw materials, parts components, merchandise, and consumable items from vendors; receiving, storing, and disseminating inputs from suppliers; inspection; and inventory management.

- **Operations**—Activities, costs, and assets associated with converting inputs into final product form (production, assembly, packaging, equipment maintenance, facilities operations, quality assurance, environmental protection).

- **Outbound logistics**—Activities, costs, and assets dealing with physically distributing the product to buyers (finished goods warehousing, order processing, order picking and packing, shipping, delivery vehicle operations).

- **Sales and marketing**—Activities, costs, and assets related to sales force efforts, advertising and promotion, market research and planning, and dealer/distributor support.

- **Service**—Activities, costs, and assets associated with providing assistance to buyers, such as installation, spare parts delivery, maintenance and repair, technical assistance, buyer inquiries and complaints.

Support Activities

- **Research, technology, and systems development**—Activities, costs, and assets relating to product R&D, process R&D, process design improvement, equipment design, computer software development, telecommunications systems, computer-assisted design and engineering, new database capabilities, development of computerized support systems.

- **Human resources**—Activities, costs, and assets associated with the recruitment, hiring, training, development, and compensation of all types of personnel; labor relations activities; development of knowledge-based skills.

- **General administration**—Activities, costs, and assets relating to general management, accounting and finance, legal and regulatory affairs, safety and security, management information systems, and other overhead functions.

Source: Adapted from Michael E Porter, *Competitive Advantage* (New York: The Free Press, 1985), pp. 37–43.

company's cost structure and locate the major cost elements. Each activity in the value chain incurs costs and ties up assets; assigning the company's operating costs and assets to each individual activity in the chain provides cost estimates of each activity. The costs a company incurs in performing each activity can be driven up or down by two types of factors: *structural drivers* (scale economies, experience curve effects, technology requirements, capital intensity, and product line complexity) and *executional drivers* (workforce commitment to continuous improvement, attitudes and capabilities regarding product quality and process quality, cycle time in getting newly developed products to market, utilization of existing capacity, efficiency of internal business processes' design and execution, and the firm's

----

Value chains are also a tool for understanding the firm's cost structure and how the costs of activities are driven up or down.

----

effectiveness in working with suppliers and/or customers to reduce its costs). Understanding a company's cost structure means understanding:

- Whether it is trying to achieve a competitive advantage based on (1) lower costs (managerial efforts to lower costs along the company's value chain should be highly visible) or (2) differentiation (managers may have deliberately spent more in performing those activities responsible for creating the differentiating attributes).
- Cost behavior in each activity in the value chain and how the costs of one activity spill over to affect the costs of other activities.
- Whether the linkages among activities in the company's value chain present opportunities for cost reduction (e.g., Japanese VCR producers were able to reduce prices from $1,300 in 1977 to under $300 in 1984 by spotting the impact of an early step in the value chain, product design, on a later step, production, and drastically reducing the number of parts in VCRs).[3]

However, there's more to strategic cost analysis and a company's cost competitiveness than just how the cost of its activities compare with rivals'. Competing companies often differ in their degrees of vertical integration across all the stages of business activity involved in providing a product or service to the final user. Comparing the value chain for a partially integrated rival against the chain for a fully integrated rival requires adjusting for differences in scope of activities performed. Moreover, uncompetitive prices to end-use customers can have their origins in activities performed by other companies either upstream or downstream in the market. A company's suppliers or forward channel allies may have excessively high cost structures or profit margins that put a company's cost competitiveness in jeopardy even though its own internal costs are competitive.

For example, in determining Michelin's cost competitiveness vis-a-vis Goodyear and Bridgestone in supplying replacement tires to vehicle owners, one has to look at more than whether Michelin's tire manufacturing costs are above or below Goodyear's and Bridgestone's manufacturing costs. If a replacement tire buyer has to pay $400 at retail for a set of Michelin tires and only $350 for comparable sets of Goodyear and Bridgestone tires, that leaves Michelin with a $50 price disadvantage in the replacement tire marketplace. This can stem not only from higher manufacturing costs (*perhaps* reflecting the added costs of Michelin's strategic efforts to rebuild a better-quality tire with more performance features) but also (1) from differences in what the three tiremakers pay their suppliers for materials and tiremaking components and (2) differences in the operating efficiencies, costs, and markups of Michelin's wholesale-retail dealer outlets versus those of Goodyear's and Bridgestone's dealer outlets. Thus, determining whether a company's prices and costs are competitive from an end-user's standpoint requires looking at the activities and costs of competitively relevant suppliers and forward allies, as well as the costs of internally performed activities.

A company's cost competitiveness depends not only on the costs of internally performed activities (its own value chain) but also on costs in the value chains of suppliers and forward channel allies.

As the tire industry example makes clear, a company's value chain is embedded in a larger system of activities that includes the value chains of its upstream suppliers and downstream customers or allies engaged in getting its product/service to end-users.[4] Accurately assessing a company's competitiveness in end-use markets requires that company managers understand the entire delivery system, not just the company's own value chain; at the very least, this means considering the value chains of suppliers and forward channel allies (if any)—as shown in Figure 4–2. Suppliers' value chains are relevant because suppliers perform activities and incur costs in creating and delivering the purchased inputs used in a company's own value chain; the cost and quality of these inputs influence the company's cost and/or differentiation capabilities. Anything a company can do to reduce its suppliers' costs or improve suppliers' effectiveness can enhance its own competitiveness. Forward channel value chains are relevant because (1) the costs and margins of downstream companies are part of the price the end-user pays and (2) the activities channel allies perform affect the end-user's satisfaction. Furthermore, a company can often enhance its competitiveness by undertaking activities that have a beneficial impact on its customers' value chains. For instance, some aluminum can producers have constructed plants next to beer breweries and deliver cans on overhead conveyors directly to brewers' can-filling line; this has resulted in significant savings in production scheduling, shipping, and inventory costs for both container producers and breweries.[5]

Although the value chains in Figures 4–1 and 4–2 are typical, the nature of the chains and the relative importance of the activities within them vary by industry and by company position in the value chain system. The value chain for the pulp and paper industry (timber farming, logging, pulp mills, papermaking, printing, and publishing) differs from the chain for the home appliance industry (parts and components manufacture, assembly, wholesale distribution, and retail sales). The value chain for the soft drink industry (processing of basic ingredients, syrup manufacture, bottling and can filling, wholesale distribution, and retailing) differs from the chain for the computer software industry (programming, disk loading, marketing, and distribution). A producer of bathroom and kitchen faucets depends heavily on the activities of wholesale distributors and building supply retailers to represent its products to homebuilders and do-it-yourselfers; a producer of small gasoline engines markets directly to the makers of lawn and garden equipment. A wholesaler's most important activities and costs deal with purchased goods, inbound logistics, and outbound logistics. A hotel's most important

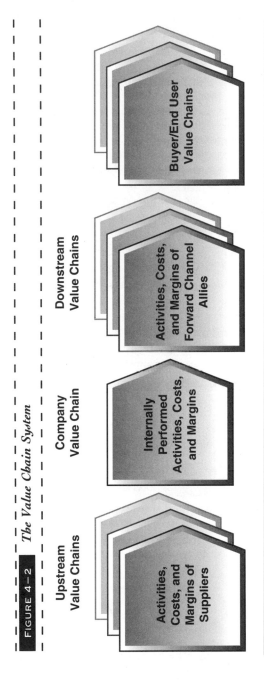

FIGURE 4-2   *The Value Chain System*

Upstream
Value Chains

Company
Value Chain

Downstream
Value Chains

Activities,
Costs, and
Margins of
Suppliers

Internally
Performed
Activities, Costs,
and Margins

Activities, Costs,
and Margins of
Forward Channel
Allies

Buyer/End User
Value Chains

Source: Adapted from Michael E Porter, *Competitive Advantage* (New York: The Free Press, 1985), p. 35.

activities and costs are in operations. A global public accounting firm's most important activities and costs are human resources management (recruiting and training a highly competent professional staff) and service. Outbound logistics is a crucial activity at Domino's Pizza, but is comparatively insignificant at Blockbuster. Sales and marketing are dominating activities at Coca-Cola, but have minor roles in the cost structure and activities of electric and gas utilities. Consequently, generic value chains like those in Figure 4–1 and 4–2 are illustrative, not absolute, and may require adaptation to fit a particular company's circumstances.

DEVELOPING THE DATA FOR STRATEGIC COST ANALYSIS

The data requirements for value chain analysis can be formidable. Typically, it requires breaking a firm's departmental cost accounting data out into the cost of performing specific activities.[6] The appropriate degree of disaggregation depends on the economics of the activities and how valuable it is to develop cross-company cost comparisons for narrowly defined activities as opposed to broadly defined activities. A good guideline is to develop separate cost estimates for activities having different economics and for activities representing a significant or growing proportion of cost.[7]

Traditional accounting identifies costs according to broad categories of expenses— wages and salaries, employee benefits, supplies, travel, depreciation, R&D, and other fixed charges. *Activity-based costing* entails assigning these broad categories of costs to the specific tasks and activities being performed, as shown in Table 4–2.[8] It also entails developing cost estimates for activities performed in the competitively relevant portions of suppliers' and downstream customers' value chains. To benchmark the firm's cost position against rivals, costs for the same activities for each rival must likewise be estimated—an advanced art in competitive intelligence in itself. But despite the tediousness of developing cost estimates activity by activity and the imprecision of some of the estimates, the payoff in exposing the costs of particular internal tasks and functions and determining the cost competitiveness of one's position vis-a-vis one's rivals makes it a valuable strategic management tool. Despite the difficulty calculating these costs, every company's managers should attempt to estimate the value chain for the business in which they are involved.[9] Illustration 9 shows a simplified value chain comparison for

---

TABLE 4–2   *The Difference between Traditional Cost Accounting and Activity-based Cost Accounting*

Cost Categories in Departmental Budget		Cost of Performing Specific Departmental Activities	
Wages and Salaries	$350,000	Evaluate supplier capabilities	$135,750
Employee benefits	115,000	Process purchase orders	82,100
Supplies	6,500	Expedite supplier deliveries	23,500
Travel	2,400	Expedite internal processing	15,840
Depreciation	17,000	Check quality of items purchased	94,300
Other fixed charges	124,000	Check incoming deliveries against purchase orders	48,450
Miscellaneous operating expenses	25,250	Resolve problems	110,000
		Internal administration	130,210
	$640,150		$640,150

ILLUSTRATION 9	*Value Chains for Anheuser-Busch and Adolph Coors Beers*

In the table below are average cost estimates for the combined brands of beer produced by Anheuser-Busch and Coors. The example shows raw material costs, other manufacturing costs, and forward channel distribution costs.

Activity-Cost Elements	Estimated Average Cost Breakdown for Combined Anheuser-Busch Brands		Estimated Average Cost Breakdown for Combined Adolph Coors Brands	
	Per 6-Pack of 12-oz. Cans	Per Barrel Equivalent	Per 6-Pack of 12-oz. Cans	Per Barrel Equivalent
1. Manufacturing costs:				
Direct production costs:				
Raw material ingredients	$0.1384	$ 7.63	$0.1082	$ 5.96
Direct labor	0.1557	8.58	0.1257	6.93
Salaries for nonunionized personnel	0.0800	4.41	0.0568	3.13
Packaging	0.5055	27.86	0.4663	25.70
Depreciation on plant and equipment	0.0410	2.26	0.0826	4.55
Subtotal	0.9206	50.74	0.8396	46.27
Other expenses:				
Advertising	0.0477	2.63	0.0338	1.86
Other marketing costs and general administrative expenses	0.1096	6.04	0.1989	10.96
Interest	0.0147	0.81	0.0033	0.18
Research and development	0.0277	1.53	0.0195	1.07
Total manufacturing costs	$1.1203	$ 61.75	$1.0951	$ 60.34
2. Manufacturer's operating profit	0.1424	7.85	0.0709	3.91
3. Net selling price	1.2627	69.60	1.1660	64.25
4. Plus federal and state excise taxes paid by brewer	0.1873	10.32	0.1782	9.82
5. Gross manufacturer's selling price to distributor/wholesaler	1.4500	79.92	1.3442	74.07
6. Average margin over manufacturer's cost	0.5500	30.31	0.5158	28.43
7. Average wholesale price charged to retailer (inclusive of taxes in item 4 above but exclusive of other taxes)	$2.00	$110.23	$1.86	$102.50
8. Plus other assorted state and local taxes levied on wholesale and retail sales (this varies from locality to locality) . .	0.60		0.60	
9. Average 20% retail markup over wholesale cost	0.40		0.38	
10. Average price to consumer at retail	$3.00		$2.84	

Note: The difference in the average cost structures for Anheuser-Busch and Adolph Coors is, to a substantial extent, due to A-B's higher proportion of super-premium beer sales. A-B's super-premium brand, Michelob, was the bestseller in its category and somewhat more costly to brew than premium and popular-priced beers.

Source: Compiled by Tom McLean, Elsa Wischkaemper, and Arthur A Thompson, Jr., from a wide variety of documents and field interviews. Based on 1982 data.

Anheuser-Busch (the U.S. industry leader) and Adolph Coors (the third ranking brewer).

The most important application of value chain analysis is to expose how a particular firm's cost position compares with those of its rivals. What is needed is competitor-versus-competitor cost estimates for each major customer group or market segment. The size of a company's cost advantage/disadvantage can vary from item to item in the product line, from customer group to customer group (if different distribution channels are used), and from geographic market to geographic market (if cost factors vary across geographic regions).

■ **BENCHMARKING THE COSTS OF KEY ACTIVITIES**

Company efforts to benchmark the costs of performing a given activity against competitors' costs (and/or against the costs of a noncompetitor in another industry that efficiently and effectively performs much the same activity or business process) have mushroomed over the past decade. Benchmarking focuses on making cross-company comparisons of how basic functions and processes in the value chain are performed—how materials are purchased, how suppliers are paid, how inventories are managed, how employees are trained, how payrolls are processed, how fast the company can get new products to the market, how the quality control function is performed, how customer orders are filled and shipped, and how maintenance is performed.[10]

Xerox, an early pioneer of benchmarking, was driven to compare its costs against competitors when in 1979 Japanese manufacturers began selling mid-size copiers in the United States for $9,600 each, an amount less than Xerox's production costs.[11] Although

Xerox management suspected its Japanese competitors were dumping, it sent a team of line managers, including the head of manufacturing, to Japan to make a detailed study of competitors' business processes and costs; fortunately, Xerox's joint

Benchmarking company activities provides hard evidence of a company's cost competitiveness.

venture partner in Japan, Fuji-Xerox, knew the competitors well. The team found that Xerox's costs were excessive due to gross inefficiencies in its manufacturing processes and business practices. The study proved instrumental in Xerox's efforts to become cost competitive and prompted Xerox to embark on a long-term program to benchmark 67 of its key work processes against companies identified as having the ultimate best practices in performing these processes. Xerox recognized that its benchmarking efforts should extend to any company regarded as being world-class in performing an activity relevant to Xerox's business, rather than restricting its benchmarking to office equipment rivals.

Sometimes benchmarking can be accomplished by collecting information from published reports, trade groups, and industry research firms and by talking to knowledgeable industry analysts, customers, and suppliers (customers, suppliers, and joint venture partners often make willing benchmarking allies). More usually, though, benchmarking requires arranging field trips to the facilities of competing or noncompeting companies to observe how things are done, ask questions, compare practices and processes, and perhaps exchange data on productivity, staffing levels, time requirements, and other cost components. However, benchmarking may involve competitively sensitive information about processes or how lower costs are achieved so rivals can't be expected to be completely open, even if they do agree to host tours and answer questions. The explosive interest of companies in benchmarking costs and identifying best practices has prompted consulting organizations (e.g., Andersen Consulting, A. T. Kearney, Best Practices Benchmarking & Consulting, and Towers Perrin) and several newly formed councils and associations (the International Benchmarking Clearinghouse and the Strategic Planning Institute's Council on Benchmarking) to gather benchmarking data, prepare benchmarking studies, and pass information about best practices and the costs of performing activities through to clients/members without identifying the sources. Over 80 percent of *Fortune 500* companies now engage in some form of benchmarking.

Managers who elect to do their own benchmarking can benefit from the guidelines and recommendations of experienced benchmarkers:[12]

- Concentrate on specific, well-defined activities like inventory management or order processing. Study the company's own procedures thoroughly and choose four to six companies to benchmark against, including two or three companies that perform the activity well. A diverse set of companies is usually best.

- Form a benchmarking team that consists mainly of company personnel directly engaged in performing the activity being benchmarked. Include workers and union leaders, as well as the managers who will have to make any changes—they need to see for themselves what others are doing. Keep the team small and visits to outside facilities short (one day per company is usually enough).

- Be prepared to exchange information with the companies being benchmarked. Be ready to answer any question about your company that you ask the other company.

- Protect the confidentiality of data obtained from other companies—just because a company agrees to sharing doesn't mean it wants the information to go any further.

- Keep things legal and aboveboard by refraining from asking questions that relate to competitively sensitive areas and proprietary data. Ethical behavior is an absolute must.

Benchmarking is a manager's best tool for determining whether the company is performing particular functions and activities efficiently, whether its costs arc in line with those of competitors, and which internal activities and business processes need to be scrutinized for improvement. It is a way of learning which companies are the best in performing certain activities and functions and then imitating—or, better still, improving on—their techniques. Toyota managers got their idea for just-in-time inventory deliveries by studying how U.S. supermarkets replenished their shelves. Southwest Airlines reduced the turnaround time of its aircraft at each scheduled stop by studying pit crews on the auto racing circuit.

■ STRATEGIC OPTIONS FOR ACHIEVING COST COMPETITIVENESS

Value chain analysis can reveal a great deal about a firm's cost competitiveness. One of the fundamental insights of strategic cost analysis is that a company's competitiveness depends on how well it manages its value chain activities relative to how well its competitors manage theirs.[13] Examining the makeup of a company's own value chain and comparing it to rivals' chains helps quantify cost advantages/disadvantages and which cost components are responsible. Such information is vital in crafting strategies to eliminate a cost disadvantage or create a cost advantage.

As can be seen from Figure 4–2, there are three main areas in a company's overall value chain system where important differences in the costs of competing firms can occur: in the suppliers' part of the value chain, in a company's own activity segments, and in the forward channel portion of the industry chain. If a firm's lack of cost competitiveness lies either in the backward (upstream) or forward (downstream) sections of the total value chain, then reestablishing cost competitiveness usually has to extend beyond its in-house operations. When a firm's cost disadvantage is principally associated with the costs of items purchased from suppliers (the upstream end of the industry chain), company managers can pursue any of several strategic actions to correct the problem:[14]

> **Strategic actions to eliminate a cost disadvantage depend on where in the value chain the cost differences originate.**

- Negotiate more favorable prices with suppliers.
- Work with suppliers to help them achieve lower costs.
- Integrate backward to gain control over the costs of purchased items.
- Try to substitute lower-priced inputs.
- Do a better job of managing the linkages between suppliers' value chains and the company's own chain; for example, careful coordination between a company and its suppliers can permit just-in-time deliveries that lower a company's inventory and internal logistics costs and that may also allow its suppliers to economize on their warehousing, shipping, and production scheduling costs—a win-win outcome (instead of a zero-sum game where a company's gains match supplier concessions).
- Try to make up the difference by cutting costs elsewhere in the chain.

A company's strategic options for eliminating cost disadvantages in the forward end of the value chain system include:[15]

- Pushing distributors and other forward channel allies to reduce their markups.
- Working closely with forward channel allies/customers to identify win-win opportunities to reduce costs—a chocolate manufacturer learned that by shipping its bulk chocolate in liquid form in tank cars instead of 10-pound molded bars, it saved its candy bar manufacturing customers the cost of unpacking and melting plus it eliminated its own costs of molding bars and packing them.
- Changing to a more economical distribution strategy, including the possibility of forward integration.
- Trying to make up the difference by cutting costs earlier in the cost chain.

When the source of a firm's cost disadvantage is internal, managers can use any of nine strategic approaches to restore cost parity:[16]

- Initiate internal budget reductions.
- Reengineer business processes and work practices to boost employee productivity, improve the efficiency of performing key activities, increase the utilization of company assets, and otherwise do a better job of managing cost drivers.

- Try to eliminate some cost-producing activities altogether by revamping the value chain system—for example, change technologies or perhaps bypass the value chains of forward channel allies and market directly to end-users.

- Relocate high-cost activities to geographic areas where they can be performed less expensively.

- Use contractors or outside vendors for activities that can be performed externally at a lower cost than if done internally.

- Invest in cost-saving technological improvements (i.e., automation, robotics, flexible manufacturing techniques, computerized controls).

- Innovate around the troublesome cost components as new investments are made in plant and equipment.

- Simplify the product design so that it can be manufactured more economically.

- Try to make up the internal cost disadvantage by achieving savings in the backward and forward portions of the value chain system.

■ VALUE CHAIN ANALYSIS, CORE COMPETENCIES, AND COMPETITIVE ADVANTAGE

How well a company manages its value chain activities relative to competitors is key to building valuable core competencies and leveraging them into sustainable competitive advantage. With rare exceptions, a firm's products or services themselves are not a source of competitive advantage—it is too easy for a resourceful company elsewhere to clone, improve upon, or find an effective substitute for them.[17] Rather, a company's competitive edge is usually grounded in its skills and capabilities relative to rivals and, more specifically, in the scope and depth of its ability to perform competitively crucial value chain activities better than its rivals can.

Core competencies emerge from a company's experience, learned skills, and focused efforts in performing one or more related value chain components. Merck and Glaxo, two of the world's most competitively capable pharmaceutical companies, have built their strategic positions around expert performance of a few key activities: extensive R&D to develop new drugs, careful patenting, skill in gaining rapid and thorough

Value chain analysis helps managers identify which activities have competitive advantage potential.

clinical clearance through regulatory bodies, and creating an unusually strong distribution and sales force.[18]

To arrive at a sound diagnosis of a company's true competitive capabilities, managers need to do four things:

- Construct a value chain of company activities.

- Examine the linkages among internally performed activities and the linkages with suppliers' and customers' chains.

- Identify the activities and competencies critical to customer satisfaction and market success.

- Make appropriate internal and external benchmarking comparisons to determine how well the company performs activities and how its cost structure compares with competitors.

The strategy-making lesson of value chain analysis is that increased company competitiveness hinges on managerial efforts to concentrate company resources and talent on those skills and activities where the company can gain dominating expertise in serving its target market.

▶ QUESTION 4: HOW STRONG IS THE COMPANY'S COMPETITIVE POSITION?

Using value chain concepts and other strategic cost analysis tools to determine a company's competitiveness is necessary but not sufficient. A more all-inclusive assessment needs to be made of a company's competitive position and competitive strength. Particular elements to evaluate include: (1) the regard customers have for the company's product and service, (2) whether the firm's position can be expected to improve or deteriorate if the present strategy is continued (allowing for fine-tuning), (3) how the firm ranks *relative to key rivals* on each important measure of competitive strength and industry key success factor, (4) whether the firm enjoys a competitive advantage or is currently at a disadvantage, and (5) the firm's ability to defend its position in light of industry driving forces, competitive pressures, and the anticipated moves of rivals.

Systematic assessment of a company's competitive position relative to its rivals is an essential step in company situation analysis.

Table 4–3 lists some indicators of whether a firm's competitive position is improving or slipping. Company managers, however, need to do more than just identify areas of competitive strength and weakness. They have to form judgments about whether the company has a net competitive advantage or disadvantage vis-a-vis its key competitors and whether the company's market position and performance can be expected to improve or deteriorate under the current strategy.

Managers can begin the task of evaluating the company's competitive strength by benchmarking the company against industry rivals not just on cost but also on product

---

TABLE 4–3   *The Signs of Strength and Weakness in a Company's Competitive Position*

Signs of Competitive Strength	Signs of Competitive Weakness
• Important core competences	• Confronted with competitive disadvantages
• Strong market share (or a leading market share)	• Losing ground to rival firms
• A pacesetting or distinctive strategy	• Below-average growth in revenues
• Growing customer base and customer loyalty	• Short on financial resources
• Above-average market visibility	• A slipping reputation with customers
• In a favorably situated strategic group	• Trailing in product development
• Concentrating on fastest-growing market segments	• In a strategic group destined to lose ground
• Strongly differentiated products	• Weak in areas where there is the most market potential
• Cost advantages	• A higher-cost producer
• Above-average profit margins	• Too small to be a major factor in the marketplace
• Above-average technological and innovational capability	• Not in good position to deal with emerging threats
• A creative, entrepreneurially alert management	• Weak product quality
• In position to capitalize on opportunities	• Lacking skills and capabilities in key areas

quality, customer service, customer satisfaction, financial strength, technological skills, and product cycle time (how quickly new products can be gotten from the idea or design stage into the marketplace). It is not enough to benchmark the costs of activities and identify best practices; a company should benchmark itself against competitors on all strategically and competitively important aspects of its business.

■ COMPETITIVE STRENGTH ASSESSMENTS

The most telling way to determine how strongly a company holds its competitive position comes from quantitatively assessing whether the company is stronger or weaker than close rivals on each key success factor and each important indicator of competitive strength. Much of the information for competitive position assessment comes from previous analyses. Industry and competitive analysis reveals the key success factors and competitive measures that will separate industry winners and losers. Competitor analysis and benchmarking data provide a basis for judging the strengths and capabilities of key rivals. The first step is to make a list of the industry's key success factors and most telling measures of competitive strength or weakness (6 to 10 measures usually suffice). Second, rate the firm and its key rivals on each factor. Rating scales from 1 to 10 are best to use, although ratings of *stronger* (+), *weaker* (−), and *about equal* (=) may be appropriate when information is scanty and assigning numerical scores conveys a false appearance of precision. Third, sum the individual strength ratings to get an overall measure of competitive strength for each competitor. Finally, draw conclusions about the size and extent of the company's net competitive advantage or disadvantage taking specific note of areas where the company's competitive position is strongest and weakest.

Table 4–4 provides two examples of competitive strength assessment. The first employs an *unweighted rating scale;* with unweighted ratings each key success factor/competitive strength measure is assumed to be equally important. Whichever company has the highest strength rating on a given measure has an implied competitive edge on that factor; the size of its edge is mirrored in the margin of difference between its rating and the ratings assigned to rivals. Summing a company's strength ratings on all the measures produces an overall strength rating. The higher a company's

High competitive-strength ratings signal competitive advantage; low ratings signal competitive disadvantage.

overall strength rating, the stronger its competitive position. The wider the gap between a company's overall rating and the scores of lower-rated rivals, the greater is its implied net competitive advantage. Thus, ABC's total score of 61 (see the top half of Table 4–4) signals a greater net competitive advantage over Rival 4 (with a score of 32) than over Rival 1 (with a score of 58).

However, using a weighted rating system is a better methodology because the different measures of competitive strength are unlikely to be *equally* important. In a commodity-product industry, for instance, having low unit costs relative to rivals is nearly always the most important determinant of competitive strength. In an industry with strong product differentiation the most significant measures of competitive strength may be brand awareness, amount of advertising, reputation for quality, and distribution capability. In a *weighted rating system* each

A weighted competitive strength analysis is conceptually stronger than an unweighted analysis because not all strength measures are equally important.

TABLE 4–4   *Illustrations of Unweighted and Weighted Competitive Strength Assessments*

A. Sample of an Unweighted Competitive Strength Assessment

Rating scale: 1 = Very weak; 10 = Very strong

Key Success Factor/Strength Measure	ABC Co.	Rival 1	Rival 2	Rival 3	Rival 4
Quality/product performance	8	5	10	1	6
Reputation/image	8	7	10	1	6
Raw material access/cost	2	10	4	5	1
Technological skills	10	1	7	3	8
Manufacturing capability	9	4	10	5	1
Marketing/distribution	9	4	10	5	1
Financial strength	5	10	7	3	1
Relative cost position	5	10	3	1	4
Advertising effectiveness	5	7	10	1	4
Unweighted overall strength rating	61	58	71	25	32

B. Sample of a Weighted Competitive Strength Assessment

Rating scale: 1 = Very weak; 10 = Very strong

Key Success Factor/Strength Measure	Weight	ABC Co.	Rival 1	Rival 2	Rival 3	Rival 4
Quality/product performance	0.10	8/0.80	5/0.50	10/1.00	1/0.10	6/0.60
Reputation/image	0.10	8/0.80	7/0.70	10/1.00	1/0.10	6/0.60
Raw material access/cost	0.10	2/0.20	10/1.00	4/0.40	5/0.50	1/0.10
Technological skills	0.05	10/0.50	1/0.05	7/0.35	3/0.15	8/0.40
Manufacturing capability	0.05	9/0.45	4/0.20	10/0.50	5/0.25	1/0.05
Marketing/distribution	0.05	9/0.45	4/0.20	10/0.50	5/0.25	1/0.05
Financial strength	0.10	5/0.50	10/1.00	7/0.70	3/0.30	1/0.10
Relative cost position	0.35	5/1.75	10/3.50	3/1.05	1/0.35	4/1.40
Advertising effectiveness	0.15	5/0.75	7/1.05	10/1.50	1/0.15	4/1.60
Sum of weights	1.00					
Weighted overall strength rating		6.20	8.20	7.00	2.10	2.90

measure of competitive strength is assigned a weight based on its perceived importance in shaping competitive success. The largest weight could be as high as .75 (maybe even higher) in situations where one particular competitive variable is overwhelmingly decisive, or as low as .20 when two or three strength measures are more important than the rest. Lesser competitive strength indicators can carry weights of .05 or .10. No matter whether the differences between the weights are big or little, *the sum of the weights must add up to 1.0.*

Weighted strength ratings are calculated by deciding how a company stacks up on each strength (using the 1-to-10 rating scale) and multiplying the assigned rating by the assigned weight (a rating score of 4 times a weight of .20 gives a weighted rating of .80). Again, the company with the highest rating on a given strength has an implied competitive edge, with the size of its edge reflected in the difference between its rating and rivals' ratings. The weight attached to the measure indicates how important the edge is.

Summing a company's weighted strength ratings for all the measures yields an overall strength rating. Comparisons of the weighted overall strength scores indicate which competitors are in the strongest and weakest competitive positions and who has how large a net competitive advantage over whom.

The bottom half of Table 4–4 shows a sample competitive strength assessment for ABC Company using a weighted rating system. Note that the unweighted and weighted rating schemes produce a different ordering of the companies. In the weighted system, ABC Company dropped from second to third in strength, and Rival 1 jumped from third into first because of its high strength ratings on the two most important factors. Weighting the importance of the strength being measured can thus make a significant difference in the outcome of the assessment.

Competitive strength assessments provide useful conclusions about a company's competitive situation. The ratings show how a company compares to rivals, factor by factor and measure by measure, thus revealing where it is strongest and weakest and against whom. Moreover, the overall competitive strength scores indicate whether the company has a net competitive advantage or is at a disadvantage against each rival. The firm with the largest overall competitive strength rating can be said to have a net competitive advantage over each of its rivals.

> **Competitive strengths and competitive advantages enable a company to improve its long-term market position.**

Knowing where a company is strong and where it is weak is essential in crafting a strategy to strengthen its long-term competitive position. As a general rule, a company should try to convert its strengths into sustainable competitive advantage and take strategic actions to protect against its weaknesses. At the same time, competitive strength ratings point to which rival companies may be vulnerable to competitive attack and the areas where they are weakest. When a company has important competitive strengths in areas where one or more rivals are weak, it makes sense to consider offensive moves to exploit rivals' competitive weaknesses.

▶ QUESTION 5: WHAT STRATEGIC ISSUES DOES THE COMPANY NEED TO ADDRESS?

The final analytical task is to hone in on the strategic issues management needs to address in order to form an effective strategic action plan. Here, managers need to draw upon all the prior analyses, put the company's overall situation into perspective, and determine exactly where they need to focus their strategic attention. This step should not be taken lightly. Without a precise definition of the issues, managers are not prepared to craft a strategy—a good strategy must offer a plan for dealing with all of the strategic issues that need to be addressed.

> **Effective strategy making requires thorough understanding of the strategic issues a company faces.**

To pinpoint issues for the company's strategic action agenda, managers ought to consider the following:

- Whether the present strategy is adequate in light of driving forces at work in the industry.

- How closely the present strategy matches the industry's *future* key success factors.

- How good a defense the present strategy offers against the five competitive forces—particularly those that are expected to intensify in strength.
- In what ways the present strategy may not be adequate to protect the company from external threats and internal weaknesses.
- Where and how the company may be vulnerable to competition from one or more rivals.

TABLE 4-5   *Company Situation Analysis Worksheet*

---

1. Strategic Performance Indicators

Performance Indicator	19___	19___	19___	19___	19___
Market share	_____	_____	_____	_____	_____
Sales growth	_____	_____	_____	_____	_____
Net profit margin	_____	_____	_____	_____	_____
Return on equity investment	_____	_____	_____	_____	_____
Other?	_____	_____	_____	_____	_____

2. Internal Strengths

Internal Weaknesses

External Opportunities

External Threats

3. Competitive Strength Assessment

Rating scale: 1 = Very weak; 10 = Very strong.

Key Success Factor/ Competitive Variable	Weight	Firm A	Firm B	Firm C	Firm D	Firm E
Quality/product performance	_____	_____	_____	_____	_____	_____
Reputation/image	_____	_____	_____	_____	_____	_____
Raw material access/cost	_____	_____	_____	_____	_____	_____
Technological skills	_____	_____	_____	_____	_____	_____
Manufacturing capability	_____	_____	_____	_____	_____	_____
Marketing/distribution	_____	_____	_____	_____	_____	_____
Financial strength	_____	_____	_____	_____	_____	_____
Relative cost position	_____	_____	_____	_____	_____	_____
Other?	_____	_____	_____	_____	_____	_____
Overall strength rating	_____	_____	_____	_____	_____	_____

4. Conclusions Concerning Competitive Position
(Improving/slipping? Competitive advantages/disadvantages?)

5. Major Strategic Issues/Problems the Company Must Address

- Whether the company has competitive advantage or must work to offset competitive disadvantage.

- Where the strong spots and weak spots are in the present strategy.

- Whether additional actions are needed to improve the company's cost position, capitalize on emerging opportunities, and strengthen the company's competitive position.

These considerations should indicate whether the company can continue the same basic strategy with minor adjustments or whether major overhaul is necessary.

The better matched a company's strategy is to its external environment and internal situation, the less need there is to contemplate big shifts in strategy. On the other hand, when the present strategy is not well suited for the road ahead, managers need to give top priority to the task of crafting a new strategy.

Table 4–5 provides a format for completing a company situation analysis. It incorporates the concepts and analytical techniques discussed in this chapter and provides a way of reporting the results of company situation analysis in a systematic, concise manner.

Strategy and Competitive Advantage

Competing in the marketplace is like war. You have injuries and casualties, and the best strategy wins.

John Collins

The essence of strategy lies in creating tomorrow's competitive advantages faster than competitors mimic the ones you possess today.

Gary Hamel and C. K. Prahalad

You've got to come up with a plan. You can't wish things will get better.

**John F. Welch
CEO, General Electric**

Winning business strategies are grounded in sustainable competitive advantage. A company has *competitive advantage* whenever it has an edge over rivals in attracting customers and defending against competitive forces. There are many sources of competitive advantage: having the best-made product on the market, being able to deliver superior customer service, achieving lower costs than rivals, being in a more convenient geographic location, proprietary technology, features and styling with more buyer appeal, shorter lead times in developing and testing new products, a well-known brand name and reputation, and providing buyers more value for the money (a combination of good quality, good service, and acceptable price). Essentially, though, to succeed in building a competitive advantage, a company's

> Investing aggressively in creating sustainable competitive advantage is a company's single most dependable way to achieve above-average profitability.

strategy must aim at providing buyers with what they perceive as superior value—a good product at a lower price or a better product that is worth paying more for.

This chapter focuses on how a company can achieve or defend a competitive advantage.[1] We begin by describing the basic types of competitive strategies and then examine how these approaches rely on offensive moves to build competitive advantage and on defensive moves to protect competitive advantage. In the concluding two sections we survey the pros and cons of a vertical integration strategy and look at the competitive importance of timing strategic moves—when it is advantageous to be a first-mover or a late-mover.

▶ THE FIVE GENERIC COMPETITIVE STRATEGIES

A company's competitive strategy consists of the business approaches and initiatives it takes to attract customers, withstand competitive pressures, and strengthen its market position. The objective, quite simply, is to knock the socks off rival companies, earn a competitive advantage in the marketplace, and cultivate a clientele of loyal customers. A company's strategy for competing typically contains both offensive and defensive actions, with emphasis shifting from one to the other as market conditions warrant. And it includes short-lived tactical maneuvers designed to deal with immediate conditions, as well as actions calculated to have lasting impact on the firm's long-term competitive capabilities and market position.

Competitive strategy has a narrower scope than business strategy. Business strategy not only concerns the issue of how to compete, but it also embraces functional area strategies, how management plans to respond to changing industry conditions of all kinds (not just those that are competition-related), and how management intends to address the full-range of strategic issues confronting the business. Competitive strategy, however, deals exclusively with management's action plan for competing successfully and creating customer value.

Companies the world over have tried every conceivable approach to attracting customers, earning their loyalty on repeat sales, outcompeting rivals, and winning an edge in the marketplace. And since managers tailor short-run tactics and long-term maneuvers to fit their company's specific situation and market environment, there are countless strategy variations and nuances in emphasis. In this sense, there are as many competitive strategies as there are competitors. However, minor differences aside, there are impressive similarities when one considers (1) the company's market target and (2) the type of competitive advantage the company is trying to achieve. Five categories of competitive strategy approaches stand out:[2]

1. *A low-cost leadership strategy*—striving to be the overall low-cost provider of a product or service that appeals to a broad range of customers.

2. *A broad differentiation strategy*—seeking to differentiate the company's product offering from rivals' in ways that will appeal to a broad range of buyers.

3. *A best-cost provider strategy*—giving customers more value for the money by combining an emphasis on low cost with an emphasis on upscale differentiation. The target is to have the best (lowest) costs and prices relative to producers of comparable products.

4. *A focus or market niche strategy based on lower cost*—concentrating on a narrow buyer segment and outcompeting rivals on the basis of lower cost in serving niche members.

5. *A focus or market niche strategy based on differentiation*—offering niche members a product or service customized to their tastes and requirements.

The five generic competitive approaches are shown in Figure 5–1; each stakes out a different market position and involves fundamentally different approaches to managing the business. Table 5–1 highlights the distinctive features of these generic competitive strategies (for simplicity, the two strains of focus strategies are combined under one heading since they differ only on one feature—the basis of competitive advantage).

■ LOW-COST PROVIDER STRATEGIES

Striving to be the industry's overall low-cost provider is a powerful competitive approach in markets where many buyers are price-sensitive. The aim is to open up a sustainable cost advantage over competitors and then use the company's lower-cost edge as a basis for

---

| FIGURE 5–1 | *The Five Generic Competitive Strategies* |

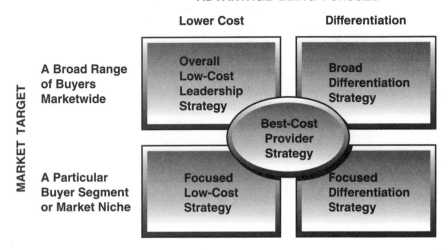

Source: Adapted from Michael E Porter, *Competitive Strategy* (New York: Free Press, 1980), pp. 35–40.

---

either underpricing competitors and gaining market share at their expense or earning a higher profit margin selling at the going market price. A cost advantage will generate superior profitability unless it is used up in aggressive price-cutting efforts to win sales from rivals. Achieving low-cost leadership typically means making low costs *relative to competitors* the theme of the firm's entire business strategy. A low-cost

> A low-cost leader's basis for competitive advantage is overall lower costs than its competitors' costs.

strategy, however, should not be pursued so zealously that a firm's product or service ends up being too spartan and frills-free to generate buyer appeal. Illustration 10 describes ACX Technologies' strategy to be a low-cost provider of aluminum cans.

OPENING UP A COST ADVANTAGE

To achieve a cost advantage, a firm's cumulative costs across its value chain must be lower than its competitors' cumulative costs. There are two ways to accomplish this:[3]

- Do a better job than rivals of performing activities efficiently and managing the factors that drive the costs of value chain activities.

- Revamp the firm's value chain to bypass some cost-producing activities altogether.

Let's look at each of the two avenues for gaining a cost advantage.

CONTROLLING THE COST DRIVERS

A firm's cost position is the result of the behavior of costs in each activity in its total value chain. The major cost drivers which come into play in determining a company's costs in each activity segment of the chain fall into two categories:[4]

TABLE 5—1 *Distinctive Features of the Generic Competitive Strategies*

Type of Feature	Low-Cost Leadership	Broad Differentiation	Best-Cost Provider	Focused Low-Cost and Focused Differentiation
Strategic target	• A broad cross-section of the market.	• A broad cross-section of the market.	• Value-conscious buyers.	• A narrow market niche defined by distinctive buyer needs and preferences.
Basis of competitive advantage	• Lower costs than competitors.	• An ability to offer buyers something different from competitors.	• Give customers more value for the money.	• Lower cost in serving the niche or an ability to offer niche buyers something customized to their requirements and tastes.
Product line	• A good basic product with few frills (acceptable quality and limited selection).	• Many product variations, wide selection, strong emphasis on differentiating features.	• Good-to-excellent attributes, several-to-many upscale features.	• Customized to fit the specialized needs of the target segment.
Production emphasis	• A continuous search for cost reduction without sacrificing acceptable quality and essential features.	• Invent ways to create value for buyers; strive for product superiority.	• Incorporate upscale features and attributes at low cost.	• Tailor-made for the niche.
Marketing emphasis	• Try to make a virtue out of product features that lead to low cost.	• Build in whatever features buyers are willing to pay for. • Charge a premium price to cover the extra costs of differentiating features.	• Underprice rival brands with comparable features.	• Communicate the focuser's unique ability to satisfy the buyer's specialized requirements.
Sustaining the strategy	• Economical prices/ good value. • All elements of strategy aim at contributing to a sustainable cost advantage—the key is to manage costs down, year after year, in every area of the business.	• Communicate the points of difference in credible ways. • Stress constant improvement; keep innovating to stay ahead of imitative competitors. • Emphasize a few key differentiating features; tout them to create a reputation and brand image.	• Unique expertise in managing costs down and product/ service caliber up simultaneously.	• Remain totally dedicated to serving the niche better than other competitors; don't blunt the firm's image and efforts by entering other segments or adding other product categories to widen market appeal.

ILLUSTRATION 10

ACX Technologies' Strategy to Become a Low-Cost Producer of Aluminum Cans

ACX Technologies began as an idea of William Coors, CEO of Adolph Coors beer company, to recycle more used aluminum cans back into new cans. Typical aluminum can-making operations involved producing thick aluminum slabs from a smelter using bauxite ore combined with as much as 50% scrap aluminum, including used aluminum beverage cans; the slabs of aluminum ingot were fed into a rolling mill to achieve the required thickness. Cans were then formed by stamping pieces of thin aluminum sheet into a seamless can with the top open for filling.

Coors' idea was to produce aluminum-can sheet from 95 percent recycled cans. He began by purchasing rights to technology that his company had helped to develop in Europe; the technology used lower-cost electric arc furnaces to melt aluminum scrap directly, short-cutting the smelter process which required heavy capital investment and big production volumes to be competitive. Coors then built a plant in Colorado that could grind and melt used cans and pour hot aluminum through a continuous caster to make aluminum sheet suitable for the tops and tabs of beverage cans. It took seven years to develop alloys with the desired attributes and finetune the process—Coors originally believed it could be done in less than two years.

In mid-1991 Coors announced it would build a new $200 million mill in Texas to make sheet aluminum for the body of the can—the product with the most exacting specifications but also the No. 1 end-use for aluminum in the United States. Production was expected to begin by mid-1992, but problems and delays soon pushed the startup date into fall 1993. The new plant's low-cost advantages stemmed from several factors:

- Lower capital investment.
- Use of 95% recycled aluminum cans as feedstock—reducing raw material costs in producing aluminum sheet by 10% to 15%.
- Lower electricity requirements—electric arc technology used only about one-fifth of the electricity of bauxite-smelter technology.
- Comparatively low electric rates at the Texas location.
- Reduced labor costs as compared to bauxite-smelter technology.

Overall, production costs were expected to be anywhere from 20% to 35% below the costs of aluminum can producers using traditionally produced aluminum sheet, depending on the prevailing market prices for aluminum ingot and scrap aluminum. In addition, the mill had greater flexibility than traditional producers to vary its alloy mixes to meet different customer specifications.

Meanwhile, in December 1992 during construction of the Texas plant, Coors decided to spin off the whole aluminum can operations (along with a paper-packaging operation making patented polyethylene cartons with high-quality metallic graphics—packaging for Cascade boxes and Lever 2000 soap bars are examples— a ceramics unit making materials for high-tech applications, and several developmental businesses) into a new publicly owned company called ACX Technologies. The new company had 1992 revenues of $570 million, about 28% of which were sales to Coors. The breakdown of revenues in 1992 was as follows: aluminum for cans, 17%; graphics packaging, 37%; ceramics materials, 32%; and developmental businesses, 14% (including corn wet milling, biotechnology, defense electronics, and biodegradable polymers).

In summer 1993, the Texas plant was in startup, and can makers began testing the quality of its aluminum sheet. Coors was the first to qualify ACX's output for use; at year-end 1993 four other can users were testing the suitability of the plant's output for their products. ACX expected the plant to ship close to 50 million pounds of aluminum by year-end 1993 and to ship 100 million pounds or more in 1994 as new customers placed orders. Analysts believed that ACX could, given its cost advantage, grow its annual volume to the 1.0-billion to 1.5-billion-pound range in 10 years as it perfected the process and gained acceptance for the quality of its output.

The company's new shares had been issued at $10.75 in December 1992 when it went public. In the first 20 days of trading the price climbed to $21.75. Later in 1993, it traded as high as $46. In January 1994 it was trading in the high 30s.

Source: Based on information published by The Robinson-Humphrey Company and on Marc Charlier, "ACX Strives to Become Aluminum's Low-Cost Producer," *The Wall Street Journal*, September 29, 1993, p. B2.

Structural cost drivers

1. *Economies or diseconomies of scale.* Economies and diseconomies of scale can be found or created in virtually every segment of the activity cost chain. For example, manufacturing economies can sometimes be achieved by simplifying the product line and scheduling longer production runs for fewer models. A geographically organized sales force can realize economies as regional sales volume grows because a salesperson can write larger orders at each sales call and/or because of reduced travel time between calls. On the other hand, a sales force organized by product line can encounter travel-related diseconomies if salespersons have to spend disproportionately more time traveling to call on distantly spaced customers. In global industries, modifying products by country instead of selling a standard product worldwide tends to boost unit costs because of time spent in model changeovers, shorter production runs, and inability to reach the most economic scale of production for each model. Boosting local or regional market share can lower sales and marketing costs per unit, whereas opting for a larger national share by entering new regions can create scale diseconomies unless and until the market penetration in the newly entered regions reaches efficient proportions.

2. *Learning and experience curve effects.* Experience-based cost savings can come from improved layout, gains in labor efficiency, debugging of technology, product design modifications that enhance manufacturing efficiency, redesign of machinery and equipment to gain increased operating speed, getting samples of a rival's products and having design engineers study how they are made, and tips from suppliers, consultants, and ex-employees of rival firms. Learning time varies with the amount of management attention devoted to capturing the benefits of available experience. Learning benefits can be kept proprietary by building or modifying production equipment in-house, retaining key employees, limiting the amount and kind information disseminated through employee publications, and enforcing strict nondisclosure provisions in employment contracts.

3. *Linkages with other activities in the chain.* When the cost of one activity is affected by how other activities are performed, there is opportunity to lower the costs of the linked activities through better coordination and/or joint optimization. Linkages with suppliers tend to center on suppliers' product design characteristics, quality assurance procedures, delivery and service policies, and the manner by which the supplier's product is furnished. For example, delivery of nails in prepackaged 1-lb., 5-lb., and 10-lb. assortments instead of 100-lb. bulk cartons can reduce a hardware dealer's labor costs in filling individual customer orders. The easiest supplier linkages to exploit are those where both the supplier's and the firm's costs fall because of coordination and/or joint optimization. Linkages with forward channels tend to center on location of warehouses, materials handling, outbound shipping, and packaging.

4. *Sharing opportunities with other business units within the enterprise.* When an activity can be shared with a sister unit, there can be significant cost savings. Cost sharing is one way to potentially achieve scale economies, shorten the time spent on the learning curve of a new technology, and/or achieve fuller capacity utilization. Sometimes the experience gained in one division can be used to help lower costs in

another; sharing knowledge is significant when the activities are similar and expertise can be readily transferred from one unit to another.

5. *The benefits of vertical integration versus outsourcing.* Partially or fully integrating into the activities of either suppliers or forward channel allies can allow an enterprise to detour suppliers or buyers with considerable bargaining power; vertical integration can also result in cost savings when it is feasible to coordinate or merge adjacent activities in the value chain. On the other hand, it is sometimes cheaper to outsource certain functions and activities to outside specialists, who by virtue of their expertise and volume, can perform the activity/function cheaper.

6. *Locational variables.* Locations differ in their prevailing wage levels, tax rates, energy costs, inbound and outbound shipping and freight costs, and so on. Opportunities may exist for reducing costs by relocating plants, field offices, warehouses, or headquarters. Moreover, whether sister facilities are near or far apart affects the costs of shipping intrafirm inventory, outbound freight on goods shipped to customers, and coordination.

Executional cost drivers

1. *Timing considerations associated with first-mover advantages and disadvantages.* The first major brand in the market is sometimes able to establish and maintain its brand name at a lower cost than later brands. Late-movers, however, in fast-paced technology or product development situations, can benefit from purchasing second- or third-generation equipment or avoiding the high product/market development costs of first-moving pioneers.

2. *The percentage of capacity utilization.* High fixed costs as a percentage of total costs create a stiff unit-cost penalty for underutilization of existing capacity. Increased utilization of capacity spreads indirect and overhead costs over a larger unit volume and enhances the efficiency of fixed assets. The more capital-intensive the business, the more important this cost driver becomes. Finding ways to minimize the ups and downs in seasonal capacity utilization can be an important cost advantage.[5]

3. *Strategic choices and operating decisions.* Managers at various levels can impact a firm's costs through a variety of the decisions they make:
    *   Increasing/decreasing the number of products offered.
    *   Adding/cutting the services provided to buyers.
    *   Incorporating more/less performance and quality features into the product.
    *   Paying higher/lower wages and fringe benefits to employees relative to rivals and firms in other industries.
    *   Increasing/decreasing the number of different forward channels used in distributing the firm's product.
    *   Raising/lowering the levels of R&D support relative to rivals.
    *   Putting more/less emphasis on achieving higher levels of productivity and efficiency, as compared to rivals.
    *   Raising/lowering the specifications set for purchased materials.

Managers intent on achieving low-cost leader status have to understand the structural and executional cost drivers for each activity in the firm's total value chain. Then they have to use their knowledge about the cost drivers to reduce costs for every activity where there is a potential cost saving. The task of continuing to push costs down (to the point of not incurring some costs at all) is seldom simple or painless; rather, it is a task that managers have to attack with ingenuity and single-minded toughness.

REVAMPING THE MAKE-UP OF THE VALUE CHAIN

Dramatic cost advantages can emerge from finding innovative ways to restructure processes and tasks, to cut out frills, and to provide the basics in more economical fashion. The primary ways companies can achieve a cost advantage by reconfiguring their value chains include:

- Simplifying the product design.

- Stripping away all the extras and offering only a basic, no-frills product or service, thereby cutting out activities and costs associated with multiple features and options.

- Reengineering core business processes to cut out unnecessary steps and low-value-added activities.

- Shifting to a simpler, less-capital-intensive or more streamlined technological process.

- Finding ways to bypass the use of costly raw materials or components.

- Using direct-to-end-user sales and marketing approaches that cut out the often large costs and margins of wholesalers and retailers. It is not unusual for costs and margins in the wholesale-retail portions of the value chain to represent 50 percent of the price paid by the final consumer.

- Relocating facilities nearer suppliers or customers, or both, to curtail inbound and outbound logistics costs.

- Achieving a more economical degree of forward or backward vertical integration relative to competitors.

- Going against the "something for everyone" approach of others and focusing on a limited product/service to meet a special, but important, need of the target buyer segment, thereby eliminating activities and costs associated with numerous product versions.

Successful low-cost producers usually achieve their cost advantages by exhaustively pursuing cost savings throughout the value chain. All avenues are used and no area of potential is overlooked. Normally, low-cost producers have a very cost-conscious corporate culture that features spartan facilities, limited perks and frills for executives, intolerance of waste, intensive screening of budget requests, and broad employee participation in cost control efforts. But while low-cost providers are champions of frugality, they are usually aggressive in committing funds to projects and programs that promise to drive costs out of the business.

THE KEYS TO SUCCESS

Managers intent on pursuing a low-cost provider strategy have to study each cost-creating activity to identify what drives its cost. Then they have to use that knowledge to continually force those costs down. Completely reengineering how activities are

---

| ILLUSTRATION 11 | *Winning a Cost Advantage: Iowa Beef Packers and Federal Express* |

Iowa Beef Packers (IBP) and Federal Express have been able to win strong competitive positions by restructuring the traditional value chains in their industries. In beef packing, the traditional value chain involved raising cattle on scattered farms and ranches, shipping them live to labor-intensive, unionized slaughtering plants, and then transporting whole sides of beef to grocery retailers whose butcher departments cut them into smaller pieces and package them for sale to grocery shoppers.

Iowa Beef Packers revamped the traditional chain with a radically different strategy—large automated plants employing nonunion labor were built near economically transportable supplies of cattle, and the meat was partially butchered at the processing plant into smaller high-yield cuts (sometimes sealed in plastic casing ready for purchase), boxed, and shipped to retailers. IBP's inbound cattle transportation expenses, traditionally a major cost item, were cut significantly by avoiding the weight losses that occurred when live animals were shipped long distances; major outbound shipping cost savings were achieved by not having to ship whole sides of beef with their high waste factor. Iowa Beef's strategy was so successful that it was, in 1985, the largest U.S. meatpacker, surpassing the former industry leaders, Swift, Wilson, and Armour.

Federal Express innovatively redefined the value chain for rapid delivery of small parcels. Traditional firms like Emery and Airborne Express operated by collecting freight packages of varying sizes, shipping them to their destination points via air freight and commercial airlines, and then delivering them to the addressee. Federal Express opted to focus only on the market for overnight delivery of small packages and documents. These were collected at local drop points during the late afternoon hours, flown on company-owned planes during early evening hours to a central hub in Memphis where from 11 P.M. to 3 A.M. each night, all parcels were sorted, then reloaded on company planes, and flown during the early morning hours to their destination points, where they were delivered the next morning by company personnel using company trucks. The cost structure so achieved by Federal Express was low enough to permit it to guarantee overnight delivery of a small parcel anywhere in the United States for a price as low as $11. In 1986, Federal Express had a 58 percent market share of the air-express package delivery market versus a 15 percent share for UPS, 11 percent for Airborne Express, and 10 percent for Emery/Purolator.

Source: Based on information in Michael E Porter, *Competitive Advantage* (New York: Free Press, 1985), p. 109.

---

performed and coordinated can often yield savings of 30 to 70 percent, compared to the 5 to 10 percent savings possible with creative tinkering and adjusting. Where possible, though, managers need to be entrepreneurially creative in cutting some activities out of the value chain system altogether. As the two examples in Illustration 11 indicate, companies can sometimes achieve dramatic cost advantages from restructuring their value chains and slicing out a number of cost-producing activities.

Companies that have successfully pursued low-cost leadership strategies include Lincoln Electric in arc welding equipment, Briggs and Stratton in small horsepower gasoline engines, BIC in ballpoint pens, Black and Decker in power tools, Stride Rite in footwear, Beaird-Poulan in chain saws, Ford in heavy-duty trucks, General Electric in major home appliances, Wal-Mart in discount retailing, and Southwest Airlines in commercial airline travel.

THE COMPETITIVE DEFENSES OF LOW-COST LEADERSHIP
Being the low-cost provider in an industry offers some attractive defenses against the five competitive forces.

- In meeting the challenges of *rival competitors,* the low-cost company is in the best position to compete offensively on the basis of price, to defend against price wars, to use the appeal of a lower price as a weapon for grabbing sales and market share from rivals, and to earn above-average profits (based on bigger profit margins or greater sales volume). Low-cost is a powerful defense in markets where price competition thrives.

- In defending against the bargaining power of *buyers,* low costs provide a company with partial profit margin protection, since powerful customers are rarely able to bargain price down past the survival level of the next most cost-efficient seller.

A low-cost leader is in the strongest position to set the floor on market price.

- In countering the bargaining leverage of *suppliers,* the low-cost producer is more insulated than competitors from powerful suppliers *if* the primary source of its cost advantage is greater internal efficiency. (A low-cost provider whose cost advantage stems from being able to buy components at favorable prices from outside suppliers may actually be more vulnerable to growing leverage on the part of its suppliers.)

- As concerns *potential entrants,* the low-cost leader can use price cutting to make it harder for a new rival to win customers; the pricing power of the low-cost provider acts as a barrier to new entrants.

- In competing against *substitutes,* a low-cost leader is better positioned than higher-cost rivals to use low price as a defense against companies trying to gain market inroads with a substitute product or service.

Consequently, a low-cost company's ability to set the industry's price floor and still earn a profit erects barriers around its market position. Anytime price competition becomes a major market force, less efficient rivals are squeezed the most. Firms in a low-cost position relative to rivals have a competitive edge in meeting the demands of buyers who base their purchase decision on low price.

WHEN A LOW-COST PROVIDER STRATEGY WORKS BEST
A competitive strategy predicated on low-cost leadership is particularly powerful when:

1. Price competition among rival sellers is especially vigorous.

2. The industry's product is an essentially standardized, commodity-type item readily available from a host of sellers—a condition that allows buyers to shop for the best price.

3. There are few ways to achieve product differentiation that have value to buyers (the differences from brand to brand do not matter much to buyers), in which case buyers are very sensitive to price difference among sellers.

4. Most buyers use the product in the same way—thus a standardized product is satisfactory, and price, not features or quality, becomes the dominant competitive force.

5. Switching from one product to another can be done cheaply, thus giving buyers

the flexibility to switch readily to lower-priced sellers having equally good products.

6.   Buyers are large and have significant power to bargain down prices.

As a rule, the more price-sensitive buyers are and the more inclined they are to base their purchasing decision on which seller offers the best price, the more appealing a low-cost strategy becomes. In markets where rivals compete mainly on price, low-cost relative to competitors is the only competitive advantage that matters.

THE RISKS OF A LOW-COST PROVIDER STRATEGY

A low-cost competitive approach does have its drawbacks. Technological breakthroughs can open up cost reductions for rivals that nullify a low-cost leader's past investments and hard-won gains in efficiency. Rival firms may find it easy and/or inexpensive to imitate the leader's low-cost methods, thus making any advantage short-lived. A company driving zealously to push its costs down can become so fixated on cost reduction that it fails to react to subtle but significant market swings—like growing buyer interest in added features or service, new developments in related products that alter how buyers use the company's product, or declining buyer sensitivity to price. The fixated company risks getting left behind as buyers opt for enhanced quality, innovative performance features, faster service, and other differentiating features. Heavy investments in cost reduction can also lock a firm into both its present technology and present strategy, leaving it vulnerable to new technologies and to growing customer interest in something other than a cheaper price.

To avoid the risks and pitfalls of a low-cost leadership strategy, managers must understand that the strategic target is *low cost relative to competitors,* not absolute low cost. In pursuing low-cost status, managers must take care not to strip away features and services that buyers consider essential. Furthermore, how valuable a cost advantage is from a competitive strategy perspective depends on its sustainability. Sustainability, in turn, hinges upon whether the company's means of achieving its cost advantage are difficult for rivals to mimic.

■ DIFFERENTIATION STRATEGIES

Differentiation strategies become an attractive competitive approach whenever buyers' needs and preferences are too diverse to be fully satisfied by a standardized product. To be successful with a differentiation strategy, a company has to study buyers' needs and behavior carefully to understand their opinions about what is important, what constitutes value, and what they are willing to pay for. Then the company has to incorporate one or more attributes and features with buyer appeal into its product/service offering—enough to make its product/service distinct from that of its rivals. Competitive advantage results once a sufficient number of buyers become strongly attached to the attributes and features a differentiator has incorporated into its product offering; the stronger the buyer appeal of a company's differentiating features, the stronger the competitive advantage.

A differentiator's basis for competitive advantage is a product whose attributes differ significantly from the products of rivals.

TYPES OF DIFFERENTIATION THEMES

Companies can pursue differentiation from many angles: a different taste (Dr. Pepper and Listerine), special features (Jenn Air's indoor cooking tops with a vented built-in grill for barbecuing), superior service (Federal Express in overnight package delivery), spare parts availability (Caterpillar guarantees 48-hour spare parts delivery to any customer anywhere in the world or else the part is furnished free), more for the money (McDonald's and Wal-Mart), engineering design and performance (Mercedes Benz automobiles), prestige and distinctiveness (Rolex watches), product reliability (Johnson & Johnson baby products), quality manufacture (Karastan carpets and Honda automobiles), technological leadership (3M Corporation in bonding and coating products), a full range of services (Merrill Lynch), a complete line of products (Campbell's Soup), and top-of-the-line image and reputation (Brooks Brothers and Ralph Lauren menswear, Kitchen Aid dishwashers, and Cross writing instruments).

Successful differentiation allows a firm (1) to command a premium price for its product, and/or (2) to increase unit sales (because additional buyers are won over by the differentiating features), and/or (3) to gain buyer loyalty to its brand. Differentiation enhances profitability whenever the extra price the product commands outweighs the added costs of achieving differentiation. Company differentiation strategies are easily defeated when the distinctions a company pursues aren't valued highly by enough buyers to cause them to choose its brand over a rivals' and/or when a company's approach to differentiation is easily copied or matched by its rivals.

ACTIVITIES WHERE DIFFERENTIATION OPPORTUNITIES EXIST

Differentiation is not something that is hatched in marketing and advertising departments and it isn't limited to just quality and service. The possibilities for successfully differentiating products/services exist throughout the value chain system. The most common places in the chain where differentiation opportunities exist include:

1. *Purchasing and procurement activities* that ultimately affect the performance or quality of the company's end product. McDonald's, for example, gets high ratings on its french fries partly because it has strict specifications on the potatoes it purchases from suppliers.

2. *Product-oriented R&D activities* that have potential for improving designs and performance features, expanding end-uses and applications, increasing product variety, shortening lead times in developing new models, more frequent first-on-the-market victories, added user safety, greater recycling capability, and enhanced environmental protection.

3. *Production process-oriented R&D activities* that allow custom-order manufacture, environmentally safe production methods, and improved product quality, reliability, or appearance.

4. *Manufacturing activities* that can reduce product defects, prevent premature product failure, extend product life, allow better warranty coverage, improve economy of use, result in more end-user convenience, and enhance product appearance. For example, the quality edge enjoyed by Japanese automakers stems from their superior performance of manufacturing and assembly-line activities.

5. *Outbound logistics and distribution activities* that allow for faster delivery, more accurate order filling, and fewer warehouse and on-the-shelf stockouts.

6. *Marketing, sales, and customer service activities* that can result in such differentiating attributes as superior technical assistance to buyers, faster maintenance and repair services, more and better product information for customers, more and better training materials for end-users, better credit terms, quicker order processing, more frequent sales calls, and greater customer convenience. For example, IBM boosts buyer value by providing its mainframe computer customers with extensive technical support and round-the-clock operating maintenance.

A full understanding of the sources of differentiation and the activities that drive uniqueness is necessary managerial preparation for devising a sound differentiation strategy and evaluating the competitive advantage potential of various differentiation approaches.[6]

ACHIEVING A DIFFERENTIATION-BASED COMPETITIVE ADVANTAGE

One key to a successful differentiation strategy is to create buyer value in ways unmatched by rivals. There are three approaches to creating buyer value. One is to incorporate product attributes and user features that lower the buyer's overall costs of using the company's product—Illustration 12 lists options for making a company's product more economical to use. A second approach is to incorporate features that raise the performance a buyer gets from the product—Illustration 13 contains differentiation avenues that enhance product performance and buyer value.

A third approach is to incorporate features that enhance buyer satisfaction in noneconomic or intangible ways. Goodyear's new Aquatread tire design appeals to safety-conscious motorists wary of slick roads in rainy weather. Wal-Mart's campaign to feature products ''Made in America'' appeals to customers concerned about the loss of American jobs to foreign manufacturers. Rolex, Jaguar, Cartier, Ritz-Carlton, and Gucci have differentiation-based competitive advantages linked to buyer desires for status, image, prestige, upscale fashion, superior craftsmanship, and the finer things in life. L. L. Bean makes its mail-order customers feel secure in their purchases by providing an unconditional guarantee with no time limit: ''All of our products are guaranteed to give 100 percent satisfaction in every way. Return anything purchased from us at anytime if it proves otherwise. We will replace it, refund your purchase price, or credit your credit card, as you wish.''

REAL VALUE, PERCEIVED VALUE, AND SIGNALS OF VALUE

Buyers seldom pay for value they don't perceive, no matter how real the unique extras may be.[7] Thus the price premium that a differentiation strategy commands reflects *the value actually delivered* to the buyer and *the value perceived* by the buyer (even if not actually delivered). A buyer's initial perception of a product's value is influenced by the buyer's assessment of what their experience with the product will be. Incomplete knowledge on the part of buyers often results in value judgments based on such *signals* as price (where price connotes quality), attractive packaging, saturation ad campaigns, ad

> A firm that signals extra value effectively may command a higher price than a firm that actually delivers higher value but signals it poorly.

ILLUSTRATION 12   *Differentiating Features That Lower Buyer Costs*

A company doesn't have to lower price to make it cheaper for a buyer to use its product. An alterative is to incorporate features and attributes into the company's product/service package that:

- Reduce the buyer's scrap and raw materials waste. Example of differentiating feature: cut-to-size components.
- Lower the buyer's labor costs (less time, less training, lower skill requirements). Example of differentiating feature: snap-on assembly features, modular replacement of worn-out components.
- Cut the buyer's down-time or idle time. Examples of differentiating features: greater product reliability, ready spare parts availability, or less frequent maintenance requirements.
- Reduce the buyer's inventory costs. Example of differentiating feature: just-in-time delivery.
- Reduce the buyer's pollution control costs or waste disposal costs. Example of differentiating feature: provide scrap pickup for use in recycling.
- Reduce the buyer procurement and order-processing costs. Example of differentiating feature: computerized online ordering and billing procedures.
- Lower the buyer's maintenance and repair costs.

Example of differentiating feature: superior product reliability.
- Lower the buyer's installation, delivery, or financing costs. Example of differentiating feature: 90-day payment same as cash.
- Reduce the buyer's need for other inputs (energy, safety equipment, security personnel, inspection personnel, other tools and machinery). Example of differentiating feature: fuel-efficient power equipment.
- Raise the trade-in value of used models
- Lower the buyer's replacement or repair costs if the product unexpectedly fails later. Example of differentiating feature: longer warranty coverage.
- Lower the buyer's need for technical personnel. Example of differentiating feature: provide free technical support and assistance.
- Boost the efficiency of the buyer's production process. Example of differentiating feature: faster processing speeds, better interface with ancillary equipment.

Source: Adapted from Michael E Porter, *Competitive Advantage* (New York: Free Press, 1985), pp. 135–37.

content and image, the quality of brochures and sales presentations. Buyer perception is also influenced by the seller's facilities, customer list, market share, length of time in business, and the professionalism, appearance, and personality of customer contact personnel. Signals of value may be as important as actual value (1) when the nature of product/service differentiation is subjective or hard to quantify, (2) when buyers are making a first-time purchase, (3) when repurchase is infrequent, and (4) when buyers are unsophisticated.

KEEPING THE COST OF DIFFERENTIATION IN LINE
Once company managers have identified which approach to creating buyer value and establishing a differentiation-based competitive advantage makes the most sense, actions have to be taken to build value-creating attributes into the product at an acceptable cost. Attempts to achieve differentiation usually raise costs. The trick to profitable product/service differentiation is either to keep the costs of achieving it below the added price premium that the differentiating attributes can command (thus increasing the profit margin per unit sold) or to offset thinner profit margins with enough added volume to increase

---

ILLUSTRATION 13   *Differentiating Features That Raise the Performance a User Gets*

To enhance the performance a buyer gets from using its product/service, a company can incorporate features and attributes that:

- Provide buyers greater reliability, durability, convenience, or ease of use.
- Make the company's product/service cleaner, safer, quieter, or more maintenance-free than rival brands.
- Exceed environmental or regulatory standards.
- Meet the buyer's needs and requirements more completely, compared to competitors' offerings.

- Give buyers the option to add on or to upgrade later as new product versions come on the market.
- Give buyers more flexibility to tailor their own products to the needs of their customers.
- Do a better job of meeting the buyer's future growth and expansion requirements.

Source: Adapted from Michael E Porter, *Competitive Advantage,* (New York: Free Press, 1985), pp. 135–38.

---

total profits. It usually makes sense to add extra differentiating features that are not costly but add to buyer satisfaction. Fine restaurants, for example, typically provide such extras as a slice of lemon in the water glass, valet parking, and complimentary after-dinner mints. The overriding condition in pursuing differentiation is that a firm not to get its overall unit costs so far out of line with competitors that it has to charge a higher price than buyers are willing to pay.

WHAT MAKES A DIFFERENTIATION STRATEGY ATTRACTIVE

Differentiation offers a buffer against rival strategies when it results in enhanced buyer loyalty to a company's brand or model and greater willingness to pay a little (perhaps a lot!) more for it. In addition, successful differentiation (1) erects entry barriers in the form of customer loyalty and product/service distinction that newcomers find hard to hurdle, (2) mitigates buyers' bargaining power since the products of alternative sellers are less attractive to them, and (3) helps a firm fend off threats from substitutes. In addition, to the extent that differentiation allows a company to charge a higher price and have bigger profit margins, then the company is in a stronger position to withstand the efforts of powerful vendors to get a higher price for the items they supply. Thus, as with cost leadership, successful differentiation creates lines of defense for dealing with the five competitive forces.

As a rule, differentiation strategies work best in markets where (1) there are many ways to differentiate the product or service and many buyers perceive these differences as having value, (2) buyer needs and uses of the item are diverse, and (3) few rival firms are following a similar differentiation approach.

The most appealing approaches to differentiation are those that are hard or expensive for rivals to duplicate. Easy-to-copy differentiating features have little attraction because they do not produce a sustainable competitive advantage. Indeed, resourceful competitors can, in time, clone almost any product. This is why sustainable differentiation depends so much on internal skills and core competencies. When a company has skills and capabilities that competitors cannot readily match and when its expertise can be used to perform activities in the value chain where differentiation potential exists, then it has a strong basis for sustainable differentiation. As a rule, differentiation is more likely to result in a longer-lasting and more profitable competitive edge if it is based on:

- Technical superiority.
- Product quality.
- Comprehensive customer service.
- More value for the money.

Such differentiating attributes are widely perceived by buyers as having value; moreover, the skills and expertise required to produce them tends to be tougher for rivals to copy or overcome profitably.

THE RISKS OF A DIFFERENTIATION STRATEGY

There are, of course, no guarantees that differentiation will produce a meaningful competitive advantage. If buyers see little value in the product's distinctions (i.e., a standard item meets their needs), then a low-cost strategy can easily defeat a differentiation strategy. In addition, differentiation can be defeated if competitors can quickly copy most or all of the appealing product attributes a company develops. Rapid imitation means that a firm never achieves real differentiation since competing brands keep changing in like ways each time a company moves to set its offering apart.

A low-cost producer strategy can defeat a differentiation strategy when buyers don't believe extra attributes add real value.

Thus, to be successful at differentiation, a firm must search out lasting sources of distinction that are burdensome for rivals to overcome. Aside from these considerations, other common pitfalls to pursuing differentiation include:[8]

- Trying to differentiate on the basis of something that does not lower a buyer's cost or enhance a buyer's well-being, as perceived by the buyer.
- Overdifferentiating so that price is too high relative to competitors or product quality or service levels exceed buyers' needs.
- Trying to charge too high a price premium (the bigger the premium, the more buyers can be lured away by lower-priced competitors).
- Ignoring the need to signal value and depending only on intrinsic product attributes to achieve differentiation.
- Not understanding or identifying what buyers consider as value.

■ THE STRATEGY OF BEING A BEST-COST PROVIDER

This strategy aims at giving customers *more value for the money*. It combines an emphasis on low-cost with an emphasis on *more than minimally acceptable* quality, service, features, and performance. The idea is to create superior value by meeting or exceeding buyer expectations on various product or service attributes and beating their expectations on price. The aim is to become the low-cost provider of a product or service with *good-to-excellent* attributes,

A best-cost producer is skilled at making upscale products at a lower cost than rivals.

ILLUSTRATION **14**   *Toyota's Best-Cost Producer Strategy for Its Lexus Line*

Toyota Motor Co. is widely regarded as the low-cost producer among the world's motor vehicle manufacturers. Despite its emphasis on product quality, Toyota has achieved absolute low-cost leadership because of its considerable skills in efficient manufacturing techniques and because its models are positioned in the low-to-medium end of the price spectrum where high production volumes are conducive to low unit costs. But when Toyota decided to introduce its new Lexus models to compete in the luxury-car market, it employed a classic best-cost producer strategy. Toyota's Lexus strategy had three features:

- Transferring the company's expertise in making high-quality Toyota models at low cost to making premium quality luxury cars at costs below other luxury-car makers, especially Mercedes and BMW. Toyota executives reasoned that Toyota's manufacturing skills should allow it to incorporate high-tech performance features and upscale quality into Lexus models at less cost than other luxury-car manufacturers.
- Using its relatively lower manufacturing costs to underprice Mercedes and BMW, both of which had models selling in the $40,000–$75,000 range (and some even higher). Toyota believed that with its cost advantage it could price attractively equipped Lexus models in the $38,000–$42,000 range, drawing

price-conscious buyers away from Mercedes and BMW and perhaps inducing quality-conscious Lincoln and Cadillac owners to trade up to a Lexus.

- Establishing a new network of Lexus dealers, separate from Toyota dealers, dedicated to providing a level of personalized, attentive customer service unmatched in the industry.

In the 1993–1994 model years, the Lexus 400 series models were priced in the $40,000-$45,000 range and competed against Mercedes' 300/400E series, BMW's 525i/535i series, Nissan's Infiniti Q45, Cadillac Seville, Jaguar, and Lincoln's Continental Mark VIII series. The lower-priced Lexus 300 series, priced in the $30,000-$38,000 range, competed against Cadillac Eldorado, Acura Legend, Infiniti J30, Buick Park Avenue, Mercedes new C-Class series, BMW's 315 series, and Oldsmobile's new Aurora line.

Lexus' best-cost producer strategy was so successful that Mercedes, plagued by sagging sales and concerns of overpricing, reduced its prices significantly on its 1994 models and introduced a new C-Class series, priced in the $30,000–$35,000 range, to become more competitive. The Lexus LS 400 models and the Lexus SC 300/400 models ranked first and second, respectively, in the widely watched J. D. Power & Associates quality survey for 1993 cars; the entry-level Lexus ES 300 model ranked eighth.

---

then use that cost advantage to underprice brands with comparable attributes. Such a competitive approach is termed a *best-cost provider strategy* because the producer has the best (lowest) cost relative to producers whose brands are comparably positioned.

The competitive advantage of a best-cost provider comes from matching rivals on key dimensions of quality, performance, features, or service and beating them on cost. To become a best-cost producer, a company must match quality at a lower cost than rivals, match features at a lower cost than rivals, match product performance at a lower cost than rivals, and so on. What distinguishes a successful best-cost provider is expertise in incorporating upscale product or service attributes at a low cost, or, to put it a bit differently, an ability to contain the costs of providing customers with a better product. The most successful best-cost producers have the skills to simultaneously manage unit costs down and product calibre up—see Illustration 14.

A best-cost provider strategy has great appeal from the standpoint of competitive positioning. It produces superior customer value by balancing a strategic emphasis on low cost against a strategic emphasis on differentiation. In effect, it is a *hybrid* strategy that allows a company to combine the competitive advantage appeals of both low-cost and differentiation to arrive at superior buyer value. In markets where buyer diversity makes product differentiation the norm and many buyers are price- and value-sensitive, a best-cost producer strategy can be more advantageous than either a pure low-cost producer strategy or a pure differentiation strategy keyed to product superiority. This is because a best-cost provider can position itself near the middle of the market with either a medium-quality product at a below-average price or a very good product at a medium price. Often, the majority of buyers prefer a mid-range product rather than the cheap, basic product of a low-cost producer or the expensive product of a top-of-the-line differentiator.

■ FOCUS OR MARKET NICHE STRATEGIES

What sets focus strategies apart from low-cost or differentiation strategies is concentrated attention on a narrow piece of the total market. The target segment or niche can be defined

> What sets a focus strategy apart is concentrated attention on a narrow piece of the total market.

by geographic uniqueness, by specialized requirements in using the product, or by special product attributes that appeal only to niche members. The objective is to do a better job of serving buyers in the target market niche than rival competitors. *A focuser's basis for competitive advantage is either (1) lower costs than competitors in serving the market niche or (2) an ability to offer niche members something different from other competitors.* A focus strategy based on low cost depends on a buyer segment whose requirements are less costly to satisfy as compared to the rest of the market. A focus strategy based on differentiation depends on there being a buyer segment that demands unique product attributes.

Examples of firms employing some version of a focus strategy include Tandem Computers (a specialist in "nonstop" computers for customers who need a "fail-safe" system), Rolls Royce (in superluxury automobiles), Cannondale (in top-of-the-line mountain bikes), Fort Howard paper (specializing in paper products for industrial and commercial enterprises only), commuter airlines like Horizon and Atlantic Southeast (specializing in low-traffic, short-haul flights that link major airports with smaller cities 50 to 250 miles away), and Bandag (a specialist in truck tire recapping that promotes its recaps aggressively at over 1,000 truck stops). Illustration 15 provides examples of a focused low-cost strategy and a focused differentiation strategy.

Using a focus strategy to compete on the basis of low-cost is a fairly common business approach. Budget-priced motel chains like Days Inn, Motel 6, and LaQuinta

> The competitive advantage of a focused low-cost strategy is ability to serve niche members at lower cost than rivals.

have lowered their investment and operating cost per room by using a no-frills approach and catering to price-conscious travelers. Discount stock brokerage houses have lowered costs by focusing on customers who are willing to forgo all the investment research, investment advice, and financial services offered by full-service firms in return for 30 percent or more commission savings on their buy–sell transactions. Pursuing a cost advantage via focusing works well when a firm can find ways to lower costs significantly by limiting its customer base to a well-defined buyer segment.

| ILLUSTRATION 15 | *Focus Strategies in the Lodging Industry: Motel 6 and Ritz-Carlton* |

Motel 6 and Ritz-Carlton compete at opposite ends of the lodging industry. Motel 6 employs a focus strategy keyed to low cost; Ritz-Carlton employs a focus strategy based on high-end differentiation.

Motel 6 caters to price-conscious travelers who want a clean, no-frills place to spend the night. To be a low-cost provider of overnight lodging, Motel 6 (1) selects relatively inexpensive sites on which to construct its units (usually *near* interstate exits and high traffic locations but far enough away to avoid paying prime site prices), (2) builds only basic facilities (no restaurant or bar, and only rarely a swimming pool), (3) relies on standard architectural designs that incorporate inexpensive materials and low-cost construction techniques, and (4) has simple room furnishings and decorations. These approaches lower both investment costs and operating costs. Without restaurants, bars, and all kinds of guest services, a Motel 6 unit can be operated with just front-desk personnel, room clean-up crews, and skeleton building and grounds maintenance. To promote the Motel 6 concept with travelers who have simple overnight requirements, the chain uses unique, recognizable radio ads done by nationally syndicated radio personality, Tom Bodett; the ads describe Motel 6's clean rooms, no-frills facilities, friendly atmosphere, and dependably low rates (usually under $30 per night).

In contrast, the Ritz-Carlton caters to discriminating travelers and vacationers willing and able to pay for top-of-the-line accommodations and world-class personal service. Ritz-Carlton hotels feature (1) prime locations and scenic views from many rooms, (2) custom architectural designs, (3) fine dining restaurants with gourmet menus prepared by accomplished chefs, (4) elegantly appointed lobbies and bar lounges, (5) swimming pools, exercise facilities, and leisure time options, (6) upscale room accommodations, (7) an array of guest services and recreation opportunities appropriate to the location, and (8) large, well-trained professional staffs who do their utmost to make each guest's stay an enjoyable experience.

Both companies concentrate their attention on a narrow piece of the total market. Motel 6's basis for competitive advantage is lower costs than competitors' in providing basic, economical overnight accommodations to price-constrained travelers. Ritz-Carlton's advantage is its capability to provide superior accommodations and unmatched personal service for a well-to-do clientele. Each is able to succeed, despite polar opposite strategies, because the market for lodging consists of diverse buyer segments with diverse preferences and abilities to pay.

At the other end of the market spectrum, companies like Ritz-Carlton, Tiffany's, Porsche, Haagen-Dazs, and W. L. Gore (the maker of Gore-tex) have crafted successful differentiation-based focus strategies targeted at upscale buyers wanting products/services with world-class attributes. Indeed, most markets contain a buyer segment willing to pay a big price premium for the very finest items available, thus opening the strategic window for some competitors to employ differentiation-based focus strategies aimed at the tiptop of the market pyramid.

> **The competitive advantage of a focused differentiation strategy is superior ability to provide niche buyers with specialized expertise or customized product attributes.**

WHEN FOCUSING IS ATTRACTIVE

A focus strategy based either on low-cost or differentiation becomes increasingly attractive as more of the following conditions are met:

- The segment is big enough to be profitable.
- The segment has good growth potential.

- The segment is not crucial to the success of major competitors.
- The firm has the skills and resources to serve the segment effectively.
- The focuser can defend itself against challengers based on the customer goodwill it has built up and its superior ability to serve buyers in the segment.

A focuser's specialized skills in serving the target market niche provide a basis for defending against the five competitive forces. Multisegment rivals may not have the same competitive capability to serve the focused firm's target clientele. The focused firm's competence in serving the market niche raises entry barriers, and thus makes it harder for companies outside the niche to enter. A focuser's unique capabilities in serving the niche also present a hurdle that makers of substitute products must overcome. The bargaining leverage of powerful customers is blunted somewhat by their own unwillingness to shift their business to rival companies less capable of meeting their expectations.

Focusing works best (1) when it is costly or difficult for multisegment competitors to meet the specialized needs of the target market niche, (2) when no other rival is attempting to specialize in the same target segment, (3) when a firm doesn't have the resources to go after a wider part of the total market, and (4) when the industry has many different segments, thereby allowing a focuser to pick an attractive segment suited to its strengths and capabilities.

THE RISKS OF A FOCUS STRATEGY

Focusing carries several risks. One is the chance that competitors will find effective ways to match the focused firm in serving the narrow target market. A second is the potential for buyers in the niche to shift toward the product attributes desired by the market as a whole. This erosion of the differences across buyer niches lowers entry barriers into a focuser's market niche and provides an open invitation for rivals to begin competing for the focuser's customers. A third risk is that the segment becomes so attractive it is soon inundated with competitors, causing segment profits to be splintered.

▶ ## USING OFFENSIVE STRATEGIES TO SECURE COMPETITIVE ADVANTAGE

Competitive advantage is nearly always achieved by successful offensive strategic moves; defensive strategies can protect competitive advantage but rarely are the basis for achieving competitive advantage. How long it takes for a successful offensive to create an edge is a function of the industry's competitive characteristics.[9] The *buildup period*, shown in Figure 5–2, can be short, as with service businesses which need little in the way of equipment and distribution system support to implement a new offensive move. The buildup can, however, take much longer, as with capital intensive and technologically sophisticated industries where firms may need several years to debug a new technology, bring new capacity on line, and win consumer acceptance of a new product. Ideally, an offensive move builds competitive advantage quickly. The longer it takes, the more likely rivals will spot the move, see

---

Competitive advantage is usually acquired by employing a creative offensive strategy that isn't easily thwarted by rivals.

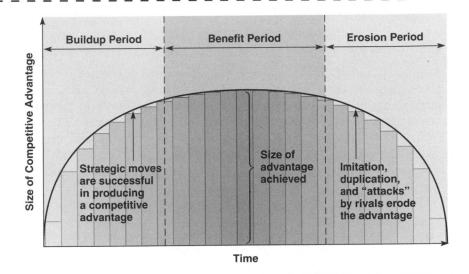

FIGURE 5–2   *The Building and Eroding of Competitive Advantage*

its potential, and begin a counterresponse. The size of the advantage (indicated on the vertical scale in Figure 5–2) can be large, as in the pharmaceutical industry where patents on an important new drug produce a substantial advantage, or small, as in the apparel industry where popular new designs can be imitated quickly.

Following a successful competitive offensive, there is a *benefit period* during which the fruits of competitive advantage can be enjoyed. The length of the benefit period depends on how much time it takes rivals to launch counteroffensives and begin closing the competitive gap. A lengthy benefit period gives a firm valuable time to earn above-average profits and recoup the investment made in creating the advantage. The best strategic offensives produce big competitive advantages and long benefit periods.

As competitors respond with serious counteroffensives to attack the advantage, the *erosion period* begins. Any competitive advantage a firm currently holds will eventually be eroded by the actions of competent, resourceful competitors.[10] Thus, to sustain an initially won advantage, a firm must devise a second strategic offensive. The groundwork for the second offensive needs to be laid during the benefit period in preparation for the competitors inevitable efforts to cut into the leader's advantage. To successfully sustain a competitive advantage, a company must stay a step ahead of rivals by initiating one creative strategic offensive after another to improve its market position and retain customer favor.

There are six basic ways to mount strategic offensives:[11]

• Initiatives to match or exceed competitor strengths

• Initiatives to capitalize on competitor weaknesses

• Simultaneous initiatives on many fronts

- End-run offensives
- Guerrilla offensives
- Preemptive strikes

■ INITIATIVES TO MATCH OR EXCEED COMPETITOR STRENGTHS

There are two good reasons to go head-to-head against rival companies, pitting one's own strengths against theirs, price for price, model for model, promotion tactic for promotion tactic, and geographic area by geographic area. The first is to try to gain market share by outcompeting weaker rivals; challenging weaker rivals where they are strongest is attractive whenever a firm has a superior product offering and the organizational capabilities to win market share away from less-competent and less-resourceful competitors. The other reason is to whittle away at a strong rival's competitive advantage; here success is measured by how much the competitive gap is narrowed. The merits of a strength-against-strength offensive challenge, of course, depend on how much it costs to wage the offensive compared to its competitive benefits. To succeed, the initiator needs enough competitive strength and resources to take at least some market share from the targeted rivals. Absent good prospects for long-term competitive gains and added profitability, such an offensive is ill-advised.

Attacking a competitor's strengths can involve initiatives on any of several fronts—price cutting, running comparison ads, adding new features that appeal to the rival's customers, constructing major new plant capacity in the rival's backyard, or bringing out new models to match their models. In a classic ploy, the aggressor challenges its rival with an equally good product offering at a lower price.[12] This can produce market share gains if the competitor has strong reasons for not resorting to price cuts of its own and if the challenger can convince buyers that its product adequately meets their needs. However, such a strategy will increase profits only if volume gains offset the impact of thinner margins per unit sold.

> One of the most powerful offensive strategies is to challenge rivals with an equally good or better product and a lower price.

Another way to mount a price-aggressive challenge is to achieve a cost advantage first and then hit competitors with a lower price.[13] Price cutting supported by a cost advantage is perhaps the strongest basis for launching and sustaining a price-aggressive offensive. Without a cost advantage, price cutting works only if the aggressor has more financial resources and can outlast its rivals in a war of attrition.

■ INITIATIVES TO CAPITALIZE ON COMPETITOR WEAKNESSES

In this offensive approach, a company tries to gain market inroads by matching its competitive strengths against the weaknesses of rivals. There are a number of entirely legitimate ways to achieve competitive gains at the expense of rivals' weaknesses:

- Concentrate on geographic regions where a rival has a weak market share or is exerting less competitive effort.
- Go after buyer segments that a rival is neglecting or is weakly equipped to serve.

- Make special sales presentations to the customers of rivals whose product quality, features, or product performance are subpar; in such cases, a challenger with a better product can often convince quality-conscious customers to switch to its brand.

- Make special sales pitches to the customers of those rivals who have done a poor job of providing adequate customer service—it may be relatively easy for a service-oriented challenger to win a rival's disenchanted customers.

- Try to move in on rivals that have weak advertising and weak brand recognition—a challenger with strong marketing skills and a recognized brand name can often win customers away from lesser-known rivals.

- Introduce new models or product versions that exploit gaps in the product lines of rivals. Sometimes ''gap-fillers'' turn out to be a market hit and develop into growth segments—witness Chrysler's success in minivans. This initiative works well when new product versions satisfy certain buyer needs that heretofore have been ignored.

As a rule, trying to exploit competitor weaknesses has a better chance of succeeding than initiatives that challenge competitor strengths, especially if the weaknesses represent significant vulnerabilities and the rival is caught by surprise with no ready defense.[14]

■ SIMULTANEOUS INITIATIVES ON MANY FRONTS

On occasions a company may see merit in launching a grand competitive offensive involving many initiatives (price cuts, increased advertising, new product introductions, free samples, coupons, in-store promotions, rebates) in many or all geographic areas. Campaigns such as these can throw a rival off-balance, diverting its attention in many directions and forcing it to protect many pieces of its customer base simultaneously. Hunt's tried such an offensive several years ago in an attempt to wrest market share away from Heinz in the ketchup market. The attack began when Hunt's introduced two new ketchup flavors (pizza and hickory) to disrupt consumers' taste preferences, create new flavor segments, and capture more scarce shelf space. Simultaneously, Hunt's lowered its price to 70 percent of Heinz's price, offered sizable trade allowances to retailers, and raised its advertising budget to over twice the level of Heinz's.[15] The offensive failed because not enough Heinz users tried the Hunt's brands, and many of those who did soon switched back to Heinz. Grand offensives have their best chance of success when a challenger with an attractive product or service also has the financial resources to outspend rivals in courting customers. Then the challenger may be able to blitz the market with an array of promotional offers and entice a large number of buyers to switch their brand allegiance.

■ END-RUN OFFENSIVES

End-run offensives seek to avoid head-on challenges tied to aggressive price cutting, escalated advertising, or costly efforts to outdifferentiate rivals. Instead the idea is to maneuver *around* competitors and be the first to enter unoccupied market territory. Examples of end-run offensives include moving aggressively into geographic areas where rivals have little or no market presence, trying to create new segments by

End-run offensives dodge head-to-head confrontations that escalate competitive intensity and risk cutthroat competition.

introducing products with features to better meet the needs of selected buyers, and leapfrogging into next-generation technologies to supplant existing products and/or production processes. With an end-run offensive, a company can gain a significant first-mover advantage in a new arena and force competitors to play catch-up. The most successful end-runs change the rules of the competitive game in the aggressor's favor.

■ GUERRILLA OFFENSIVES

Guerrilla offensives are particularly well suited to small challengers who have neither the resources nor the market visibility to mount a full-fledged campaign to win business away from industry leaders. A guerrilla offensive employs the hit-and-run principle, selectively targeting buyer groups and market segments that an underdog can exploit to its own advantage. There are several ways to wage a guerrilla offensive:[16]

1. Concentrate on market segments that are not important to rivals or where buyer loyalty to rivals' brands is weakest.

2. Focus on areas where rivals are overextended and have spread their resources most thinly. Possibilities include selecting customers located in isolated geographic areas, enhancing delivery schedules at times when competitors' deliveries are running behind, upgrading quality when rivals have quality control problems, and boosting technical support services when buyers are confused by competitors' proliferation of models and optional features.

3. Make small, scattered, random raids on the leaders' customers with such tactics as occasional lowballing on price to win a big order or steal a key account.

4. Surprise key rivals with sporadic but intense bursts of promotional activity to pick off the business of buyers who might otherwise choose rivals' brands.

5. If rivals employ unfair or unethical competitive tactics and the situation merits it, file legal actions charging antitrust violations, patent infringement, or unfair practices.

■ PREEMPTIVE STRATEGIES

Preemptive strategies involve moving first to secure an advantageous position that rivals are foreclosed or discouraged from duplicating. There are several ways to win a prime strategic position with preemptive moves:[17]

•   Expand production capacity ahead of market demand to discourage rivals from following with expansions of their own. If rivals can be bluffed out of adding capacity by a fear of creating long-term excess supply and having to struggle with the bad profit economics of underutilized plants, the preemptor stands to win a bigger market share as market demand grows and it has the plant capacity to take on new orders.

> Preemptive strategies create competitive advantage by catapulting the aggressor into a prime competitive position which rivals are prevented or discouraged from matching.

•   Tie up the best (or the most) raw material sources and/or the most reliable, high-quality suppliers via long-term contracts or backward vertical integration. This move can relegate rivals to struggling for second-best supply positions.

- Secure the best geographic locations. An attractive first-mover advantage can often be locked in by getting the most favorable site along a heavily traveled thoroughfare, at a new interchange or intersection, in a new shopping mall, in a natural beauty spot, close to cheap transportation or raw material supplies or market outlets, and so on.

- Obtain the business of prestigious customers.

- Build an image in consumer's minds that is distinct and and compelling. Examples include Avis's well-known "We try harder" theme, Frito-Lay's guarantee to retailers of "99.5% service," Holiday Inn's assurance of "no surprises," and Prudential's "piece of the rock" image.

- Secure exclusive or dominant access to the best distributors in an area.

General Mills' Red Lobster restaurant chain has been notably successful in tying up access to excellent seafood suppliers. DeBeers became the dominant world distributor of diamonds by buying up the production of most of the important diamond mines. DuPont's aggressive capacity expansions in titanium dioxide, while not blocking all competitors from expanding, did discourage enough to give it a leadership position in the titanium dioxide industry. Fox's stunning $6.3 billion preemptive bid over CBS for rights to televise NFL games on weekends is widely regarded as a strategic move to catapult Fox into the ranks of the major television networks, alongside ABC, NBC, and CBS.

To be successful, a preemptive move doesn't have to totally block rivals from following or copying; it merely needs to give a firm a prime position. A prime position is one that puts rivals at a competitive disadvantage and is not easily circumvented.

■ CHOOSING WHOM TO ATTACK

Aggressor firms need to analyze which of their rivals to challenge as well as how to challenge them. There are basically four types of firms to launch offensive campaigns against:[18]

1. *Market leader(s)*. Offensive attacks on a major competitor make the best sense when the market share leader is not the true leader in terms of serving the market well. Signs of leader vulncrability include unhappy buyers, sliding profits, strong commitment to dated technologies, outdated plants and equipment, a preoccupation with diversification, an inferior product line, and a competitive strategy that lacks real strength based on low-cost leadership or strong differentiation. Attacks on leaders can also succeed when the challenger is able to revamp its value chain or innovate to gain a fresh cost-based or differentiation-based competitive advantage.[19] Attacks on leaders need not have the objective of making the aggressor the new leader, however; a challenger may win by simply wresting enough sales from the leader to make the challenger a stronger runner-up. Nonetheless, waging an offensive against strong leader(s) risks squandering valuable resources in a futile effort and perhaps even precipitating a fierce and profitless industrywide battle for market share—caution is well-advised.

2. *Runner-up firms*. Launching offensives against weaker runner-up firms whose positions are vulnerable entails relatively low risk. This is especially attractive when a challenger's competitive strengths match the runner-up's weaknesses.

3. *Struggling enterprises that are on the verge of going under.* Challenging a hard-pressed rival in ways that further sap its financial strength and competitive position can weaken its resolve and hasten its exit from the market.

4. *Small local and regional firms.* Because these firms typically have limited expertise, a challenger with broader capabilities is well-positioned to raid their biggest and best customers—particularly those who are growing rapidly, have increasingly sophisticated requirements, and may already be thinking about switching to a supplier with more full-service capability.

As we have said, successful strategies are grounded in competitive advantage. This goes for offensive strategies, too. The kinds of competitive advantages that usually offer the strongest basis for a strategic offensive include:[20]

- Having a lower-cost product design.
- Having lower-cost production capability.
- Having product features that deliver either superior performance or lower user costs.
- An ability to deliver more after-sale support.
- Having the resources to escalate the marketing effort in an undermarketed industry.
- Pioneering a new distribution channel.
- Having the capability to bypass wholesale distributors and sell direct to the end-user.

Almost always, a strategic offensive should be tied to what a firm does best—its competitive strengths and capabilities. As a rule, these strengths should take the form of a *key skill* (cost reduction capabilities, customer service, technical expertise) or a *strong functional competence* (engineering and product design, manufacturing, advertising and promotion, marketing) or superior ability to perform key activities in the value chain that lower cost or enhance differentiation.[21]

▶ USING DEFENSIVE STRATEGIES TO PROTECT COMPETITIVE ADVANTAGE

In a competitive market, all firms are subject to challenges from rivals. Market offensives can come both from new entrants in the industry and from established firms seeking to improve their market positions. The purpose of defensive strategy is to lower the risk of being attacked, weaken the impact of any attack that occurs, and influence challengers to aim their efforts at other rivals. While defensive strategy usually doesn't enhance a firm's competitive advantage, it should definitely help fortify a firm's competitive position and help sustain whatever competitive advantage it may have.

The foremost purpose of defensive strategy is to protect competitive advantage and fortify the firm's competitive position.

There are several basic ways for a company to protect its competitive position. One approach involves blocking the challenger's offensive opportunities. Specific options include:[22]

- Broadening the firm's product line to close off any niches or gaps through which challengers might enter.

- Introducing models or brands that match or preempt what challengers offer.

- Keeping prices low on models that most closely match competitors' offerings.

- Signing exclusive agreements with dealers and distributors to restrict competitors' distribution options.

- Granting dealers and distributors sizable volume discounts to discourage them from experimenting with other suppliers.

- Offering free or low-cost training to product users.

- Making it harder for competitors to get buyers to try their brands by (1) giving special price discounts to buyers who are considering trial use of rival brands, (2) resorting to high levels of couponing and sample giveaways to buyers most prone to experiment, and (3) making early announcements about impending new products or price changes to induce potential buyers to postpone switching.

- Raising the amount of financing provided to dealers and/or to buyers.

- Reducing delivery times for spare parts.

- Increasing warranty coverages.

- Patenting alternative technologies.

- Maintaining participation in alternative technologies.

- Protecting proprietary knowledge in R&D, product design, production technologies, and other competitively sensitive value chain activities.

- Signing exclusive contracts with the best suppliers to block aggressive rivals' access.

- Purchasing natural resource reserves ahead of present needs to keep them from competitors.

- Avoiding suppliers that also serve competitors.

- Challenging rivals' products or practices in regulatory proceedings.

These actions not only buttress a firm's present position, they also present competitors with a moving target. It is not enough just to try to protect the status quo. A good defense requires quick adjustments to changing industry conditions and, on occassion, being a first-mover to block or preempt moves by would-be aggressors. A mobile defense is thus preferable to a stationary defense.

A second approach to defensive strategy involves signaling challengers that there is real potential of strong retaliation if attacked. The goal is to dissuade challengers from attacking at all by raising their expectations that the resulting battle will be more costly than it is worth, or at least divert them to options that are less threatening to the defender. Would-be challengers can be signaled by:[23]

- Publicly announcing management's commitment to maintain the firm's present market share.

- Publicly announcing plans to construct adequate production capacity to meet and possibly surpass forecasted growth in volume.

- Giving out advance information about a new product, technology breakthrough, or the planned introduction of new brands or models in hopes that challengers will be induced to delay moves of their own until they see if the signalled actions are accurate.

- Publicly committing the company to a policy of matching the prices or other terms offered by competitors.

- Maintaining a war chest of cash and marketable securities.

- Making an occasional strong counterresponse to the moves of a weaker competitor to enhance the firm's image as a tough defender.

Another way to dissuade rivals involves trying to lower the profit inducement for challengers to launch an offensive. When a firm's or industry's profitability is enticingly high, challengers are more willing to tackle high defensive barriers and combat strong retaliation. A defender can deflect attacks, especially from new entrants, by deliberately forgoing some short-run profits and by using accounting methods that obscure profitability.

▶ VERTICAL INTEGRATION STRATEGIES AND COMPETITIVE ADVANTAGE

Vertical integration extends a firm's competitive scope within its industry. It involves expanding the firm's scope either backward into sources of supply and/or forward toward end-users of the final product. Thus, if a manufacturer elects to build a new plant to make certain component parts rather than purchase them from outside suppliers, it remains in essentially the same industry as before. However, now it has business units in two production stages of the industry's value chain system. Similarly, if a personal computer manufacturer opens 100 retail stores to market its brands directly to users, it remains in the personal computer business even though its competitive scope extends further forward in the industry chain.

Vertical integration strategies can aim at *full integration* (i.e., participating in all stages of the industry value chain), or *partial integration* (i.e., building positions in just some stages of the industry's value chain). A firm can accomplish vertical integration by starting its own operations in other stages in the industry's value chain or by acquiring a company already performing the activities it wants to bring in-house.

■ STRATEGIC ADVANTAGES OF VERTICAL INTEGRATION

The only good reason for investing company resources in vertical integration is to strengthen the firm's competitive position.[24] Unless vertical integration produces sufficient cost savings to justify the extra investment or yields a competitive advantage, it has no real payoff profitwise or strategywise.

A vertical integration strategy has appeal *only* if it significantly strengthens a firm's competitive position.

Integrating backward generates cost savings only when the volume needed is big enough to capture the same scale economies suppliers have and when suppliers' production efficiency can be matched or exceeded. The potential of backward integration to generate a cost advantage over rivals is usually biggest when suppliers have sizable profit margins, when the item being supplied is a major cost component, and when the necessary technological skills are easily mastered. Backward vertical integration can produce a competitive advantage when a company, by performing activities in-house that were previously outsourced, ends up with a better-quality product/service offering, improves the calibre of its customer service, or in other ways enhances the performance or value of its final product. Occasionally, integrating into more stages along the value chain can add to a company's differentiation capabilities by allowing it to build or strengthen its core competencies, better master key skills or critical technologies, or add features that deliver greater customer value.

Backward integration can spare a company the uncertainty of being dependent on suppliers for crucial components or support services. It can lessen a company's vulnerability to powerful suppliers that don't hesitate to raise prices at every opportunity. Stockpiling, fixed-price contracts, multiple-sourcing, long-term cooperative partnerships, or the use of substitute inputs may not be attractive ways for dealing with uncertain supply conditions or with economically powerful suppliers. Companies that are low on a key supplier's customer priority list can find themselves waiting on shipments every time supplies get tight. If this occurs often and wrecks havoc in a company's own production and customer relations activities, backward integration can be an advantageous strategic solution.

The strategic impetus for forward integration has much the same roots. In many industries, independent sales agents, wholesalers, and retailers handle competing brands of the same product; they have no allegiance to any one company's brand and tend to push what sells and earns them the biggest profits. Undependable sales and distribution channels can give rise to costly inventory pileups and frequent underutilization of capacity, thereby undermining the economies of a steady, near-capacity production operation. In such cases, it can be advantageous for a manufacturer to integrate forward into wholesaling and/or retailing in order to build a committed group of dealers and outlets representing its products to end-users. Sometimes even a few percentage points' increase in the average rate of capacity utilization can boost manufacturing margins enough to profit from company-owned distributorships, franchised dealer networks, and/or a chain of retail stores. On other occasions, integrating forward into the activity of selling directly to end-users can, by cutting out many of the costs of going through regular wholesale-retail channels, result in a relative cost advantage and lower selling prices to ultimate customers.

For a raw materials producer, integrating forward into manufacturing may permit greater product differentiation and provide an avenue of escape from the price-oriented competition of a commodity business. Often, in the early phases of an industry's value chain, intermediate goods are commodities in the sense that they have essentially identical technical specifications regardless of their producer (as is the case with crude oil, poultry, sheet steel, cement, and textile fibers). Competition in the markets for commodity or commoditylike products is usually fiercely price-competitive, with the shifting balance between supply and demand giving rise to volatile profits. However, the closer the activities in the chain get to the ultimate consumer, the greater the opportunities for a firm to break out of commodity competition and differentiate its end-product via design, service, quality features, packaging, promotion, and so on. Often, product differentiation causes the importance of price to shrink in comparison to other value-creating activities and allows for improved profit margins.

■ STRATEGIC DISADVANTAGES OF VERTICAL INTEGRATION

Vertical integration has some substantial drawbacks, however. It boosts a firm's capital investment in the industry, increasing business risk (what if the industry goes sour?) and perhaps denying financial resources to more worthwhile pursuits. A vertically integrated firm has vested interests in protecting its present investments in technology and production facilities even though they may be starting to become obsolete. Because of the high costs of abandoning such investments before they are worn out, fully integrated firms are often slower to adopt new technologies than partially integrated or nonintegrated firms. Second, integrating forward or backward locks a company in to fixed sources of supply (that later may prove costly) and potentially results in less flexibility in accommodating buyer demands for greater product variety.

Third, vertical integration can pose problems of balancing capacity at each stage in the value chain. The most efficient scale of operation at each activity link in the value chain can vary substantially. Exact self-sufficiency at each interface is the exception, not the rule. Where internal capacity is deficient to supply the next stage, the difference has to be bought externally. Where internal capacity is excessive, customers need to be found for the surplus. And if by-products are generated, they require arrangements for disposal.

Fourth, integration forward or backward often calls for radically different skills and business capabilities. Manufacturing, wholesale distribution, and retailing are different businesses with different key success factors, even though the physical products are the same. Managers of a manufacturing company should consider carefully whether it makes good business sense to invest time and money in developing the expertise and merchandising skills to integrate forward into wholesaling or retailing. Many manufacturers have learned the hard way that owning and operating wholesale-retail networks present many headaches, fit poorly with what they do best, and do not always add the kind of value to their core business they thought would result. Integrating backward into parts and components manufacture isn't as simple or profitable as it sometimes sounds either. Personal computer makers, for example, frequently have trouble getting timely deliveries of the latest semiconductor chips at favorable prices, but most don't come close to having the resources or capabilities to integrate backward into chip manufacture; the semiconductor business is technologically sophisticated, entails heavy capital requirements and ongoing R&D effort, and mastering the manufacturing process takes a long time.

Fifth, vertical integration can reduce a company's manufacturing flexibility, lengthening the time it takes to make design and model changes and to bring new products to market. Companies that alter designs and models frequently in response to shifting buyer preferences often find vertical integration into parts and components burdensome because of constant retooling and redesign costs and the time it takes to implement coordinated changes throughout the value chain. Outsourcing is often quicker and cheaper than vertical integration, allowing a company to be more flexible and more nimble in adapting its product offering to fast-changing buyer preferences. Most of the world's automakers, despite their expertise in automotive technology and manufacturing, have concluded that they are better off from the standpoints of quality, cost, and design flexibility purchasing many of their key parts and components from manufacturing specialists, rather than integrating backward to supply their own needs.

UNBUNDLING AND OUTSOURCING STRATEGIES

In recent years, some vertically integrated companies have found vertical integration to be so competitively burdensome that they have adopted vertical deintegration (or unbundling) strategies. Deintegration involves withdrawing from certain stages/activities in the value chain system and relying upon outside vendors to supply the needed products, support services, or functional activities. Outsourcing pieces of the value chain formerly performed in-house makes strategic sense whenever:

- An activity can be performed better or more cheaply by outside specialists.

- The activity is not crucial to the firm's ability to achieve sustainable competitive advantage and won't hollow out its core competencies, essential skills, or technical know-how.

- It reduces the company's risk exposure to changing technology and/or changing buyer preferences.

- It streamlines company operations in ways that improve organizational flexibility, cut cycle time, speed decision making, and reduce coordination costs.

- It allows a company to concentrate on its core business and doing what it does best.

Often, many of the advantages of vertical integration can be captured and many of the disadvantages avoided via long-term cooperative partnerships with key suppliers.

All in all, therefore, a strategy of vertical integration can have both important strengths and weaknesses. Which direction the scales tip on vertical integration depends on (1) whether it can enhance the performance of strategy-critical activities in ways that lower cost or increase differentiation; (2) its impact on investment costs, flexibility and response times, and administrative overheads associated with coordinating operations across more stages; and (3) whether it creates competitive advantage. Absent solid benefits, vertical integration is not likely to be an attractive business strategy option.

> Unless vertical integration builds competitive advantage, it is a strategic move of questionable value.

▶ FIRST-MOVER ADVANTAGES AND DISADVANTAGES

When to make a strategic move is often as crucial as *what* move to make. Timing is especially important when *first-mover advantages* or *disadvantages* exist.[25] Being first to initiate a strategic move can have a high payoff when (1) pioneering helps build a firm's image and reputation with buyers; (2) early commitments to supplies of raw materials, new technologies, distribution channels, and so on, can produce an absolute cost advantage over rivals; (3) first-time customers remain strongly loyal to pioneering firms in making repeat purchases; and (4) moving first constitutes a preemptive strike, making imitation extra hard or unlikely. The bigger the first-mover advantages, the more attractive that making the first move becomes.

> Because of first-mover advantages and disadvantages, competitive advantage is often attached to *when* a move is made as well as to *what* move is made.

However, a wait-and-see approach doesn't always carry a competitive penalty. Being a first-mover may entail greater risks than being a late-mover. First-mover disadvantages (or late-mover advantages) arise when (1) pioneering leadership is much more costly than followership and only negligible experience curve effects accrue to the leader, (2) rapid technological improvements quickly render early investments obsolete (thus allowing following firms to gain the advantages of next-generation products and processes), (3) it is easy for latecomers to crack the market because customer loyalty to pioneering firms is weak, and (4) the hard-earned skills and know-how developed by the market leaders during the early competitive phase are easily copied or even surpassed by late movers. Good timing, therefore, is an important ingredient in deciding whether to be aggressive or cautious in pursuing a particular move.

Matching Strategy to a Company's Situation

Strategy isn't something you can nail together in slap-dash fashion by sitting around a conference table . . .

Terry Haller

The essence of formulating competitive strategy is relating a company to its environment . . . the best strategy for a given firm is ultimately a unique construction reflecting its particular circumstances.

Michael E. Porter

You do not choose to become global. The market chooses for you; it forces your hand.

**Alain Gomey
CEO, Thomson S.A.**

The task of matching strategy to a company's situation is complicated because of the many, and sometimes conflicting, external and internal factors managers have to weigh. However, while the number and variety of considerations is necessarily lengthy, the most important drivers shaping a company's strategic options fall into two broad categories:

• The nature of industry and competitive conditions.

• The firm's own competitive capabilities, market position, and best opportunities.

The dominant strategy-shaping industry and competitive conditions revolve around the particular life cycle stage of the industry (emerging, rapid growth, mature, declining), its structure (fragmented versus concentrated), the nature and relative strength of the five competitive forces, and scope of competitive rivalry (most particularly whether the company's market is globally competitive). The pivotal company-specific considerations hinge on whether the company is an industry leader, an up-and-coming challenger, a satisfied runner-up, or a struggling also-ran and the company's particular set of strengths, weaknesses, opportunities, and threats. But even these few categories of considerations result in too many situational combinations to cover here. However, we can adequately demonstrate what the task of matching strategy to the situation involves by considering five classic types of industry environments:

1. Competing in an emerging and rapidly growing industry.
2. Competing in a maturing industry.
3. Competing in stagnant or declining industries.
4. Competing in fragmented industries.
5. Competing in international markets.

and three classic types of company situations:

- Strategies for industry leaders.
- Strategies for runner-up firms.
- Strategies for weak and crisis-ridden firms.

▶ STRATEGIES FOR COMPETING IN EMERGING INDUSTRIES

An emerging industry is one in the early formative stage. Most companies are in a start-up mode, adding people, acquiring or constructing facilities, gearing up production, trying to broaden distribution, and gain buyer acceptance. Often, there are important product design problems and technological problems to be worked out as well. Emerging industries present managers with some unique strategy-making challenges:[1]

- Because the market is new and unproven, there are uncertainties about how it will function, how fast it will grow, and how big it will get. The little historical data that may be available is virtually useless in projecting future trends.

- Much of the technology tends to be proprietary and closely guarded, having been developed in-house by pioneering firms; some firms may file patents to secure competitive advantage.

- Often, there is no consensus regarding which of several competing production technologies will be most successful or which product attributes will gain the most buyer favor. Until the market sorts these things out, wide differences in product quality and performance from producer to producer are typical. Rivalry centers around each firm's efforts to get the market to ratify its own strategic approach to technology, product design, marketing, and distribution.

- Entry barriers tend to be relatively low, even for entrepreneurial start-up companies. Well-financed, opportunistic companies are likely to enter if the industry has promise for explosive growth.

- Experience curve effects often permit significant cost reductions as volume builds.

- Firms have little hard information about competitors, how fast products are gaining buyer acceptance, and users' experiences with the product; the industry receives little coverage in the business press and there are no trade associations gathering and distributing information.

- Since all buyers are first-time users, the marketing task is to induce initial purchase and overcome customer concerns about product features, performance reliability, and conflicting claims of rival firms.

- Many potential buyers expect first-generation products to be rapidly improved, so they choose to delay purchase until technology and product design mature.

- Initially, firms have trouble securing ample supplies of raw materials and components until suppliers gear up to meet the industry's needs.

- Those companies that find themselves short of funds to support needed R&D get through several lean years until the product catches on often end up merging with competitors or being acquired by outsiders looking to invest in a growth market.

The two critical strategic issues confronting firms in an emerging industry are (1) how to finance the start-up phase and (2) what market segments and competitive advantages to go after in trying to secure a leading industry position.[2] Competitive strategies keyed either to low cost or differentiation are usually viable. Focusing should be considered when financial resources are limited and the industry has too many technological frontiers to pursue at once. One option for financially constrained enterprises is to form a strategic alliance or joint venture to gain access to needed skills and resources. Because an emerging industry has no established market rules and industry participants employ widely varying strategic approaches, a well-financed firm with a powerful strategy can shape the rules and become a recognized industry leader.

Dealing with the risks and opportunities of an emerging industry represents one of the most challenging business strategy problems. To be successful in an emerging industry, companies usually have to pursue one or more of the following strategic avenues:[3]

1. Try to win the early race for industry leadership with risk-taking entrepreneurship and a bold creative strategy. Broad or focused differentiation strategies tied to product superiority typically offer the best chance for early competitive advantage.

> Strategic success in an emerging industry calls for a willingness to pioneer and take risks, an intuitive feel for what buyers will like, and quick response to new developments.

2. Push to perfect technology, improve product quality, and develop attractive performance features.

3. Try to capture any first-mover advantages associated with more models, better styling, early commitments to technologies and raw materials suppliers, experience curve effects, and new distribution channels.

4. Search out new customer groups, new geographical areas to enter, and new user applications. Make it easier and cheaper for first-time buyers to try the industry's first-generation product.

5. Gradually shift the advertising emphasis from building product awareness to increasing frequency of use and creating brand loyalty.

6. As a dominant technology emerges, adopt it quickly. While there's merit in trying to pioneer the "dominant design" approach, such a strategy is quite risky when there are many competing technologies, each developing quickly, and R&D is expensive.

7. Use price cuts to attract the next layer of price-sensitive buyers into the market.

8. Expect well-financed outsiders to move in with aggressive strategies as the perceived risk of investing in the industry lessens. Try to prepare for the entry of powerful competitors by forecasting (a) who the entrants may be (based on present and future entry barriers) and (b) the types of strategies they are likely to use.

The short-term value of winning the early race for growth and market share leadership has to be balanced against the longer-range need to build a durable competitive edge and a defendable market position.[4] New entrants, attracted by the growth and profit potential, may crowd the market. Aggressive newcomers, aspiring for industry leadership, can quickly become major players by acquiring and merging the operation of weaker competitors. Young companies in fast-growing markets face three strategic hurdles: (1) managing their own rapid expansion, (2) defending against competitors trying to horn in on their success, and (3) building a competitive position extending beyond their initial product or market. Such companies can help their cause by selecting knowledgeable members for their board of directors, hiring entrepreneurially oriented managers with experience in guiding young businesses through the start-up and takeoff stages, perhaps merging with or acquiring another firm to gain added expertise and a stronger resource base, and concentrating on out-innovating the competition.

▶ ## STRATEGIES FOR COMPETING IN A MATURING INDUSTRY

The rapid-growth environment of a young industry cannot go on forever. However, the transition to a slower-growing, maturing industry does not have a clearly differentiated beginning point; it can be forestalled by a steady stream of technological advances, product innovations, or other driving forces that keep rejuvenating market demand. Nonetheless, when growth rates slacken, the transition to market maturity usually produces fundamental changes in the industry's competitive environment:[5]

1. *Slowing growth in buyer demand generates more competition for market share.* Firms that want to continue on a rapid-growth track start looking for ways to take customers away from their competitors. Price cutting, increased advertising, and other aggressive tactics are common.

2. *Buyers become more sophisticated, often driving a harder bargain on repeat purchases.* Since buyers have experience with the product and familiarity with competing brands, they are better able to evaluate brands and negotiate a better deal with sellers.

3. *Competition often produces a greater emphasis on price and service.* As sellers all begin to offer the product attributes buyers prefer, buyer choices increasingly depend on which seller offers the best combination of price and service.

4. *Firms have a "topping out" problem in adding production capacity.* Slower rates of industry growth mean slowdowns in capacity expansion. Each firm has to monitor rivals' expansion plans and time its own capacity additions to minimize oversupply in the industry. With slower industry growth, adding too much capacity too soon is a mistake that can adversely affect company profits well into the future.

5. *Product innovation and new product applications are harder to educe.* Producers find it increasingly difficult to create new product features, find further uses for the product, and sustain buyer excitement.

6. *International competition increases.* Growth-minded domestic firms seek sales opportunities in foreign markets. Some companies, looking for ways to cut costs, relocate plants to countries with lower wage rates. Product standardization and diffusion of technology reduce entry barriers and make it possible for companies to become market contenders in more countries. Industry leadership passes to companies that build strong competitive positions in most of the world's major geographic markets and achieve the largest global market shares.

7. *Industry profitability falls temporarily or permanently.* Slower growth, increased competition, more-sophisticated buyers, and occasional periods of overcapacity put

pressure on industry profit margins. Weaker, less-efficient firms are usually the hardest hit.

8. *Stiffening competition induces mergers and acquisitions among competitors, drives the weakest firms out of the industry, and, results in industry consolidation.* Inefficient firms and firms with weak competitive strategies can survive in a fast-growing industry with booming sales. But the intensifying competition that accompanies industry maturity exposes competitive weakness and throws second- and third-tier competitors into a survival-of-the-fittest contest.

As industry maturity begins to hit full force, firms can make several strategic moves to strengthen their competitive positions.[6]

PRUNING THE PRODUCT LINE

While a wide selection of models, features, and product options has competitive value during the growth stage when buyers' needs are still evolving, such variety can become too costly as price competition stiffens and profit margins are squeezed. Too many product versions prevent firms from achieving the economies of long production runs. In addition, the prices of slow-selling versions may not cover their true costs. Pruning marginal product offerings lowers costs and permits more concentration on items whose margins are highest and/or where the firm has a competitive advantage.

In a maturing industry, strategic emphasis needs to be on reducing costs, accelerating sales promotion efforts, expanding internationally, and acquiring distressed competitors.

MORE EMPHASIS ON PROCESS INNOVATION

Efforts to reinvent the manufacturing process can have a fourfold payoff: lower costs, better production quality, greater capability to turn out multiple product versions, and shorter design-to-market cycles. Process innovation may involve improving labor efficiency by revamping production lines, creating self-managed work teams, reengineering manufacturing processes, instituting total quality programs, and increasing the use of advanced technology such as robotics, computerized controls, and automatic guided vehicles. Japanese firms have become remarkably adept at using manufacturing process innovation to become lower-cost producers of higher-quality products.

A STRONGER FOCUS ON COST REDUCTION

Stiffening price competition gives firms extra incentive to reduce unit costs. Companies can push suppliers for better prices, switch to lower-priced components, develop more economical product designs, cut low-value activities out of the value chain, streamline distribution channels, and reengineer internal processes.

INCREASING SALES TO PRESENT CUSTOMERS

In a mature market, growing by taking customers away from rivals may not be as appealing as expanding sales to existing customers. Strategies to increase the purchases of existing customers can involve providing complementary items and ancillary services, and finding more ways for customers to use the product. Convenience food stores, for example, have boosted average sales per customer by adding video rentals, automatic bank tellers, and deli counters.

PURCHASING RIVAL FIRMS AT BARGAIN PRICES

Sometimes the facilities and assets of distressed rivals can be acquired cheaply. Bargain-priced acquisitions can help create a low-cost position if they present opportunities for greater operating efficiency. In addition, an acquired firm's customer base can provide expanded market coverage. The most desirable acquisitions are those that will significantly enhance the acquiring firm's competitive strength.

EXPANDING INTERNATIONALLY

As its domestic market matures, a firm may seek foreign markets where attractive growth potential still exists and competitive pressures are not so strong. Several manufacturers in highly industrialized nations found international expansion attractive because equipment no longer suitable for domestic operations could be used in plants in less-developed foreign markets. Such possibilities arise (1) when foreign buyers have less-sophisticated needs and have simpler, old-fashioned end-use applications, and (2) when foreign competitors are smaller, less formidable, and do not employ the latest production technology. Strategies to expand internationally also make sense when a domestic firm's skills, reputation, and product appeal to foreign markets. Even though the U.S. market for soft drinks is mature, Coca-Cola has remained a growth company through increased sales efforts in foreign markets where soft drink sales are expanding rapidly.

■ STRATEGIC PITFALLS

Perhaps the biggest strategic snare a company can fall into as an industry matures is to steer the middle course among low-cost, differentiation, and focusing. Such compromises guarantee that a firm will end up stuck in the middle with a fuzzy strategy, a lack of commitment to achieving competitive advantage based on low-cost or differentiation, and a mediocre image with buyers. Other pitfalls include sacrificing long-term competitive position for short-term profit, waiting too long to respond to price cutting, getting caught with too much capacity as growth slows, overspending on marketing efforts to boost sales growth, and failing to pursue cost reduction soon enough and aggressively enough.

> One of the greatest strategic mistakes a firm can make is pursuing a compromise among low-cost, differentiation, and focusing that leaves it stuck in the middle with a fuzzy strategy, a mediocre image, and no competitive advantage.

▶ STRATEGIES FOR FIRMS IN STAGNANT OR DECLINING INDUSTRIES

Many firms operate in industries where demand is declining, or growing at a slower pace than the average throughout the economy. Although harvesting the business to obtain the greatest cash flow, selling out, and closing down are obvious end-game strategies for uncommitted competitors with dim long-term prospects, strong competitors may be able to sustain good performance in a stagnant market environment.[7] Stagnant demand by itself is not enough to make an industry unattractive. Selling out may or may not be practical, and closing operations is always a last resort.

Businesses competing in slow-growth/declining industries have to accept the difficult realities of being stagnant; they must resign themselves to performance targets consistent with available market opportunities. Cash flow and return-on-investment criteria are more appropriate than growth-oriented performance measures; however, sales and market share growth are by no means ruled out. Strong competitors may be able to take sales from weaker rivals, and the acquisition or exit of weaker firms creates opportunities for the remaining companies to capture greater market share.

In general, companies that have succeeded in stagnant industries have relied heavily on one of the following strategic themes:[8]

1. *Pursue a focus strategy by identifying, creating, and exploiting the growth segments within the industry.* Stagnant or declining markets, like other markets, are composed of numerous segments or niches. Frequently, one or more of these segments is growing rapidly, despite a lack of growth in the industry as a whole. An astute competitor, the first to concentrate on the most attractive segments, can escape stagnating sales and profits and possibly achieve competitive advantage in the target segments.

2. *Stress differentiation based on quality improvement and product innovation.* Either enhanced quality or innovation can rejuvenate demand by creating important, new growth segments or inducing buyers to trade up. Successful product innovation opens up additional avenues for competing besides meeting or beating rivals' prices. Differentiation based on successful innovation has the additional advantage of being difficult and expensive for rival firms to imitate.

3. *Work diligently and persistently to drive costs down.* When increases in sales cannot be counted on to generate increases in earnings, companies can improve profit margins and return on investment by continuous productivity improvement and cost reduction year after year. Potential cost-saving actions include *(a)* outsourcing functions and activities that can be performed more cheaply by outsiders, *(b)* reengineering internal processes, *(c)* consolidating underutilized production facilities, *(d)* adding more distribution channels to ensure the unit volume needed for low-cost production, *(e)* closing low-volume, high-cost distribution outlets, and *(f)* cutting marginally useful activities from the value chain.

These three strategic themes are not mutually exclusive.[9] Attempts to introduce new versions of a product can *create* a fast-growing market segment. Similarly, relentless pursuit of operating efficiencies permits price reductions that stimulate increased purchases by price-conscious buyers. Note, that all three themes are spin-offs of the generic competitive strategies, adjusted to fit the circumstances of a tough industry environment.

The most attractive declining industries are those in which sales erode slowly, there is a large base of built-in demand, and some profitable niches remain. The most common strategic mistakes companies make in stagnating or declining markets are (1) getting trapped in a profitless war of attrition, (2) diverting too much cash out of the business too quickly (thus accelerating a company's demise), and (3) being overly optimistic about the industry's future and waiting for things to get better.

Illustration 16 describes the creative approach taken by Yamaha to reverse declining market demand for pianos.

| ILLUSTRATION 16 | *Yamaha's Strategy in the Piano Industry* |

For some years now, worldwide demand for pianos has been declining—in the mid-1980s the decline was 10% annually. Modern-day parents have not put the same stress on music lessons for their children as prior generations of parents did. In an effort to see if it could revitalize its piano business, Yamaha conducted a market research survey to learn what use was being made of pianos in households that owned one. The survey revealed that the overwhelming majority of the 40 million pianos in American, European, and Japanese households were seldom used. In most cases, the reasons the piano had been purchased no longer applied. Children had either stopped taking piano lessons or were grown and had left the household; adult household members played their pianos sparingly, if at all—only a small percentage were accomplished piano players. Most pianos were serving as a piece of fine furniture and were in good condition despite not being

tuned regularly. The survey also confirmed that the income levels of piano owners were well above average.

Yamaha's piano strategists saw the idle pianos in these upscale households as a potential market opportunity. The strategy that emerged entailed marketing an attachment that would convert the piano into an old-fashioned automatic player piano capable of playing a wide number of selections recorded on 3½-inch floppy disks (the same kind used to store computer data). The player piano conversion attachment carried a $2,500 price tag. Concurrently, Yamaha introduced Disklavier, an upright acoustic player piano model that could play *and record* performances up to 90 minutes long; the Disklavier retailed for $8,000. At year-end 1988 Yamaha offered 30 prerecorded disks for $29.95 each and planned to release a continuing stream of new selections. Yamaha believed that these new high-tech products held potential to reverse the downtrend in piano sales.

▶ STRATEGIES FOR COMPETING IN FRAGMENTED INDUSTRIES

A number of industries are populated with hundreds, even thousands, of small and medium-sized companies, many of which are privately held and have only a tiny share of total industry sales.[10] The standout competitive feature of a fragmented industry is the absence of market leaders with king-sized market shares or widespread buyer recognition. Examples of fragmented industries include book publishing, landscaping and plant nurseries, kitchen cabinets, oil tanker shipping, auto repair, restaurants and fast-food, public accounting, women's dresses, metal foundries, meat packing, paperboard boxes, log homes, hotels and motels, and furniture.

Any of several reasons can account for the fragmentation of the supply side of an industry:

- Low entry barriers allow small firms to enter quickly and cheaply.

- An absence of large-scale production economies permit small companies to compete on an equal cost footing with larger firms.

- Buyers require relatively small quantities of customized products (as in business forms, interior design, and advertising); because demand for any particular product version is small, sales volumes are inadequate to support producing, distributing, or marketing on a scale that yields advantages to a large firm.

- The market for the industry's product/service is local (dry cleaning, residential construction, medical services, automotive repair), giving competitive advantage to local businesses familiar with local buyers and local market conditions.

- Market demand is so large and so diverse that it takes very large numbers of firms to accommodate buyer requirements (health care, energy, apparel).

- High transportation costs limit the radius a plant can economically service—as in concrete blocks, mobile homes, milk, and gravel.

- Local regulatory requirements differ in different geographic areas.

- The industry is so new that no firms have yet developed the skills and resources to command a significant market share.

Some fragmented industries consolidate naturally as they mature. The stiffer competition that accompanies slower growth produces a shakeout of weak, inefficient firms and a greater concentration of larger, more visible sellers. Other fragmented industries remain atomistically competitive because it is inherent to the nature of their business. Still others get stuck in a fragmented state because existing firms lack the resources or ingenuity to employ a strategy powerful enough to drive industry consolidation.

Competitive rivalry in fragmented industries can vary from moderately strong to fierce. Low barriers make entry of new competitors an ongoing threat. Competition from substitutes may or may not be a major factor. The relatively small size of companies in fragmented industries puts them in a weak position to bargain with powerful suppliers and buyers, although sometimes small companies can form a cooperative and use their combined leverage to negotiate better sales and purchase arrangements. In a fragmented and weak environment, however, the best a firm can expect is to cultivate a loyal customer base and grow a bit faster than the industry average. Competitive strategies based either on low cost or differentiation are viable unless the industry's product is highly standardized. Focusing on a well-defined market niche or buyer segment usually offers more potential for competitive advantage than striving for broad market appeal. Suitable competitive strategy options in a fragmented industry include:

In fragmented industries competitors usually have the strategic latitude to pursue either a low-cost or a differentiation-based competitive advantage.

- *Constructing and operating "formula" facilities*—This strategic approach is frequently employed in restaurant and retailing businesses operating at multiple locations. It involves constructing standardized outlets in favorable locations at minimum cost and then polishing to a science how to operate them in super-efficient manner. McDonald's, Red Lobster, and 7-Eleven have pursued this strategy to perfection, earning excellent profits in their respective industries.

- *Becoming a low-cost operator*—When price competition is intense and profit margins are under constant pressure, companies can stress no-frills operations featuring low overhead, use of high-productivity/low-cost labor, lean capital budgets, high fixed-asset utilization, and dedicated pursuit of total operating efficiency. Successful low-cost producers in a fragmented industry can cut prices and earn profits above the industry average.

- *Increasing customer value through integration*—Backward or forward integration may contain opportunities to lower costs or enhance the value given to customers.

Examples include assembling components before shipment to customers, providing technical advice, or opening regional distribution centers.

- *Specializing by product type*—When a fragmented industry's products include a range of styles or services, a strategy to focus on one product/service category can be very effective. Some firms in the furniture industry specialize in only one type of furniture, such as brass beds, rattan and wicker, lawn and garden, and early American. In auto repair, companies specialize in transmission repair, body work, and fast oil changes.

- *Specializing by customer type*—A firm can cope with the intense competition of a fragmented industry by catering to those customers (1) who have the least bargaining leverage because they are small or purchase small amounts, (2) who are the least price-sensitive, or (3) who are interested in unique product attributes, a customized product/service, or other extras.

- *Focusing on a limited geographic area*—Even though a firm in a fragmented industry can't win a big share of total industrywide sales, it can still try to dominate a local/regional geographic area. Concentrating company efforts on a limited territory can produce greater operating efficiency, speed delivery and other customer services, promote strong brand awareness, and permit saturation advertising, while avoiding the diseconomies of stretching operations out over a much wider geographic area. Supermarkets, banks, and sporting goods retailers have been successful in operating multiple locations within a limited geographic area.

In fragmented industries, firms generally have the strategic freedom to pursue broad or narrow buyer groups and low-cost or differentiation-based competitive advantages.

▶ STRATEGIES FOR COMPETING IN INTERNATIONAL MARKETS

Companies are motivated to expand into international markets for any of three basic reasons: a desire for new markets, a need to achieve lower costs, or a desire to access the natural resources located in other countries. Whatever the reason, an international strategy has to be situation-driven. Special attention has to be paid to how national markets differ in buyer needs and habits, distribution channels, long-run growth potential, driving forces, and competitive pressures. In addition to the basic market differences from country to country, there are four other situational considerations unique to international operations: cost variations among countries, fluctuating exchange rates, host government trade policies, and the pattern of international competition.

Competing in international markets poses a bigger strategy-making challenge than competing in only the company's home market.

MANUFACTURING COST VARIATIONS

Differences in wage rates, worker productivity, inflation rates, energy costs, tax rates, government regulations, and the like, create sizable variations in manufacturing costs from country to country. It is common for plants in some countries to have manufacturing cost advantages over plants in other countries because of their lower input costs (especially labor), less-strict government regulations, or their unique natural resources. In such cases, the low-cost countries become principal production sites, and most of the output is exported to markets in other parts of the world. Companies with facilities in these locations (or which source their products from contract manufacturers in these countries) have a competitive advantage over those that do not. The competitive role of low manufacturing costs is most evident in low-wage countries such as Taiwan, South Korea, Mexico, and Brazil, which have become production havens for goods with high labor content.

Another important manufacturing cost consideration in international competition is the concept of *manufacturing share* as distinct from brand share or market share. For example, although less than 40 percent of all the video recorders sold in the United States carry a Japanese brand name, Japanese companies do 100 percent of the manufacturing—all sellers source their video recorders from Japanese manufacturers.[11] In microwave ovens, Japanese brands have less than a 50 percent share of the U.S. market, but the manufacturing share of Japanese companies is over 85 percent. *Manufacturing share is significant because it is a better indicator than market share of the industry's low-cost producer.* In a globally competitive industry where some competitors are intent on global dominance, being the worldwide low-cost producer is a powerful competitive advantage. Achieving low-cost producer status often requires a company to have the largest worldwide manufacturing share, with production centralized in one or more superefficient plants. However, important marketing and distribution economies associated with multinational operations can also yield low-cost leadership.

FLUCTUATING EXCHANGE RATES

The volatility of exchange rates greatly complicates the issue of locational cost advantages. Exchange rates can fluctuate as much as 20 to 40 percent annually. Changes of this magnitude can totally wipe out a country's low-cost advantage or transform a high-cost location into a competitive-cost location. A strong U.S. dollar makes it more attractive for U.S. companies to manufacture in foreign countries. Declines in the value of the dollar against foreign currencies can eliminate much of the cost advantage that foreign manufacturers have over U.S. manufacturers and can even prompt foreign companies to establish production plants in the United States.

HOST GOVERNMENT TRADE POLICIES

National governments have enacted all kinds of measures affecting international trade and the operation of foreign companies in their markets. Host governments may impose import tariffs and quotas, set local-content requirements on goods made inside their borders by foreign-based companies, and regulate the prices of imported goods. In addition, outsiders may face myriad regulations regarding technical standards, product certification, prior approval of capital spending projects, withdrawal of funds from the country, and minority (sometimes majority) ownership by local citizens. Some governments also provide subsidies and low-interest loans to domestic companies to help them compete against foreign-based companies. Other governments, anxious to obtain new plants and jobs, offer foreign companies a helping hand in the form of subsidies, privileged market access, and technical assistance.

■ MULTICOUNTRY COMPETITION VERSUS GLOBAL COMPETITION

There are important differences in the patterns of international competition from industry to industry.[12] At one extreme, competition can be termed *multicountry* because it takes place country by country; competition in each national market is essentially independent of competition in other national markets. For example, there is a banking industry in France, one in Brazil, and one in Japan, but competitive conditions in banking differ markedly in all three countries. Moreover, a bank's reputation, customer base, and competitive position in one nation has little or no bearing on its ability to compete successfully in another nation. In industries where multicountry competition prevails, the power of a company's strategy in any one nation does not transfer to other nations, and any competitive advantage the strategy yields is largely confined to that nation and does not spill over to other countries where it operates. With multicountry competition there is no international market, just a collection of self-contained national markets. Industries characterized by multicountry competition include many types of food products (coffee, cereals, canned goods, frozen foods), many types of retailing, beer, life insurance, apparel, and metals fabrication.

Multicountry competition exists when there is no international market, just a collection of self-contained country markets.

At the other extreme is *global competition* where prices and competitive conditions across national markets are strongly linked and the term international or global market has true meaning. In a globally competitive industry, a company's competitive position in one country both affects and is affected by its position in other countries. Rival companies compete against each other in many different countries, but especially so in countries where sales volumes are large and where having a competitive presence is strategically important to building a strong global position in the industry. In global competition, a firm's overall competitive advantage grows out of its entire worldwide operation. The competitive advantage it has created at its home base is supplemented by advantages growing out of its operations in other countries. These advantages can include having plants in low-wage countries, a capability to serve customers with multinational operations of their own, and a brand reputation that is transferable from country to country. *A global competitor's market strength is directly proportional to its portfolio of country-based competitive advantages.* Global competition exists in automobiles, television sets, tires, telecommunications equipment, copiers, watches, and commercial aircraft.

Global competition exists when leading competitors to compete head-to-head in many different countries.

An industry can have segments that are globally competitive and segments where competition is country by country.[13] In the hotel-motel industry, for example, the low- and medium-priced segments are characterized by multicountry competition because competitors mainly serve travelers within the same country. In the business and luxury segments, however, competition is more globalized. Companies like Nikki, Marriott, Sheraton, and Hilton have hotels at many international locations and use worldwide reservation systems and common quality and service standards to gain marketing advantages in serving businesspeople and

In multicountry competition, rival firms vie for national market leadership. In globally competitive industries, rival firms vie for worldwide leadership.

travelers who make international trips. In lubricants, the marine engine segment is globally competitive because ships move from port to port and require the same oil everywhere they stop. Brand reputations have a global scope and successful marine engine lubricant producers (Exxon, British Petroleum, and Shell) operate globally. In automotive motor oil, however, multicountry competition dominates. Countries have different weather conditions and driving patterns, production is subject to limited scale economies, shipping costs are high, and retail distribution channels differ markedly from country to country. Thus domestic firms, like Quaker State and Pennzoil in the United States and Castrol in Great Britain, can be market leaders.

All these situational considerations, along with the obvious cultural and political differences among countries, shape a company's strategic approach in international markets.

■ TYPES OF INTERNATIONAL STRATEGIES

There are six distinct strategic options for a company participating in international markets. It can:

1. *License foreign firms to use the company's technology or produce and distribute the company's products* (in which case international revenues will equal the royalty income from the licensing agreement).

2. *Maintain a national (one-country) production base and export goods to foreign markets,* using either company-owned or foreign-controlled forward distribution channels.

3. *Follow a multicountry strategy* whereby a company's international strategy is crafted country by country to be responsive to buyer needs and competitive conditions in each country where it operates. Strategic moves in one country are made independently of actions taken in another country; strategy coordination across countries is considered secondary to matching company strategy to national conditions.

4. *Follow a global low-cost strategy* where the company strives to be a low-cost supplier to buyers in most or all strategically important markets of the world. The company's strategic efforts are coordinated worldwide to achieve a low-cost position relative to competitors.

5. *Follow a global differentiation strategy* where a firm differentiates its product from other companies' products on the same attributes in all countries to create a consistent image and a consistent competitive theme. The firm's strategic moves are coordinated across countries to achieve consistent differentiation worldwide.

6. *Follow a global focus strategy* where company strategy is aimed at serving the same identifiable niche in each of many strategically important country markets. Strategic actions are coordinated globally to achieve a consistent low-cost or differentiation-based competitive approach in its target niche worldwide.

Licensing makes sense when a firm with either valuable technology or a unique patented product has neither the internal organizational capability nor the resources in foreign markets. By licensing the technology or the production rights to foreign-based firms, it at least realizes income from royalties.

Using domestic plants as a production base for exporting goods to foreign markets is an excellent initial strategy for pursuing international sales. It minimizes both risk and capital requirements, and is a conservative way to test international markets. With an export strategy, a manufacturer can limit its involvement in foreign markets by contracting with foreign wholesalers experienced in importing to handle the entire distribution and marketing function in their countries or region of the world. If it is more advantageous to maintain control over these functions, a manufacturer can establish its own distribution and sales organizations in some or all of the target foreign markets. Either way, a firm minimizes its direct investments in foreign countries because of its home base production and export strategy. Such strategies are commonly favored by Korean and Italian companies—products are designed and manufactured at home and only marketing activities are performed abroad. Whether such a strategy can be pursued successfully over the long run hinges on the relative cost competitiveness of a home country production base. In some industries, firms gain additional scale economies and experience curve benefits from centralizing production in one or several large plants whose output capability exceeds demand in any one national market. To capture such large economies of scale, a company must export to markets in other countries. However, this strategy is competitively vulnerable when manufacturing costs in the home country are substantially higher than in countries where rivals have plants.

The pros and cons of a multicountry strategy versus a global strategy are a bit more complex.

■ A MULTICOUNTRY STRATEGY OR A GLOBAL STRATEGY?

The need for a multicountry strategy derives from the sometimes vast differences in cultural, economic, political, and competitive conditions in different countries. The more diverse national market conditions are, the stronger the case for a *multicountry strategy* where the company tailors its strategic approach to fit each host country's market. In such cases, the company's overall international strategy is an amalgamation of its country strategies.

While multicountry strategies are best suited for industries where multicountry competition dominates, global strategies are best suited for globally competitive industries. With a *global strategy*, the company's strategy for competing is mostly the same in all countries. Although *minor* country-to-country differences in strategy do exist to accommodate specific competitive conditions in host countries, the company's fundamental competitive approach (low-cost, differentiation, or focus) remains the same

> When competing internationally, choose the strategy that is appropriate to the competition in the target market—a multicountry strategy for multicountry markets and a global strategy for global markets.

worldwide. Moreover, a global strategy involves (1) integrating and coordinating the company's strategic moves worldwide and (2) selling in many if not all nations where there is significant buyer demand. Table 6–1 provides a point-by-point comparison of multicountry versus global strategies. The question of which to pursue is the foremost strategic issue firms face when they compete in international markets.

| TABLE 6-1 | *Differences between Multicountry and Global Strategies* |

	Multicountry Strategy	**Global Strategy**
Strategic arena	Selected target countries and trading areas.	Most countries which constitute critical markets for the product (at least North America, the European Community, and the Pacific Rim— Australia, Japan, South Korea, and Southeast Asia).
Business strategy	Custom strategies to fit the circumstances of each host country situation; little or no strategy coordination across countries.	Same basic strategy worldwide; minor country-by-country variations where essential.
Product-line strategy	Adapted to local needs.	Mostly standardized products sold worldwide.
Production strategy	Plants scattered across many host countries.	Plants located on the basis of maximum competitive advantage (in low-cost countries, close to major markets, geographically scattered to minimize shipping costs, or use of a few world-scale plants to maximize economies of scale—as most appropriate).
Source of supply for raw materials and components	Suppliers in host country preferred (local facilities meeting local buyer needs; some local sourcing may be required by host government).	Attractive suppliers from anywhere in the world.
Marketing and distribution	Adapted to practices and culture of each host country.	Much more worldwide coordination; minor adaption to host country situations if required.
Company organization	Form subsidiary companies to handle operations in each host country; each subsidiary operates more or less autonomously to fit host country conditions.	All major strategic decisions are closely coordinated at global headquarters; a global organizational structure is used to unify the operations in each country.

The strength of a multicountry strategy is that it matches the company's competitive approach to host country circumstances. This matching becomes essential as more of the following conditions prevail:

- There are significant country-to-country differences in customers' needs and buying habits (see Illustration 17).
- Buyers in a country insist on special-order or highly customized products.
- Buyer demand for the product exists in comparatively few national markets.
- Host governments enact regulations requiring that products sold locally meet strict manufacturing specifications or performance standards.
- The trade restrictions of host governments are so diverse and complicated they preclude a uniform, coordinated worldwide market approach.

A multicountry strategy does, however, have two significant drawbacks: It entails very little strategic coordination across country boundaries and it is not closely tied to achieving competitive advantage. The primary orientation of a multicountry strategy is responsiveness to local country conditions, not building a multinational-based competitive

---

ILLUSTRATION **17**   *Nestlé's Multicountry Strategy in Instant Coffee*

Nestlé is the world's largest food company with over $33 billion in revenues, market penetration on all major continents, and plants in over 60 countries. The star performer in Nestlé's food products lineup is coffee, with sales of over $5 billion and operating profits of $600 million. Nestlé is the world's largest producer of coffee; it is also the world's market leader in mineral water (Perrier), condensed milk, frozen food, candies, and infant food.

In 1992 the company's Nescafé brand was the leader in the instant coffee segment in virtually every national market but the United States, where it ranked Number 2 behind Maxwell House. Nestlé produced 200 types of instant coffee, from lighter blends for the U.S. market to dark expressos for Latin America. To keep its instant coffees matched to consumer tastes in different countries (and areas within some countries), Nestlé operated four coffee research labs, with a combined budget of $50 million annually, to experiment with new blends in aroma, flavor, and color. The strategy was to match the

blends marketed in each country to the tastes and preferences of coffee drinkers in that country, introducing new blends to develop new segments when opportunities appeared and altering blends as needed to respond to changing tastes and buyer habits.

Although instant coffee sales were declining worldwide due to the comeback of new-style automatic coffeemakers, they were rising in two tea-drinking countries, Britain and Japan. In Britain, Nescafé was promoted extensively to build a bigger base of instant coffee drinkers. In Japan, where Nescafé was considered a luxury item, the company made its Japanese blends available in fancy containers suitable for gift giving. In 1993 Nestlé began introducing Nescafé instant coffee and Coffee-Mate creamer in several large cities in China.

Sources: Shawn Tully, "Nestlé Shows How to Gobble Markets," *Fortune,* January 16, 1989, pp. 74–78; "Nestlé: A Giant in a Hurry," *Business Week,* March 22, 1993, pp. 50–54; and company annual reports.

---

advantage over other international competitors and the domestic companies of host countries. A global strategy, because it is more uniform from country to country, can concentrate on securing a sustainable low-cost or differentiation-based competitive advantage over both international and domestic rivals. Whenever country-to-country differences are small enough to be accommodated within the framework of a global strategy, a global strategy is preferable to a multicountry strategy because of the value of uniting a company's competitive efforts worldwide to pursue lower cost or differentiation.

■ GLOBAL STRATEGY AND COMPETITIVE ADVANTAGE

A firm can gain competitive advantage (or offset domestic disadvantages) with a global strategy in two ways.[14] One involves a global competitor's ability to locate its activities (R&D, parts manufacture, assembly, distribution centers, sales and marketing, customer service centers) among nations to lower costs or achieve greater product differentiation. The second advantage is an enhanced ability to coordinate dispersed activities in ways that a domestic-only competitor cannot.

A global company can pursue sustainable competitive advantage by coordinating its strategic actions worldwide and locating activities in the most advantageous nations; a domestic-only competitor forfeits such opportunities.

LOCATING ACTIVITIES

To use location to build competitive advantage, a global firm must consider two issues: (1) whether to concentrate its activities in one or two countries or disperse them more broadly and (2) in which countries to locate particular activities. Activities tend to be concentrated in one or two locations when there are significant economies of scale to performing that activity, when there are advantages in locating related activities in the same area to achieve better coordination, and when there is a steep learning or experience curve associated with performing the activity. Thus, in some industries scale economies in parts manufacture or assembly are so great that a company establishes one large plant from which it serves the world market. Where just-in-time inventory practices yield big cost-savings and/or where an assembly plant has partnering arrangements with large suppliers, parts manufacturing plants may be clustered around final assembly plants.

Dispersing activities is more advantageous than concentrating activities in several instances. Buyer-related activities—such as distribution to dealers, sales and advertising, and after-sale service—usually are best undertaken near the customer. This means physically locating the capability to perform these activities in every country market where a global firm has major customers (unless buyers in several adjoining countries can be served quickly from a nearby central location). For example, firms that make mining and oil-drilling equipment maintain operations in many international locations to support customers' needs for speedy equipment repair and technical assistance. Large public accounting firms have numerous international offices to service the foreign operations of their multinational corporate clients. A global competitor that effectively disperses its buyer-related activities can gain a service-based competitive edge in world markets over rivals whose buyer-related activities are more concentrated. This is one reason the Big Six public accounting firms have been so successful relative to second-tier firms. Dispersing activities to many locations is also competitively advantageous when high transportation costs, diseconomies of scale, and trade barriers make it too expensive to operate from a central location. Many companies operate geographically scattered distribution centers out of the need to shorten delivery times to customers or quickly replenish stocks in their own retail outlets. In addition, it is strategically advantageous to disperse activities to hedge against the risks of fluctuating exchange rates, supply interruptions (due to strikes, mechanical failures, and transportation delays), and adverse political developments. Such risks are greater when activities are concentrated in a single location.

The classic reason for locating an activity in a particular country is to lower costs.[15] Even though a global firm has strong reason to disperse buyer-related activities to many international locations regardless of cost incentives, such activities as materials procurement, parts manufacture, technology research, finished goods assembly, and new product development can frequently be decoupled from buyer locations and performed wherever cost advantage lies. Components can be made in Mexico, technology research done in Frankfurt, new products developed and tested in Phoenix, and assembly plants located in Spain, Brazil, Taiwan, and South Carolina. Capital can be raised in whatever country it is available for the best terms.

Low cost is not the only locational consideration, however. A research unit may be located in a particular nation because of its pool of technically trained personnel. A customer service center or sales office may be located in a particular country to help develop strong relationships with pivotal customers. An assembly plant may be located in a country in return for the host government's allowing freer import of components from large-scale, centralized component plants located elsewhere.

COORDINATING ACTIVITIES AND STRATEGIC MOVES

Aligning and coordinating company activities located in different countries contribute to sustainable competitive advantage in several different ways. If a firm learns how to assemble its product more efficiently at its Brazilian plant, the accumulated knowledge and expertise can be transferred to its assembly plant in Spain. Knowledge gained in marketing a company's product in Great Britain can be used to introduce the product in New Zealand and Australia. A company can shift production from one country location to another to take advantage of exchange rate fluctuations, to enhance its leverage with host country governments, and to respond to changing wage rates, energy costs, or trade restrictions. A company can enhance its brand reputation by consistently positioning its products with the same differentiating attributes on a worldwide basis. The reputation for quality that Honda established worldwide, first in motorcycles and then in automobiles, gave it competitive advantage in positioning Honda lawnmowers at the upper end of the market—the Honda name gave the company instant credibility with buyers.

A global competitor can choose where and how to challenge rivals. It may decide to retaliate against aggressive rivals in the country market where the rival has its biggest sales volume or its best profit margins in order to reduce the rival's financial resources for competing in other country markets. It may decide to wage a price-cutting offensive against weak rivals in their home markets, capturing greater market share and subsidizing any short-term losses with profits earned in other country markets.

A company which competes only in its home country has access to none of the competitive advantage opportunities associated with international locations or coordination. By shifting from a domestic strategy to a global strategy, a domestic company that finds itself at a competitive disadvantage to global companies can begin to restore its competitiveness.

■ STRATEGIC ALLIANCES

Strategic alliances are cooperative agreements between firms that go beyond normal company-to-company dealings but that fall short of merger or full partnership.[16] An alliance can involve joint research efforts, technology sharing, joint use of production facilities, marketing one another's products, or joining forces to manufacture components or assemble finished products. Strategic alliances are a means for firms in the same industry yet based in different countries to compete on a more global scale while still preserving their independence. Historically, export-minded firms in industrialized nations sought alliances with firms in less-developed countries to import and market their products locally—such arrangements were often necessary to gain access to the less-developed country's market. More recently, leading companies from different parts of the world have formed strategic alliances to strengthen their mutual ability to serve whole continental areas and move towards more global market participation. Both Japanese and American companies have been active in forming alliances with European companies to strengthen their ability to compete in the 12-nation European Community and to capitalize on the opening up of Eastern European markets. Illustration 18 describes Toshiba's successful use of strategic alliances.

> Strategic alliances can help companies in global markets strengthen their competitive positions while preserving their independence.

| ILLUSTRATION 18 | *Toshiba's Use of Strategic Alliances and Joint Ventures* |

Toshiba, Japan's oldest and third largest electronics company (after Hitachi and Matsushita), over the years has made technology licensing agreements, joint ventures, and strategic alliances a cornerstone of its corporate strategy. Using such partnerships to complement its own manufacturing and product innovation capabilities, it has become a $37 billion maker of electrical and electronics products—from home appliances to computer memory chips to telecommunication equipment to electric power generation equipment.

Fumio Sato, Toshiba's CEO, contends that joint ventures and strategic alliances are a necessary component of strategy for a high-tech electronics company with global ambitions:

> It is no longer an era in which a single company can dominate any technology or business by itself. The technology has become so advanced, and the markets so complex, that you simply can't expect to be the best at the whole process any longer.

Among Toshiba's two dozen major joint ventures and strategic alliances are:

- A five-year old joint venture with Motorola to design and make dynamic random access memory chips (DRAMs) for Toshiba and microprocessors for Motorola. Initially the two partners invested $125 million apiece in the venture and have since invested another $480 million each.
- A joint venture with IBM to make flat-panel liquid crystal displays in color for portable computers.
- Two other joint ventures with IBM to develop computer memory chips (one a "flash" memory chip that remembers data even after the power is turned off).
- An alliance with Sweden-based Ericsson, one of the world's biggest telecommunications manufacturers, to develop new mobile telecommunications equipment.
- A partnership with Sun Microsystems, the leading maker of microprocessor-based workstations, to provide portable versions of the workstations to Sun and to incorporate Sun's equipment in Toshiba products to control power plants, route highway traffic, and monitor automated manufacturing processes.
- A $1 billion strategic alliance with IBM and Siemens to develop and produce the next-generation DRAM—a single ship capable of holding 256 million bits of information (approximately 8,000 typewritten pages).
- An alliance with Apple Computer to develop CD-ROM-based multimedia players that plug into a TV set.
- A joint project with the entertainment division of Time Warner to design advanced interactive cable television technology.

Other alliances and joint ventures, with General Electric, United Technologies, National Semiconductor, Samsung (Korea), LSI Logic (Canada), and with European companies like Olivetti, SCS-Thomson, Rhone-Poulenc, Thomson Consumer Electronics, and GEC Alstholm, are turning out such products as fax machines, copiers, medical equipment, computers, rechargeable batteries, home appliances, and nuclear and steam power generating equipment.

So far, none of Toshiba's relationships with partners have gone sour despite potential conflicts among related projects with competitors (Toshiba has partnerships with nine other chip-makers to develop or produce semiconductors). Toshiba attributes this to its approach to alliances: choosing partners carefully, being very open about Toshiba's connections with other companies, carefully defining the role and rights of each partner in the original pact (including who get what if the alliance doesn't work out), and cultivating easy relations and good friendships with each partner. Toshiba's management believes that strategic alliances and joint ventures have been an effective way for the company to move into new businesses quickly, share the design and development costs of ambitious new products with competent partners, and achieve greater access to important geographic markets outside Japan.

Source: Based on Brenton R Schlender, "How Toshiba Makes Alliances Work," *Fortune*, October 4, 1993, pp. 116–20.

Companies enter into alliances for several strategically beneficial reasons.[17] The three most important are to gain economies of scale in production and/or marketing, to fill gaps in their technical and manufacturing expertise, and to acquire market access. By joining forces in producing components, assembling models, and marketing their products, companies can realize cost savings not achievable with their own smaller volumes. Allies learn much from one another in performing joint research, sharing technology, and studying one another's manufacturing methods. Alliances are often used by outsiders to meet governmental requirements for local ownership, and allies can share distribution facilities and dealer networks, thus mutually strengthening their access to buyers. In addition, alliances affect competition; not only can alliances offset competitive disadvantages, but they also can result in the allied companies' directing their competitive energies more toward mutual rivals and less toward one another. Many runner-up companies, wanting to preserve their independence, have resorted to alliances rather than mergers to try to close the competitive gap on leading companies.

Alliances have their pitfalls, however. Achieving effective coordination between independent companies, each with different motives and perhaps conflicting objectives, is a challenging task. It requires many meetings of many people to resolve what is to be shared, what is to remain proprietary, and how the cooperative arrangements will work. The transactions costs are high. Allies may have to overcome language and cultural barriers as well. Often, after the honeymoon period is past, partners discover they have deep differences about how to proceed and conflicting objectives and strategies. Tensions build, working relationships cool, and the hoped-for benefits never materialize.[18] Allies often have difficulty collaborating effectively in competitively sensitive areas, thus raising questions about mutual trust and forthright exchanges of information and expertise. Also, egos clash, as do company cultures, and the key people—on whom success or failure depends—may be unable to work closely together as partners or arrive at consensus on implementation and joint operations.

Most important, though, is the danger of depending on another company for essential expertise and capabilities over the long term. To be a serious market contender, a company must ultimately develop internal capabilities to strengthen its competitive position and build a sustainable competitive advantage. Where this is not feasible, merger is a better solution than strategic alliance. Strategic alliances are best used as a transient means to combat competitive disadvantage in international markets; rarely if ever can they be relied upon to create competitive advantage. Illustration 19 relates the experiences of companies with strategic alliances.

> Strategic alliances are more effective in combating competitive disadvantage than in gaining competitive advantage.

To realize the most from a strategic alliance, companies should observe five guidelines:[19]

- Pick a compatible partner; take the time to build strong communication and trust and don't expect immediate payoffs.

- Choose an ally whose products and markets *complement,* rather than compete with, the company's own products and customer base.

ILLUSTRATION 19   *Company Experiences With Strategic Alliances*

As the chairman of British Aerospace recently observed, a strategic alliance with a foreign company is "one of the quickest and cheapest ways to develop a global strategy." AT&T has formed joint ventures with many of the world's largest telephone and electronics companies. Boeing, the world's premier manufacturer of commercial aircraft, has partnered with Kawasaki, Mitsubishi, and Fuji to produce a long-range, wide-body jet for delivery in 1995. General Electric and Snecma, a French maker of jet engines, have a 50–50 partnership to make jet engines to power aircraft made by Boeing, McDonnell-Douglas, and Airbus Industrie (the leading European maker of commercial aircraft and a company that was formed through an alliance among aerospace from Britain, Spain, Germany, and France); this particular alliance was regarded as a model because not only had it been in existence for 17 years but it had also produced orders for 10,300 engines, totaling $38 billion.

Since the early 1980s, hundreds of strategic alliances have been formed in the motor vehicle industry as car and truck manufacturers and automotive parts suppliers moved aggressively to get in stronger position to compete globally. Not only have there been alliances between automakers strong in one region of the world and automakers strong in another region, but there have also been strategic alliances between vehicle-makers and key parts suppliers (especially those with high-quality parts and strong technological capabilities). General Motors and Toyota in 1984 formed a 50–50 partnership called New United Motor Manufacturing, Inc. (NUMMI), to produce cars for both companies at an old GM plant in Fremont, California. The strategic value of the GM–Toyota alliance was that Toyota would learn how to deal with suppliers and workers in the United States (as a prelude to building its own plants in the United States) while GM would learn about Toyota's approaches to manufacturing and management. Each company sent managers to the NUMMI plant to work for two or three years to learn and absorb all they could, then transferred their NUMMI graduates to jobs where they could be instrumental in helping their company apply what had been learned. Toyota moved quickly to capitalize on its experiences at NUMMI; by 1991 Toyota had opened two plants on its own in North America, was constructing a third plant, and was producing 50 percent of the vehicles it sold in North America in its North American plants. While General Motors had incorporated much of it NUMMI learning into the management practices and manufacturing methods it was using at its newly opened Saturn plant in Tennessee, it proceeded more slowly than Toyota. American and European companies are generally regarded as less skilled than the Japanese in transferring the learning from strategic alliances into their own operations.

Many alliances fail or are terminated when one partner ends up acquiring the other. A 1990 survey of 150 companies involved in terminated alliances found that three-fourths of the alliances had been taken over by Japanese partners. A nine-year alliance between Fujitsu and International Computers, Ltd. (ICL), a British manufacturer, ended when Fujitsu acquired 80 percent of ICL. According to one observer, Fujitsu deliberately maneuvered ICL into a position of having no better choice than to sell out to its partner; Fujitsu began as a supplier of components for ICL's mainframe computers, then expanded its role over the next nine years to the point where it was ICL's only source of new technology. When ICL's parent, a large British electronics firm, saw the mainframe computer business starting to decline and decided to sell, Fujitsu was the only buyer it could find.

Source: Adapted from Jeremy Main, "Making Global Alliances Work," *Fortune*, December 17, 1990, pp. 121–26.

- Learn thoroughly and rapidly about a partner's technology and management; transfer valuable ideas and practices into one's own operations promptly.
- Be careful not to divulge competitively sensitive information to a partner.
- View the alliance as temporary (5 to 10 years); continue the alliance if it's beneficial but don't hesitate to terminate it when that ceases to be the case.

■ STRATEGIC INTENT, PROFIT SANCTUARIES, AND CROSS-SUBSIDIZATION

Competitors in international markets can be distinguished not only by their strategies but also by their long-term objectives and strategic intent. Four types of competitors stand out:[20]

- Firms whose strategic intent is *global dominance* or, at least, high rank among the global market leaders; such firms pursue some form of global strategy.

- Firms whose primary strategic objective is *defending domestic dominance* in their home market, even though they may derive some of their sales internationally (usually under 20 percent) and have operations in other foreign markets.

- Firms that aspire to a growing share of worldwide sales and whose primary strategic orientation is *host country responsiveness;* such firms have a multicountry strategy and may already derive a large fraction of their revenues from foreign operations.

- *Domestic-only firms* whose strategic intent does not extend beyond building a strong competitive position in their home country market; such firms base their competitive strategies on domestic market conditions and watch events in the international market only for their domestic impact.

These types of firms are *not* equally well positioned to be successful in markets where they compete head on. Consider, the case of a purely domestic U.S. company competing against a Japanese company operating in many country markets and aspiring to global dominance. The Japanese company can cut its prices in the U.S. market to gain market share at the expense of the U.S. company, while subsidizing any losses with profits earned in its home sanctuary and in other foreign markets. The U.S. company has no effective way to retaliate. It is vulnerable even if it is the U.S. market leader. However, if the U.S. company is a multinational competitor and operates in Japan as well as elsewhere, it can counter Japanese pricing in the United States with retaliatory price cuts in its competitor's main profit sanctuary, Japan, and in other countries where it competes against the same Japanese company. This scenario can happen today with almost any domestic-only company in any country market with active multinational competitors.

Thus, a domestic-only competitor is not on a level playing field competing against a multinational rival. When aggressive global competitors enter a domestic-only company's market, one of the domestic-only competitor's best defenses is to switch to a multinational or global strategy to give it the same cross-subsidizing capabilities the aggressors have.

PROFIT SANCTUARIES AND CRITICAL MARKETS

Profit sanctuaries are country markets where a company has a strong or protected market position and derives substantial profits. Japan, for example, is a profit sanctuary for most Japanese companies because trade barriers and import restrictions erected around Japanese industries by the Japanese government effectively block foreign companies from competing for a large share of Japanese sales. Protected from the threat of foreign competition in their home market, Japanese companies have been able to charge higher prices to their Japanese customers and earned attractively large profits on sales made in Japan. In most cases, a company's biggest and

---

A particular nation is a company's *profit sanctuary* when the company derives a substantial amount of its total profits from sales in that nation.

most strategically crucial profit sanctuary is its home market. However, multinational companies also have profit sanctuaries in those country markets where they have strong competitive positions, big sales volumes, and attractive profit margins.

Profit sanctuaries are valuable competitive assets in global industries. Companies with large, protected profit sanctuaries have competitive advantage over companies that don't have a dependable sanctuary. Companies with multiple profit sanctuaries are more favorably positioned than companies with a single sanctuary. Normally, a global competitor with multiple profit sanctuaries can successfully outcompete a domestic competitor whose only profit sanctuary is its home market.

To defend against global competitors, companies don't have to compete in all or even most foreign markets, but they do have to compete in all critical markets; *critical markets* are markets in countries:

- That are the profit sanctuaries of key competitors.
- That have big sales volumes.
- That contain prestigious customers whose business it is strategically important to have.
- That offer exceptionally good profit margins due to weak competitive pressures.[21]

The more critical markets a company participates in, the greater its ability to use cross-subsidization as a defense against competitors intent on global dominance.

THE COMPETITIVE POWER OF CROSS-SUBSIDIZATION

Cross-subsidization is a powerful competitive weapon. It involves using profits earned in one or more country markets to support a competitive offensive against key rivals or to gain increased penetration of a critical market. A typical offensive involves matching (or nearly matching) rivals on product quality and service, then charging a low enough price to draw customers away from rivals. While price cutting may result in a company earning lower profits (or even incurring losses) in the critical market it is attacking, the challenger may still realize acceptable overall profits when the above-average earnings from its other profit sanctuaries are added in.

Cross-subsidization is most powerful when a global firm with multiple profit sanctuaries is aggressively intent on achieving global market dominance over the long term. Both a domestic-only competitor and a multicountry competitor having no strategic coordination between its locally responsive country strategies are vulnerable to competition from rivals intent on global dominance. A global strategy can defeat a domestic-only strategy because a one-country competitor cannot effectively defend its market share over the long term against a global competitor with cross-subsidization capability. The global competitor can use lower prices to siphon away the domestic company's customers, all the while gaining market share, building its name recognition, and supporting its offensive campaign with profits earned in its other critical markets. Furthermore, it can gauge the depth of its price cuts to move in and capture market share quickly, or it can price a shade under domestic

A competent global competitor with multiple profit sanctuaries can outcompete a domestic competitor whose only profit sanctuary is its home market.

firms to make gradual market inroads over a decade or more so as not to threaten domestic firms precipitiously and perhaps arouse protectionist government actions. A domestic company's best short-term hope is immediate and perhaps dramatic cost reduction, combined with government protection in the form of tariff barriers, import quotas, and antidumping penalties. In the long term, the domestic company has to find ways to compete on a more equal footing—a difficult challenge when it needs to charge a price to cover full unit costs while the global competitor can charge a price only high enough to cover the incremental costs of selling in the domestic company's profit sanctuary. The best long-term defenses for a domestic company are to enter into strategic alliances with foreign firms or adopt a global strategy and compete on an international scale. Occasionally, it is possible to drive enough costs out of the business over the long term to survive with a domestic-only strategy. As a rule, however, competing only domestically is a perilous strategy in an industry populated with global competitors.

While a company with a multicountry strategy has some cross-subsidy defense against a company with a global strategy, its vulnerability comes from a lack of competitive advantage and a probable cost disadvantage. A global competitor with a large manufacturing share and state-of-the-art plants is almost certain to be a lower-cost producer than a multicountry strategist with many small plants and short production runs turning out specialized products country by country. Companies pursuing a multicountry strategy thus need differentiation and focus-based advantages keyed to local responsiveness to defend against a global competitor. Such a defense is adequate in industries with national differences significant enough to impede a global strategy. But if an international rival can accommodate necessary local needs within a global strategy and still retain a cost edge, then a global strategy can defeat a multicountry strategy.

► STRATEGIES FOR INDUSTRY LEADERS

Industry leaders typically enjoy a well-known reputation, and often possess proven strategies (keyed either to low-cost leadership or to differentiation). Some of the best-known industry leaders are Anheuser-Busch (beer), IBM (mainframe computers), McDonald's (fast food), Gillette (razor blades), Campbell's Soup (canned soups), Gerber (baby food), AT&T (long-distance telephone service), Eastman Kodak (camera film), and Levi Strauss (jeans). Sustaining leadership or perhaps becoming *the dominant leader* as opposed to *a leader* are the most significant concerns of industry leaders. However, the pursuit of industry leadership and large market share per se is important primarily because of the competitive advantage and profitability that accrues to being the industry's biggest company.

Three contrasting strategic postures are open to industry leaders and dominant firms:[22]

1. *Stay-on-the-offensive strategy*—This strategy relies on the principle that the best defense is a good offense. Offensive-minded leaders stress being ''first-movers,'' to sustain their competitive advantage (lower cost or differentiation) and reinforce their reputation as *the* leader. A low-cost provider aggressively pursues cost reduction and a differentiator consistently tries new ways to set its product apart from rivals' brands. The theme of a stay-on-the-offensive strategy is relentless pursuit of continuous improvement and innovation. Striving to be first—with new products, better

performance features, quality enhancements, improved customer services, or ways to cut production costs—not only helps a leader avoid complacency but it also keeps rivals on the defensive and scrambling to keep up. The array of offensive options can also include initiatives to expand overall industry demand—discovering new uses for the product, attracting new users to the product, and promoting more frequent use of the product. Offensive leaders can also look for ways to make it easier and less costly for potential customers to switch to their products. Unless a leader's market share is already so dominant that it presents a threat of antitrust action (a market share under 60 percent is usually safe), then a stay-on-the-offensive strategy involves trying to grow *faster* than the industry as a whole and wrest market share from rivals. A leader whose growth does not equal or outpace the industry average is losing ground to competitors.

2. *Fortify-and defend strategy*—The essence of fortify and defend is to make it more difficult for new firms to enter the market and for challengers to gain market share. The goals of a strong defense are to hold onto the firm's present market share, strengthen its current market position, and protect the firm's competitive advantage. Specific defensive actions can include:
   - Attempting to raise the competitive ante for challengers and new entrants via increased spending for advertising, customer service, and R&D.
   - Introducing more of the company's own brands to match the product attributes that challenger brands have or could incorporate.
   - Providing new value-added services and other extras that boost customer loyalty and make it harder or more costly for customers to switch to rival products.
   - Broadening the product line to close off possible vacant niches for competitors to slip into.
   - Keeping prices reasonable and quality attractive.
   - Building new capacity ahead of market demand to try to block the market expansion potential of smaller competitors.
   - Patenting the feasible alternative technologies.
   - Signing exclusive contracts with the best suppliers and dealer/distributors.

   A fortify-and-defend strategy best suits firms that have already achieved industry dominance and don't wish to risk antitrust action. It is also a good strategy for increasing profits and cash flow when the industry's prospects for growth are low or when further gains in market share do not appear profitable to pursue. The fortify-and-defend theme always entails trying to grow as fast as the market as a whole (to stave off market share slippage) and reinvesting enough capital in the business to protect the leader's ability to compete.

3. *Follow-the-leader strategy*—Here the leader's strategic posture encourages runner-up firms to be content followers rather than aggressive challengers. Specific actions to meet competitive threats can include matching or exceeding challengers' price cuts, using large-scale promotional campaigns to counter challengers' moves to gain market share, and offering better deals to the major customers of maverick firms. Leaders can also court distributors assiduously to dissuade them of the need to carry rivals' products, provide salespersons with documented information about the

weaknesses of aggressor's products, or try to fill vacant positions by making attractive offers to the better executives of encroaching rivals. When a leader consistently meets competition with strong retaliatory tactics, it sends clear signals that offensive attacks on the leader's position will be met and probably won't pay off. However, leaders pursuing this strategic approach should choose their battles carefully. It may be more strategically productive to assume a hands-off posture and not respond when smaller rivals attack each others' customer base.

▶ STRATEGIES FOR RUNNER-UP FIRMS

Runner-up firms occupy weaker market positions than industry leaders. Some runner-up firms are *market challengers* employing offensive strategies to gain market share and a stronger market position. Others are *content followers,* comfortable in their current position because profits are adequate. Follower

---
Rarely can a runner-up firm successfully challenge an industry leader by imitating its strategy.

---

firms have no urgent strategic issue to confront beyond maintaining their strategies by matching industry leader changes appropriately.

Any firm interested in improving its market standing needs a strategy aimed at building a competitive advantage all its own. Rarely can a runner-up firm improve its competitive position by imitating the strategies of leading firms. A cardinal rule in offensive strategy is to avoid challenging a leader head-on with an imitative strategy, regardless of the resources and staying power of the challenger.[23] Moreover, if a challenger has a 5 percent market share and needs a 20 percent share to earn attractive returns, it needs a more creative approach to competing than just "try harder."

In industries where large size yields significantly lower unit costs and thus gives large-share competitors an important cost advantage, small-share firms have only two viable strategic options: try to increase market share to achieve cost parity with their larger rivals, or withdraw from the business. The competitive strategies most underdogs use to build market share are based on (1) becoming a lower-cost producer and using the appeal of a lower price to win customers from weak, higher-cost rivals, and (2) using differentiation strategies based on quality, technological superiority, better customer service, best-cost, or innovation. Achieving low-cost leadership is usually open to a runner-up company only when one of the market leaders is not already solidly positioned as the industry's low-cost producer. But a small-share competitor may still be able to reduce its cost disadvantage by acquiring or merging with smaller firms; the combined market shares may provide the needed access to size-related economies. Other options include revamping its value chain to produce the needed cost savings and finding ways to better manage executional cost drivers.

In situations where scale economies or experience curve effects are small and a large market share produces no cost advantage, runner-up companies have more strategic flexibility and can consider any of the following six approaches:[24]

1. *Vacant niche strategy*—This version of a focus strategy concentrates on customer or end-use applications that market leaders have bypassed or neglected. An ideal vacant niche is sufficiently large to be profitable, has some growth potential, is well-suited

to a firm's own capabilities and skills, and is outside the interest of leading firms. Two examples where vacant-niche strategies have worked successfully are regional commuter airlines serving cities with too few passengers to attract the interest of major airlines and organic foods producers (like Health Valley, Hain, and Tree of Life) that cater to organic foods customers—a market segment traditionally ignored by Pillsbury, Kraft General Foods, Heinz, Nabisco, Campbell Soup, and other leading food products firms.

2. *Specialist strategy*—A specialist firm focuses its competitive efforts on one market segment: a single product, a particular end-use, or a customer group with special needs. The aim is to build competitive advantage through expertise in special purpose products or specialized customer services. Smaller companies that have successfully used a specialist-focus strategy include Formby's (a specialist in stains and finishes for wood furniture, especially refinishing), Liquid Paper Co. (a leader in correction fluid for typists), Canada Dry (known for its ginger ale, tonic water, and carbonated soda water), and American Tobacco (a leader in chewing tobacco and snuff).

3. *Ours is-better-than-theirs strategy*—The approach here is to use a differentiation-based focus strategy keyed to superior quality or unique attributes. Sales and marketing efforts are aimed directly at quality-conscious and performance-oriented buyers. Fine craftsmanship, prestige, frequent product innovations, and/or close contact with customers to develop a better product usually undergird this approach. Some examples include Beefeater and Tanquerary in gin, Tiffany in diamonds and jewelry, Chicago Cutlery in premium-quality kitchen knives, Baccarat in fine crystal, Cannondale in mountain bikes, Bally in shoes, and Patagonia in apparel for outdoor recreation enthusiasts.

4. *Satisfied-follower strategy*—Follower firms deliberately refrain from initiating trend-setting strategic moves and from aggressive attempts to build market share at the expense of the leader's market share. Followers prefer approaches that will not provoke competitive retaliation, often opting for focus and differentiation strategies that keep them out of the leaders' paths. They react and respond rather than initiate and challenge. They prefer defense to offense. And they rarely get out of line with the leaders on price. Union Camp (in paper products) has been a successful market follower by consciously concentrating on selected product uses and applications for specific customer groups, focused R&D, profits rather than market share, and cautious but efficient management.

5. *Growth-through-acquisition strategy*—One way to strengthen a company's position is to merge with or acquire weaker firms to form a stronger enterprise with a larger share of the market. Commercial airline companies such as Northwest, USAir, and Delta owe their market share growth during the past decade to acquisition of smaller regional airlines. Similarly, the Big Six public accounting firms have enhanced their national and international coverage by merging or forming alliances with other CPA firms at home and abroad.

6. *Distinctive-image strategy*—Some runner-up companies build their strategies by making themselves stand out from competitors. A variety of strategic approaches can be used: creating a reputation for charging the lowest prices, providing prestige

quality at a good price, extensive and superior customer service, distinct product attributes, new product introduction, or creative advertising. Examples include Dr. Pepper's strategy of calling attention to its distinctive taste, Apple Computer's approach to user-friendly personal computing, and Honda's emphasis on the quality and dependability of its cars.

In industries where size is a significant success factor, firms with low market shares have some formidable obstacles to overcome: (1) less access to economies of scale in manufacturing, distribution, or sales promotion; (2) difficulty in gaining customer recognition; (3) an inability to afford comprehensive mass media advertising campaigns; and (4) difficulty in funding capital requirements.[25] But *it is erroneous to view runner-up firms as inherently less profitable or unable to hold their own against the largest firms.* Many smaller firms earn healthy profits and enjoy good reputations with customers. Often, the handicaps of smaller size can be surmounted and a profitable competitive position established by (1) focusing on a few market segments where the company's strengths can yield a competitive edge, (2) developing technical expertise that will be highly valued by customers, (3) aggressively pursuing the development of new products for customers in the target market segments, and (4) using innovative entrepreneurial approaches to outmanage stodgy, slow-to-change market leaders. Runner-up companies have a good opportunity to gain market share and industry prominence if they make a leapfrog technological breakthrough, if leaders stumble or become complacent, or if they have the patience to nibble away at the leaders and build up their own customer base over a long period of time.

▶ STRATEGIES FOR WEAK BUSINESSES

A firm in an also-ran or declining competitive position has four basic strategic options. If it has the financial resources, it can launch an *offensive turnaround strategy,* keyed either to low-cost or new differentiation themes, and spend enough money and talent to move up in the industry and become a respectable market contender within five years or so. It can employ a *fortify-and-defend* strategy, using variations of its present strategy and fighting to keep sales, market share, profitability, and competitive position at current levels. It can opt for an *immediate abandonment* strategy and get out of the business, either by selling out to another firm or by closing down operations if a buyer can not be found. It can also employ a *harvest strategy,* keeping reinvestment to a minimum and taking actions to maximize short-term cash flows in preparation for an orderly market exit. The gist of the first three options is self-explanatory. The fourth merits more discussion.

The strategic options for a competitively weak company include waging a modest offensive to improve its position, defending its present position, being acquired by another company, or harvesting.

A *harvest strategy* steers a middle course between preserving the status quo and a speedy exit from the market. Harvesting is a phasing down or endgame strategy that involves sacrificing market position in return for improved cash flows or short-term profitability. The overriding financial objective is to reap the greatest possible amount of cash and use that cash to fund other business endeavors.

A harvesting operation is fairly straightforward. The operating budget is steadily cut; reinvestment in the business is minimized. Capital expenditures for new equipment are put on hold or given low financial priority (unless replacement needs are unusually urgent); instead, efforts are made to stretch the life of existing equipment and make do with present facilities as long as possible. Price may be raised gradually, promotional expenses slowly cut, quality reduced in not so visible ways, nonessential customer services curtailed, and the like. Although harvesting results in shrinking sales and market share, if cash expenses can be cut even faster, then after-tax cash flows may rise (at least temporarily) and the company's profits will erode slowly rather than rapidly.

Harvesting is a reasonable strategic option for a weak business in the following circumstances:[26]

1. When the industry's long-term prospects are unattractive.
2. When rejuvenating the business would be too costly or at best marginally profitable.
3. When the firm's market share is becoming increasingly costly to maintain or defend.
4. When reduced levels of competitive effort will not trigger an immediate or rapid falloff in sales.
5. When the enterprise can redeploy the freed resources in higher opportunity areas.
6. When the business is *not* a crucial component of a diversified company's portfolio of business interests (harvesting a noncore business is strategically preferable to harvesting a core business).
7. When the business does not contribute other desired features, such as sales stability, prestige, or a well-rounded product line, to a company's overall business portfolio.

The more of these seven conditions that are present, the more ideal the business is for harvesting.

Harvesting strategies make the most sense for diversified companies that have sideline or noncore business units in weak competitive positions or in unattractive industries. Such companies can take the cash flows from these business units and reallocate them to business units with greater profit potential or to financing the acquisition of new businesses.

■ TURNAROUND STRATEGIES FOR BUSINESSES IN CRISIS

Turnaround strategies are needed when a business worth rescuing goes into crisis. The objective is to arrest and reverse the sources of competitive and financial weakness as quickly as possible. Management's first task in formulating a suitable turnaround strategy is to diagnose what lies at the root of poor performance. Is it an unexpected downturn in sales brought on by a weak economy? An ill-chosen competitive strategy? Poor execution of an otherwise workable strategy? An overload of debt? Can the business be saved or is the situation hopeless? Understanding accurately what is wrong with the business and the seriousness of its strategic problems is essential because different diagnoses lead to different turnaround strategies.

Some of the most common causes of business trouble are taking on too much debt, overestimating the potential for sales growth, ignoring the profit-depressing effects of an overly aggressive effort to buy market share with deep price cuts, being burdened with heavy fixed costs because of an inability to utilize plant capacity, betting on R&D efforts to boost competitive position and profitability and failing to come up with effective innovations, betting on technological long-shots, being too optimistic about the ability to penetrate new markets, making frequent changes in strategy (because the previous strategy didn't work out), and being overpowered by the competitive advantages enjoyed by more successful rivals. Curing these kinds of problems and achieving a successful business turnaround can involve any of the following actions:

- Revising the existing strategy.
- Launching efforts to boost revenues.
- Pursuing cost reduction.
- Selling off assets to raise cash to save the remaining part of the business.
- Any combination of the above.

STRATEGY REVISION

When weak performance is caused by poor strategy, overhauling that strategy can proceed along any of several paths: (1) shifting to a new competitive approach to rebuild the firm's market position, (2) changing internal operations and functional area strategies to better support the same overall business strategy, (3) merging with another firm in the industry and forging a new strategy incorporating the newly merged firm's strengths, and (4) retrenching into a reduced core of products and customers more closely matched to the firm's strengths. The most appealing path depends on prevailing industry conditions, the firm's particular strengths and weaknesses, its competitive capabilities vis-a-vis rival firms, and the severity of the crisis. A situation analysis of the industry, major competitors, the firm's own competitive position, and its skills and resources are prerequisites to action. As a rule, successful strategy revision must be tied to the ailing firm's strengths and near-term competitive capabilities and directed at its best market opportunities.

BOOSTING REVENUES

Revenue-increasing turnaround efforts aim at generating increased sales volume. There are a number of revenue-building options: price cuts, increased promotion, a larger sales force, added customer services, and quickly achieved product improvements. Attempts to increase revenues and sales volumes are necessary (1) when there is little or no room in the operating budget to cut expenses and still break even and (2) when the key to restoring profitability is increased utilization of existing capacity. If buyer demand is not especially price-sensitive because of differentiating features, the quickest way to boost short-term revenues may be to raise prices, rather than opt for volume-building price cuts.

CUTTING COSTS

Cost-reducing turnaround strategies work best when an ailing firm's value chain and cost structure are flexible enough to permit radical surgery, when operating inefficiencies are identifiable and readily correctable, and when costs are obviously bloated and savings can be quickly achieved in several places. It also helps if the firm is relatively close to its break-even point. Accompanying a general belt tightening can be an increased emphasis on paring administrative overhead, eliminating low value-added or nonessential activities, modernizing existing plant and equipment for greater productivity, delaying nonessential capital expenditures, and debt restructuring to reduce interest costs and stretch out repayments.

SELLING OFF ASSETS

Assets reduction/retrenchment strategies are essential when cash flow is critical and when the most practical way to generate cash is (1) through sale of some of the firm's assets such as plant and equipment, land, patents, inventories, or profitable subsidiaries, and (2) through retrenchment—pruning of marginal products from the product line, closing or selling older plants, reducing the workforce, withdrawing from outlying markets, and cutting back customer service. Sometimes crisis-ridden companies sell off assets not so much to unload losing operations and stem cash drains as to raise funds to save and strengthen the remaining activities. In such cases, the choice is usually to dispose of noncore business assets to support strategy renewal in the firm's core business(es).

COMBINATION EFFORTS

Combination turnaround strategies are usually essential in grim situations that require fast action on a broad front. Likewise, combination actions are frequently used when new managers are brought in to make whatever changes they see fit. The tougher the problems, the more likely the solutions will involve multiple strategic initiatives.

Turnaround efforts tend to be high-risk undertakings and often fail. A landmark study of 64 companies found no successful turnarounds among the most troubled companies in eight basic industries.[27] Many waited too long to begin a turnaround. Others found themselves short of both cash and entrepreneurial talent to compete in a slow-growth industry characterized by a fierce battle for market share; better positioned rivals simply proved too strong to defeat. Many troubled companies go through a series of aborted or failed turnaround attempts and management changes before long-term competitive viability and profitability is finally restored.

■ THIRTEEN COMMANDMENTS FOR CRAFTING SUCCESSFUL BUSINESS STRATEGIES

Business experiences through the years prove over and over that disastrous strategies can be avoided by adhering to certain principles. The wisdom of these past experiences can be distilled into 13 commandments that, if faithfully observed, help strategists craft better action plans.

1. *Place top priority on crafting and executing strategic moves that enhance the company's competitive position for the long term.* An ever-stronger competitive position pays off year after year, but the glory of meeting one quarter's and one year's financial performance targets quickly passes. Shareholders are never well-served by managers who let short-term financial performance considerations rule out strategic initiatives that will significantly bolster the company's long-term competitive position and competitive strength. The best way to protect a company's long-term profitability is with a strategy that strengthens the company's long-term competitiveness.

2. *Understand that a clear, consistent competitive strategy, when well crafted and well executed, builds reputation and recognizable industry position; a frequently changed strategy aimed at capturing momentary market opportunities yields fleeting benefits.*

The pursuit of short-run financial opportunism, absent any long-term strategic consistency, tends to produce the worst kind of profits: one-shot rewards that are unrepeatable. A company that has a well-conceived, consistent competitive strategy aimed at securing a strong market position will outperform and defeat a rival whose main desire is to meet Wall Street's short-term expectations. In an ongoing enterprise, the game of competition ought to be played for the long term, not the short term.

3. *Avoid stuck-in-the-middle strategies that represent compromises between achieving lower costs or achieving greater differentiation and between broad-versus-narrow market appeal.* Compromise strategies rarely produce sustainable competitive advantage or a distinct competitive position—well-executed best-cost producer strategies are the only exception where a compromise between low cost and differentiation succeeds. Usually, companies with compromise or middle-of-the-road strategies end up with average costs, average differentiation, an average image and reputation, a middle-of-the-pack industry ranking, and little prospect of becoming an industry leader.

4. *Invest in creating a sustainable competitive advantage*—it is the single most dependable contributor to above-average profitability.

5. *Play aggressive offense to build competitive advantage and aggressive defense to protect it.*

6. *Avoid strategies capable of succeeding only in the most optimistic circumstances*—there is every reason to expect competitors to employ countermeasures and, besides, there are always times when market conditions are unfavorable.

7. *Be cautious in pursuing a rigid or inflexible strategy that locks the company in for the long-term with little room to maneuver—inflexible strategies can be made obsolete by changing market conditions.* Strategies to achieve top quality or lowest cost should be interpreted as *relative to competitors* and/or customer needs rather than based on arbitrary management absolutes. While long-term strategic consistency is usually a virtue, strategic absolutes and constants are usually flaws.

8. *Don't underestimate the reactions and the commitment of rival firms*—especially when they are pushed into a corner and their well-being is threatened.

9. *Be wary of attacking strong, resourceful rivals without solid competitive advantage and ample financial strength.*

10. *Attacking competitive weakness is usually more profitable than attacking competitive strength.*

11. *Be judicious in cutting prices without an established cost advantage*—only a low-cost producer can win at price cutting over the long term.

12. *Be aware that aggressive moves to wrest market share away from rivals often provoke aggressive retaliation in the form of a marketing "arms race" and/or price wars*—to the detriment of everyone's profits. Aggressive moves to capture a bigger market share invite cutthroat competition particularly when the market is plagued with high inventories and excess production capacity.

TABLE 6-2   *Sample Worksheet for a Strategic Action Plan*

---

1. Strategic vision and mission

2. Strategic objectives:
   • Short term

   • Long term

3. Financial objectives:
   • Short term

   • Long term

4. Overall business strategy

5. Supporting functional strategies:
   • Production

   • Marketing/sales

   • Finance

   • Personnel/human resources

   • Other

6. Recommended actions:
   • Immediate

   • Longer-range

---

13. *Strive to open up conspicuous gaps in quality or service or performance features when pursuing a differentiation strategy*—tiny differences between rivals' product offerings may not be visible or important to buyers.

Table 6–2 provides an easily used format for covering all the bases in a strategic plan for a single-business enterprise.

Corporate Diversification Strategies

To acquire or not to acquire: that is the question.

Robert J. Terry

Strategy is a deliberate search for a plan of action that will develop a business's competitive advantage and compound it.

Bruce D. Henderson

In this chapter and the next, we move up one level in the strategy-making hierarchy as we shift attention from formulating strategy for a single-business enterprise to formulating strategy for a diversified enterprise. Because a diversified company is a collection of individual businesses, corporate strategy making is a bigger-picture exercise than crafting line-of-business strategy. In a single-business enterprise, management has to contend with only one industry cnvironment and how to compete successfully in it. But in a diversified company corporate managers have to craft a multibusiness, multi-industry strategic action plan for a number of different business divisions competing in diverse industry environments.

As explained in Chapter 2, the task of crafting corporate strategy for a diversified company involves:

1. Deciding on moves to position the company in the industries chosen for diversification. The basic strategic options for such positioning are to acquire a company in the target industry, form a joint venture with another company to enter the target industry, or start a new company internally and try to grow it from the ground up.

2. Devising actions to improve the long-term performance of the corporation's portfolio of businesses once diversification has been achieved. This can involve strengthening the competitive positions of existing businesses, divesting businesses that no longer fit into management's long-range plans, and adding new businesses to the portfolio.

3. Capturing whatever strategic fit benefits exist within the portfolio of businesses and then turning them into competitive advantages.

4. Evaluating the profit prospects of each business unit and steering corporate resources into the most attractive strategic opportunities.

These tasks are sufficiently time-consuming and demanding that corporate-level decision-makers generally refrain from becoming immersed in the details of crafting and implementing business-level strategies, preferring instead to delegate lead responsibility for business-level strategy making to the head of each business unit.

In this chapter we survey the generic types of corporate diversification strategies and describe how a company can use diversification to create or compound competitive advantage for its business units. In Chapter 8 we will examine the techniques and procedures for assessing the strategic attractiveness of a diversified company's business portfolio.

▶ FROM SINGLE-BUSINESS CONCENTRATION TO DIVERSIFICATION

Most companies begin as small single-business enterprises serving a local or regional market. During a company's early years, its product line tends to be limited, its capital base thin, and its competitive position vulnerable. Usually, a young company's strategic emphasis is on increasing sales volume, boosting market share, and cultivating a loyal clientele. Profits are reinvested, and new debt is taken on to grow the business as fast as conditions permit. Price, quality, service, and promotion are tailored more precisely to customer needs. As soon as practical, the product line is broadened to meet variations in customer wants and capture sales for related end-use applications.

Opportunities for geographical market expansion are normally pursued next. The natural sequence of geographic market expansion proceeds from local to regional to national to international, though the degree of penetration may be uneven from area to area because of varying profit potentials. Geographic expansion may, of course, stop well short of global or even national proportions because of intense competition, lack of resources, or the unattractiveness of further market coverage.

Somewhere along the way the potential of vertical integration, either backward to sources of supply or forward to the ultimate consumer, may become a strategic consideration. Generally, vertical integration makes sense only if it significantly enhances a company's profitability and competitive strength.

So long as the company's energies are absorbed trying to capitalize on profitable growth opportunities in its present industry, there is no urgency to pursue diversification. But when company growth potential starts to wane, the strategic options are either to become more aggressive in taking market share away from rivals or pursue diversification into other businesses. A decision to diversify raises the question of, "What kind and how much diversification?" The strategic possibilities are wide open. A company can diversify into closely related businesses or into totally unrelated businesses. It can diversify to a small extent (less than 10 percent of total revenues and profits) or to a large extent (up to 50 percent of revenues and profits). It can move into one or two large, new businesses or a greater number of small ones. Once diversification has been achieved, the time may come when management has to consider divesting or liquidating businesses that are no longer attractive.

> Diversification doesn't need to become a strategic priority until a company begins to run out of growth opportunities in its core business.

■ WHY A SINGLE-BUSINESS STRATEGY IS ATTRACTIVE

Companies that concentrate on a single business can achieve enviable success over many decades without relying upon diversification to sustain their growth. McDonald's, Delta Airlines, Coca-Cola, Domino's Pizza, Apple Computer, Wal-Mart, Federal Express, Timex, Campbell Soup, Anheuser-Busch, Xerox, Gerber, and Polaroid all won their reputations in a single business. In the nonprofit sector, continued emphasis on a single activity has proved beneficial for the Red Cross, Salvation Army, Christian Children's Fund, Girl Scouts, Phi Beta Kappa, and the American Civil Liberties Union.

Concentrating on a single line of business (totally or with a small dose of diversification) has some useful organizational and managerial advantages. First, a single business is less ambiguous about its identity and mission. The energies of the *total* organization are directed down *one* business path. A single business lessens the chance that either senior management's time or limited organizational resources will be stretched too thinly over too many diverse activities. Entrepreneurial efforts can be directed exclusively to focusing the firm's business strategy and competitive approach on changes in industry and customer needs. All the firm's managers, especially top executives, can be intimately knowledgeable about the core business and opera-

There are important organizational and managerial advantages to concentrating on a single business.

tions. In many cases, senior officers will have risen through the ranks and possess first-hand experience in field operations. This is strikingly different from broadly diversified enterprises where corporate managers seldom have worked in more than one or two of the company's businesses. Finally, concentrating on one business carries a heftier incentive for managers to direct the company toward capturing a stronger long-term competitive position in the industry, as opposed to pursuing the fleeting benefits of juggling corporate assets to produce temporarily higher profits. The company can devote the full force of its organizational resources to becoming better at what it does. Important competencies and competitive skills are more likely to emerge. With management's attention focused exclusively on one business, the probability is higher that ideas will emerge on how to improve production technology, better meet customer needs with innovative new product features, and enhance efficiencies or differentiation capabilities anywhere in the value chain. The more successful a single-business enterprise is, the more able it is to parlay its accumulated experience and distinctive expertise into a sustainable competitive advantage and a prominent leadership position in its industry.

■ THE RISK OF A SINGLE-BUSINESS STRATEGY

The big risk of single-business concentration is putting all of a firm's eggs in one industry basket. If the industry stagnates or becomes competitively unattractive, company prospects dim and superior profit performance is much harder to achieve. At times, changing customer needs, technological innovation, or new substitute products can undermine or wipe out a single-business firm—consider, for example, what the word processing capabilities of personal computers have done to the electric typewriter business and what the advent of compact discs has done to long-playing records and is doing to the market for cassette tapes. For this reason most single-business companies turn their strategic attention to diversification when their business starts to show signs of peaking out.

■ WHEN DIVERSIFICATION STARTS TO MAKE SENSE

To analyze when diversification makes the most strategic sense, consider Figure 7–1 in which the variable of competitive position is plotted against various rates of market growth to create four distinct strategic alternatives for an undiversified company.[1] Firms that fall into the rapid market growth/strong competitive position box have several logical strategy options, the strongest of which in the near term may be continuing to pursue single-business concentration. Given the industry's high growth rate (and implicit long-term attractiveness), it makes sense for firms in this position to push hard to maintain or increase their market share, further develop core competencies, and make whatever

---

FIGURE 7–1   *Matching Corporate Strategy Alternatives to Fit an Undiversified Firm's Situation*

COMPETITIVE POSITION

	WEAK	STRONG
RAPID	**STRATEGY OPTIONS** (in probable order of attractiveness) • Reformulate single-business concentration strategy (to achieve turnaround). • Acquire another firm in the same business (to strengthen competitive position). • Vertical integration (forward or backward if it strengthens competitive position). • Diversification. • Be acquired by/sell out to a stronger rival. • Abandonment (a last resort in the event all else fails).	**STRATEGY OPTIONS** (in probable order of attractiveness) • Continue single-business concentration –International expansion (if market opportunities exist). • Vertical integration (if it strengthens the firm's competitive position). • Related diversification (to transfer skills and expertise built up in the company's core business to adjacent businesses).
SLOW	**STRATEGY OPTIONS** (in probable order of attractiveness) • Reformulate single-business concentration strategy (to achieve turnaround). • Merger with a rival firm (to strengthen competitive position). • Vertical integration (only if it strengthens competitive position substantially). • Diversification. • Harvest/divest. • Liquidation (a last resort in the event all else fails).	**STRATEGY OPTIONS** (in probable order of attractiveness) • International expansion (if market opportunities exist). • Related diversification. • Unrelated diversification. • Joint ventures into new areas. • Vertical integration (if it strengthens competitive position). • Continue single-business concentration (achieve growth by taking market share from weaker rivals).

MARKET GROWTH RATE

capital investments are necessary to continue in a strong industry position. At some juncture, a company in this box may contemplate vertical integration if this would add to its competitive strength. Later, when market growth starts to slow, it can consider a diversification strategy to spread business risk and transfer the skills or expertise the company has built up into closely *related* businesses.

When **to diversify depends partly on a company's growth opportunities in its present industry and partly on its competitive position.**

Firms in the rapid growth/weak position category should first address the questions of (1) why their current approach to the market has resulted in a weak competitive position and (2) what it will take to become an effective competitor. Second they should consider their options for rejuvenating their present competitive strategy (given the high rate of market growth). In a rapidly expanding market, even weak firms should be able to improve their performance and make headway in building a stronger market position. If the firm is young and struggling, it usually has a better chance for survival in a growing market, where plenty of new business is up for grabs, than in a stable or declining industry. However, if a weakly positioned company in a rapid-growth market lacks the resources and skills to hold its own, its best option is to merge either with another company in the industry that has the missing pieces or with a cash-rich outsider that can support the firm's development. Vertical integration, whether forward or backward or both, is an option for weakly positioned firms whenever such integration can materially strengthen the firm's competitive position. A third option is diversification into related or unrelated areas (if adequate financing can be found). If all else fails, abandonment— divestiture in the case of a multibusiness firm or liquidation in the case of a single-business firm—has to become an active strategic option. While abandonment may seem extreme because of the high growth potential, a company unable to make a profit in a booming market probably does not have the ability to make a profit at all—particularly if competition stiffens or industry conditions sour.

Companies with a weak competitive position in a relatively slow-growth market should look at (1) revising their present competitive strategy to reverse their situation and create a more attractive competitive position, (2) integrating forward or backward if good profit improvement and competitive positioning opportunities exist, (3) diversifying into related or unrelated areas, (4) merging with another firm, (5) harvesting and then divesting, and (6) liquidating by either selling out to another firm or closing down operations.

Companies that are strongly positioned in a slow-growth industry should consider taking the excess cash flow from their existing business to finance a diversification strategy. Diversification into businesses where a firm can leverage its core competencies and competitive strengths is usually the best strategy. Diversification into totally unrelated businesses, however, has to be considered if none of its related business opportunities offer attractive profit prospects. Joint ventures with other organizations into new fields of endeavor are another logical possibility. Vertical integration should be a last resort (since it provides no escape from the industry's slow-growth condition) and makes strategic sense only if a firm can expect

Companies with strong competitive positions in slow-growth industries are prime candidates for diversifying into new businesses.

sizable profit gains. Unless it sees important growth *segments* within the industry that merit further invest-and-build actions, a strong company in a slow-growth industry would be wise to curtail new investment in its present business to free cash for new endeavors.

When to diversify is therefore partly a function of a firm's competitive position and partly a function of the remaining opportunities in its home base industry. There really is no well-defined point at which companies in the same industry should diversify. Indeed, companies in the same industry can rationally choose different diversification approaches and launch them at different times.

BUILDING SHAREHOLDER VALUE: THE ULTIMATE JUSTIFICATION FOR DIVERSIFYING

The underlying purpose of corporate diversification is to build shareholder value. For diversification to enhance shareholder value, corporate strategy must do more than simply diversify the company's business risk by investing in more than one industry. Shareholders can achieve the same risk diversification on their own by purchasing stock in companies in different industries. Strictly speaking, *diversification does not create shareholder value unless a diversified group of businesses perform better under a single corporate umbrella than they would perform operating as independent, stand-alone businesses.* For example, if company A diversifies by purchasing company B and if A and B's consolidated profits in the years to come prove no greater than what each would have earned on its own, then A's diversification into business B won't provide its shareholders with added value. Company A's shareholders could have achieved the same $2 + 2 = 4$ result on their own by purchasing stock in company B. Shareholder value is not *created* by diversification unless it produces a $2 + 2 = 5$ effect where sister businesses perform better together as part of the same firm than they could perform as independent companies.

> To create shareholder value, a diversifying company must get into businesses that can perform better under common management than they could perform as stand-alone enterprises.

THREE TESTS FOR JUDGING A DIVERSIFICATION MOVE

To determine whether diversification has enhanced shareholder value requires difficult and speculative judgments about how well a diversified company's businesses would have performed on their own. Comparisons of actual performance against hypothetical performance are never very satisfactory and, besides, they represent after-the-fact assessments. Although strategists have to base diversification decisions on future expectations, attempts to gauge the impact of particular diversification moves on shareholder value do not have to be abandoned. Corporate strategists can assess whether a particular diversification move is capable of increasing shareholder value by using three tests:[2]

1. *The attractiveness test:* The industry chosen for diversification must be attractive enough to yield consistently good returns on investment. Whether an industry is attractive depends chiefly on the presence of favorable competitive conditions and a

market environment conducive to long-term profitability. Such indicators as rapid growth or a sexy product are unreliable proxies of attractiveness.

2. *The cost-of-entry test:* The cost to enter the target industry must not be so high as to erode the potential for good profitability. A catch-22 can prevail here, however. The more attractive an industry, the more expensive it can be to get into. Entry barriers for start-up companies are nearly always high—were they low, a rush of new entrants would soon erode the high profit potential. And purchasing a company already in the business typically entails a high acquisition cost because of the industry's strong appeal. Costly entry undermines the potential for enhancing shareholder value.

3. *The better-off test:* The diversifying company must either bring potential for competitive advantage to its new business or the new business must offer the potential for additional competitive advantage to the company's present businesses. The opportunity to create sustainable competitive advantage where none existed before means there is also opportunity for added profitability and shareholder value.

Diversification moves that satisfy all three tests have the greatest potential to build shareholder value over the long term. Diversification moves that can pass only one or two tests are suspect.

▶ DIVERSIFICATION STRATEGIES

Once the decision is made to diversify, any of several different paths can be taken. Figure 7–2 shows the choices a company can make in moving from a single-business enterprise to a diversified enterprise. Vertical integration strategies may or may not be considered depending on the extent to which forward or backward integration strengthens a firm's competitive position or helps it secure a competitive advantage. When diversification becomes a serious strategic option, a choice must be made whether to pursue related diversification, unrelated diversification, or some of both. Once diversification has been accomplished, management's task is to figure out how to manage the existing business portfolio; the basic strategic options boil down to the six postdiversification alternatives shown in the last box in Figure 7–2.

We can get a better understanding of the strategic issues corporate managers face in creating and managing a diversified group of businesses by looking at six types of diversification strategies:

1. Strategies for entering new industries—acquisition, start-up, and joint ventures.
2. Related diversification strategies.
3. Unrelated diversification strategies.
4. Divestiture and liquidation strategies.
5. Corporate turnaround, retrenchment, and restructuring strategies.
6. Multinational diversification strategies.

The first three involve ways to diversify; the last three involve strategies to strengthen the positions and performance of companies that have already diversified.

FIGURE 7–2 *Corporate Strategy Alternatives*

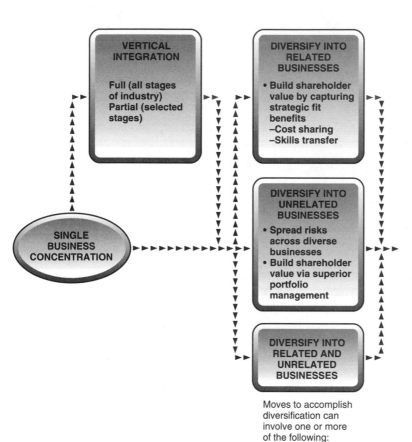

VERTICAL INTEGRATION

Full (all stages of industry)
Partial (selected stages)

DIVERSIFY INTO RELATED BUSINESSES

• Build shareholder value by capturing strategic fit benefits
  –Cost sharing
  –Skills transfer

DIVERSIFY INTO UNRELATED BUSINESSES

• Spread risks across diverse businesses
• Build shareholder value via superior portfolio management

DIVERSIFY INTO RELATED AND UNRELATED BUSINESSES

SINGLE BUSINESS CONCENTRATION

Moves to accomplish diversification can involve one or more of the following:

• Acquisition/merger

• Start-up of own new businesses from scratch

• Joint venture partnerships

POST-DIVERSIFICATION STRATEGIC MOVE ALTERNATIVES

• Make new acquisitions (or seek merger partnerships)
  –To build positions in new related/unrelated industries
  –To strengthen the position of business units in industries where the firm already has a stake

• Divest some business units
  –To eliminate weak-performing businesses from portfolio
  –To eliminate businesses that no longer fit

• Restructure makeup of whole portfolio if many business units are performing poorly
  –By selling selected business units
  –By using cash from divestitures plus unused debt capacity to make new acquisitions

• Retrench/narrow the diversification base
  –By pruning weak businesses
  –By shedding all noncore businesses
  –By divesting one or more core businesses

• Become a multinational, multi-industry enterprise (DMNC)
  –To succeed in globally competitive core businesses against international rivals
  –To capture strategic fit benefits and win a competitive advantage via multinational diversification

• Liquidate/close down money-losing businesses that cannot be sold

In recent years, takeovers have become an increasingly used approach to acquisition. The term *takeover* refers to the attempt (often sprung as a surprise) of one firm to acquire ownership or control over another firm against the wishes of the latter's management (and perhaps some of its stockholders).

■ STRATEGIES FOR ENTERING NEW BUSINESSES

Entering new businesses can take any of three forms: acquisition, internal start-up, and joint ventures. *Acquisition of an existing business* is the most popular means of diversifying into another industry and has the advantage of a quick entry into the target market. At the same time, business acquisitions can help a diversifier overcome such entry barriers as technological inexperience, establishing supplier relationships, matching rivals' efficiency and unit costs, introductory advertising and promotional costs, and adequate distribution. In many industries, developing the knowledge, resources, scale of operation, and market reputation necessary to become an effective competitor from scratch can take years. However, finding the right kind of company to acquire sometimes presents a challenge.[3] The dilemma an acquisition-minded firm faces is whether to buy a successful company at a high price

> One of the difficulties of entering attractive industries by acquisition is finding a suitable company at a price that satisfies the cost-of-entry test.

or a struggling company at a "bargain" price. If the firm has little knowledge of the industry but ample capital, it is often better off purchasing a capable, strongly positioned firm—unless the acquisition price is unreasonably high. On the other hand, when the acquirer sees promising ways to transform a weak firm into a strong one and has the money, the capability, and the patience to do it, a struggling company can be the better long-term investment.

The cost-of-entry test requires that the expected profit stream of an acquired business provide an attractive return on the total acquisition cost and on any capital investment needed to sustain or expand its operations. A high acquisition price can make that improbable or difficult. For instance, suppose that the price to purchase a company is $3 million and that the business is earning after-tax profits of $200,000 on an equity investment of $1 million (a 20 percent annual return). Simple arithmetic requires that the acquired business's profits be tripled for the purchaser to earn the same 20 percent return on the $3 million acquisition price that the previous owners were getting on their $1 million equity investment. Building the acquired firm's earnings from $200,000 to $600,000 annually could take several years—and require additional investment on which the purchaser would also have to earn a 20 percent return. Since the owners of a successful and growing company usually demand a price that reflects their business's future profit prospects, it's easy for such an acquisition to flunk the cost-of-entry test. A diversifier can't count on finding a successful company in an appealing industry at a price that still permits attractive returns on investment.

Achieving diversification through *internal start-up* involves creating a new company under the corporate umbrella to compete in the desired industry. A newly formed organization not only has to overcome entry barriers, it also has to invest in new production capacity, develop sources of supply, hire and train employees, build channels of distribution, grow a customer base, and so on. Generally, forming a start-up company to enter a new industry is more attractive when (1) there is ample time to launch the business,

> The biggest drawbacks to internal diversification are the costs of overcoming entry barriers and the added time required to build a strong and profitable competitive position.

(2) incumbent firms are likely to be slow or ineffective in responding to a new entrant, (3)

internal entry has lower costs than entry by acquisition, (4) the company already has most or all of the skills it needs to compete effectively, (5) adding new production capacity will not adversely impact the supply-demand balance in the industry, and (6) the targeted industry is made up of relatively small firms so the new start-up does not have to compete against larger, more powerful rivals.[4]

Joint ventures are a useful way to gain access to a new business in at least three types of situations.[5] First, a joint venture is a good device for a project that is uneconomical or risky to do alone. Second, joint ventures make sense when pooling resources and competencies produces an organization with more of the skills needed to be a strong competitor. Third, joint ventures with foreign partners are sometimes the only or best way to surmount foreign entry barriers such as import quotas, tariffs, nationalistic political interests, and cultural roadblocks. Foreign partners offer the benefits of local knowledge, managerial and marketing personnel, and access to distribution channels. However, such joint ventures often pose complicated questions about how to divide efforts among the partners and who has effective control.[6] Conflicts between foreign and domestic partners can arise over local sourcing of components, how much production to export, whether operating procedures should conform to the foreign company's standards or to local preferences, and control over cash flows and the disposition of profits.

▶ RELATED DIVERSIFICATION STRATEGIES

In choosing which industries to diversify into, the two basic options are to pick industries *related* to the organization's core business or *unrelated* to the organization's core business. A related diversification strategy involves diversifying into businesses that possess some kind of strategic fit. *Strategic fit* exists when different businesses have sufficiently related value chains that there are important opportunities for (1) transferring skills and expertise from one business to another or (2) combining the related activities of separate businesses into a single operation and reducing costs.[7] *A diversified firm that exploits these value chain interrelationships and captures the benefits of strategic fit achieves a consolidated performance greater than the sum of what the businesses can earn pursuing independent strategies.* The presence of strategic fit within a diversified firm's business portfolio, together with corporate management's skill in capturing the benefits of the interrelationships, makes related diversification a $2 + 2 = 5$ phenomenon and becomes a basis for competitive advantage. The greater the strategic fit benefits, the bigger the competitive advantage of related diversification and the more that related diversification satisfies the better-off test for building shareholder value.

Related diversification involves diversifying into businesses whose value chains have good strategic fit.

Strategic fit relationships can arise out of technology sharing, common labor skills and requirements, common suppliers and raw material sources, the potential for joint manufacture of parts and components, similar operating methods, similar managerial competence, reliance on the same types of marketing and merchandising skills, ability to share a common sales force, ability to use the same wholesale distributors or retail dealers in accessing consumers, potential for combining after-sale service activities, or potential to use a common brand name. The fit can occur anywhere along the value chains of the respective businesses. Strategic fit relationships are important because they represent opportunities for cost-saving efficiencies, technology or skills transfers, added differentiation, or brand name advantages, all of which are avenues for gaining competitive advantages over business rivals that have not diversified or that have diversified but not in ways that give them access to such strategic fit benefits.

_ _ _ _ _ _ _ _ _ _ _ _ _ _ _ _
What makes related diversification attractive is the opportunity to turn strategic fits into competitive advantage.
_ _ _ _ _ _ _ _ _ _ _ _ _ _ _ _

Some of the most commonly used approaches to related diversification are:

- Entering businesses where sales force, advertising, and distribution activities can be shared (a bread bakery buying a maker of crackers and salty snack foods).

- Exploiting similar technologies (a maker of agricultural seeds and fertilizers diversifying into chemicals for insect and plant disease control).

- Transferring expertise from one business to another (a successful operator of hamburger outlets acquiring a chain specializing in Mexican fast foods).

- Transferring the organization's brand name and reputation with consumers to a new product/service (a tire manufacturer diversifying into automotive repair centers).

- Acquiring new businesses that will specially help the firm's position in its existing businesses (a cable TV broadcaster purchasing a sports team and a movie production company to provide original programming).

Examples of related diversification abound. BIC Pen, which pioneered inexpensive disposable ballpoint pens, used its core competencies in low-cost manufacturing and mass merchandising as its basis for diversifying into disposable cigarette lighters and disposable razors—both of which required low-cost production ability and skilled consumer marketing for competitive success. Tandy Corp. practiced related diversification when its chain of Radio Shack outlets, which originally handled mostly radio and stereo equipment, added telephones, intercoms, calculators, clocks, electronic and scientific toys, personal computers, and peripheral computer equipment. The Tandy strategy was to use the marketing access provided by its thousands of Radio Shack locations to become one of the world's leading retailers of electronic technology to individual consumers. Philip Morris, a leading cigarette manufacturer, employed a marketing-related diversification strategy when it purchased Miller Brewing, General Foods, and Kraft and transferred its skills in cigarette marketing to the marketing of beer and food products. Lockheed pursued a customer needs-based diversification strategy in creating business units to supply the U.S. Department of Defense with missiles, rocket engines, aircraft, electronic equipment, ships, and contract R&D for weapons. The product line of Procter & Gamble (P&G) includes Jif peanut butter, Duncan Hines cake mixes, Folger's coffee, Tide laundry detergent, Crisco vegetable oil, Crest toothpaste, Ivory soap, Charmin toilet tissue, and Head and Shoulders shampoo—all different businesses with different competitors and different production requirements. But P&G's products still represent related diversification because they all move through the same wholesale distribution systems, are sold in common retail settings to the same shoppers, are advertised and promoted in the same ways, and use the same marketing and merchandising skills.

ILLUSTRATION 20   *Examples of Companies with*
Related Business Portfolios

Presented below are the business portfolios of four companies that have pursued some form of related diversification:

Gillette

- Blades and razors
- Toiletries (Right Guard, Silkience, Foamy, Dry Idea, Soft & Dry, Oral-B toothbrushes, White Rain, Toni)
- Writing instruments and stationery products (Paper Mate pens, Liquid Paper correction fluids, Waterman pens)
- Braun shavers, cordless curlers, coffeemakers, alarm clocks, and electric toothbrushes

PepsiCo

- Soft drinks (Pepsi, Mountain Dew, Slice)
- Kentucky Fried Chicken
- Pizza Hut
- Taco Bell
- Frito-Lay
- 7Up International (non-U.S. sales of 7Up)

Phillip Morris Companies

- Cigarettes (Marlboro, Virginia Slims, Benson & Hedges, and Merit)
- Miller Brewing Company
- Kraft General Foods (Maxwell House, Sanka, Oscar Mayer, Kool-Aid, Jell-O, Post cereals, Birds-Eye frozen foods, Kraft cheeses, Sealtest dairy products, Breyer's ice cream)
- Mission Viejo Realty

Johnson & Johnson

- Baby products (powder, shampoo, oil, lotion)
- Disposable diapers
- Band-Aids and wound care products
- Stayfree, Carefree, Sure & Natural, and Modess feminine hygiene products
- Tylenol
- Prescription drugs
- Surgical and hospital products
- Dental products
- Oral contraceptives
- Veterinary and animal health products

Source: Company annual reports.

Illustration 20 shows the business portfolios of several companies that have pursued a strategy of related diversification.

■ STRATEGIC FIT, ECONOMIES OF SCOPE, AND COMPETITIVE ADVANTAGE

A related diversification strategy has considerable appeal. It allows a firm to preserve some unity in its business activities, reap the competitive advantage benefits of skills transfer or lower costs, and still spread investor risks over a broader base. A company that has developed valuable skills and competencies in its original business can employ a related diversification strategy to exploit what it does best and transfer its competencies and competitive skills to another business. Successful skills or technology transfers can lead to competitive advantage in the new business.

> Strategic fits offer the potential competitive advantage of *(a)* lower costs, *(b)* transfer of key skills, technological expertise, or managerial competence, or *(c)* use of the same brand name.

Diversifying into businesses where technology, facilities, functional activities, or distribution channels can be shared can lead to lower costs because of economies of scope. *Economies of scope* exist whenever it is less costly for two or more businesses to be operated under centralized management than to function as independent businesses. The economies of operating over a wider range of businesses or product lines can arise from cost-saving opportunities to share resources or combine activities anywhere along the respective value chains of the businesses and from shared use of an established brand name. The greater the economies of scope

> *Economies of scope* arise from cost-saving opportunities anywhere along the value chains of related businesses.

associated with the particular businesses a company has diversified into, the greater the potential for creating a competitive advantage based on lower costs.

Both skills transfer and activity sharing enable the diversifier to earn greater profits from its businesses than the businesses could earn operating independently. The key to skills transfer and activity-sharing opportunities is diversification into businesses with strategic fit. While strategic fit relationships can occur throughout the value chain, most fall into one of three broad categories.

MARKET-RELATED FITS

When the value chains of different businesses overlap such that the products are used by the same customers, distributed through common dealers and retailers, or marketed and promoted in similar ways, then the businesses exhibit a market-related strategic fit. A variety of cost-saving opportunities (or economies of scope) spring from a market-related strategic fit: Using a single sales force for all related products rather than having separate sales forces for each business, advertising related products in the same ads and brochures, using the same brand names, coordinating delivery and shipping, combining after-sale service and repair organizations, coordinating order processing and billing, using common promotional tie-ins (cents-off coupons, free samples and trial offers, seasonal specials), and combining dealer networks. Such market-related strategic fits usually allow a firm to economize on its marketing, selling, and distribution costs.

In addition to economies of scope, market-related fit can generate opportunities to transfer selling skills, promotional skills, advertising skills, and product differentiation skills from one business to another. Moreover, a company's brand name and reputation in one product can often be transferred to other products. Honda's name in motorcycles and automobiles gave it instant credibility and recognition in entering the lawnmower business without spending large sums on advertising. Canon's reputation in photographic equipment was a competitive asset that facilitated the company's diversification into copying equipment. Panasonic's name in radios and televisions was readily transferred to microwave ovens, making it easier and cheaper for Panasonic to diversify into the microwave oven market.

OPERATING FIT

Businesses have an *operating fit* when there is potential for cost sharing or skills transfer in procuring materials, conducting R&D, mastering a new technology, manufacturing components, assembling finished goods, or performing administrative support functions. Sharing related operating fits usually present cost-saving opportunities; some derive from the economies of combining activities into a larger-scale operation *(economies of scale)* and some derive from the ability to eliminate costs by performing certain functions together rather than independently *(economies of scope)*. The greater the proportion of cost that a shared activity represents, the more significant the shared cost savings become and the greater the cost advantage that can result. With operating fit, the most important skills transfer opportunities usually relate to situations where technological or manufacturing expertise in one business has beneficial applications in another.

MANAGEMENT FIT

This type of fit occurs when different business units have comparable types of entrepreneurial, administrative, or operating problems, thereby allowing a company to benefit from transferring its demonstrated managerial competence in one line of business to managing another business. Opportunities to transfer managerial expertise can occur anywhere in the value chain. Ford Motor Co. transferred its automobile financing and credit management expertise to the savings and loan industry when Ford acquired some failing savings and loan associations during the 1989 bailout of the crisis-ridden S&L industry. Emerson Electric transferred its skills in low-cost manufacture to its newly acquired Beaird-Poulan chain saw business division. The transfer of management expertise drove Beaird-Poulan's new strategy, changed the way its chain saws were designed and manufactured, and paved the way for new pricing and distribution emphasis.

CAPTURING STRATEGIC FIT BENEFITS

It is one thing to diversify into industries with strategic fit and another to actually realize the benefits. To capture the benefits of activity sharing, related activities must be merged into a single functional unit and coordinated; then the cost-savings (or differentiation advantages) must be squeezed out. Merged functions and coordination can entail reorganization costs, and management must determine that the benefit of *some* centralized strategic control is great enough to warrant sacrifice of business-unit autonomy. Likewise, where skills transfer is the cornerstone of strategic fit, managers must find a way to make the transfer effective without stripping too many skilled personnel from the business with the expertise. The more a company's diversification strategy is tied to skills transfer, the more it has to develop a big enough and talented enough pool of specialized personnel not only to supply new businesses with the skill but also to master the skill sufficiently to create competitive advantage.

> Competitive advantage achieved through strategic fits among related businesses allows related diversification to have a 2 + 2 = 5 effect on shareholder value.

► UNRELATED DIVERSIFICATION STRATEGIES

Despite the strategic fit benefits associated with related diversification, a number of companies opt for unrelated diversification strategies. In unrelated diversification, the underlying strategic theme is to consider diversifying into any industry with a good profit opportunity. Corporate managers exert no deliberate effort to find businesses having strategic fit with the firm's other businesses. While companies with an unrelated diversification strategy may try to make certain their diversification targets meet the industry attractiveness and cost-of-entry tests, the conditions needed for the better-off test are either disregarded or relegated to secondary status. Decisions to diversify into one industry versus another are the product of an opportunistic search for good companies to acquire. *The basic premise of unrelated diversification is that any company that can be acquired on good financial terms and has satisfactory profit prospects represents a choice for diversification no matter what business the company is in.* Much time and effort goes into finding and screening acquisition candidates. Typically, corporate strategists screen candidate companies using such criteria as:

A strategy of unrelated diversification is more concerned with potential for financial gain than with competitive advantage potential of strategic fit.

- Whether the business can meet corporate targets for profitability and return on investment.
- Whether the new business will require substantial infusions of capital to replace fixed assets, fund expansion, and provide working capital.
- Whether the business is in an industry with significant growth potential.
- Whether the business is big enough to contribute significantly to the parent firm's bottom line.
- Whether there are potential union difficulties or adverse government regulations on product safety or the environment.
- Whether the industry is vulnerable to recession, inflation, high interest rates, or shifts in government policy.

Sometimes, companies with an unrelated diversification strategy concentrate on identifying businesses that offer quick opportunities for financial gain; three types of acquisition candidates may hold such attraction:

- *Companies whose assets are undervalued*—opportunities may exist to acquire such companies for less than full market value and make substantial capital gains by reselling their assets and businesses for more than their acquired costs.
- *Companies that are financially distressed*—such businesses can often be purchased at a bargain price, their operations turned around with the aid of the parent companies' financial resources and managerial expertise, and then held either as a long-term investment in the acquirer's business portfolio (because of their strong earnings or cash flow potential) or sold at a profit.
- *Companies that have bright growth prospects but are short on investment capital*—capital-poor, opportunity-rich companies are usually coveted acquisition candidates for a financially strong, opportunity-seeking firm.

Companies that pursue unrelated diversification nearly always enter new businesses by acquiring an established company rather than by forming a start-up subsidiary within its own corporate structure. Their premise is that growth by acquisition translates into

---

ILLUSTRATION 21   *Diversified Companies with Unrelated Business Portfolios*

Union Pacific Corporation	United Technologies
• Railroad operations (Union Pacific Railroad Company) • Oil and gas exploration • Mining • Microwave and fiber optic transportation information and control systems • Hazardous waste management disposal • Trucking (Overnite Transportation Company) • Oil refining • Real estate	• Pratt & Whitney aircraft engines • Carrier heating and air-conditioning equipment • Otis elevators • Sikorsky helicopters • Essex wire and cable products • Norden defense systems • Hamilton Standard controls • Space transportation systems • Automotive components

Westinghouse Electric Corp.	Textron, Inc.
• Electric utility power generation equipment • Nuclear fuel • Electric transmission and distribution products • Commercial and residential real estate financing • Equipment leasing • Receivables and fixed asset financing • Radio and television broadcasting • Longines-Wittnauer Watch Co. • Beverage bottling • Elevators and escalators • Defense electronic systems (missile launch equipment, marine propulsion) • Commercial furniture • Community land development	• Bell helicopters • Paul Revere Insurance • Missile reentry systems • Lycoming gas turbine engines and jet propulsion systems • E-Z-Go golf carts • Homelite chain saws and lawn and garden equipment • Davidson automotive parts and trims • Specialty fasteners • Avco Financial Services • Jacobsen turf care equipment • Tanks and armored vehicles

Source: Company annual reports.

enhanced shareholder value. Suspending application of the better-off test is seen as justifiable so long as unrelated diversification results in sustained growth in corporate revenues and earnings and so long as none of the acquired businesses end up performing badly.

Illustration 21 shows the business portfolios of several companies that have pursued unrelated diversification. Such companies are frequently labeled as *conglomerates* because there is no strategic theme in their diversification makeup and because their business interests range broadly across diverse industries.

■ PROS AND CONS OF UNRELATED DIVERSIFICATION

Unrelated or conglomerate diversification has appeal from several financial angles:

1. Business risk is scattered over a variety of industries, making the company less dependent on any one business. While the same can be said for related diversification, unrelated diversification places no restraint on how risk is spread. An argument can be made that unrelated diversification is a superior way to diversify financial risk as

compared to related diversification because the company's investments can span a greater variety of totally different businesses.

2. Capital resources can be invested in whatever industries offer the best profit prospects; cash flows from company businesses with lower profit prospects can be diverted to acquiring and expanding business units with higher growth and profit potentials. Corporate financial resources are thus employed to maximum advantage.

3. Company profitability is somewhat more stable because hard times in one industry may be partially offset by good times in another—ideally, cyclical downswings in some of the company's businesses are counterbalanced by cyclical upswings in the company's other businesses.

4. To the extent that corporate managers are exceptionally astute at spotting bargain-priced companies with big upside profit potential, shareholder wealth can be enhanced.

While entry into an unrelated business can often pass the attractiveness and the cost-of-entry tests (and sometimes even the better-off test), a strategy of unrelated diversification has drawbacks. Unrelated diversification places great demands on corporate-level management to make sound decisions regarding fundamentally different businesses operating in fundamentally different industry and competitive environments. The greater the number of businesses a company is in and the more diverse they are, the harder it is for corporate managers to oversee each subsidiary and spot problems early, to become expert in evaluating the attractiveness of each business's industry and competitive environment, and to judge the calibre of strategic actions and plans proposed by business-level managers. As one president of a diversified firm expressed it:

> **The drawbacks to unrelated diversification are the difficulties of managing so much business diversity and the absence of strategic opportunities to turn diversification into competitive advantage.**

> We've got to make sure that our core businesses are properly managed for solid, long-term earnings. We can't just sit back and watch the numbers. We've got to know what the real issues are out there in the profit centers. Otherwise, we're not even in a position to check out our managers on the big decisions.[8]

In broadly diversified enterprises, the challenge for corporate managers is to be shrewd and talented enough (1) to discern a good acquisition from a bad acquisition, (2) to select capable managers to run each of many different businesses, (3) to discern when the major strategic proposals of business-unit managers are sound, and (4) to know what to do if a business unit stumbles. Because every business tends to encounter rough sledding, a good way to gauge the risk of diversifying into new, unrelated areas is to ask, ''If the new business got into trouble, would we know how to bail it out?'' When the answer is no, unrelated diversification can pose significant financial risk and the business's profit prospects are more chancy.[9] As the former chairman of a Fortune 500 company advised, ''Never acquire a business you don't know how to run.'' It only takes one or two big strategic mistakes—such as misjudging industry attractiveness, not having the expertise for the unexpected problems in a newly acquired business, or being too optimistic about the difficulties of turning a struggling new acquisition around—to cause a precipitous drop in corporate earnings and crash the company's stock price.

Second, without some kind of strategic fit and the added measure of competitive advantage it offers, consolidated performance of an unrelated multibusiness portfolio tends to be no better than the sum of what the individual business units could achieve if they were independent. Furthermore, to the extent that corporate managers meddle unwisely in business unit operations or hamstring them with corporate policies, it may be worse. Except, perhaps, for the added financial backing that a cash-rich corporate parent can provide, a strategy of unrelated diversification does nothing for the competitive strength of the individual business units. Each business has to build a competitive edge on its own — the unrelated nature of sister businesses offers no basis for cost reduction, skills transfer, or technology sharing. In a widely diversified firm, the value added by corporate managers depends primarily on the quality of the guidance they give to the general managers of their subsidiaries and on how good they are at deciding what new businesses to add, which ones to get rid of, how best to deploy available financial resources.

Third, although in theory unrelated diversification offers the potential of greater sales-profit stability over the course of the business cycle, in practice attempts at countercyclical diversification fall short of the mark. Few attractive businesses have opposite up-and-down cycles; the great majority of businesses are similarly affected by economic good times and hard times. There's no convincing evidence that the consolidated profits of broadly diversified firms are more stable or less subject to reversal in periods of recession and economic stress than the profits of less-diversified firms.[10]

Despite these drawbacks, unrelated diversification can sometimes be a desirable corporate strategy. It certainly merits consideration when a firm needs to move away from an unattractive industry and has no distinctive skills it can transfer to an adjacent industry. There's also a rationale for pure diversification if owners have a strong preference to invest in several unrelated businesses instead of in a family of related ones. Otherwise, the case for unrelated diversification hinges on the prospects for financial gain.

A key issue in unrelated diversification is how broad a net to cast in building the business portfolio. In other words, should the corporate portfolio contain few businesses or many unrelated ones? How much business diversity can corporate executives successfully manage? A reasonable way to resolve the issue comes from answering two questions: "What is the least diversification it will take to achieve acceptable growth and profitability?" and "What is the most diversification that can be managed given the complexity it adds?"[11] The optimal answer usually lies between these two extremes.

■ UNRELATED DIVERSIFICATION AND SHAREHOLDERS VALUE

Unrelated diversification is, fundamentally, a finance-driven approach to creating shareholder value whereas related diversification is fundamentally strategy-driven. *Related diversification represents a strategic approach to creating value* because it is predicated on exploiting the linkages between the value chains of different businesses to lower costs, transfer skills and technological expertise across businesses, and gain benefit from other kinds of strategic fit. The objective is to convert the strategic fits among the firm's businesses into an additional competitive advantage beyond what business subsidiaries are able to achieve on their own. The competitive advantage a firm

------

Unrelated diversification is a financial approach to creating shareholder value whereas related diversification represents a strategic approach.

------

achieves through related diversification is the driver for building greater shareholder value.

In contrast, *unrelated diversification is principally a financial approach to creating value* because shareholder benefits accrue from astute deployment of corporate financial resources and from executive skill in spotting financially attractive business opportunities. Since unrelated diversification produces no strategic fit opportunities of consequence, corporate strategists can't build shareholder value by acquiring companies that create or compound competitive advantage for its business subsidiaries. In a conglomerate, competitive advantage doesn't extend beyond what each business subsidiary can achieve independently through its own competitive strategy. Consequently, for unrelated diversification to result in enhanced shareholder value corporate strategists must exhibit superior skills in creating and managing a portfolio of diversified business interests. This specifically means the following:

- Doing a superior job of diversifying into new businesses that can produce consistently good returns on investment (i.e., satisfying the attractiveness test).

- Doing an excellent job of negotiating favorable acquisition prices (i.e., satisfying the cost-of-entry test).

- Making astute moves to sell previously acquired business subsidiaries at their peak and getting premium prices. To do this requires being able to discern when a business subsidiary is on the verge of confronting adverse industry and competitive conditions and consequent declines in long-term profitability.

> For corporate strategists to build shareholder value through a conglomerate, they must be smart enough to produce financial results from a group of businesses that exceed what business-level managers can produce.

- Being shrewd in shifting corporate financial resources out of businesses where profit opportunities are dim and into businesses where rapid earnings growth and high returns on investment are occurring.

- Doing such a good job overseeing the firm's business subsidiaries and contributing to their management that the businesses perform at a higher level than they would otherwise be able to do (i.e., the better-off test).

To the extent that corporate executives can craft and execute a strategy of unrelated diversification that produces enough of the above outcomes for the enterprise to consistently outperform other firms in generating dividends and capital gains for stockholders, then a case can be made that shareholder value will truly be enhanced. Achieving such results consistently requires supertalented corporate executives, however. Without them, unrelated diversification is a very dubious way to try to build shareholder value—there are far more examples of failure than success.

▶ DIVESTITURE AND LIQUIDATION STRATEGIES

Even a shrewd corporate diversification strategy can result in the acquisition of business units that, down the road, just do not work out. Misfits or partial fits cannot be completely avoided because it is impossible to predict precisely how getting into a new line of business will actually work out. In addition, long-term industry attractiveness changes over time. Subpar performance by some business units is bound to occur, thereby raising questions of whether to keep them or divest them. Other business units, despite adequate financial performance, may not mesh as well with the rest of the firm as was originally expected.

A business must be considered for divestiture when corporate strategists conclude it no longer fits or is no longer an attractive investment.

Sometimes, a diversification move that seems sensible from a strategic fit standpoint turns out to lack the compatibility of values essential to a *cultural fit*.[12] Several pharmaceutical companies had just this experience. When they diversified into cosmetics and perfume, they discovered their personnel had little respect for the "frivolous" nature of such products compared to the far "nobler" task of developing "miracle" drugs to cure the ill. The absence of shared values and cultural compatibility between the medical-research/chemical-compounding expertise of the pharmaceutical companies and the fashion-marketing orientation of the cosmetics business was the undoing of what otherwise was diversification into businesses with technology-sharing potential, product development fit, and some overlap in distribution channels.

When a particular line of business loses its appeal, the most attractive solution usually is to sell it. Normally such businesses should be divested as quickly as is practical. To prolong divestiture decisions serves no purpose unless time is needed to get it in better shape to sell. The more business units in a diversified firm's portfolio, the more likely that it will have occasion to divest poor performers, dogs, and misfits. A useful guide to determine if and when to divest a business subsidiary is to ask the question, "If we were not in this business today, would we want to get into it now?"[13] When the answer is no or probably not, divestiture should be considered.

Divestiture can take either of two forms. The parent can spin off a business as a financially and managerially independent company in which the parent company may or may not retain partial ownership. Or the parent may sell the unit outright, in which case a buyer needs to be found. As a rule, divestiture should not be approached from the angle of, "Who can we pawn this business off on and what is the most we can get for it?"[14] Instead, it is wiser to ask, "For what sort of organization would this business be a good fit, and under what conditions would it be viewed as a good deal?" Organizations for which the business is a good fit are likely to pay the highest price.

Of all the strategic alternatives, liquidation is the most unpleasant and painful, especially for a single-business enterprise where it means the organization ceases to exist. For a multi-industry, multibusiness firm to liquidate one of its lines of business is less traumatic. The hardships of job eliminations, plant closings, and so on, while not to be minimized, still leave an ongoing organization, which may be healthier after its pruning. In hopeless situations, an early liquidation effort usually serves owner–stockholder interests better than an inevitable bankruptcy. Prolonging the pursuit of a lost cause exhausts an organization's resources and leaves less to liquidate; it can also mar reputations and ruin management careers. Unfortunately, it is seldom simple for management to differentiate between an achieveable turnaround and one that is not. This is particularly true when emotions such as pride overcome judgment—as often is the case.

▶ CORPORATE TURNAROUND, RETRENCHMENT, AND PORTFOLIO RESTRUCTURING STRATEGIES

Turnaround, retrenchment, and portfolio restructuring strategies are used when corporate management has to restore an ailing business portfolio to good health. Poor performance can be caused by large losses in one or more business units that pull the corporation's overall financial performance down, a disproportionate number of businesses in unattractive industries, a bad economy adversely impacting many of the firm's business units, an excessive debt burden, or ill-chosen acquisitions that haven't lived up to expectations.

Corporate turnaround strategies focus squarely on efforts to restore money-losing businesses to profitability as opposed to divesting them. The intent is to get the whole company back in the black by successfully addressing the problems of those businesses in the portfolio most responsible for pulling down overall performance. Turnaround strategies are most appropriate in situations where the reasons for poor performance are short-term, the ailing businesses are in attractive industries, and divesting the money-losers does not make long-term strategic sense.

Corporate retrenchment strategies involve reducing the scope of diversification to a smaller number of businesses. Retrenchment is usually undertaken when corporate management concludes that the company is in too many businesses and needs to concentrate its efforts on a few core businesses. Sometimes diversified firms retrench because they can't make individual businesses profitable after several frustrating years of trying or because they lack funds to support the investment needs of all of their business subsidiaries. More commonly, however, corporate executives conclude that the firm's diversification efforts have ranged too far afield and that the key to improved long-term performance lies in concentrating on building strong positions in a fewer number of businesses. Retrenchment is usually accomplished by divesting businesses that are too small to make a significant contribution to earnings or that have little or no strategic fit with the company's core businesses. Divesting such businesses frees resources that can be used to reduce debt or support expansion of the company's core businesses.

Portfolio restructuring strategies involve radical surgery on the mix and percentage makeup of the types of businesses in the portfolio. For instance, one company over a two-year period divested 4 business units, closed down the operations of 4 others, and added 25 new lines of business to its portfolio, 16 through acquisition and 9 through internal start-up. Restructuring can be prompted by any of several conditions: (1) a strategy review reveals that the firm's long-term performance prospects have become unattractive because the portfolio contains too

Portfolio restructuring involves bold strategic action to revamp the diversified company's business makeup through a series of divestitures and new acquisitions.

many slow-growth, declining, or competitively weak business units; (2) one or more of the firm's core businesses fall prey to hard times; (3) a new CEO takes over and decides to redirect where the company is headed; (4) cutting-edge technologies or products emerge and a major shakeup of the portfolio is needed to build a position in a potentially big new industry; (5) the firm has a unique opportunity to make an acquisition so large that it has to sell several business units to finance the new acquisition; or (6) major businesses in the portfolio have become increasingly unattractive, forcing a shakeup in the portfolio in order to produce satisfactory long-term corporate performance.

Portfolio restructuring typically involves both divestitures and new acquisitions. Candidates for divestiture include not only weak or up-and-down performers or those in unattractive industries, but also those that no longer fit (even though they may be profitable and in attractive industries). Many broadly diversified companies, disenchanted with the performance of some acquisitions and having only mixed success in overseeing so many unrelated business units, have restructured their business portfolios to a narrower core of activities. In other cases, business units incompatible with newly established related diversification criteria have been divested, the remaining units regrouped and aligned to capture more strategic fit benefits, and new acquisitions made to strengthen their positions in the industries chosen for emphasis.

The trend to demerge and deconglomerate has been driven by a growing preference toward gearing diversification to creating strong, competitive positions in a few, well-selected industries. Indeed, in response to investor disenchantment with the conglomerate approach to diversification (evident in the fact that conglomerates often have *lower* price-earnings ratios than companies with related diversification strategies), some conglomerates have undertaken portfolio restructuring and retrenchment in a deliberate effort to escape being regarded as a conglomerate.

▶ MULTINATIONAL DIVERSIFICATION STRATEGIES

The distinguishing characteristic of a multinational diversification strategy is a *diversity of businesses* and a *diversity of national markets*.[15] Here, corporate managers have to conceive and execute a substantial number of strategies—at least one for each industry, with as many multinational variations as is appropriate to the situation. At the same time, managers of diversified multinational corporations (DMNCs) need to be alert for beneficial ways to coordinate the firm's strategic actions across industries and countries. The goal of strategic coordination at the headquarter's level is to bring the full force of corporate resources and capabilities to the task of securing sustainable competitive advantages in each business and national market.[16]

■ THE EMERGENCE OF MULTINATIONAL DIVERSIFICATION

Until the 1960s, multinational companies (MNCs) operated fairly autonomous subsidiaries in each host country, each catering to the special requirements of its own national market.[17] Management tasks at company headquarters primarily involved finance functions, technology transfer, and export coordination. In pursuing a national responsiveness strategy, the primary competitive advantage of an MNC was grounded in its ability to transfer technology, manufacturing know-how, brand name identification, and marketing and management skills from country to country at costs lower than could be achieved by host country competitors. Standardized administrative procedures helped minimize overhead costs, and once an initial organization for managing foreign subsidiaries was put in place, entry into additional national markets could be accomplished at low incremental costs. Frequently, an MNC's presence and market position in a country was negotiated with the host government rather than driven by international competition.

During the 1970s, however, multicountry strategies based on national responsiveness began to lose their effectiveness. Competition broke out on a global scale in more and more industries as Japanese, European, and U.S. companies pursued international expansion in the wake of trade liberalization and the opening up of market opportunities in both industrialized and less-developed countries.[18] The relevant market arena in many industries shifted from national to global principally because the strategies of global competitors, most notably the Japanese companies, involved gaining a market foothold in host country markets via lower-priced, higher-quality offerings than those of established companies. To fend off global competitors, traditional MNCs were driven to integrate their operations across national borders in a quest for better efficiencies and lower manufacturing costs. Instead of separately manufacturing a complete product range in each country, plants became more specialized in their production operations to gain the economies of longer production runs, permit the use of faster automated equipment, and capture experience curve effects. Country subsidiaries obtained the rest of the product range they needed from sister plants in other countries. Gains in manufacturing efficiencies from converting to state-of-the-art, world-scale manufacturing plants more than offset increased international shipping costs, especially in light of the other advantages globalized strategies offered. With a global strategy, an MNC could locate plants in countries with low labor costs—a key consideration in industries whose products have high labor content. With a global strategy, an MNC could also exploit differences in tax rates, setting transfer prices in its integrated operations to produce higher profits in low-tax countries and lower profits in high-tax countries. Global strategic coordination also gave MNCs increased ability to take advantage of country-to-country differences in interest rates, exchange rates, credit terms, government subsidies, and export guarantees. As a consequence of these advantages, it became increasingly difficult for a company that produced and sold its product in only one country to succeed in an industry populated with aggressive competitors intent on achieving global dominance.

During the 1980s another source of competitive advantage began to emerge: using the strategic-fit advantages of related diversification to build stronger competitive positions simultaneously in several related global industries. Being a diversified MNC (DMNC) became competitively superior to being a single-business MNC in cases where strategic fits and economies of scope existed across global industries. Related diversification is most capable of producing competitive advantage for a multinational company where expertise in a core technology can be applied in different industries (at least one of which is global) and where there are important economies of scope and brand name advantages to being in a family of related businesses.[19] Illustration 22 indicates Honda's strategy in exploiting gasoline engine technology and its well-known name by diversifying into a variety of products with engines.

■ SOURCES OF COMPETITIVE ADVANTAGE FOR A DMNC

When a multinational company has expertise in a core technology and has diversified into a series of related products and businesses to exploit that core, a centralized R&D effort coordinated at the headquarters level holds real potential for competitive advantage. By channeling corporate resources directly into a strategically coordinated R&D/technology effort, as opposed to letting each business unit perform its own R&D function, the DMNC can launch a world-class, global-scale assault to advance the core technology, generate

ILLUSTRATION 22   *Honda's Competitive Advantage*

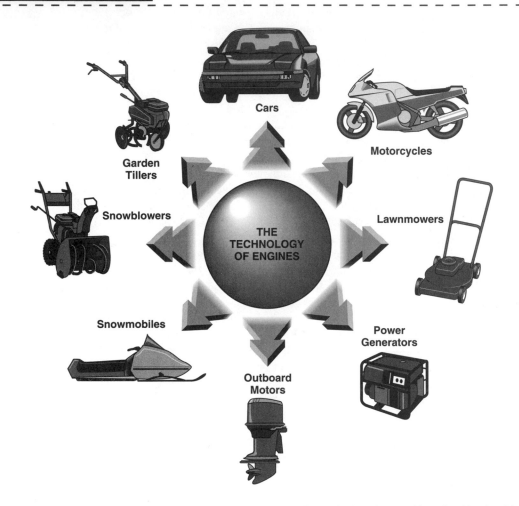

The Technology of Engines

At first blush anyone looking at Honda's lineup of products—cars, motorcycles, lawn mowers, power generators, outboard motors, snowmobiles, snowblowers, and garden tillers—might conclude that Honda has pursued unrelated diversification. But underlying the obvious product diversity is a common core: the technology of engines.

The basic Honda strategy is to exploit the company's expertise in engine technology and manufacturing and to capitalize on its brand recognition. One Honda ad teases consumers with the question, "How do you put six Hondas in a two-car garage?" It then shows a garage containing a Honda car, a Honda motorcycle, a Honda snowmobile, a Honda lawnmower, a Honda power generator, and a Honda outboard motor.

Source: Adapted from CK Prahalad and Yves L Doz, *The Multinational Mission* (New York: Free Press, 1987), p. 62.

technology-based manufacturing economies within and across product/business lines, make across-the-board product improvements, and develop complementary products—all significant advantages in a globally competitive marketplace. In the absence of centralized coordination, R&D/ technology investments are likely to be scaled down to match each business's product-market perspec-

---

A multinational corporation can gain competitive advantage by diversifying into global industries having related technologies.

---

tive, setting the stage for the strategic fit benefits of coordinated technology management to slip away.[20]

The second source of competitive advantage for a DMNC concerns the distribution and brand name advantages that can accrue from diversifying into related global industries. Consider, for instance, the competitive strength of such Japanese DMNCs as Sanyo and Matsushita. Both have diversified into a range of globally competitive consumer goods industries—TVs, stereo equipment, radios, VCRs, small domestic appliances such as microwave ovens, and personal computers. By widening their scope of operations in products marketed through similar distribution channels, Sanyo and Matsushita have not only exploited related technologies but also built stronger distribution capabilities, captured logistical and distribution-related economies, and established greater brand awareness for their products.[21] Such competitive advantages are unavailable to a domestic-only company pursuing single-business concentration. Moreover, with a well-diversified product line and a multinational market base, a DMNC can enter new country markets or new product markets and gain market share through below-market pricing or, if necessary, below-average-cost-pricing, subsidizing the entry with earnings from one or more of its country market profit sanctuaries and/or earnings in other businesses.

A multinational corporation can attain competitive advantage by diversifying into related global industries where the strategic fits produce economies of scope and the benefits of brand name transfer.

Both a one-business multinational company and a one-business domestic company are weakly positioned to defend their markets against a determined DMNC willing to accept lower short-term profits in order to establish itself in a desirable new market. A one-business domestic company has only one profit sanctuary—its home market. A one-business multinational company may have profit sanctuaries in several country markets but all are in the same business. Each is vulnerable to a DMNC that launches a major strategic offensive in their profit sanctuaries and low-balls its prices to win market share at their expense. A DMNC's ability to keep hammering away at competitors with low prices year after year may be supported by a cost advantage growing out of its related diversification strategy, a willingness to cross-subsidize low profits or even losses with earnings from its profit sanctuaries in other country markets and/or its earnings from other businesses. Sanyo, for example, by pursuing related diversification keyed to product-distribution-technology types of strategic fit and managing its product families on a global scale has the ability to encircle domestic companies like Zenith (which manufactures TVs and small computer systems) and Maytag (which manufactures home appliances) and put them under serious competitive pressure. In Zenith's case, Sanyo can peck away at Zenith's market share in televisions and in the process weaken the loyalty of television

ILLUSTRATION 23   *Mitsubishi: The Competitive Power of a Keiretsu*

Mitsubishi is Japan's largest *keiretsu*—a family of affiliated companies. With combined 1992 sales of $175 billion, the Mitsubishi *keiretsu* consists of 28 core companies: Mitsubishi Corp. (the trading company), Mitsubishi Heavy Industries (the group's biggest manufacturer—shipbuilding, air conditioners, forklifts, robots, gas turbines), Mitsubishi Motors, Mitsubishi Steel, Mitsubishi Aluminum, Mitsubishi Oil, Mitsubishi Petrochemical, Mitsubishi Gas Chemical, Mitsubishi Plastics, Mitsubishi Cable, Mitsubishi Electric, Mitsubishi Construction, Mitsubishi Paper Mills, Mitsubishi Mining and Cement, Mitsubishi Rayon, Nikon, Asahi Glass, Kirin Brewery, Mitsubishi Bank (the world's fifth largest bank and the lead bank for family companies), Tokio Marine and Fire Insurance (one of the world's largest insurance companies), and 8 others. Beyond this core group are hundreds of other Mitsubishi-related subsidiaries and affiliates.

The 28 core companies of the Mitsubishi *keiretsu* are bound together by cross-ownership of each other's stock (the percentage of shares of each core company owned by other members ranges from 17% to 100%, with an average of 27%), by interlocking directorships (it is standard for officers of one company to sit on the boards of other *keiretsu* members), joint ventures, and long-term business relationships. They use each others' products and services in many instances—among the suppliers to Mitsubishi Motor's Diamond Star plant in Bloomington, Illinois, are 25 Mitsubishi and Mitsubishi-related suppliers. It is common for them to join forces to make acquisitions—five Mitsubishi companies teamed to buy a cement plant in California; Mitsubishi Corp. bought an $880 million chemical company in Pittsburgh with financial assistance from Mitsubishi Bank and Mitsubishi Trust, then sold pieces to Mitsubishi Gas Chemical, Mitsubishi Rayon, Mitsubishi Petrochemical, and Mitsubishi Kasei. Mitsubishi Bank and occasionally other Mitsubishi financial enterprises serve as a primary financing source for new ventures and as a financial safety net if *keiretsu* members encounter tough market conditions or have financial problems.

Despite these links, there's no grand Mitsubishi strategy. Each company operates independently, pursuing its own strategy and markets. On occasion, group members find themselves going after the same markets competing with each other. Nor do member companies usually get sweetheart deals from other members; for example, Mitsubishi Heavy Industries lost out to Siemens in competing to supply gas turbines to a new power plant that Mitsubishi Corp.'s wholly owned Diamond Energy subsidiary constructed in Virginia. But operating independence does not prevent them from recognizing their mutual interests, cooperating voluntarily without formal controls, or turning inward to *keiretsu* members for business partnerships on ventures perceived as strategically important.

A President's Council, consisting of 49 chairmen and presidents, meet monthly, usually the second Friday of the month. While the formal agenda typically includes a discussion of joint philanthropical and public relations projects and a lecture by an expert on some current topic, participants report instances where strategic problems or opportunities affecting several group members are discussed and major decisions made. It is common for a Mitsubishi company involved in a major undertaking (initiating its first foray into the U.S. or European markets or developing a new technology) to ask for support from other members. In such cases, group members who can take business actions that contribute to solutions are expected to do so. The President's Council meetings also serve to cement personal ties, exchange information, identify mutual interests, and set up follow-on actions by subordinates. Other methods used by Mitsubishi to foster an active informal network of contacts, information sharing, cooperation, and business relationships among member companies include regular get-togethers of Mitsubishi–America and Mitsubishi–Europe executives and even a matchmaking club where member company employees can meet prospective spouses.

In recent years, Mitsubishi companies have introduced a number of consumer products in the United States and elsewhere, all branded with a three-diamond logo derived from the crest of the founding samurai family—cars and trucks made by Mitsubishi Motors, big-screen TVs and mobile phones made by Mitsubishi Electric, and air conditioners produced by Mitsubishi Heavy Industries. Mitsubishi executives believe common logo usage has produced added brand awareness; for example, in the United States Mitsubishi Motors' efforts to advertise and market its cars and trucks has helped boost brand awareness of Mitsubishi TVs. In several product categories one or more Mitsubishi companies operate in stages all along the industry value chain—from components production to assembly to shipping, warehousing, and distribution.

Similar practices exist in the next five largest Japanese *keiretsu:* Dai-Ichi Kangin with 47 core companies, Mitsui Group with 24 core companies (including Toyota and Toshiba), Sanwa with 44 core companies, Sumitomo with 20 core companies (including NEC, a maker of telecommunications equipment and personal computers), and Fuyo with 29 core companies (including Nissan and Canon). Most observers agree that Japan's *keiretsu* model gives Japanese companies major competitive advantages in international markets. According to a Japanese economics professor at Osaka University, "Using group power, they can engage in cutthroat competition."

Source: Based on information in "Mighty Mitsubishi Is on the Move" and "Hands across America: The Rise of Mitsubishi," *Business Week,* September 24, 1990, pp. 98–107.

---

retailers to the Zenith brand. In Maytag's case, Sanyo can diversify into large home appliances by acquiring an established appliance maker or manufacturing on its own and cross-subsidizing a low-priced market entry against Maytag and other less-diversified home appliance firms with earnings from its many other business and product lines. If Sanyo chooses, it can keep its prices low for several years to gain market share at the expense of domestic rivals, turning its attention to profits after the battle for market share and competitive position is won.[22] Some additional aspects of the competitive power of broadly diversified enterprises are dscribed in Illustration 23.

A multinational corporation that has diversified into related global industries is well positioned to outcompete both a one-business domestic company and a one-business multinational company.

The competitive principle is clear: A DMNC has a strategic arsenal capable of defeating both a single-business MNC and a single-business domestic company over the long term. The competitive advantages of a DMNC, however, depend on employing a related diversification strategy in industries that are already globally competitive or are becoming so. Then the related businesses have to be managed so as to capture strategic fit benefits. DMNCs have the biggest competitive advantage potential in industries with technology transfer and technology-sharing opportunities and where there are important economies of scope and brand name benefits associated with competing in related product families.

A DMNC also has important cross-subsidization potential for winning its way into attractive new markets. However, while DMNCs have significant cross-subsidization powers, they rarely use them in the extreme. It is one thing to use a *portion* of the profits and cash flows from existing businesses to cover reasonable short-term losses to gain entry to a new business or a new country market; it is quite another to drain corporate profits indiscriminately to the point of impairing overall company performance to support either deep price discounting and quick market penetration in the short term or continuing losses over the longer term. At some juncture, every business and every market entered has to make a profit contribution or become

A DMNC's most potent advantages usually derive from technology sharing, economies of scope, shared brand names, and its capacity to employ cross-subsidization tactics.

a candidate for abandonment. Moreover, the company has to command consistently acceptable overall performance from the whole business portfolio. So there are limits to cross-subsidization. As a general rule, cross-subsidization is justified only if there is a good chance that short-term losses can be amply recouped in some way over the long term.

▶ COMBINATION DIVERSIFICATION STRATEGIES

The six corporate diversification approaches described above are not mutually exclusive. They can be pursued in combination and in varying sequences, allowing ample room for companies to customize their diversification strategies to fit their own circumstances. The most common business portfolios created by corporate diversification strategies are:

- A "dominant-business" enterprise with sales concentrated in one major core business but with a modestly diversified portfolio of either related or unrelated businesses amounting to no more than one-third of total corporatewide sales.

- A narrowly diversified enterprise having a *few* (two to five) *related core* business units.

- A broadly diversified enterprise made up of *many* mostly *related* business units.

- A narrowly diversified enterprise comprised of a *few* (two to five) *core* business units in *unrelated* industries.

- A broadly diversified enterprise having *many* business units in mostly *unrelated* industries.

- A multibusiness enterprise that has diversified into unrelated areas but that has a portfolio of related businesses within each area—thus giving it *several unrelated groups of related businesses*.

In each case, the geographic markets of individual businesses within the portfolio can range from local to regional to national to multinational to global. Thus, a company can be competing locally in some businesses, nationally in others, and globally in still others.

Evaluating the Strategy of a Diversified Company

If we can know where we are and something about how we got there, we might see where we are trending—and if the outcomes which lie naturally in our course are unacceptable, to make timely change.

Abraham Lincoln

No company can afford everything it would like to do. Resources have to be allocated. The essence of strategic planning is to allocate resources to those areas that have the greatest future potential.

Reginald Jones

Once a company has diversified, three strategic issues continuously challenge corporate strategy-makers:

- How attractive is the group of businesses the company is in?
- Assuming the company sticks with its present lineup of businesses, how good is its performance outlook in the years ahead?
- If the previous two answers are not satisfactory, what should the company do to get out of some existing businesses, strengthen the positions of remaining businesses, and get into new businesses to boost the performance prospects of its business portfolio?

The task of crafting and implementing action plans to improve the attractiveness and competitive strength of a company's business-unit portfolio is the heart of what corporate-level strategic management is all about.

Strategic analysis of diversified companies builds on the concepts and methods used for single-business companies. But there are also new aspects to consider and additional analytical approaches to master. We use the following eight-step process to systematically evaluate the strategy of a diversified company, assess the caliber and potential of its various businesses, and decide what strategic actions to take next:

1. Identify the present corporate strategy.
2. Construct one or more business portfolio matrixes to reveal the character of the company's business portfolio.
3. Compare the long-term attractiveness of each industry the company has diversified into.
4. Compare the competitive strength of the company's business units to determine which are strong contenders in their respective industries.
5. Rate the different business units on the basis of their historical performance and their prospects for the future.

6. Assess each business unit's compatibility with present corporate strategy and determine the value of any strategic fit relationships among existing business units.

7. Rank the business units in terms of priority for new capital investment and decide whether the general strategic posture and direction for each business unit should be aggressive expansion, fortify and defend, overhaul and reposition, or harvest/divest.

8. Craft new strategic moves to improve overall corporate performance.

The rest of this chapter discusses this eight-step process and introduces the analytical techniques needed to arrive at sound corporate strategy appraisals.

▶ IDENTIFYING THE PRESENT CORPORATE STRATEGY

Strategic analysis of a diversified company starts by probing the organization's present strategy and business makeup. Recall from Figure 2–2 in Chapter 2 that a good overall perspective of a diversified company's corporate strategy comes from looking at:

Evaluating a diversified firm's business portfolio needs to begin with a clear identification of the firm's diversification strategy.

• The extent to which the firm is diversified, as measured by the proportion of total sales and operating profits contributed by each business unit and by whether the diversification base is broad or narrow.

• Whether the firm's portfolio is keyed to related or unrelated diversification, or a mixture of both.

• Whether the scope of company operations is mostly domestic, increasingly multinational, or global.

• The nature of recent moves to boost performance of key business units and/or strengthen existing business positions.

• Any moves to add new businesses to the portfolio and build positions in new industries.

• Any moves to divest weak or unattractive business units.

• Management efforts to realize the benefits of strategic fit relationships and use diversification to create competitive advantage.

• The proportion of capital expenditures going to each business unit.

Getting a clear fix on the current corporate strategy and the rationale for it are a necessary foundation for a thorough strategy analysis and, subsequently, for any changes to improve the strategy.

▶ MATRIX TECHNIQUES FOR EVALUATING DIVERSIFIED PORTFOLIOS

One of the most used techniques for assessing the quality of the businesses a company has diversified into is portfolio matrix analysis. *A business portfolio matrix is a two-dimensional display comparing the strategic positions of each one of a diversified company's businesses.* Matrixes can be constructed using any pair of strategic position indicators. The most revealing indicators are industry growth rate, market share,

long-term industry attractiveness, competitive strength, and stage of product/market
evolution. Usually one dimension of the matrix
relates to the attractiveness of the industry environment and the other to the strength of a business
within its industry. Three types of business portfolio
matrixes are used most frequently—the growth-
share matrix developed by the Boston Consulting
Group, the industry attractiveness-business strength matrix pioneered at General Electric,
and the Hofer-A.D. Little industry life-cycle matrix.

> A business portfolio matrix is a two-dimensional display comparing the strategic positions of every business within a diversified company.

■ THE GROWTH SHARE MATRIX

The first business portfolio matrix to receive widespread usage was a four-square grid
devised by the Boston Consulting Group (BCG), a leading management consulting firm.[1]
Figure 8–1 illustrates a BCG type of matrix. The matrix is formed using *industry growth
rate* and *relative market share* as the axes. Each
business unit in the corporate portfolio appears as a
bubble, or circle, on the four-cell matrix, with the
size of each bubble scaled to the percentage of
revenues it represents in the overall corporate
portfolio.

> The BCG portfolio matrix compares a diversified company's businesses on the basis of industry growth rate and relative market share.

Early BCG methodology arbitrarily placed the dividing line between high and low
industry growth rates at around twice the real GNP growth rate plus inflation, but the
boundary percentage can be set at any percentage (5 percent, 10 percent, or whatever) that
managers consider appropriate for their company's situation. A good case can be made for
placing the line so that business units in industries growing faster than the economy as a
whole end up in the high-growth cells and those in industries growing slower than the
economywide rate fall into low-growth cells. Rarely does it make sense to put the dividing
line between high growth and low growth at less than 5 percent.

Relative market share is the ratio of a business's market share to the market share held
by the largest rival firm in the industry, with market share measured in unit volume, not
dollars. For instance, if business A has a 15 percent share of its industry's total volume
and the share held by its largest rival is 30 percent,
then A's relative market share is 0.5. If business B
has a market-leading share of 40 percent and its
largest rival has a 30 percent share, B's relative
market share is 1.33. Given this definition, only
business units that are market share leaders in their
respective industries will have relative market share values greater than 1.0; business units
that trail one or more rivals in market share will have ratios below 1.0.

> Relative market share is a better indicator of a business's competitive strength and market position than a simple percentage measure of market share.

BCG's original standard put the border between high and low relative market share
at 1.0, as shown in Figure 8–1. When the boundary is set at 1.0, circles in the two
left-side cells of the matrix represent businesses in the firm's portfolio that are market
share leaders in their industry. Circles in the two right-side cells identify portfolio
members that are in runner-up positions in their industry. The degree to which they trail
is indicated by the size of the relative market share ratio. A ratio of .10 indicates that the

---

FIGURE 8-1 *The BCG Growth Share Business Portfolio Matrix*

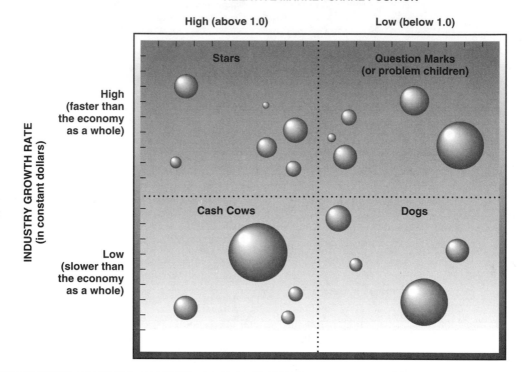

RELATIVE MARKET SHARE POSITION

High (above 1.0)   Low (below 1.0)

INDUSTRY GROWTH RATE (in constant dollars)

High (faster than the economy as a whole)

Low (slower than the economy as a whole)

Stars

Question Marks (or problem children)

Cash Cows

Dogs

Note: *Relative* market share is defined by the ratio of one's own market share to the market share held by the largest *rival* firm. When the vertical dividing line is set at 1.0, the only way a firm can achieve a star or cash cow position in the growth share matrix is to have the largest market share in the industry. Since this is a very stringent criterion, it may be fairer and more revealing to locate the vertical dividing line in the matrix at about 0.75 or 0.80.

business has a market share only 1/10 that of the largest firm in the market; whereas a ratio of .80 indicates a market share that is 4/5, or 80 percent, as big as the leading firm's. Many portfolio analysts think that putting the boundary between high and low relative market share at 1.0 is unreasonably stringent because only businesses having the largest market share in their industry can qualify for the two left-side cells of the matrix. They advocate putting the boundary at about 0.75 or 0.80 so that businesses to the left have *strong* or above-average market positions (even though they are not *the* leader) and businesses to the right are clearly in underdog or below-average positions.

Using *relative* market share instead of *actual* market share to construct the growth share matrix is analytically superior because the former measure is a better indicator of comparative market strength and competitive position. A 10 percent market share is much stronger if the leader's share is 12 percent than if it is 50 percent; the use of relative market share captures this difference. Equally important, relative market share is likely to reflect relative cost based on experience in producing the product and economies of large-scale production. Large businesses may be able to operate at lower unit costs than smaller firms because of technological and efficiency gains that attach to larger size. But the Boston Consulting Group found that the phenomenon of lower unit costs went beyond just the effects of scale economies. Based on accumulated research data, they found that as the cumulative volume of production increased, the knowledge gained from the firm's growing production experience often led to the discovery of additional efficiencies and ways to reduce cost even further. BCG labeled the relationship between cumulative production volume and lower unit costs as *the experience curve effect* (for more details, see Figure 3–2 in Chapter 3). A sizable experience curve effect in an industry's value chain places a strategic premium on market share: The competitor that gains the largest market share tends to realize important cost advantages that in turn can be used to lower prices and gain still additional customers, sales, market share, and profit. The stronger the experience curve effect in a business, the more dominant its role in strategy-making.[2]

With these features of the BCG growth share matrix in mind, we are ready to explore the portfolio implications for businesses in each cell of the matrix in Figure 8–1.

QUESTION MARKS AND PROBLEM CHILDREN

Business units falling in the upper-right quadrant of the growth share matrix have been designated by BCG as ''question marks'' or ''problem children.'' Rapid market growth makes such business units attractive from an industry standpoint. But their low relative market share (and thus reduced access to experience curve effects) raises a question about whether they have the strength to compete successfully against larger, more cost-efficient rivals—hence, the ''question mark'' or ''problem child'' designation. Question mark businesses, moreover, are typically ''cash hogs''—so labeled because their cash needs are high (owing to the large investment needed to finance rapid growth and new product development) and their internal cash generation is low (owing to low market share, less access to experience curve effects and scale economies, and consequently thinner profit margins). A question mark/cash hog business in a fast-growing industry may well require large infusions of cash just to keep up with rapid market growth and even bigger cash infusions if it must outgrow the market and gain enough market share to become an industry leader. The corporate parent of a cash hog business has to decide whether it is worthwhile to fund the perhaps considerable investment requirements of a question mark business.

A ''cash hog'' business is one whose internal cash flows are inadequate to fully fund its capital requirements.

BCG has argued that the two best strategic options for a question mark business are (1) an aggressive invest-and-expand strategy to capitalize on the industry's rapid-growth opportunities or (2) in the event that the costs of building market share outweigh the potential payoff, divestiture. Pursuing a fast-growth strategy is imperative anytime an attractive question mark business is in an industry characterized by a strong experience curve effect. Sometimes it takes major gains in market share to begin to match the lower costs of firms with greater cumulative production experience and still greater market shares. The stronger the experience curve effect, the more potent the cost advantages of rivals

The prescriptions for question mark businesses are to either invest aggressively and grow it into a star performer or else divest it and shift resources to businesses with better prospects.

with larger relative market shares. Consequently, so the BCG thesis goes, unless a question mark/problem child business can successfully pursue a fast-growth strategy and win major market share gains, it cannot hope to ever become cost competitive with large-volume firms that are further down the experience curve—in which case divestiture becomes the only other viable long-run alternative. BCG's corporate strategy prescriptions for managing question mark/problem child business units are thus straightforward: Divest those that are weaker and have less chance to catch the leaders on the experience curve; invest heavily in high-potential question marks and groom them to become tomorrow's "stars."

STARS

Businesses with high relative market share positions in high-growth markets rank as "stars" in the BCG grid because they offer excellent profit and growth opportunities. They are the business units an enterprise depends on to boost overall performance of the total portfolio.

Given their dominant market share position and rapid growth environment, stars typically require large cash investments to expand production facilities and meet working capital needs. They also tend to generate large internal cash flows due to the low-cost advantage of scale economies and cumulative production experience. Some star businesses can cover their investment needs with self-generated cash flows; others can be cash hogs requiring sizable capital infusions from their corporate parents to stay abreast of rapid industry growth. Normally, strongly positioned star businesses in industries where growth is beginning to slow tend to be self-sustaining in terms of cash flow and make little claim on the corporate parent's treasury. Young stars, however, typically require substantial investment capital *beyond what they can generate on their own* and are thus cash hogs.

"Star" businesses have strong competitive positions in rapidly growing industries, are major contributors to corporate revenue and profit growth, and may be cash hogs.

CASH COWS

Businesses with a high relative market share in a low growth market are designated by BCG as "cash cows." A *cash cow business* generates substantial cash surpluses over what is needed for reinvestment and growth. Because of the business's high relative market share and industry leadership position, it has the sales volume, market reputation, and brand loyalty to earn attractive profits. Because it is in a slow-growth industry, it typically generates more cash from current operations than is needed for capital reinvestment and financing competitive efforts to sustain its present market position.

A "cash cow" business is valuable because it generates cash for financing new acquisitions, funding the capital requirements of cash hog businesses, and paying dividends.

Many of today's cash cows were yesterday's stars, having gradually moved down on the vertical scale (dropping from the top cell into the bottom cell) as industry demand matured. Cash cows, though less attractive from a growth standpoint, are valuable businesses. The surplus cash flows they generate can be used to pay corporate dividends, finance acquisitions, and provide funds for investing in emerging stars and problem children being groomed as future stars. Every effort should be made to keep strong cash cow businesses in healthy condition to preserve their cash-generating capability over the long term. The goal should be to fortify and defend a cash cow's market position while efficiently generating dollars to redeploy elsewhere. Weakening cash cows (those drifting toward the lower right corner of the cash cow cell) may become candidates for harvesting and eventual divestiture if competition stiffens or increased capital requirements stemming from the emergence of important new technologies or replacement of major facilities cause cash flow surpluses to dry up or, in the worst case, become negative.

Dogs

Businesses with a low relative market share in a slow-growth industry are called "dogs" because of their dim growth prospects, their trailing market position, and the squeeze that being behind the leaders on the experience curve puts on their profit margins. Weak dog businesses (those positioned in the lower right corner of the dog cell) are often unable to generate attractive long-term cash flows. Sometimes they cannot even produce enough cash to support a rear-guard fortify-and-defend strategy—especially if competition is brutal and profit margins are chronically thin. Consequently, except in unusual cases, the BCG corporate strategy prescription is that weakly performing dog businesses be harvested, divested, or liquidated, depending on which alternative yields the most cash.

> **Weaker dog businesses should be harvested, divested, or liquidated; stronger dogs can be retained as long as their profits and cash flows remain acceptable.**

Implications for Corporate Strategy

The chief contribution of the BCG growth share matrix is the attention it draws to the cash flow and investment characteristics of various types of businesses and how corporate financial resources can be shifted between business subsidiaries to optimize the performance of the whole corporate portfolio. According to BCG analysis, a sound, long-term corporate strategy should utilize the excess cash generated by cash cow business units to finance market share increases for cash hog businesses. If successful, the cash hogs eventually become self-supporting stars. Then, when stars' markets begin to mature and their growth slows, they become cash cows. The "success sequence" is thus problem child/question mark to young star (but perhaps still a cash hog) to self-supporting star to cash cow.

> **The BCG growth share matrix highlights the cash flow, investment, and profitability characteristics of certain types of businesses and the benefits of shifting financial resources among them.**

Weaker, less-attractive question mark businesses are often a liability to a diversified company because of the high-cost economics associated with their low relative market share and because their cash hog nature requires the corporate parent to keep pumping enough capital into the business to keep it abreast of fast-paced market growth. According to BCG prescriptions, these question marks should be prime divestiture candidates *unless* (1) they can be kept profitable and viable with their own internally generated funds or (2) the capital infusions needed from the corporate parent are quite modest.

Not every question mark business is a cash hog or a disadvantaged competitor, however; those in industries with small capital requirements, few scale economies, and weak experience curve effects can often compete ably against larger industry leaders and contribute enough to corporate earnings and return on investment to justify retention in the portfolio. Clearly, though, weaker question marks still have a low-priority claim on corporate resources and a tenuous role in the portfolio. Question mark businesses unable to become stars are destined to drift vertically downward in the matrix, becoming dogs, as growth slows for their industry's products.

Dogs should be retained only as long as they contribute adequately to overall company performance. Strong dogs may produce a positive cash flow and show average profitability. But the further a dog business moves toward the bottom-right corner of the BCG matrix, the more likely that it is tying up assets that could be more profitably redeployed. The BCG recommendation for managing a weakening or already weak dog is to harvest it. When a harvesting strategy is no longer attractive, a weak dog should be eliminated from the portfolio.

There are two ''disaster sequences'' in the BCG scheme: (1) when a star's position in the matrix erodes over time to that of a problem child and then is dragged by slowing industry growth down into the dog cell of the matrix and (2) when a cash cow loses market leadership to the point where it becomes a dog on the decline. Other strategic mistakes include overinvesting in a safe cash cow; underinvesting in a high-potential question mark, so instead of moving into the star category it tumbles into a dog; and shotgunning resources thinly over many question marks rather than concentrating on the best question marks to boost their chances of becoming stars.

STRENGTHS AND WEAKNESSES IN THE GROWTH SHARE MATRIX APPROACH

The BCG business portfolio matrix makes a definite contribution to thinking strategically about a diversified company's businesses. Viewing a diversified group of businesses as a collection of cash flows and cash requirements (present and future) is a major step forward in understanding the financial aspects of corporate strategy. The BCG matrix highlights the financial interaction within a corporate portfolio, shows the kinds of financial considerations that must be dealt with, and explains why priorities for corporate resource allocation can differ from business to business. It also provides good rationalizations for both invest-and-expand strategies and divestiture. Yet, it is analytically incomplete and potentially misleading:

The growth-share matrix has significant shortcomings.

---

1. A four-cell matrix based on high-low classifications hides the fact that many businesses (the majority?) are in markets with an average growth rate and have relative market shares that are neither high nor low but somewhere in between. In which cells do these average businesses belong?

2. While viewing businesses as stars, cash cows, dogs, or question marks does have communicative appeal, it is a misleading simplification to pigeonhole all businesses into one of four categories. Some market share leaders have never really been stars in terms of profitability. All businesses with low relative market shares are not dogs or question marks—in many cases, runner-up firms have proven track records in terms of growth, profitability, and competitive ability, even gaining on the so-called leaders. In fact, a key characteristic to assess is the *trend* in a firm's relative market

share. Is it gaining ground or losing ground and why? This weakness can be solved by placing directional arrows on each of the circles in the matrix—see Figure 8–2.

3. The BCG matrix is not a reliable indicator of relative investment opportunities across business units.[3] For example, investing in a star is not necessarily more attractive than investing in a lucrative cash cow. The matrix doesn't indicate if a question mark business is a potential winner or a likely loser. It says nothing about whether shrewd investment can turn a strong dog into a cash cow.

4. Being a market leader in a slow-growth industry is not a surefire guarantee of cash cow status because *(a)* the investment requirements of a fortify-and-defend strategy, given the impact of inflation and changing technology on the costs of replacing worn-out facilities and equipment, can soak up much or all of the available internal cash flows, and *(b)* as markets mature, competitive forces often stiffen and the ensuing vigorous battle for volume and market share can shrink profit margins and wipe out any surplus cash flows.

FIGURE 8–2   *Present versus Future Positions in the Portfolio Matrix*

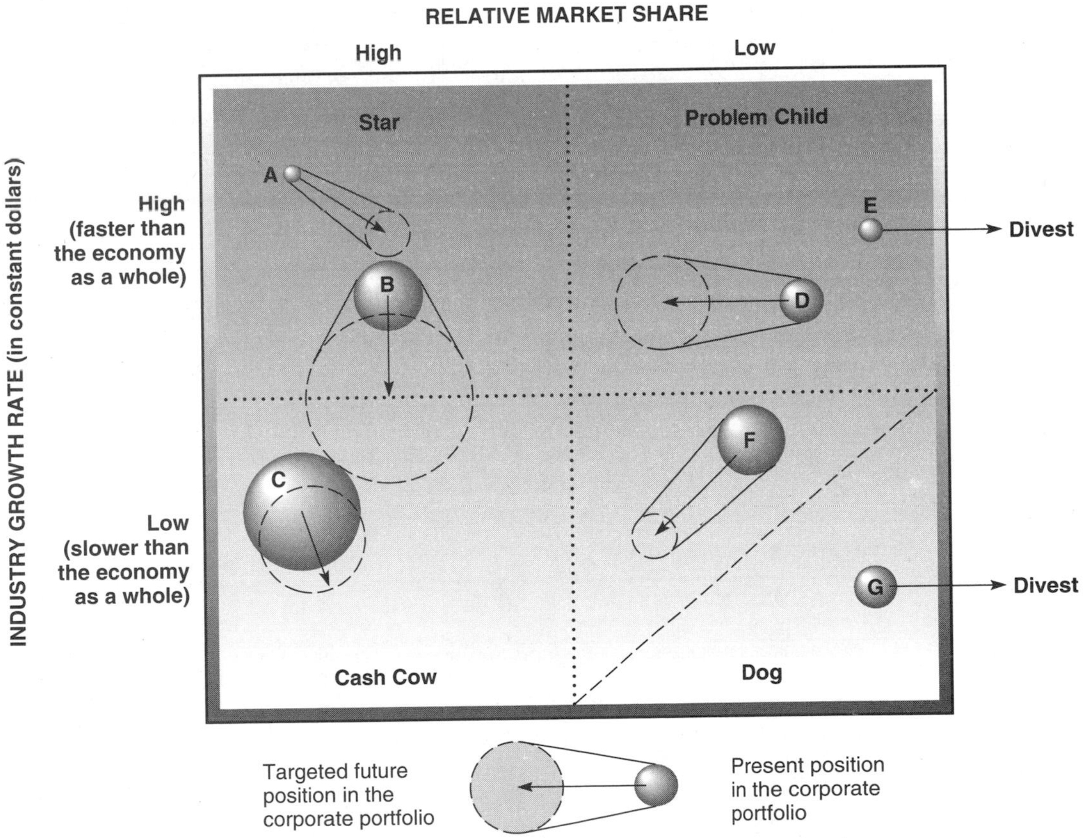

5. As our discussion in Chapter 3 clearly indicated, to thoroughly assess the relative long-term attractiveness of a group of businesses, corporate strategists need to examine more than just industry growth and relative market share.

6. The connection between relative market share and profitability is not as tight as the experience curve effect implies. The importance of cumulative production experience in lowering unit costs varies from industry to industry. Sometimes, a larger market share translates into a unit-cost advantage; sometimes it doesn't. Hence, it is wise to be cautious when prescribing strategy based on the assumption that experience curve effects are strong enough and cost differences among competitors big enough to totally drive competitive advantage. There are more sources of competitive advantage than just experience curve economics.

■ THE INDUSTRY ATTRACTIVENESS—BUSINESS STRENGTH MATRIX

An alternative matrix approach that avoids some of the shortcomings of the BCG growth share matrix was pioneered by General Electric with help from the consulting firm of McKinsey and Company. GE's effort to analyze its broadly diversified portfolio produced a nine-cell matrix based on the two dimensions of long-term industry attractiveness and business strength/competitive position (see Figure 8–3).[4] Both dimensions of the matrix are a composite of several factors as opposed to a single factor. The criteria for determining long-term industry attractiveness include market size and growth rate; technological requirements, the intensity of competition; entry and exit barriers, seasonality and cyclical influences, capital requirements, emerging industry threats and opportunities, historical and projected industry profitability, and social, environmental, and regulatory influences. To arrive at a formal, quantitative measure of long-term industry attractiveness, the chosen measures are assigned weights based on their importance to corporate management and their role in the diversification strategy. The sum of the weights must add up to 1.0. Weighted attractiveness ratings are calculated by multiplying the industry's rating on each factor (using a 1-to-5 or 1-to-10 rating scale) by the factor's weight. For example, a rating score of 8 times a weight of .25 gives a weighted rating of 2.0. The sum of weighted ratings for all the attractiveness factors yields the industry's long-term attractiveness. The procedure is shown below:

> In the attractiveness–strength matrix, each business's location depends on quantitative measures of long-term industry attractiveness and business strength/competitive position.

Industry Attractiveness Factor	Weight	Rating	Weighted Industry Rating
Market size and projected growth	.15	5	0.75
Seasonality and cyclical influences	.10	8	0.80
Technological considerations	.10	1	0.10
Intensity of competition	.25	4	1.00
Emerging opportunities and threats	.15	1	0.15
Capital requirements	.05	2	0.10
Industry profitability	.10	3	0.30
Social, political, regulatory, and environmental factors	.10	7	0.70
Industry attractiveness rating	1.00		3.90

- **Relative market share**
- **Possession of desirable core competencies**
- **Profit margins relative to competitors**
- **Ability to match or beat rivals on product quality and service**
- **Relative cost position**
- **Knowledge of customers and markets**
- **Technological capability**
- **Caliber of management**

BUSINESS STRENGTH/ COMPETITIVE POSITION

- **Market size and growth rate**
- **Industry profit margins (historical and projected)**
- **Intensity of competition**
- **Seasonality**
- **Cyclicality**
- **Technology and capital requirements**
- **Social, environmental, regulatory, and human impacts**
- **Emerging opportunities and threats**
- **Barriers to entry and exit**

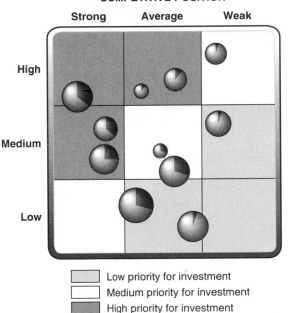

LONG-TERM INDUSTRY ATTRACTIVENESS

Strong   Average   Weak

High

Medium

Low

- Low priority for investment
- Medium priority for investment
- High priority for investment

Attractiveness ratings are calculated for each industry represented in the corporate portfolio. Each industry's attractiveness score determines its position on the vertical scale in Figure 8–3.

To arrive at a quantitative measure of business strength/competitive position, each business in the corporate portfolio is rated using the same kind of approach as for industry attractiveness. The factors used to assess business strength/competitive position include such criteria as market share, relative cost position, ability to match rival firms on product quality, knowledge of customers and markets, possession of desirable core competencies, adequacy of technological expertise, caliber of management, and profitability relative to competitors (as specified in the box in Figure 8–3). Analysts have a choice between rating each business unit on the very same generic factors (which strengthens the basis for interindustry comparisons) or rating each business unit's strength on the factors most pertinent to its own industry (which gives a sharper measure of competitive position than a generic set of factors). Each business's strength/position rating determines its position along the horizontal axis of the matrix—that is, whether it merits a strong, average, or weak designation.[5]

The industry attractiveness and business strength scores for a business provide the basis for locating it in one of the nine cells of the matrix. In the GE attractiveness-strength matrix, the area of the circles is proportional to the size of the industry, and the pie slices within the circle reflect the business's market share.

CORPORATE STRATEGY IMPLICATIONS

The most important strategic implications from the attractiveness-strength matrix are the assignment of investment priorities to each of the company's business units. Businesses in the three cells at the upper left, where long-term industry attractiveness and business strength/competitive position are favorable, are accorded top investment priority. The strategic prescription for businesses falling in these three cells is "grow and build," with businesses in the high-strong cell having the highest claim on investment funds. Next in priority come businesses positioned in the three diagonal cells stretching from the lower left to the upper right. These businesses are usually given medium priority. They merit steady reinvestment to maintain and protect their industry positions; however, if a business in one of these three cells has an unusually attractive opportunity, it can win a higher investment priority and be given the go-ahead to employ a more aggressive strategic approach. The typical strategy prescription for businesses in the three cells in the lower right corner of the matrix is harvest or divest. In exceptional cases, however, where good turnaround potential exists, a prescription of "overhaul and reposition" is appropriate.[6]

The nine-cell attractiveness-strength approach has three desirable attributes. One, it allows for intermediate rankings between high and low and between strong and weak. Two, it incorporates explicit consideration of a much wider variety of strategically relevant variables. The BCG matrix is based totally on two considerations—industry growth rate and relative market share; the nine-cell GE matrix takes many factors into

account to determine long-term industry attractiveness and many factors into account to determine business strength/competitive position. Three, and most important, it stresses the channeling of corpo-

– – – – – – – – – – – – – – – – – – –
The nine-cell attractiveness-strength matrix is conceptually stronger than the four-cell growth-share matrix.
– – – – – – – – – – – – – – – – – – –

rate resources to businesses with the greatest probability of achieving competitive advantage and superior performance. It is hard to argue against the logic of concentrating resources in those businesses that enjoy a higher degree of attractiveness and competitive strength, being very selective in making investments in businesses with ''intermediate'' positions, and withdrawing resources from businesses that are lower in attractiveness and strength unless they offer exceptional turnaround potential.

However, the nine-cell GE matrix, like the four-cell growth share matrix, provides no real guidance on the specifics of business strategy; the most that can be concluded from the GE matrix analysis is the *general* strategic posture to take in managing the business: aggressive expansion, fortify-and-defend, or harvest–divest. Such prescriptions may be valuable from an overall portfolio management perspective, but they leave untouched the whole issue of strategic coordination across related businesses, as well as what specific competitive approaches and strategic actions to take at the business-unit level. Another weakness is that the attractiveness–strength matrix effectively hides businesses that are about to emerge as winners because their industries are entering the takeoff stage.[7]

FIGURE 8-4 *The Life Cycle Portfolio Matrix*

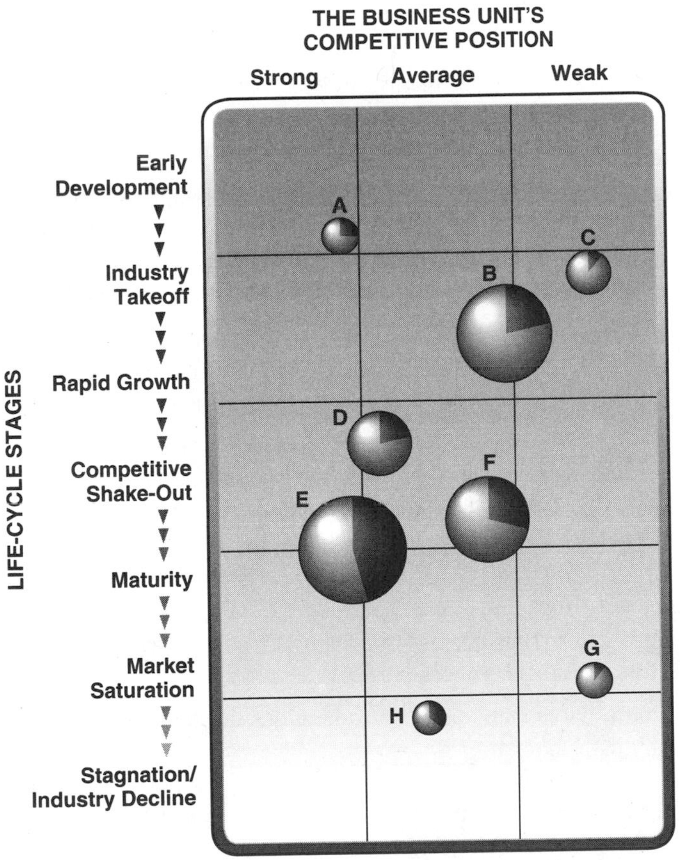

■ THE LIFE CYCLE MATRIX

To better identify a *developing-winner* type of business, analysts can use a 15-cell matrix where business units are plotted based on their stage of industry evolution and strength of competitive position, as shown in Figure 8–4.[8] Again, the circles represent the sizes of the industries and the pie wedges denote the business's market share. In Figure 8–4, business A could be labeled a *developing winner;* business C might be classified as a *potential loser,* business E as an *established winner,* business F as a *cash cow,* and business G as a *loser* or a *dog.* The power of the life cycle matrix is the story it tells about the distribution of a diversified company's businesses across the stages of industry evolution.

The life cycle matrix highlights how a diversified firm's businesses are distributed across the industry life cycle.

■ DECIDING WHICH PORTFOLIO MATRICES TO CONSTRUCT

Restricting the analysis to just one type of portfolio matrix is unwise. Each matrix has its pros and cons, and each tells a different story about the portfolio's strengths and weaknesses. If adequate data is available, all three matrices should be constructed since there's merit in assessing the company's business portfolio from different perspectives. Corporate managers need to understand the mix of industries represented in the portfolio, the strategic position each business has in its industry, the portfolio's performance potential, and relevant financial and resource allocation considerations. Using all three matrices to view a diversified portfolio enhances such understanding.

▶ COMPARING INDUSTRY ATTRACTIVENESS

A principal consideration in evaluating a diversified company's strategy is the attractiveness of the industries it has entered as a result of diversification. The more attractive the industries are that the company has invested in, the better are its long-term profit prospects. Industry attractiveness needs to be evaluated from three perspectives:

1. *The attractiveness of each industry represented in the business portfolio.* The relevant question is ''Is this a good industry for the company to be in?'' Ideally, each industry the firm has diversified into can pass the attractiveness test.

2. *Each industry's attractiveness relative to the others.* The question to answer here is, ''Which industries in the portfolio are the most attractive and which are the least attractive?'' Ranking the industries from most attractive to least attractive is a prerequisite to deciding how to allocate corporate resources.

3. *The attractiveness of all the industries as a group.* The question here is, ''How appealing is the mix of industries?'' A company whose revenues and profits come chiefly from businesses in unattractive industries probably needs to consider restructuring its business portfolio.

All the industry attractiveness considerations discussed in Chapter 3 have application in this analytical phase.

An industry attractiveness/business strength portfolio matrix provides a strong, systematic basis for judging which business units are in the most attractive industries. If such a matrix has not been constructed, quantitative rankings of industry attractiveness can be developed using the same procedure described earlier for the nine-cell GE portfolio matrix. As a rule, all the industries represented in the business portfolio should, at minimum, be judged on the following attractiveness factors:

- *Market size and projected growth rate*—faster-growing industries tend to be more attractive than slow-growing industries, other things being equal.

- *The intensity of competition*—industries where competitive pressures are relatively weak are more attractive than industries where competitive pressures are strong.

- *Technological and production skills required*—industries where the skill requirements are closely matched to company capabilities are more attractive than industries where the company's technical and/or manufacturing expertise is limited.

- *Capital requirements*—industries with low capital requirements (or amounts within the company's reach) are relatively more attractive than industries where investment requirements could strain corporate financial resources.

- *Seasonal and cyclical factors*—industries where demand is relatively stable and dependable are more attractive than industries where there are wide swings in buyer demand.

- *Industry profitability*—industries with healthy profit margins and high rates of return on investment are generally more attractive than industries where profits have historically been low or where the business risks are high.

- *Social, political, regulatory, and environmental factors*—industries with significant problems in these areas are less attractive than industries where such problems are no worse than most businesses encounter.

- *Strategic fits with other industries into which the firm has diversified*—an industry can be attractive simply because it has valuable strategic fit with other industries represented in the portfolio.

Calculation of industry attractiveness ratings for all industries in the corporate portfolio provides a basis for ranking the industries from most attractive to least attractive. If formal industry attractiveness ratings seem too cumbersome or tedious to calculate, corporate managers can rely upon their knowledge of conditions in each industry to classify individual industries as having "high," "medium," or "low" attractiveness. However, the validity of such subjective assessments depends on whether management has probed industry conditions sufficiently to make dependable judgments.

For a diversified company to be a strong performer, a substantial portion of its revenues and profits must come from business units judged to be in attractive industries. It is particularly important that core businesses be in industries with a good outlook for growth and above-average profitability. Business units in the least attractive industries may be divestiture candidates, unless they are positioned strongly enough to overcome the adverse industry environment or they are a strategically important component of the portfolio.

> The more attractive the industries into which a company diversifies, the better its performance prospects.

► ## COMPARING BUSINESS-UNIT STRENGTH

Doing an appraisal of each business unit's strength and competitive position in its industry helps corporate managers evaluate how the business is positioned in its industry and the extent to which it already is or can become a strong market contender. The two most revealing techniques for evaluating a business's industry position are SWOT analysis and competitive strength assessment. Quantitative rankings of the strength/position of the various business units in the corporate portfolio can be calculated using either the procedure described in constructing the attractiveness-strength matrix or the procedure presented in Chapter 4. Assessments of how a diversified company's business subsidiaries compare in competitive strength should be based on such factors as:

- *Relative market share*—business units with higher relative market shares normally have greater competitive strength than business units with lower shares.

- *Ability to compete on price and/or quality*—business units which are very cost-competitive and/or which have established brand names and a reputation for excellent product quality tend to be more strongly positioned in their industries than business units struggling to establish a recognized name or achieve cost parity with major rivals.

- *Technology and innovation capabilities*—business units recognized for their technological leadership and innovative ability are usually strong competitors in their industry.

- *How well the business unit's skills and competencies match industry key success factors*—the more a business unit's strengths match the industry's key success factors, the stronger its competitive position tends to be.

- *Profitability relative to competitors*—business units that consistently earn above-average returns on investment and have bigger profit margins than their rivals usually have stronger competitive positions than business units with below-average profitability for their industry. Moreover, above-average profitability signals competitive advantage, while below-average profitability usually denotes competitive disadvantage.

Other indicators of competitive strength which can be deployed include knowledge of customers and markets, production capabilities, marketing skills, reputation and brand name awareness, and the caliber of management.

Calculation of competitive strength ratings for each business unit provides a basis for judging which ones are in strong positions in their industries and which are in weak positions. If calculating competitive strength ratings is complicated by lack of sufficient data, analysts can rely upon their knowledge of each business unit's competitive situation and again use the "strong," "average," or "weak," classifications of competitive position. If trustworthy, such subjective assessments of business-unit strength can substitute for quantitative measures.

Managerial evaluations of which businesses in the portfolio enjoy the strongest competitive positions add further rationale and justification for corporate resource allocation. A company may earn larger profits over the long term by investing in a business with a competitively strong position in a moderately attractive industry than a weak business in a glamour industry. This is why a diversified company needs to consider *both* industry attractiveness and business strength in deciding where to steer resources.

> Shareholder interests are generally best served by concentrating corporate resources on businesses that can contend for market leadership in their industry.

Many diversified companies concentrate their resources on industries where they can be strong market contenders and divest businesses that are not good candidates for becoming leaders. At General Electric, the whole thrust of corporate strategy and corporate resource allocation is to put GE's businesses into a Number 1 or 2 position in both the United States and globally—see Illustration 24.

▶ COMPARING BUSINESS-UNIT PERFORMANCE

Once each business subsidiary has been rated on the basis of industry attractiveness and competitive strength, the next step is to evaluate which businesses have the best performance prospects and which ones have the worst. The most important considerations in judging business unit performance are sales growth, profit growth, contribution to company earnings, and the return on capital invested in the business. Cash flow generation can be a big consideration, especially for cash cow businesses or businesses with potential for harvesting. Information on each business's past performance can be gleaned from financial records. While past performance is not necessarily a good predictor of future performance, it does tell which businesses have been strong performers and which have been weak performers. The industry attractiveness/business strength evaluations should provide a solid basis for judging future prospects. Normally, strong business units in attractive industries have significantly better prospects than weak businesses in unattractive industries.

The growth and profit outlook for the company's core businesses generally determine whether the portfolio as a whole will turn in a strong or weak performance. Noncore businesses with subpar track records and little expectation for improvement are logical candidates for divestiture. Business subsidiaries with the brightest profit and growth prospects generally should head the list for having their capital investment projects funded.

▶ STRATEGIC FIT ANALYSIS

The next analytical step is to determine how well each business unit fits into the company's overall business picture. Fit needs to be reviewed from two angles: (1) whether a business unit has valuable strategic fit with other businesses the firm has diversified into (or has an opportunity to diversify into) and (2) whether the business unit meshes well with corporate strategy or adds a beneficial dimension to the corporate portfolio. A business is more attractive *strategically* when it has cost-sharing, skills transfer, or brand name transfer opportunities that enhance competitive advantage and when it fits in with the firm's strategic direction. A business is more valuable *financially* when it is capable

---

ILLUSTRATION 24   *Portfolio Management at General Electric*

When Jack Welch became CEO of General Electric in 1981, he launched a corporate strategy effort to reshape the company's diversified business portfolio. Early on he issued a challenge to GE's business-unit managers to become Number 1 or Number 2 in their industry; failing that, the business units either had to capture a decided technological advantage translatable into a competitive edge or face possible divestiture.

By 1989, GE was a different company. Under Welch's prodding, GE divested operations worth $9 billion—TV operations, small appliances, a mining business, and computer chips. It spent a total of $24 billion acquiring new businesses, most notably RCA, Roper (a maker of major appliances whose biggest customer was Sears), and Kidder Peabody (a Wall Street investment banking firm). Internally, many of the company's smaller business operations were put under the direction of larger "strategic business units." But, most significantly, in 1989, 12 of GE's 14 strategic business units were market leaders in the United States and globally (the company's financial services and communications units served markets too fragmented to rank):

	Market Standing In the United States	Market Standing In the World
Aircraft engines	First	First
Broadcasting (NBC)	First	Not applicable
Circuit breakers	Tied for first with 2 others	Tied for first with 3 others
Defense electronics	Second	Second
Electric motors	First	First
Engineering plastics	First	First
Factory automation	Second	Third
Industrial and power systems	First	First
Lighting	First	Second
Locomotives	First	Tied for first
Major home appliances	First	Tied for second
Medical diagnostic imaging	First	First

In 1989, having divested most of the weak businesses and having built existing businesses into leading contenders, Welch launched a new initiative within GE to dramatically boost productivity and reduce the size of GE's bureaucracy. Welch argued that for GE to continue to be successful in a global marketplace, the company had to press hard for continuous cost reduction in each of its businesses and cut through bureaucratic procedures to shorten response times to changing market conditions.

Source: Developed from information in Stratford P Sherman, "Inside the Mind of Jack Welch," *Fortune,* March 27, 1989, pp. 39–50.

Business subsidiaries that don't fit strategically should be considered for divestiture unless their financial performance is outstanding.

of contributing heavily to corporate performance objectives and when it materially enhances the company's overall worth. Just as businesses with poor profit prospects ought to become divestiture candidates, so also should businesses that don't fit strategically into the company's overall business picture. Firms that emphasize related diversification probably should divest businesses with little or no strategic fit unless such businesses are unusually good financial performers or offer superior growth opportunities.

▶ RANKING THE BUSINESS UNITS ON INVESTMENT PRIORITY

Using the information and results of the preceding evaluation steps, corporate strategists can rank business units in terms of priority for new capital investment and decide on a general strategic direction for each business unit. The task is to determine where the corporation should be investing its financial resources. Which business units should have top priority for new capital investment and financial support? Which business units should carry the lowest priority for new investment? The ranking process should clarify management thinking about what the basic strategic approach for each business unit should be—grow and build (aggressive expansion), fortify and defend (protect current position with new investments as needed), overhaul and reposition (try to move the business into a more desirable industry position and to a better spot in the business portfolio matrix), or harvest/divest. In deciding whether to divest a business unit, corporate managers should rely on a number of evaluating criteria: industry attractiveness, competitive strength, strategic fit with other businesses, performance potential (profit, return on capital employed, contribution to cash flow), compatibility with corporate priorities, capital requirements, and value to the overall portfolio.

> Improving a diversified company's long-term financial performance entails concentrating company resources on businesses with the best prospects and investing minimally, if at all, in businesses with subpar prospects.

In ranking the business units on investment priority, consideration needs to be given to whether and how corporate resources and skills can be used to enhance the competitive standing of particular business units.[9] The potential for skills transfer and infusion of new capital to make a difference in business unit performance becomes especially significant when the firm has business units in less-than-desirable competitive positions and/or where improvement in some key success area could make a big difference to the business unit's performance. It is also important when corporate strategy is predicated on strategic fits that involve transferring corporate skills to recently acquired business units to strengthen their competitiveness.[10]

▶ CRAFTING A CORPORATE STRATEGY

The preceding analysis sets the stage for crafting strategic moves to improve a diversified company's overall performance. The basic issue of "what to do?" hinges on the conclusions drawn about the overall *mix* of businesses in the portfolio.[11] Key questions include: Does the portfolio contain enough businesses in very attractive industries? Does the portfolio contain too many marginal businesses? Is the proportion of mature or declining businesses so great that corporate growth will be sluggish? Does the firm have enough cash cows to finance the stars and emerging winners? Can the company's core businesses be counted on to generate dependable profits and/or cash flow? Is the portfolio overly vulnerable to seasonal or recessionary influences? Does the portfolio contain businesses or industries that the company really doesn't need to be in. Is the firm burdened with too many businesses in average-to-weak competitive positions? Does the makeup of the business portfolio put the company in good position for the future? Answers to these questions indicate whether corporate strategists should consider divesting certain businesses, making new acquisitions, or restructuring the makeup of the portfolio.

■ THE PERFORMANCE TEST

A good test of the strategic and financial attractiveness of a diversified firm's business portfolio is whether the company can attain its performance objectives with its current lineup of businesses. If so, no major corporate strategy changes are indicated. However, if a performance shortfall is probable, corporate strategists can take any of several actions to close the gap:[12]

1. *Alter the strategic plans for some (or all) of the businesses in the portfolio.* This option involves renewed corporate efforts to get better performance out of its present business units. Corporate managers can push business-level managers for better business unit performance. However, pursuing better short-term performance too zealously can impair a business's potential to perform better over the long-term. Canceling expenditures that will bolster a business's long-term competitive position in order to squeeze out better short-term financial performance is a perilous strategy. In any case, there are limits on how much extra performance can be squeezed out to reach established targets.

2. *Add new business units to the corporate portfolio.* Boosting overall performance by making new acquisitions and/or starting new businesses internally raises some new strategy issues. Expanding the corporate portfolio means taking a close look at *(a)* whether to acquire related or unrelated businesses, *(b)* what size acquisition(s) to make, *(c)* how the new units will fit into the present corporate structure, *(d)* what specific features to look for in an acquisition candidate, and *(e)* whether acquisitions can be financed without shortchanging present business units on their new investment requirements. Nonetheless, adding new businesses is a major strategic option, one frequently used by diversified companies to escape sluggish earnings performance.

3. *Divest weak-performing or money-losing businesses.* The most likely candidates for divestiture are businesses in a weak competitive position, in a relatively unattractive industry, or in an industry that does not fit the strategic requirements of the portfolio. Funds from divestitures can, of course, be used to finance new acquisitions, pay down corporate debt, or fund new strategic ventures in the remaining businesses.

4. *Form alliances to try to alter conditions responsible for subpar performance potentials.* In some situations, alliances with domestic or foreign firms, trade associations, suppliers, customers, or special interest groups may ameliorate adverse performance prospects.[13] Forming or supporting a political action group may be an effective way of lobbying for solutions to import-export problems, tax disincentives, and onerous regulatory requirements.

5. *Lower corporate performance objectives.* Adverse market circumstances or declining fortunes in one or more core business units can render companywide performance targets unreachable, and so can overly ambitious objective setting. Closing the gap between actual and desired performance may then require revision of corporate objectives to bring them more in line with reality. Lowering performance objectives is usually a last-resort option, used only after other options have come up short.

■ FINDING ADDITIONAL DIVERSIFICATION OPPORTUNITIES

One of the major corporate strategy-making concerns in a diversified company is whether to pursue further diversification and, if so, how to identify the right kinds of industries and businesses to consider. For firms pursuing unrelated diversification, the issue of where to diversify next always remains wide open—the search for acquisition candidates is based more on financial criteria than on industry or strategic criteria.unrelated businesses to the firm's portfolio are usually based on such considerations as whether the firm has the financial ability to make another acquisition, how badly new acquisitions are needed to boost overall corporate performance,

> In firms pursuing unrelated diversification, where to diversify next is addressed by hunting for businesses that offer attractive financial returns regardless of their industry.

whether one or more acquisition opportunities need to be acted on before they are purchased by other firms, and whether corporate management can handle any new acquisitions given the company's current portfolio of businesses.

With a related diversification strategy, however, the search for new industries to diversify into needs to be aimed at identifying those that have strategic fits with one or more of the firm's present businesses.[14] This means looking for industries whose value chains have fits with the value chains of businesses represented in the company's business portfolio. The interrelationships can concern (1) product or process R&D; (2) opportunities for joint manufacturing and assembly; (3) marketing, distribution channel, or common brand name usage; (4) customer overlaps, (5) opportunities for joint after-sale

> In firms pursuing related diversification, where to diversify next is addressed by locating an attractive industry having good strategic fit with one or more of the firm's present businesses.

service; or (6) common managerial know-how requirements—essentially any area where market-related, operating, or management fits can occur.

Once strategic fit opportunities outside a diversified firm's related business portfolio are identified, corporate strategists have to distinguish between opportunities where important competitive advantage potential exists and those where the strategic fit benefits are really very minor. The size of the competitive advantage potential depends directly on whether the strategic fit benefits are competitively significant, how much it will cost to capture the benefits, and how difficult it will be to merge or coordinate the business unit interrelationships.[15] Often, careful analysis reveals that while there are many actual and potential business unit interrelationships and linkages, only a few have enough strategic importance to generate meaningful competitive advantage.

■ DEPLOYING CORPORATE RESOURCES

To get ever-higher levels of performance out of a diversified company's business portfolio, corporate managers also have to allocate corporate resources effectively. They have to steer resources out of low-opportunity areas into high-opportunity areas. Divesting marginal businesses serves this purpose by freeing unproductive assets for redeployment. Surplus funds from cash cow businesses and businesses being harvested also add to the corporate treasury. Options for allocating these funds include (1) investing in ways to strengthen or expand existing businesses, (2) making acquisitions if needed, (3) funding long-range R&D ventures, (4) paying off existing long-term debt, (5) increasing dividends, and (6) repurchasing the company's stock. The first three are *strategic* actions; the last three are *financial* moves. Ideally, a company will have enough funds to serve both its strategic and financial purposes. If not, strategic uses of corporate resources should take precedence over financial uses except in unusual and compelling circumstances.

▶ ## GUIDELINES FOR MANAGING THE CORPORATE STRATEGY FORMATION PROCESS

Although formal analysis and entrepreneurial brainstorming normally undergird the corporate strategy-making process, there is more to the formation of corporate strategy. Corporate strategy in major enterprises emerges incrementally from the unfolding of many different internal and external events, and is the result of probing the future, experimenting, gathering more information, sensing problems, building awareness of the various options, developing ad hoc responses to emergencies, communicating emerging consensus, and acquiring a feel for all the strategically relevant factors, their importance, and their interrelationships.[16]

Strategic analysis is not something that the executives of diversified companies do all at once in comprehensive fashion. Such big reviews are sometimes scheduled, but studies indicate that major strategic decisions emerge gradually, rather than from periodic, full-scale analysis followed by prompt decision. Typically, top executives approach major strategic decisions a step at a time, often starting from broad, intuitive conceptions and then embellishing, fine-tuning, and modifying their original thinking as more information is gathered, as formal analysis confirms or modifies emerging judgments about the situation, and as confidence and consensus build for deciding which strategic moves need to be made. Often attention and resources are concentrated on a few critical strategic thrusts that illuminate and integrate corporate direction, objectives, and strategies.

Implementing Strategy:
Core Competencies, Reengineering, and Structural Design

We strategize beautifully, we implement pathetically.

Executive of auto-parts firm

Just being able to conceive bold new strategies is not enough. The general manager must also be able to translate his or her strategic vision into concrete steps that "get things done."

Richard G. Hamermesh

Organizing is what you do before you do something, so that when you do it, it is not all mixed up.

A. A. Milne

Once managers have decided on a strategy, the next priority is to convert it into action and good results. Putting a strategy into place and executing it well call for a different set of managerial tasks and skills than those used for crafting strategy. Crafting strategy is largely a market-driven *entrepreneurial* activity; implementing strategy is primarily an operations-driven activity revolving around the management of people and business processes. While successful strategy making depends on vision, shrewd industry and competitive analysis, and entrepreneurial creativity, successful strategy implementation depends on leading, motivating, and working through others to create a strong fit between how the organization operates its business and the requirements for good strategy execution. Implementing strategy is a make-things-happen task that requires ability to direct organizational change, design and supervise business processes, manage people, and achieve performance targets.

Experienced managers, savvy in strategy making and strategy implementing, are emphatic in saying that it is much easier to develop a sound strategic plan than it is to accomplish what the plan envisions. According to one executive, "It's been rather easy for us to decide where we wanted to go. The hard part is to get the organization to act on the new priorities."[1] What makes strategy implementation a tougher, more time-consuming management challenge than crafting strategy is the wide sweep of managerial activities involved, managers' many different options for accomplishing each activity, the demanding people management skills required, the perseverance

---

The strategy-implementer's task is to convert strategy into action to achieve the targeted objectives.

---

needed to get a variety of initiatives launched and moving, and the resistance to change that must be overcome. Just because managers announce a new strategy doesn't mean that subordinates agree with it or will cooperate in its implementation. Some may be skeptical about the merits of the strategy and see it as contrary to the organization's best interests, unlikely to succeed, or threatening to their own careers. Moreover, company personnel may have varying interpretations about what the new strategy actually means and thus differing ideas about what internal changes the new strategy will entail. They may be concerned about how the new strategy will affect their work unit, particularly if job losses are involved. Long-standing attitudes, vested interests, inertia, and ingrained organizational practices don't just melt away when managers decide on and begin implementation of a new strategy. It takes adept leadership to overcome the doubt and disagreement, to build consensus for how to proceed, and to get all of the implementation pieces in place. Depending on how much consensus building and organizational change is involved, the implementation process can take several months to several years.

Companies don't implement strategies; people do.

A FRAMEWORK FOR IMPLEMENTING STRATEGY

Like crafting strategy, implementing strategy is a job for the whole management team, not just a few senior managers. While the organization's chief executive officer and other senior managers (heads of business divisions, functional departments, and key operating units) are ultimately responsible for implementing strategy successfully, the implementation process typically impacts every part of the organizational structure, from the largest operating unit to the smallest frontline work group. Every manager has to think through the answer to, ''What has to be done in my area to implement our part of the strategic plan, and what should I be doing to get these things accomplished?'' It's a change-driven process where all managers are strategy implementers, and all employees are participants. Key to successful implementation is communicating the case for organizational change clearly enough and persuasively enough to generate commitment throughout the organization for carrying out the strategy and meeting performance targets. Ideally, managers can turn the implementation process into something of a crusade. Managers can consider implementation successful when strategic objectives and the targeted levels of financial and operating performance are achieved.

Every manager has an active role in the process of implementing and executing the firm's strategic plan.

Unfortunately, there are no 10-step checklists, no proven paths, and few concrete guidelines for tackling the job—managing strategy implementation is the least charted, most open-ended area of strategic management. The best guidelines are anecdotal, available only from personal experiences and case studies, and the wisdom they impart is often inconsistent. What's worked well for some managers has been tried by other managers and found lacking. The reasons are understandable. Not only are some managers more effective than others in employing the recommended approaches to organizational change, but each strategy-implementing challenge takes place in a different organizational context.

Managing strategy implementation is more art than science.

Different business practices and competitive circumstances, different work environments and cultures, different policies, different compensation incentives, different mixes of personalities and organizational histories are substantive enough from situation to situation to require a customized approach to strategy implementation.

■ THE PRINCIPAL TASKS

While the approaches managers take to implement strategy should be tailored to the organization's circumstances, certain bases need to be covered no matter what the organization's circumstances. These include:

- Building an organization capable of carrying out the strategy successfully.

- Developing budgets to steer ample resources into those value chain activities critical to strategic success.

- Establishing strategically appropriate policies and procedures.

- Instituting best practices and mechanisms for continuous improvement.

- Installing support systems that enable company personnel to carry out their strategic roles successfully day-in and day-out.

- Tying rewards and incentives to achieving performance objectives and good strategy execution.

- Creating a strategy-supportive work environment and corporate culture.

- Exerting the internal leadership needed to drive implementation forward and to keep improving on how the strategy is being executed.

These requirements appear repeatedly in the strategy implementation process, no matter what the specifics of the situation, and drive the action priorities on the strategy-implementer's agenda—as depicted in Figure 9–1. Some of these tasks usually end up being more crucial or time-consuming than others, depending on the organization's circumstances—its financial and competitive condition, the resulting availability of important resources, the nature and extent of the proposed strategic change, the requirements of the strategy being implemented, the corporate culture and the strength of ingrained behavior patterns that have to be changed, and any pressures for quick results and near-term financial improvements.

To devise an action agenda, strategy implementers first need to assess what the organization must do differently and better to carry out the strategy successfully, then consider the options for making the changes as rapidly as is practical. Almost without exception, the strategy-implementer's action priorities need to concentrate on fitting how the organization performs its value chain activities and conducts its internal business to the requirements for first-rate strategy execution. A series of fits are needed:

- *Between strategy and necessary organizational skills and capabilities*. Decisive action to build core competencies is especially important when the chosen strategy is predicated on a competence-based competitive advantage.

- *Between strategy and the company's reward structure, policies, information systems, and operating practices*. The manner in which internal operations are conducted must reinforce the push for effective strategy execution.

- *Between strategy and corporate culture*. Managers have to manage in a style that creates and nurtures a strategy-supportive work environment.

The stronger these fits, the better the chances for successful strategy implementation. Systematic efforts to match how the organization conducts its business with the

FIGURE 9–1   *The Eight Big Managerial Components of Implementing Strategy*

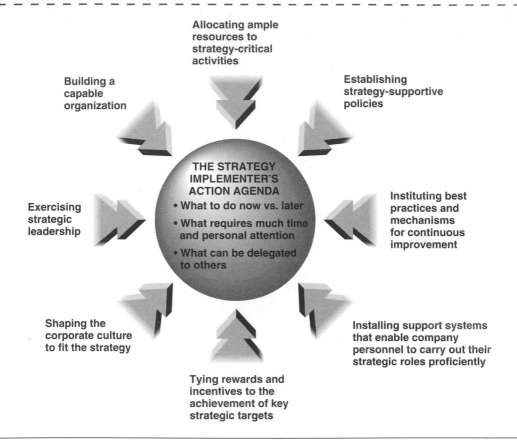

needs of the stated strategy is the best medicine against cynicism. It helps unite the organization in a team effort to achieve the intended performance outcomes. Successful strategy implementers have a knack for diagnosing what their organizations need to do to execute the chosen strategy in first-rate fashion and they are creative in establishing tight fits between those needs and how strategy-critical value chain activities are performed.

■ LEADING THE IMPLEMENTATION PROCESS

Perhaps the biggest determinant of successful strategy implementation is how well management leads the process. Implementers can exercise leadership in many ways. They can be active and visible or work quietly behind the scenes. They can make decisions authoritatively or on the basis of consensus, delegate much or little, be personally involved in the details of implementation or stand back and coach others carrying the day-to-day tasks, proceed swiftly by launching implementation initiatives on many fronts or move deliberately by being content with gradual progress over a long time frame. How managers lead the implementation task tends to be a function of (1) their experience and accumulated knowledge about the business; (2) whether they are new to the job or seasoned incumbents; (3) their network of personal relationships within the organization; (4) their diagnostic, administrative, interpersonal, and problem-solving skills; (5) their level of authority; (6) their leadership style; and (7) their view of the role they need to play to get things done. How well managers lead and how successfully they push for change tend to be decisive: Good leadership usually results in successful implementation and poor leadership usually results in frustration and wheel spinning.

Although major initiatives to implement corporate and business strategies usually have to be led by the CEO and other senior officers, top-level managers still have to rely on the active support and cooperation of middle and lower managers to push strategy changes in functional areas and operating units and to carry out the strategy effectively on a daily basis. Mid- and lower-level managers are responsible not only for initiating and supervising the implementation process in their areas of authority, but they are also instrumental in seeing that performance targets are met. It is frontline managers, working with the actual doers, who have to devise ways to improve strategy execution in the operating units where key value chain activities are performed.

The action agenda of senior-level strategy-implementers, especially in big organizations with geographically scattered operating units, involves communicating the case for change to others, building consensus for how to proceed, installing allies in key organizational units where they can push implementation along, urging and empowering subordinates to get the process moving, establishing measures of progress and deadlines, recognizing and rewarding those who achieve implementation milestones, reallocating resources to areas that need them, and personally presiding over the change process. The bigger the organization, the more the chief strategy implementer's success depends on the cooperation and implementation skills of operating managers out on the front line. In small organizations, the chief strategy implementer doesn't have to work through middle managers and can deal directly with managers and employees in operating units, personally orchestrating the action steps and implementation sequence, observing firsthand how implementation is progressing, and deciding how hard and how fast to push the process. Regardless of organization size and whether implementation involves sweeping or minor strategic change, the most

> The real skill to implementing strategy is talent at figuring out what is needed to execute the strategy proficiently.

important leadership trait is a strong, confident sense of what to do to achieve the desired results. Knowing what to do comes from a savvy understanding of the business and the organization's circumstances.

In the remainder of this chapter and in the next two chapters, we survey the manager's role as chief strategy implementer. The framework of our discussion will be organized around the eight managerial components shown in Figure 9-1 and the recurring issues associated with each. This chapter explores the management tasks of building a capable organization. Chapter 10 looks at budget allocations, policies, best practices, internal support systems, and strategically appropriate reward structures. Chapter 11 covers how to build a strategy-supportive corporate culture and exercise strategic leadership.

▶ BUILDING A CAPABLE ORGANIZATION

Proficient strategy execution depends greatly on competent personnel, better-than-adequate skills and competitive capabilities, and effective internal organization. Building a capable organization is thus always a top priority of strategy implementation. Three types of organization-building actions are paramount:

1. Selecting able people for key positions.
2. Making certain that the organization has the skills, core competencies, managerial talents, technical expertise, and competitive capabilities it needs.
3. Developing an organizational structure that is conducive to successful strategy execution.

■ SELECTING PEOPLE FOR KEY POSITIONS

Assembling a capable management team is one of the first cornerstones of the organization-building task. Strategy implementers must decide what kind of core management team is needed to execute the strategy successfully and then find experienced people who know how to get things done to fill each slot. Sometimes the existing management team is suitable; sometimes it needs to be strengthened and/or expanded by promoting qualified people from within or by bringing in outsiders whose background, thinking, and leadership style suit the situation. In turnaround and rapid-growth situations, or when a company doesn't have insiders with the requisite experience, filling key management positions from the outside is a fairly standard organization-building approach.

Putting together a strong management team with the right personal chemistry and professional skills is one of the first steps in strategy implementation.

The important skill in assembling a core executive group is the ability to discern what mix of backgrounds, experiences, areas of expertise, values, beliefs, styles of managing, and personalities will reinforce and contribute to successful strategy execution. The personal chemistry needs to be right and the talent base needs to be appropriate for the chosen strategy. Picking a solid management team is an essential organization-building function—often the first strategy implementation step to undertake.[2] Until key slots are filled with able people, it is hard for strategy implementation to proceed at full speed.

■ BUILDING CORE COMPETENCIES

An equally dominant organization-building concern is staffing operating units with the specialized talent, skills, and technical expertise needed to give the firm a competitive edge in performing critical activities in the value chain. When it is difficult, if not impossible, to outstrategize rivals, the other main avenue to industry leadership is to outexecute them. Superior strategy execution is essential in situations where rival firms have similar strategies and can readily imitate one another's strategic maneuvers. Building core competencies and organizational capabilities that rivals can't match is one of the best ways to outexecute them. This is why one of management's most

Building core competencies and organizational capabilities that rivals can't match is the best foundation for sustainable competitive advantage.

important strategy-implementing tasks is to guide the building of core competencies in competitively advantageous ways.

Core competencies can relate to any strategically relevant factor: greater proficiency in product development, manufacturing expertise, the capability to provide customers better after-sale services, an ability to respond quickly to changing customer requirements, superior ability to minimize costs, an ability to reengineer and redesign products more quickly than rivals, superior inventory management capabilities, marketing and merchandising skills, specialized depth in unique technologies, or greater effectiveness in promoting union-management cooperation. Honda's core competence is its depth of expertise in gasoline engine technology and small engine design. Intel's is in the design of complex chips for personal computers. Procter & Gamble's core competencies reside in its superb marketing-distribution skills and its R&D capabilities in five core technologies — fats, oils, skin chemistry, surfactants, and emulsifiers.[3] Sony's core competencies are based in its electronic technology expertise and its ability to translate this expertise into developing and manufacturing innovative products such as minia-turized radios, video cameras, televisions, and VCRs with unique features. Most often, a company's core competencies emerge incrementally as it moves either to bolster those skills that have contributed to earlier

Core competencies aren't born, nor can they reach fruition without management's conscious attention.

successes or to respond to customer problems, new technological and market opportunities, and the competitive maneuverings of rivals.[4] Ideally, company managers will correctly foresee changes in customer-market requirements and proactively build up new sets of competencies that offer a competitive edge.

Four traits concerning core competencies are important to a strategy-implementer's organization-building task:[5]

- Core competencies rarely consist of a narrow skill or the work efforts of a single department. Rather, they are usually a composite of skills and activities performed at different locations in the firm's value chain that, when linked, create unique organizational capability.

- Because core competencies typically emerge from the combined efforts of different work groups and departments, supervisors and department heads can't be expected to see building the overall corporation's core competencies as their domain of responsibility.

- The key to leveraging a company's core competencies into long-term competitive advantage is concentrating more effort and talent than rivals on deepening and strengthening these competencies.

- Because customers' needs change in often unpredictable ways and the specific skills needed for competitive success cannot always be accurately forecasted, a company's selected bases of competency need to be broad enough and flexible enough to respond to an unknown future.

The multiskill, multiactivity character of core competencies makes building and strengthening them an exercise in (1) managing human skills, knowledge bases, and intellect and (2) coordinating and networking the efforts of different work groups and departments at every place in the value chain related to such competencies. It's an exercise best orchestrated by senior managers who understand how the organization's core competence is created and who have the power to enforce the necessary networking and cooperation among functional departments and managers who are protective of their turf. Moreover, organization-builders have to concentrate enough resources and management attention on core competence-related activities to achieve the *dominating depth* needed for competitive advantage.[6] This does not necessarily mean spending more money on competence-related activities than present or potential competitors, but it does mean consciously focusing more talent on them and making appropriate internal and external benchmarking comparisons to move toward best-in-industry, if not best-in-world, status. To achieve dominance on lean financial resources, companies like Cray in large computers, Lotus in software, and Honda in small engines leveraged the expertise of their talent pool by frequently reforming high-intensity tasks or innovation teams and systematically reusing key people on special projects aimed at boosting the value provided to customers.[7] In leveraging internal knowledge and skills rather than physical assets or market position, the usual keys to success are superior selection, training, powerful cultural influences, cooperative networking, motivation, empowerment, attractive incentives, organizational flexibility, short deadlines, and good databases—not big operating budgets.[8]

Strategy implementers can't afford to become complacent once core competencies are in place and functioning. It's a constant organization-building challenge to broaden, deepen, or otherwise modify them in response to ongoing customer-market changes. But it's a task worth pursuing. Core competencies that are finely honed and kept current with shifting circumstances can provide an advantage in implementing strategy. Really distinctive core competencies and organizational capabilities are not easily duplicated by rival firms; any competitive advantage that results is likely to be sustainable for some time to come, thus paving the way for above-average organizational performance. This is why conscious management attention to the task of building strategically relevant internal skills and capabilities into the overall organizational scheme is one of the central tasks of organization building and effective strategy implementation.

EMPLOYEE TRAINING

Training and retraining are important aspects of implementation when a company shifts to a strategy requiring different skills, managerial approaches, and operating methods. Training is also strategically important in organizational efforts to build skills-based competencies. And it is a key activity in businesses where technology changes so rapidly that a company loses its ability to compete unless its skilled people are kept current on the latest techniques. Successful strategy implementers see that the training function is adequately funded and that effective training programs are in place. Normally, if the chosen strategy calls for new skills or different expertise, providing the necessary training should be placed near the top of the action agenda because it needs to be done early in the strategy implementation process.

■ MATCHING ORGANIZATION STRUCTURE TO STRATEGY

There are few hard and fast rules for organizing the work effort in a strategy-supportive fashion. Every firm's organization chart is partly idiosyncratic, reflecting prior organizational patterns, executive views about how best to arrange reporting relationships, the politics of who gets which assignments, and varying internal circumstances. Moreover, every strategy is grounded in its own set of key success factors and value chain activities. Thus, some sort of customized organization structure is appropriate. The following four guidelines can be helpful in fitting structure to strategy:

1. Pinpoint the primary activities and key tasks in the value chain that are pivotal to successful strategy execution and make them the main building blocks in the organization structure.

2. Whenever it doesn't make organizational sense to group all facets of a strategy-related activity under a single manager, establish ways to bridge departmental lines and achieve the necessary coordination.

3. Determine the degrees of authority needed to manage each organizational unit, endeavoring to strike an effective balance between capturing the advantages of both centralization, and decentralization.

4. Determine whether noncritical activities can be outsourced more efficiently or effectively than they can be performed internally.

PINPOINTING STRATEGY-CRITICAL ACTIVITIES

In any business, some activities in the value chain are always more critical to strategic success than others. From a strategy perspective, a certain portion of an organization's total work effort is routine and falls under the rubric of administrative good housekeeping and necessary detail. Examples include doing the payroll, managing cash flows, handling grievances and the usual assortment of people problems, providing corporate security, managing stockholder relations, maintaining fleet vehicles, and complying with regulations. Other activities are primarily support functions (data processing, accounting, training, public relations, market research, legal and legislative affairs, and purchasing). Yet there are usually certain crucial value chain activities and business processes that have to be performed exceedingly well for the strategy to be successful. For instance, hotel/motel enterprises have to be good at fast check-in/check-out, room maintenance, food service, and creating a pleasant ambiance. A manufacturer of chocolate bars must be skilled in purchasing quality cocoa beans at low prices, efficient production (a fraction of a cent in cost savings per bar can mean seven-figure improvement in the bottom line), merchandising, and promotional activities. In discount stock brokerage, the strategy-critical activities are fast access to information, accurate order execution, efficient recordkeeping and transactions processing, and good customer service. In specialty chemicals, the critical activities tend to be R&D, product innovation, getting newly developed products out of the lab and onto the market quickly, effective marketing, and expertise in assisting customers. Strategy-critical activities vary according to the particulars of a firm's strategy, value chain makeup, and competitive requirements.

Two questions help identify an organization's strategy-critical activities: "What functions have to be performed extra well or in timely fashion to achieve sustainable competitive advantage?" and, " In what value chain activities would malperformance seriously endanger strategic success?"[9] The answers generally point squarely at activities and organizational areas that are crucial and indicate where to concentrate organization-building efforts.

The rationale for making strategy-critical activities the main building blocks in the organization structure is compelling: If activities crucial to strategic success are to get the attention and organizational support they merit, they have to be centerpieces in the organizational scheme. When key business units and strategy-critical functions are put on a par with—or worse, superseded by—less important activities, the most significant activities usually end up with fewer resources and have less clout in the organization's power structure than they need. On the other hand, when the primary value-creating activities form the core of a company's organization structure and their managers hold key positions on the organization chart, their role and power is ingrained in daily operations and decision making. Senior executives seldom send a stronger signal about what is strategically important than by making key business units and critical activities prominent organizational building blocks and, further, giving the managers of these units a visible, influential position in the organizational pecking order. In many cases, there is merit in operating each of these main organizational units as a profit center.

Matching structure to strategy requires that strategy-critical activities and strategy-critical organizational units be the cornerstones of organizational structure.

In deciding how to graft routine and staff support activities onto the basic building block structure, company managers should be alert to the strategic relationships among the primary and support functions that make up its value chain. Activities can be related in any of several ways:

- By the flow of work along the value chain.
- By the type of customer served.
- By the distribution channels used.
- By the technical skills and expertise needed to perform them.
- By their contribution to building a core competence.
- By their role in a work process that spans traditional departmental lines.
- By their role in how customer value is created.
- By their sequence in the value chain.
- By the skills transfer opportunities they present.
- By the potential for combining or coordinating them in a manner that will reduce total costs.

Such relationships are important because one or more such linkages usually signal how to structure reporting relationships and where there's a need for close cross-functional coordination. If the needs of successful strategy execution are to drive organization design, then the relationships to look for are those that (1) can be melded into a core competence and (2) link one work unit's performance to another.

Managers need to be particularly alert to the fact that in traditional functionally organized structures, pieces of strategically relevant activities often end up scattered across many departments. The process of filling customer orders accurately and promptly is a case in point. The order fulfillment process begins when a customer places an order, ends when the goods are delivered, and typically includes a dozen or so steps performed by different people in different departments.[10] Someone in customer service receives the order, logs it in, and checks it for accuracy and completeness. It may then go to the finance department, where someone runs a credit check on the customer; another person may be needed to approve credit terms or special financing. Someone in sales calculates or verifies the correct pricing. When the order gets to inventory control, someone has to determine if the goods are in stock. If not, a back order may be issued or the order routed to production planning so that it can be factored into the production schedule. When the goods are ready, warehouse operations prepares a shipment schedule. Personnel in the traffic department determine the shipment method (rail, truck, air, water) and choose the route and carrier. Product handling retrieves the

----

Functional specialization can result in the pieces of strategically relevant activities being scattered across many departments.

----

product from the warehouse, verifies the item against the order, and packages the goods for shipment. Traffic releases the goods to the carrier, which takes responsibility for delivery to the customer. Each handoff from one department to the next entails queues and delays. Although organizations like the one described above incorporate Adam Smith's division of labor principle (i.e. every person involved has specific responsibility for performing one simple task) and allows for tight management control (i.e. everyone in the process is accountable to a manager for efficiency and adherence to prescribed procedures), *no one oversees the whole process and its result*.[11] Accurate, timely order fulfillment, despite its relevance to effective strategy execution, ends up being no single person's job, nor is it the job of any one functional department.[12]

Managers have to guard against organization designs that unduly fragment strategically relevant activities. Parceling strategy-critical work across many specialized departments contributes to an obsession with activity (performing the assigned tasks in the prescribed manner) rather than result (customer satisfaction, competitive advantage, lower costs). So many handoffs lengthen completion time and frequently increase overhead costs since coordinating the fragmented pieces can soak up hours of effort on the part of many people. Nonetheless, some fragmentation is necessary, even desirable in the case of support activities like finance and accounting, human resource management, engineering, technology development, and information systems, where functional centralization is advantageous, if not essential. The key in weaving support activities into the organization design is to establish reporting and coordinating arrangements that:

- Maximize how support activities contribute to enhanced performance of the primary, strategy-critical tasks in the firm's value chain.
- Contain the costs of support activities and minimize the time and energy internal units have to spend doing business with each other.

Absent such arrangements, the cost of transacting business internally becomes excessive, and functional managers, forever diligent in guarding their turf and protecting their prerogatives, can weaken the strategy execution effort and become part of the strategy-implementing problem rather than part of the solution.

REPORTING RELATIONSHIPS AND CROSS-FUNCTIONAL COORDINATION

The classical way to coordinate the activities of organizational units is to position them in the authority hierarchy so that the most closely related ones report to a single person. Senior managers generally have authority over more organizational units and thus the clout to coordinate, integrate, and arrange for the cooperation of units under their supervision. In such structures, the chief executive officer, chief operating officer, and business-level managers become central points of coordination as a result of their authority over the whole unit. When a firm is pursuing a related diversification strategy, effectively coordinating the related activities of otherwise independent business units often requires the centralizing authority of a single corporate-level officer. Also, companies with either related or unrelated diversification strategies commonly centralize such staff support functions as public relations, finance and accounting, employee benefits, and data processing at the corporate level.

But, as the customer order fulfillment example illustrates, it isn't always feasible to position closely related value chain activities and/or organizational units vertically under the coordinating authority of a single executive. Formal reporting relationships have to be supplemented. Options for unifying the strategic efforts of interrelated organizational units include the use of coordinating teams, cross-functional task forces, dual reporting relationships, informal organizational networking, voluntary cooperation, incentive compensation tied to group performance measures, and strong executive-level insistence on teamwork and interdepartmental cooperation (including a willingness to remove managers who stonewall cooperative efforts).

DETERMINING THE DEGREE OF AUTHORITY AND INDEPENDENCE TO GIVE EACH UNIT

Companies must decide how much authority and decision-making latitude to give managers of each organization unit, especially the heads of business subsidiaries and functional departments. In a highly centralized organization structure, top executives retain authority for most strategic and operating decisions and direct the work of business-unit heads and department heads; comparatively little discretionary authority is granted to subordinate managers. The weakness of centralized organization is that its vertical, hierarchical character tends to foster excessive bureaucracy and stall decision making until the review-approval process runs its course through the various management layers. In decentralized organization structures, managers (and, increasingly, other employees as well) are empowered to act on their own judgments in their assigned areas of responsibility. In a diversified company operating on the principle of decentralized decision making, for example, business unit heads have broad authority to run the subsidiary as they see fit with comparatively little interference from corporate headquarters; the business head gives functional department heads considerable decision-making latitude; and customer-contact personnel are empowered to do what it takes to please customers.

Resolving which decisions to centralize and which to decentralize is always a big issue in organization design.

Delegating greater authority to subordinate managers and employees creates a more horizontal organization structure with fewer management layers. Whereas in a centralized vertical structure managers and workers have to go up the ladder of authority for an answer, in a decentralized horizontal structure they develop their own answers and action plans—making decisions and being accountable for results is part of their job. Such streamlining of the decision-making process usually shortens the time it takes an organization to respond to competitors' actions, changing customer preferences, and other market developments. It also encourages new ideas, creative thinking, innovation, and greater involvement on the part of subordinate managers and employees.

In recent years, there's been a decided shift away from authoritarian, multilayered hierarchical structures to flatter, less hierarchical structures that stress decentralized decision-making and employee empowerment. The new preference for leaner management structures and empowered employees is grounded in two tenets: (1) Decision-making authority should be pushed down to the lowest organizational level capable of making a timely, informed, competent decision—to those people, whether managers or not, nearest the scene who are knowledgeable about the issue and trained to exercise responsible judgment. As far as strategic management is concerned, decentralization means that the managers of each organizational unit should not only lead the crafting of their unit's strategy but also lead the decision making on its implementation. Decentralization thus requires selecting strong managers to head each organizational unit and holding them accountable for crafting and executing an appropriate strategy for their unit; managers that consistently produce unsatisfactory results and have a poor track record in strategy making and strategy implementing have to be weeded out. (2) Employees below the management ranks should be empowered to make decisions on matters pertaining to their job. The case for empowering employees and holding them accountable for their performance is based on the belief that a company which draws on the combined talent of all its employees can outperform a company where the approach to people management consists of transferring ideas from the heads of bosses into the actions of employees. To ensure that the decisions of empowered employees are as well informed as possible, significant effort must be undertaken to get accurate, timely data into everyone's hands and to make sure they understand the link between their performance and company performance. Flattening corporate hierarchies and incorporating information technologies make greater empowerment feasible. It's possible now to create "a wired company" where people have direct electronic access to data, key managers, and each other, allowing them to make fast, informed decisions on job-related matters. Typically, there are genuine morale gains when people have ready access to needed information and are allowed to operate in a self-directed way.

One of the biggest exceptions to decentralizing strategy-related decisions and giving lower-level managers more operating authority arises in diversified companies with related businesses in their portfolio; in such cases, capturing the strategic-fit benefits of related activities is often best done by either centralizing decision-making authority or enforcing cooperation and shared decision making. Suppose, for instance, that businesses with overlapping process and product technologies have their own independent R&D departments, each operating as a silo or stovepipe pursuing its own priorities, projects, and strategic agenda. Without a coordinating mechanism, such as combining operations into a single department, it is hard to prevent duplication of effort, capture either economies of scale or economies of scope, or effectively broaden the vision of the company's R&D effort to include new technological pathways, product families, end-use applications, and customer groups. Likewise, centralizing control over the related activities of separate businesses makes sense when

> Centralizing strategy-implementing authority at the corporate level has merit when the related activities of related businesses need to be tightly coordinated.

there are opportunities to share a common sales force, utilize common distribution channels, rely upon a common field service organization to handle customer requests for technical assistance or provide maintenance and repair services, and so on. And for reasons previously discussed, limits also have to be placed on the independence of functional managers when pieces of strategy-critical processes are located in different organizational units and require close coordination for maximum effectiveness.

REASONS TO CONSIDER OUTSOURCING NONCRITICAL ACTIVITIES

Each supporting activity in a firm's value chain and within its traditional staff groups can be considered a service.[13] Most overheads, for example, are just services the company has chosen to produce internally. Often, such services are readily purchased externally from outside vendors. An outsider, by concentrating specialists and technology in its area of expertise, can sometimes perform these services better or more cheaply than a company which performs that activity only for itself. Outsourcing activities not crucial to its strategy allows a company to concentrate its energies and resources on those value chain activities where it can create unique value, where it can be best in the industry (or, better still, best in the world), and where it needs strategic control to build core competencies, achieve competitive advantage, and manage key customer-supplier relationships.[14] Managers too often spend inordinate amounts of time, psychic energy, and resources wrestling with functional support groups and other internal bureaucracies, a condition which diverts attention away from the company's strategy-critical activities. Approached from a strategic point of view, outsourcing noncrucial support activities (and maybe a few selected primary activities in the value chain if they are not a basis for competitive advantage) can usefully serve to decrease internal bureaucracies, flatten the organization structure, provide the company with heightened strategic focus, and increase competitive responsiveness.[15]

Outsourcing noncritical activities has many advantages.

Critics contend that extensive outsourcing can hollow out a company, leaving it at the mercy of outside suppliers and barren of the skills and organizational capabilities important to its survival.[16] However, a number of companies have been successful relying on outside components suppliers, product designers, distribution channels, advertising agencies, and financial services firms. For years Polaroid Corporation bought its film medium from Eastman Kodak, its electronics from Texas Instruments, and its cameras from Timex and others, while it concentrated on developing and producing its patented self-developing film packets and designing its next generation of cameras and films. Nike concentrates on design, marketing, and distribution to retailers, while outsourcing virtually all production of its shoes and sporting apparel. Many mining companies outsource geological work, assaying, and drilling to specialists. Ernest and Julio Gallo Winery outsources 95 percent of its grape production, letting farmers handle the weather and other risks of growing grapes while it concentrates on wine production and the marketing-sales function.[17] The major airlines outsource their in-flight meals even though food quality is important to travelers' perception of overall service quality. Eastman Kodak, Ford, Exxon, Merrill Lynch, and Chevron have outsourced their data processing activities to computer service firms, believing that outside specialists can perform the needed services at lower costs and equal or better quality. Outsourcing certain value chain activities makes strategic sense whenever outsiders can perform them at lower cost and/or with higher value-added than the buyer company can perform them internally.[18]

■ WHY STRUCTURE FOLLOWS STRATEGY

The merits of matching organization design and structure to the particular needs of strategy are lodged in research evidence about actual company experiences. A landmark study by Alfred Chandler found that changes in an organization's strategy bring about new administrative problems which, in turn, require a new or refashioned structure to successfully implement the strategy.[19] His study of 70 large corporations revealed that structure tends to follow the growth strategy of the firm—but often not until inefficiency and internal operating problems provoke a structural adjustment. The experience of these firms followed a consistent sequential pattern: new strategy creation, emergence of new administrative problems, a decline in profitability and performance, a shift to a more appropriate organizational structure, and then recovery to more profitable

Attempting to carry out a new strategy with an old organizational structure is usually unwise.

levels and improved strategy execution. That managers should reassess their company's internal organization whenever strategy changes is pretty much common sense. A new strategy is likely to entail new or different skills and key activities; if these go unrecognized, the resulting mismatch between strategy and structure can lead to problems with both implementation and performance.

HOW STRUCTURE EVOLVES AS STRATEGY EVOLVES

As firms develop from small, single-business companies into more complex enterprises employing vertical integration, geographic expansion, and diversification strategies, their organizational structures tend to evolve from one-person management to functional departments to divisions to decentralized business units. Single-business companies are organized almost always around functional departments. In vertically integrated firms, the major building blocks are divisional units, each of which performs one or more of the major processing steps along the value chain; each division in the value chain sequence may operate as a profit center for performance measurement purposes. Companies with broad geographic coverage typically are divided into regional operating units, each of which has profit-loss responsibility for its assigned geographic area. The typical building blocks of a diversified company are its individual businesses. The authority for business unit decisions is delegated to business-level managers with each business unit operating as an independent, profit center, and corporate headquarters performing assorted support functions for all the businesses.

■ STRATEGIC ADVANTAGES AND DISADVANTAGES OF DIFFERENT ORGANIZATIONAL STRUCTURES

There are five formal approaches to matching structure to strategy: (1) functional specialization, (2) geographic organization, (3) decentralized business divisions, (4) strategic business units, and (5) matrix structures featuring dual lines of strategic priority and authority. Each has strategy-related advantages and disadvantages and each usually needs to be supplemented with formal or informal organizational arrangements to fully coordinate the work effort.

FUNCTIONAL ORGANIZATION STRUCTURES

Organizational structures anchored to functionally specialized departments are the most frequently used to match structure to strategy in single-business enterprises. However, just what form the functional specialization takes varies according to customer-product-technology considerations. For instance, a technical instruments manufacturer may be organized around research and development, engineering, production, technical services, quality control, marketing, personnel, and finance and accounting. A hotel may have an organization based on front desk operations, housekeeping, building maintenance, food service, convention services and special events, guest services, personnel and training, and accounting. A discount retailer may divide its organizational units into purchasing, warehousing and distribution, store operations, advertising, merchandising and promotion, and corporate administrative services. Two representative types of functional organizational approaches are diagrammed in Figure 9–2.

Making specialized functions the main organizational building blocks works best when a firm's value chain consists of a series of discipline-specific activities, each requiring specialized skills, experience, and expertise. In such instances, staffing departmental units with experts in every facet of the activity is an attractive way (1) to exploit any learning/experience curve benefits or economy-of-scale opportunities associated with division of labor and the use of specialized technology and equipment and (2) to develop deep expertise in an important business function. When expertise in one or more functional specialities enhances operating efficiency and/or organizational capability it becomes a basis for competitive advantage. Functional structures work well so long as activities critical to strategy match functional specialities, there is minimal need for interdepartmental cooperation, and top-level management is able to short-circuit departmental rivalries and, instead, create a spirit of interdepartmental teamwork and trust.

A functional structure has two Achilles heels: excessive functional myopia and fragmentation of strategy-critical business processes across traditional departmental lines. It's tough to achieve strategic coordination across entrenched functional bureaucracies that don't talk the same language and view mandates for cross-functional cooperation as interference. In addition, functional specialists are prone to focus inward on departmental matters and upward at their boss's priorities but not outward on the business, the customer, or the industry.[20] Members of functional departments usually have strong departmental loyalties and are protective of departmental interests. Despite giving lip service given to cooperation and ''what's best for the company,'' there's a natural tendency for each functional department to push for solutions and decisions that advance its well-being and organizational influence.

> Functional departments develop strong functional mindsets and are prone to approach strategic issues more from a functional perspective than from a business perspective.

All this creates an organizational environment where functional departments operate as vertical silos, or stovepipes, a breeding ground for departmental bureaucracies, excessive layers of management, authoritarian decision making, and narrow perspectives. In addition, functionally dominated structures, because of preoccupation with developing deeper expertise and improving functional performance, have tunnel vision when it comes to devising entrepreneurially creative responses to major customer, market, or techno-

FIGURE 9–2   *Functional Organizational Structures*

A. The Building Blocks of a "Typical" Functional Organizational Structure

B. The Building Blocks of a Process-Oriented Functional Structure

STRATEGIC ADVANTAGES	STRATEGIC DISADVANTAGES
• Centralized control of strategic results.	• Excessive fragmentation of strategy-critical processes.
• Very well suited for structuring a single business.	• Can lead to interfunctional rivalry and conflict, rather than team-play and cooperation—GM must referee functional politics.
• Structure is linked tightly to strategy by designating key activities as functional departments.	• Multilayered management bureaucracies and centralized decision-making slow response times.
• Promotes in-depth functional expertise.	• Hinders development of managers with cross-functional experience because the ladder of advancement is up the ranks within the same functional area.
• Well suited to developing functional skills and functional-based competencies.	
• Conducive to exploiting learning/experience curve effects associated with functional specialization.	• Forces profit responsibility to the top.
• Enhances operating efficiency where tasks are routine and repetitive.	• Functional specialists often attach more importance to what's best for the functional area than to what's best for the whole business—can lead to functional empire-building.
	• Functional myopia often works against creative entrepreneurship, adapting to change, and attempts to create cross-functional core competencies.

logical changes. They are quick to kill ideas or discard alternatives that aren't compatible with the present functional structure. Classical functional structures also exacerbate process fragmentation whenever a firm's value chain includes strategy-critical activities that, by their very nature, are cross-functional rather than discipline specific. Process fragmentation not only complicates the problems of achieving interdepartmental coordination but also poses serious hurdles to developing cross-functional core competencies.

Interdepartmental politics, empire building, functional myopia, and process fragmentation can impose a time-consuming administrative burden on the general manager (GM), the only person with authority to resolve cross-functional differences and enforce interdepartmental cooperation. In a functional structure, much of a GM's time and energy is spent opening lines of communication across departments, tempering departmental rivalries, convincing stovepipe thinkers of the merits of broader solutions, devising ways to secure cooperation, and working to mold desirable cross-functional core competencies. To be successful, a GM has to be tough and uncompromising in insisting that department managers be team players and that functional specialists work together closely as needed; failure to cooperate fully has to carry negative consequences (specifically a lower job performance evaluation and perhaps even reassignment).

To strike a balance between being function-driven and team-driven, the formal functional structure has to be supplemented with coordinating mechanisms—frequent use of interdisciplinary task forces to work out procedures for coordinating otherwise fragmented processes and strategy-critical activities, incentive compensation tied to joint performance measures, empowering cross-functional teams to perform strategy-critical processes in a unified, timely manner, and forming interdisciplinary teams to build internal organizational bridges that will create competitively important cross-functional organizational capabilities. Instead of continuing to scatter related pieces of a business process across several functional departments and trying to integrate their efforts, it is sometimes more efficient to reengineer the work effort and create *process* departments by pulling the people who performed the pieces in functional departments into a group that works together to perform the whole process.[21] Bell Atlantic did this in cutting through its bureaucratic procedures for connecting a telephone customer to its long-distance carrier.[22] In Bell Atlantic's functional structure, when a business customer requested a connection between the Bell Atlantic system and a long-distance carrier for data services, the request traveled from department to department, taking two to four weeks to complete all the internal processing steps. In reengineering that process, Bell Atlantic pulled workers doing the pieces of the process from the many functional departments and put them on teams which, working together, could handle most customer requests in a matter of days and sometimes hours. Because the work was recurring—similar customer requests had to be processed daily—the teams were permanently grouped into a "process department."

GEOGRAPHIC FORMS OF ORGANIZATION

Organizing on the basis of geographic areas or territories is a common structural form for enterprises operating in diverse geographic markets or serving an expansive geographic area. As indicated in Figure 9–3, geographic organization has its advantages and disadvantages, but the chief reason for its popularity is that it promotes improved performance.

In the private sector, a territorial structure is typically utilized by discount retailers, power companies, cement firms, restaurant chains, and dairy products enterprises. In the

FIGURE 9-3 *A Geographic Organizational Structure*

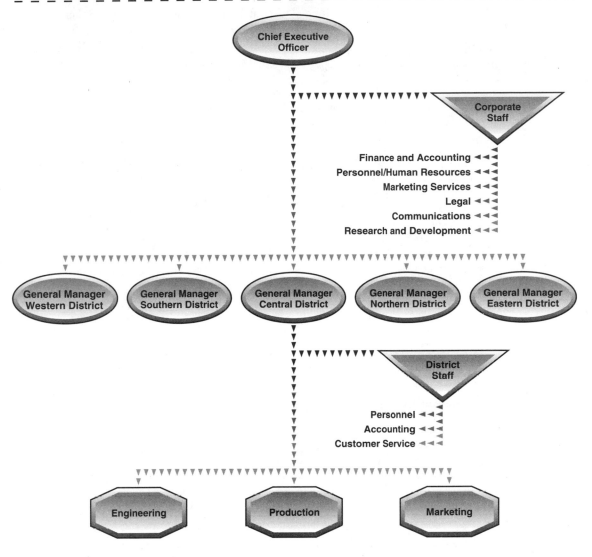

Chief Executive Officer

Corporate Staff

Finance and Accounting ◄◄◄
Personnel/Human Resources ◄◄◄
Marketing Services ◄◄◄
Legal ◄◄◄
Communications ◄◄◄
Research and Development ◄◄◄

General Manager Western District

General Manager Southern District

General Manager Central District

General Manager Northern District

General Manager Eastern District

District Staff

Personnel ◄◄◄
Accounting ◄◄◄
Customer Service ◄◄◄

Engineering

Production

Marketing

STRATEGIC ADVANTAGES

- Allows tailoring of strategy to needs of each geographical market.
- Delegates profit/loss responsibility to lowest strategic level.
- Improves functional coordination within the target market.
- Takes advantage of economies of local operations.
- Area units make an excellent training ground for higher-level general managers.

STRATEGIC DISADVANTAGES

- Poses a problem of how much geographic uniformity headquarters should impose versus how much geographic diversity should be allowed.
- Greater difficulty in maintaining consistent company image/reputation from area to area when area managers exercise much strategic freedom.
- Adds another layer of management to run the geographic units.
- Can result in duplication of staff services at headquarters and district levels, creating a cost disadvantage.

public sector, such organizations as the Internal Revenue Service, the Social Security Administration, the federal courts, the U.S. Postal Service, state troopers, and the Red Cross have adopted territorial structures to be directly accessible to geographically dispersed clienteles. Multinational enterprises use geographic structures to manage the diversity they encounter in operating across national boundaries.

A geographic organization structure is well suited for firms pursuing different strategies in different geographic regions.

Corey and Star cite Pfizer International as a good example of a company whose strategic requirements made geographic decentralization advantageous:

> Pfizer International operated plants in 27 countries and marketed products in more than 100 countries. Its product lines included pharmaceuticals (antibiotics and other ethical prescription drugs); agriculture and veterinary products (animal feed supplements, vaccines, and pesticides); chemicals (fine chemicals, bulk pharmaceuticals, petrochemicals, and plastics); and consumer products (cosmetics and toiletries).
>
> Ten geographic area managers reported directly to the president of Pfizer International and exercised line supervision over country managers. According to a company position description, it was ''the responsibility of each area manager to plan, develop, and carry out Pfizer International's business in the assigned foreign area in keeping with company policies and goals.''
>
> Country managers had profit responsibility. In most cases a single country manager managed all Pfizer activities in his country. In some of the larger, well-developed countries of Europe there were separate country managers for pharmaceutical and agricultural products and for consumer lines.
>
> Except for the fact that New York headquarters exercised control over the to-the-market prices of certain products, especially prices of widely used pharmaceuticals, area and country managers had considerable autonomy in planning and managing the Pfizer International business in their respective geographic areas. This was appropriate because each area, and some countries within areas, provided unique market and regulatory environments. In the case of pharmaceuticals and agriculture and veterinary products (Pfizer International's most important lines), national laws affected formulations, dosages, labeling, distribution, and often price. Trade restrictions affected the flow of bulk pharmaceuticals and chemicals and packaged products, and might in effect require the establishment of manufacturing plants to supply local markets. Competition, too, varied significantly from area to area.[23]

DECENTRALIZED BUSINESS UNITS

Grouping activities along business and product lines has been a favored organizing device among diversified enterprises for the past 70 years, beginning with the pioneering efforts of DuPont and General Motors in the 1920s. Separate business/product divisions emerged because diversification made a functionally specialized manager's job incredibly complex. Imagine the problems a manufacturing executive and his or her staff would have if put in charge of, say, 50 different plants using 20 different technologies to produce 30 different products in eight different businesses/industries. In a multibusiness enterprise, the needs of strategy virtually dictate that the organizational sequence be corporate to business to functional area within a business, rather than corporate to functional area (where a single functional department is responsible for its same function in all of the company's businesses).

In a diversified firm, the basic organizational building blocks are its business units; each business is operated as a stand-alone profit center.

Thus, while functional departments and geographic divisions are the standard organizational building blocks in a single business enterprise, in a multibusiness corporation the basic building blocks are the businesses the firm has diversified into. Authority over each business unit is typically delegated to a business-level manager. The approach, very simply, is to put entrepreneur-minded general managers in charge of each business unit, give them authority to formulate and implement a business strategy, motivate them with performance-based incentives, and hold them accountable for the results they produce. Each business unit then operates as a stand-alone profit center and is organized around whatever functional departments and geographic units suit the business's strategy, key activities, and operating requirements.

Fully independent business units, however, pose an organizational obstacle to companies pursuing related diversification: *There is no mechanism for coordinating related activities across business units*. It can be difficult to get autonomous business unit managers to cooperate in coordinating and sharing related activities; they are prone to argue long and hard about turf and about being held accountable for activities outside their control. To capture strategic-fit benefits in a diversified company, corporate headquarters must devise some internal organizational means for achieving strategic coordination across related business-unit activities. One option is to centralize the related functions at

> A decentralized business-unit structure can block success of a related diversification strategy unless specific organizational arrangements are devised to coordinate the related activities of related businesses.

the corporate level; examples include having a corporate R&D department if there are technology and product development fits to be managed, creating a special corporate sales force to call on customers who purchase from several of the company's business units, combining the dealer networks and sales force organizations of closely related businesses, merging the order processing and shipping functions of businesses having common customers, and consolidating the production of related components and products into fewer, more efficient plants. Alternatively, corporate officers can develop bonus arrangements that give business unit managers strong incentives to work together to achieve the full benefits of strategic fit. If these relationships involve skills or technology transfers across businesses, corporate headquarters can arrange to transfer people with the requisite skills and expertise from one business to another and can create interbusiness teams to open the flow of proprietary technology, managerial expertise, and related skills from one business to another.

A typical line-of-business organizational structure is shown in Figure 9–4, along with the strategy-related pros and cons of this organizational form.

STRATEGIC BUSINESS UNITS

In broadly diversified companies, the number of decentralized business units can be so great that the span of control is too much for a single chief executive. Then it may be useful to group related businesses and to delegate authority over them to a senior executive who reports directly to the chief executive officer. While this imposes a layer of management between business-level managers and the chief executive, it may improve strategic planning and top-management coordination of diverse business interests. This explains both the popularity of the concept of group vice president among multibusiness companies and the creation of strategic business units.

FIGURE 9-4 *A Decentralized Line-of-Business Type of Organization Structure*

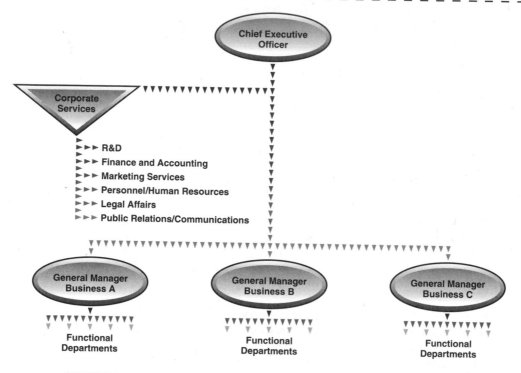

STRATEGIC ADVANTAGES

- Offers a logical and workable means of decentralizing responsibility and delegating authority in diversified organizations.

- Puts responsibility for business strategy in closer proximity to each business's unique environment.

- Allows each business unit to organize around its own value chain system, key activities and functional requirements.

- Frees CEO to handle corporate strategy issues.

- Puts clear profit/loss accountability on shoulders of business-unit managers.

STRATEGIC DISADVANTAGES

- May lead to costly duplication of staff functions at corporate and business-unit levels, thus raising administrative overhead costs.

- Poses a problem of what decisions to centralize and what decisions to decentralize (business managers need enough authority to get the job done, but not so much that corporate management loses control of key business-level decisions).

- May lead to excessive division rivalry for corporate resources and attention.

- Business/division autonomy works against achieving coordination of related activities in different business units, thus blocking to some extent the capture of strategic-fit benefits.

- Corporate management becomes heavily dependent on business-unit managers.

- Corporate managers can lose touch with business-unit situations, end up surprised when problems arise, and not know much about how to fix such problems.

A *strategic business unit* (SBU) is a grouping of business subsidiaries based on significant and commonly held strategic elements. The related elements can be an overlapping set of competitors, closely related value chain activities, a common need to compete globally, emphasis on the same kind of competitive advantage (low cost or differentiation), common key success factors, or technologically related growth oppor-tunities. At General Electric, a pioneer in the concept of SBUs, 190 businesses were grouped into 43 SBUs and then aggregated further into six "sectors."[24] At Union Carbide, 15 groups and divisions were reorganized into 150 "strategic planning units" and then regrouped and combined into 9 new "aggregate planning units." At General Foods, SBUs were originally defined on a product-line basis but were later redefined according to menu segments (breakfast foods, beverages, main meal products, desserts, and pet foods). SBUs make headquarters' reviews of the strategies of lower-level units less imposing since there is no practical way for a CEO to conduct in-depth reviews of a hundred or more different businesses. A CEO can, however, effectively review the strategic plans of a lesser number of SBUs, leaving detailed business strategy reviews and direct supervision of individual businesses to the SBU managers. Figure 9–5 illustrates the SBU form of organization, along with its strategy-related pros and cons.

> A strategic business unit (SBU) is a grouping of related businesses under the supervision of a senior executive.

The SBU concept provides broadly diversified companies with a way to rationalize the organization of many different businesses and a management arrangement for capturing strategic fit benefits and streamlining strategic planning and budgeting processes. The group vice president provides the SBU with cohesive direction, enforces strategic coordination across related businesses, and troubleshoots at the business-unit level, providing counsel and additional corporate support as needed. As strategic coordinator for all businesses in the SBU, the group vice president is in a position to facilitate resource sharing and skills transfers where appropriate and to unify the strategic decisions and actions of busi-nesses within the SBU. The SBU, in effect, becomes a strategy-making, strategy-implementing unit with a wider field of vision and operations than a single business unit. The SBU serves as a diversified company's organizational mechanism for capturing strategic-fit benefits across businesses and adding to the competitive advantage that each business in the SBU is able to build on its own. Moreover, it affords opportunity to "cross-pollinate" the activities of separate businesses, ideally creating enough new capability to stretch a company's strategic reach into adjacent products, technologies, and markets. Aggressive pursuit of resource sharing, skills transfer, and cross-pollination opportunities is one of the best avenues companies can use to develop the internal capabilities needed to enter new business arenas.

> SBU structures are a means for managing broad diversifica-tion and enforcing strategic coordination across related businesses.

MATRIX FORMS OF ORGANIZATION

A matrix organization is a structure with two (or more) channels of command, two lines of budget authority, and two sources of performance and reward. The key feature of the matrix is that authority over a business/product/project/venture and authority over a

FIGURE 9–5 *An SBU type of Organization Structure*

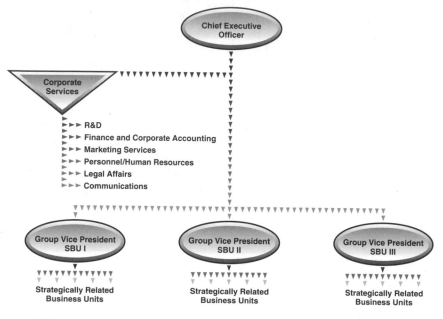

STRATEGIC ADVANTAGES

- Provides a strategically relevant way to organize the business-unit portfolio of a broadly diversified company.

- Facilitates the coordination of related activities within an SBU, thus helping to capture the benefits of strategic fits in the SBU.

- Promotes more cohesiveness among the new initiatives of separate but related businesses.

- Allows strategic planning to be done at the most relevant level within the total enterprise.

- Makes the task of strategic review by top executives more objective and more effective.

- Helps allocate corporate resources to areas with greatest growth opportunities.

STRATEGIC DISADVANTAGES

- It is easy for the definition and grouping of businesses into SBUs to be so arbitrary that the SBU serves no other purpose than administrative convenience. If the criteria for defining SBUs are rationalizations and have little to do with the nitty-gritty of strategy coordination, then the groupings lose real strategic significance.

- The SBUs can still be myopic in charting their future direction.

- Adds another layer to top management.

- The roles and authority of the CEO, the group vice president, and the business-unit manager have to be carefully worked out or the group vice president gets trapped in the middle with ill-defined authority.

- Unless the SBU head is strong willed, very little strategy coordination is likely to occur across business units in the SBU.

- Performance recognition gets blurred; credit for successful business units tends to go to corporate CEO, then to business-unit head, last to group vice president.

function/process are overlaid to form a matrix or grid, and decision-making responsibility over the activities in each unit/cell of the matrix is shared between the business/project/ product/venture team manager and the functional/process manager—as shown in Figure 9–6. In a matrix structure, subordinates have a continuing dual responsibility: to the business/project/product/venture and to their home base function. The outcome is a compromise between functional specialization (engineering, R&D, manufacturing, marketing, finance), and product-line, project, line-of-business or special venture divisions where all of the specialized talent needed for the product-line/project/line-of-business/venture is assigned to the same divisional or departmental unit.

A matrix type of organization is a genuinely different structural form from any of the others we have considered here because it breaks the unity-of-command principle. In a matrix structure there are two reporting channels, two bosses, and shared authority; the result is a different kind of organizational climate. In essence, matrix organization is a conflict resolution system through which strategic and operating priorities are negotiated, power is shared, and resources are allocated internally on the basis of the "strongest case for what is best overall for the unit".[25]

Matrix structures, although complex to manage and sometimes unwieldy, allow a firm to be organized in two different strategy-supportive ways at the same time.

The impetus for matrix organizations stems from growing use of strategies that create a simultaneous need for process teams, special project managers, product managers, functional managers, geographic area managers, new venture managers, and business-level managers—all of whom have a valid strategic role to perform. A matrix organization can be an effective structural form when an organization has at least two areas of roughly equal strategic priority. This is because a matrix promotes internal checks and balances among competing viewpoints and perspectives, with separate managers for different dimensions of strategic initiative. A matrix arrangement enables several strategic functions to be managed directly and to be formally represented in the organization structure. In this sense, it helps middle managers make trade-off decisions from an organizationwide perspective.[26] The other big advantage of matrix organization is that it can serve as a mechanism for capturing strategic fit. When the strategic fits in a diversified company are related to one specific functional area (R&D, technology, marketing, after-sale service) or when they cross traditional functional lines, matrix organizations can be a reasonable structural arrangement for coordinating activity sharing and skills transfer.

Companies using matrix structures include General Electric, Texas Instruments, Citibank, Shell Oil, TRW, Bechtel, Boeing, and Dow Chemical. Illustration 25 describes how one broadly diversified company with global strategies in each of its businesses has developed a matrix structure to manage its operations worldwide. However, in most companies, use of matrix organization is confined to discrete and important functions of what the firm does rather than its whole organizing scheme.

Many companies and managers shun matrix organization because of its chief weakness.[27] It is a complex structure to manage; employees become confused and frustrated over whom to report to for what. Moreover, because the matrix signals a need for communication and consensus it can result in a "transactions logjam." People in one area are required to transact business with people in another area and network their way through internal bureaucracies. Action turns into paralysis since, with shared authority, it is hard to move decisively without first checking with other people and getting clearance. Much time and psychic energy get eaten up in meetings and in communicating back and forth. Sizable transactions costs and longer decision times can result with little value-added. Even so, in some situations the benefits of conflict resolution, consensus building, and coordination outweigh these weaknesses, as the ABB example indicates (Illustration 25).

FIGURE 9–6 *A Matrix Organization Structure**

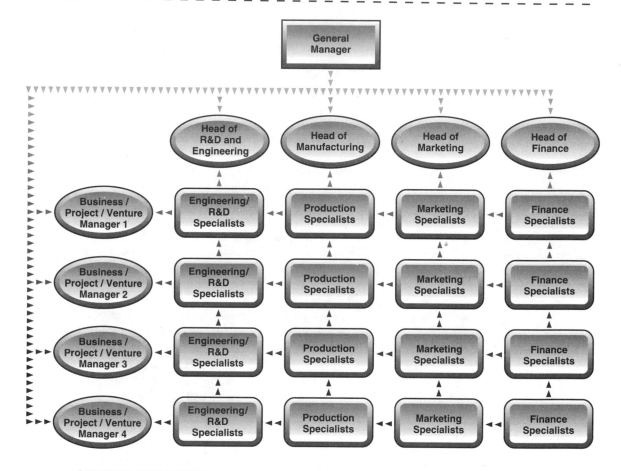

STRATEGIC ADVANTAGES

- Gives formal attention to each dimension of strategic priority.
- Creates checks and balances among competing viewpoints.
- Facilitates capture of functionally based strategic fits in diversified companies.
- Promotes making trade-off decisions on the basis of "what's best for the organization as a whole."
- Encourages cooperation, consensus-building, conflict resolution, and coordination of related activities.

STRATEGIC DISADVANTAGES

- Very complex to manage.
- Hard to maintain "balance" between the two lines of authority.
- So much shared authority can result in a transactions logjam and disproportionate amounts of time being spent on communications.
- It is hard to move quickly and decisively without getting clearance from many other people.
- Promotes an organizational bureaucracy and hamstrings creative entrepreneurship.

*Arrows indicate reporting channels

ILLUSTRATION 25   *Matrix Organization in a Diversified Global Company: The Case of Asea Brown Boveri*

Asea Brown Boveri (ABB) is a diversified multinational corporation headquartered in Zurich, Switzerland. ABB was formed in 1987 through the merger of Asea, one of Sweden's largest industrial enterprises, and Brown Boveri, a major Swiss company. Both companies manufactured electrical products and equipment. Following the merger, ABB acquired or took minority positions in 60 companies, mostly outside Europe. In 1991 ABB had annual revenues of $25 billion and employed 240,000 people around the world, including 150,000 in Western Europe, 40,000 in North America, 10,000 in South America, and 10,000 in India. The company was a world leader in the global markets for electrical products, electrical installations and service, and power-generation equipment and was the dominant European producer. European sales accounted for 60 percent of revenues, while North America accounted for 30 percent and Asia 15 percent.

To manage its global operations, ABB had devised a matrix organization that leveraged its core competencies in electrical-power technologies and its ability to achieve global economies of scale while, at the same time, maximizing its national market visibility and responsiveness. At the top of ABB's corporate organization structure was an executive committee composed of the CEO, Percy Barnevik, and 12 colleagues; the committee consisted of Swedes, Swiss, Germans, and Americans, several of whom were based outside Switzerland. The group, which met every three weeks at various locations around the world, was responsible for ABB's corporate strategy and performance.

Along one dimension of ABB's global matrix were 50 or so business areas (BAs), each representing a closely related set of products and services. The BAs were grouped into eight "business segments"; each segment was supervised by a different member of the executive committee. Each BA had a leader charged with responsibility for (1) devising and championing a global strategy, (2) setting quality and cost standards for the BA's factories worldwide, (3) deciding which factories would export to which country markets, (4) rotating people across borders to share technical expertise, create mixed-nationality teams to solve BA problems,

and build a culture of trust and communication, and (5) pooling expertise and research funds for the benefit of the BA worldwide. BA leaders worked out of whatever world location made the most sense for their BA. For example, the BA leader for power transformers, who had responsibility for 25 factories in 16 countries, was a Swede who worked out of Mannheim, Germany; the BA leader for electric metering was an American based in North Carolina.

Along the other dimension of the matrix was a group of national enterprises with presidents, boards of directors, financial statements, and career ladders. The presidents of ABB's national enterprises had responsibility for maximizing the performance and effectiveness of all ABB activities within their country's borders. Country presidents worked closely with the BA leaders to evaluate and improve what was happening in ABB's business areas in his/her country.

Inside the matrix were 1,200 "local" ABB companies with an average of 200 employees, each headed by a president. The local company president reported both to the national president in whose country the local company operated and to the leader of the BA to which its products/services were assigned. Each local company was a subsidiary of the ABB national enterprise where it was located. Thus, all of ABB's local companies in Norway were subsidiaries of ABB Norway, the national company for Norway; all ABB operations in Portugal were subsidiaries of ABB Portugal, and so on. The 1,200 presidents of ABB's local companies were expected to be excellent profit center managers, able to answer to two bosses effectively. The local president's global boss was the BA manager who established the local company's role in ABB's global strategy and, also, the rules a local company had to observe in supporting this strategy. The local president's country boss was the national CEO, with whom it was necessary to cooperate on local issues.

ABB believed that its matrix structure allowed it to optimize its pursuit of global business strategies and, at the same time, maximize its performance in every country market where it operated. The matrix was a way of being global and big strategically, yet small and local operationally. Decision making was decentralized (to BA leaders, country presidents, and local company presidents), but reporting and control was centralized (through the BA leaders, the country presidents, and the executive committee). ABB saw itself as a federation of national companies with a global coordination center.

Only 100 professionals were located in ABB's corporate headquarters in Zurich. A management information system collected data on all profit centers monthly, comparing actual performance against budgets and forecasts. Data was collected in local currencies but translated into U.S. dollars to allow for cross-border analysis. ABB's corporate financial statements were reported in U.S. dollars, and English was ABB's official language. All high-level meetings were conducted in English.

Source: Compiled from information in William Taylor, "The Logic of Global Business: An Interview with ABB's Percy Barnevik," *Harvard Business Review* 69, no. 2 (March-April 1991), pp. 90–105.

SUPPLEMENTING THE BASIC ORGANIZATION STRUCTURE

None of the basic structural designs is wholly adequate for organizing the total work effort in strategy-supportive ways. Some weaknesses can be corrected by using two or more of the structural designs simultaneously—many companies are large enough and diverse enough to have SBUs, functionally organized business units, geographic organizational structures in one or more businesses, units employing matrix principles, and several functionally specialized departments. But in many companies strategy-supportive organization requires supplementing the formal structure with special coordinating mechanisms and creative "disorganization"—cross-functional task forces, project teams, venture teams, self-sufficient work teams that perform whole processes, and specially empowered key individuals to push actions through the bureaucracy when necessary. Six of the most frequently used devices for supplementing the formal organization structure to promote better strategy execution include:

1. *Special project teams*—creating a separate, largely self-sufficient work group to oversee the completion of a special activity such as setting up a new technological process, bringing out a new product, starting up a new venture, consummating a merger with another company, seeing through the completion of a government contract, or supervising the construction and opening of a new plant. Teams are especially suitable for one-of-a-kind projects with a finite life expectancy when the normal organization is ill-equipped to achieve the same results in addition to its regular duties.

2. *Cross-functional task forces*—bringing a number of top-level executives and/or specialists together to solve problems requiring specialized expertise from several parts of the organization, coordinate strategy-related activities that span departmental boundaries, or explore ways to leverage the skills of different functional specialists into broader core competencies. Task forces seem to be most effective when they have fewer than 10 members, membership is voluntary, the seniority of the members is proportional to the importance of the problem, the task force moves swiftly to deal with its assignment, they are used sparingly (only on an as-needed basis), no staff is assigned, and documentation is scant.[28] Companies that have used task forces successfully form them to solve real problems and produce some solution efficiently; then they disband them.

3. *Venture teams*—forming a group of individuals to direct introduction of a new product, entry into a new geographic market, or the launch of a specific new business. Dow, General Mills, Westinghouse, General Electric, and Monsanto have used the venture team approach to regenerate an entrepreneurial spirit. The difficulties with venture teams include deciding who the venture manager should report to; whether funding for ventures should come from corporate, business, or departmental budgets; how to keep the venture clear of bureaucratic and vested interests; and how to coordinate large numbers of different ventures.

4. *Self-contained work teams*—a group of people drawn from different disciplines who work together on a semipermanent basis to continuously improve organizational performance in specific strategy-related areas—shortening the lab-to-market cycle time, boosting product quality, improving customer service, cutting delivery times, eliminating stockouts, reducing the costs of purchased materials and components, increasing assembly line productivity, trimming equipment downtime and maintenance expenses, or designing new models. American Express cut out three layers of hierarchy when it developed self-managed teams to handle all types of customer inquiries in a single-call, quick-resolution manner.[29]

5. *Process teams*—putting functional specialists who perform pieces of a business process together on a team instead of assigning them to their home base functional department. Such teams can be empowered to reengineer the process, held accountable for results, and rewarded on the basis of how well the process is performed. Much of Chrysler's revitalization is due to dramatically revamping its new model development process using "platform teams."[30] Each platform team consists of members from engineering, design, finance, purchasing, and marketing. The team is responsible for the car's design from beginning to end, has broad decision-making power, and is held accountable for the success or failure of their design. Teams coordinate their designs with manufacturing so that the models will be easier to build, and consult regularly with purchasing agents regarding parts quality. In one case Chrysler purchasing agents elected to pay 30 percent more for a better part because the engineer on the platform team believed the added cost would be offset by the time saved during assembly.

6. *Contact managers*—providing a single point of contact for customers when the steps of a process either are very complex or are dispersed such that integrating them for a single person or team to perform is impractical.[31] Acting as a buffer between internal processes and the customer, the contact person endeavors to answer customer questions and solve customer problems as if he or she is responsible for performing the called-for-activities. To do this, contact persons need access to all the information systems that the persons actually performing the process use and the ability to contact those people with questions and requests for further assistance when necessary. The best results are achieved when contact persons are empowered to act on their own judgment to get things done in a manner that will please customers. Duke Power, a Charlotte-based electric utility, uses empowered customer service representatives to resolve the problems of residential customers while shielding them from whatever goes on behind the scenes to produce solutions.

■ PERSPECTIVES ON ORGANIZING THE WORK EFFORT

There's no perfect or ideal organization structure. All of the basic designs have their strategy-related strengths and weaknesses. To do a good job of matching structure to strategy, strategy-implementers have to pick a basic design, modify it as needed to fit the company's particular business make-up, and then supplement it with the coordinating mechanisms and communication arrangements needed to support effective execution of the firm's strategy. While practical realities dictate giving some consideration to existing reporting relationships, personalities, internal politics, and other situational idiosyncrasies, strategy/structure factors have to predominate if the needs of effective strategy implementation are to be well served. Adjusting reporting relationships and departmental groupings to accommodate particular individuals and situational constraints should modify the strategy-structure fit in only minor ways.

Peter Drucker, one of the foremost authorities on managing, gives the following advice on organization design:

> The simplest organization structure that will do the job is the best one. What makes an organization structure "good" are the problems it does not create. The simpler the structure, the less that can go wrong.
>
> Some design principles are more difficult and problematic than others. But none is without difficulties and problems. None is primarily people-focused rather than task-focused; none is more "creative," "free," or "more democratic." Design principles are tools; and tools are neither good nor bad in themselves. They can be used properly or improperly, and that is all. To obtain both the greatest possible simplicity and the greatest "fit," organization design has to start out with a clear focus on *key activities* needed to produce *key results*. They have to be structured and positioned in the simplest possible design. Above all, the architect of organization needs to keep in mind the purpose of the structure he [or she] is designing.[32]

CURRENT ORGANIZATIONAL TRENDS

Many of today's companies are remodeling their traditional hierarchical structures built around functional specialization and centralized authority. Such structures make good strategic and organizational sense so long as (1) activities can be divided into simple, repeatable tasks that can be mastered quickly and performed efficiently in mass quantity, (2) there are important benefits to deeper functional expertise in each managerial discipline, and (3) customer needs are sufficiently standardized that it is easy to prescribe procedures for satisfying them. But these structures become a liability in businesses where customer preferences are shifting from standardized products to custom orders and special features, product life cycles are growing shorter, flexible manufacturing methods are replacing mass production techniques, customers want to be treated as individuals, the pace of technological change is accelerating, and market conditions are fluid. Multilayered management hierarchies and functionalized bureaucracies which require people to look upward in the organizational structure for answers and authority bog down in such environments. They can't deliver responsive customer service or adapt fast enough to changing conditions. Functional silos, task-oriented work, process fragmentation, layered management hierarchies, centralized decision making, growing functional and middle management bureaucracies, lots of checks and controls, and long response times can undermine competitive success in the 1990s. Today, companies need a new array of organizational capabilities to compete successfully: quick response to shifting customer preferences, short design-to-market cycles, superb quality the first time around, custom-order and multiversion production, expedited delivery, personalized customer service, accurate order filling, rapid assimilation of new technologies, creativity and innovation, and speedy reactions to competitive developments.

These new components of business strategy are driving a revolution in corporate organization.[33] Much of the corporate downsizing movement is aimed at busting functional and middle-management bureaucracies and recasting authoritarian pyramidal organizational structures into flatter, decentralized structures. The latest organizational designs for matching structure to strategy feature fewer layers of management, small-scale business units, reengineering work processes to cut back on fragmentation by functional departments, the creation of process teams and interdisciplinary work groups, lean staffing of corporate support functions, partnerships with key suppliers, empowerment of first-line supervisors and nonmanagement employees, open communications vertically and laterally, use of computers and telecommunications technologies to provide fast access to and dissemination of information, and accountability for results rather than emphasis on activity. The new organizational themes are lean, flat, responsive, and innovative. The new tools of organizational design are managers and workers able to act on their own judgment, reengineered work processes, and self-directed work teams.

The old command-and-control paradigm of vertically layered structures assumes that the people actually performing the tasks have neither the time nor the inclination to monitor and control their work and that they lack the knowledge to make informed decisions about how best to do their jobs. Such assumptions justified the need for prescribed procedures, close supervision, and managerial control of decision making. In flat, decentralized structures, these assumptions are discarded. Jobs are defined more broadly; where possible several tasks are integrated into a single job. People are more self-directed, armed with the information they need to get the job done. Fewer managers are needed because deciding how to do things becomes part of each person's or team's job.

REENGINEERING CAN PROMOTE BETTER IMPLEMENTATION

Reengineering strategy-critical business processes to reduce fragmentation across traditional departmental lines and to cut bureaucratic overhead has proven to be a legitimate, albeit little understood, organization design tool. It's not a passing fad or another management program of the month. Process organization is every bit as valid an organizing principle as functional specialization. Strategy execution is improved when the pieces of strategy-critical activities and core business processes performed by different departments are properly integrated and coordinated.

Companies that have reengineered some of their business processes have ended up compressing formerly separate steps and tasks into jobs performed by a single person and integrating jobs into team activities. Reorganization then follows, a natural consequence of task synthesis and job redesign. The experiences of companies that have successfully reengineered and restructured their operations in strategy-supportive ways suggest attacking process fragmentation and overhead reduction in the following fashion:[34]

- Develop a flow chart of the total business process, including where it interfaces with other value chain activities.

Reengineer, then reorganize.

- -

ILLUSTRATION 26   *Organizational Approaches for International and Global Markets*

- -

A 1993 study of 43 large U.S.-based consumer products companies, conducted by McKinsey & Co., a leading management consulting firm, identified internal organizational actions with the strongest and weakest links to rapidly growing sales and profits in international and global markets.

Organizational Actions Strongly Linked to International Success

- Centralizing international decision making in every area except new product development.
- Having a worldwide management development program and more foreigners in senior management posts.
- Requiring international experience for advancement into top management.
- Linking global managers with video-conferencing and electronic mail.
- Having product managers of foreign subsidiaries report to a country general manager.
- Using local executives to head operations in foreign countries (however, this is rapidly ceasing to distinguish successful companies because nearly everyone has implemented such a practice.

Organizational Actions Weakly Linked to International Success

- Creating global divisions.
- Forming international strategic business units.
- Establishing centers of excellence (where a single company facility takes global responsibility for a key product or emerging technology (too new to evaluate pro or con).
- Using cross-border task forces to resolve problems and issues.
- Creating globally integrated management information systems.

However, the lists of organizational dos and don'ts are far from decisive one way or the other. In general, the study found that internal organizational structure "doesn't matter that much," compared to having products with attractive prices and features. It is wrong to expect good results just because of good organization. Moreover, certain organizational arrangements (i.e.

centers of excellence) are too new to determine whether they positively affect sales and profit growth.

Source: Based on information reported by Joann S Lublin, "Study Sees U.S. Businesses Stumbling on the Road to Globalization," *The Wall Street Journal,* March 22, 1993, p. B4B.

- Try to simplify the process first, eliminating tasks and steps where possible and analyzing how to streamline the performance of what remains.
- Determine which parts of the process can be automated. Usually they will be repetitive, time-consuming tasks that require little thought or decision. Consider introducing advanced technologies that can be upgraded to next-generation capability and provide a basis for further productivity gains in the future.
- Evaluate each activity in the process to determine whether it is critical to strategy. Strategy-critical activities are candidates for benchmarking to achieve best-in-industry or best-in-world performance status.
- Weigh the pros and cons of outsourcing activities that are noncritical or that contribute little to organizational capabilities and core competencies.

- Design a structure for performing the activities that remain; reorganize the personnel and groups who perform these activities into the new structure.

Reengineering can produce dramatic gains in productivity and organizational capability when done properly. In the order processing section of General Electric's circuit breaker division, the elapsed time from order receipt to delivery was cut from three weeks to three days by consolidating six production units into one, reducing a variety of inventory and handling steps, automating the design system to replace a human custom-design process, and cutting the organizational layers between managers and workers from three to one.[35] Productivity rose 20 percent in one year and unit manufacturing costs dropped 30 percent.

There's no escaping the reality that reengineering, in concert with advanced office technologies and the use of self-directed, empowered work teams, provides company managers with important new organization design options. Organizational hierarchies can be flattened and middle management layers removed. Responsibility and decision-making authority can be pushed downward and outward to those places in the organization where customer contacts are made. Strategy-critical processes can be unified, performed more quickly, at lower cost, and made more responsive to changing customer preferences and expectations. Used properly, these new design approaches can trigger big gains in organizational creativity and employee productivity.

Illustration 26 reports the results of a study concerning effective and ineffective organizational arrangements in multinational companies.

Implementing Strategy:
Budgets, Policies, Best Practices, Support Systems, and Rewards

CHAPTER
TEN

Winning companies know how to
do their work better.

**Michael Hammer and James
Champy**

While a corporation can come up
with a plan for the future, it takes
everybody's help—and commitment—to implement it.

**Ronald W. Allen
CEO, Delta Airlines**

If you talk about change but don't
change the reward and recognition
system, nothing changes.

**Paul Allaire
CEO, Xerox Corporation**

In the previous chapter we emphasized the importance of building an organization capable of performing strategy-critical activities in a coordinated and highly competent manner. In this chapter we cover five additional strategy-implementing tasks:

1. Reallocating resources as needed to match the budgetary and staffing requirements of the new strategy.
2. Establishing strategy-supportive policies.
3. Instituting best practices and mechanisms for continuous improvement.
4. Installing support systems that enable company personnel to carry out their strategic roles proficiently day-in and day-out.
5. Employing motivational practices and incentive compensation methods that enhance organizationwide commitment to good strategy execution.

► LINKING BUDGETS TO STRATEGY

Getting an organization down the strategy implementation path throws a manager squarely into the budget-making process. Organizational units need enough resources to carry out their part of the strategic plan. This includes having enough of the right kinds of people and sufficient operating funds for them to do their work successfully. Strategy implementers are obligated to screen subordinates' requests for new capital projects and bigger operating budgets, distinguishing between what would be nice and what can make a cost-justified contribution to strategy execution. Moreover, they have to make a persuasive, documented case to superiors on what additional resources, if any, it will take to implement and execute their assigned piece of company strategy.

How well managers link budget allocations to the needs of strategy implementation will either promote or impede the process. Too little funding slows progress and impedes the ability of organizational units to execute their piece of the strategic plan proficiently. Too much funding wastes organizational resources and reduces financial performance. Both outcomes argue for strategy-implementers to be deeply involved in the budgeting process, closely reviewing the programs and budget proposals of strategy-critical organization units.

Depriving strategy-critical groups of the funds needed to execute their piece of the strategy can undermine the implementation process.

Managers must also be willing to shift resources from one area to another to support new strategic initiatives and priorities. A change in strategy nearly always calls for budget reallocations. Units that were important in the old strategy may now be oversized and overfunded. Units that now have a bigger and more critical strategic role may need more people, new equipment, additional facilities, and above-average increases in their operating budgets. Strategy implementers need to be active and forceful in shifting resources, downsizing some areas, upsizing others, and amply funding activities with a critical role in the new strategy. They have to exercise their power to allocate resources to make things happen and make the tough decisions to kill projects and activities that are no longer justified. The essential condition is that the funding requirements of the new strategy must drive the allocation of capital and each unit's operating budgets. Underfunding organizational units and activities pivotal to strategic success can defeat the whole implementation process.

New strategies usually call for significant budget reallocations.

Aggressive resource reallocation can have a positive strategic payoff. For example, at Harris Corporation, where the strategy was to diffuse research ideas into areas that were commercially viable, top management regularly shifted groups of engineers out of government projects and moved them (as a group) into new commercial venture divisions. Boeing has used a similar approach to reallocating ideas and talent; according to one Boeing officer: "We can do it (create a big new unit) in two weeks. We couldn't do it in two years at International Harvester."[1] Forceful actions to reallocate operating funds and move people into new organizational units signal a strong commitment to implementing strategic change, and they are frequently needed to catalyze the implementation process and give it credibility.

Fine-tuning the implementation of a company's existing strategy usually involves less reallocation and more of an extrapolation approach. Big movements of people and money from one area to another are seldom necessary. Improvement can usually be accomplished by incrementally increasing or decreasing the budgets and staffing of existing organization units. The chief exception occurs when a significant ingredient of corporate/business strategy is to generate fresh, new products and business opportunities from within the organization. Then, as proposals and business plans worth pursuing bubble up from below, decisions have to be made regarding capital expenditures, operating budgets, and from where the needed personnel will come. Companies like 3M, GE, and Boeing shift resources and people from area to area on an as-needed basis to support the launch of new products and new business ventures. They empower "product champions" and small bands of would-be entrepreneurs by giving them financial and technical support and by setting up organizational units and programs to help new ventures blossom more quickly.

▶ **CREATING STRATEGY-SUPPORTIVE POLICIES AND PROCEDURES**

Changes in strategy generally call for some changes in work practices and how internal operations are conducted. Asking people to alter established procedures and behavior always upsets the internal order of things. Pockets of resistance and employees anxious about how the changes will affect them are normal responses; this is especially true when the changes hold the potential for eliminating jobs. Questions are also likely to arise over what needs to be done in common fashion and where there needs to be leeway for independent action.

Prescribing policies and operating procedures aids the task of implementing strategy in several ways:

1. New or freshly revised policies and procedures provide top-down guidance to operating managers, supervisory personnel, and employees regarding how certain things now need to be done and what behavior is expected, thus establishing some degree of regularity, stability, and dependability in how management has decided to execute the strategy and operate the business on a daily basis.

2. Policies and procedures help align actions and behavior with strategy throughout the organization, placing limits on independent action and channeling individual and group efforts along the intended path of accomplishment. Policies and procedures counteract tendencies for parts of the organization to resist or reject common approaches—most people refrain from ignoring established practices or violating company policy without first gaining clearance or else having strong justification.

3. Policies and standardized operating procedures establish and help enforce needed consistency in how strategy-critical activities are performed in geographically scattered operating units. The existence of significant differences in the operating practices and procedures among organizational units performing common functions sends mixed messages to internal personnel about how to do their job and also to customers who do business with the company at multiple locations.

4. Because the process of dismantling old policies and procedures and instituting new ones invariably alters the character of the internal work climate, managers charged with implementing the strategy can use the policy-changing process as a powerful lever for changing the corporate culture to produce better alignment with the new strategy.

From a strategy implementation perspective, therefore, company managers need to be inventive in devising policies and practices that can provide vital support to effective strategy execution. McDonald's policy manual, in an attempt to steer "crew members" into stronger quality and service behavior patterns, spells out detailed procedures: "Cooks must turn, never flip, hamburgers. If they haven't been purchased, Big Macs must be discarded in 10 minutes after being cooked and french fries in 7 minutes. Cashiers must make eye contact with and smile at every customer." At Delta Airlines, it is corporate policy to test the aptitudes of all flight attendant applicants for friendliness, cooperativeness, and teamwork. Caterpillar Tractor has a policy of guaranteeing its customers 24-hour parts delivery anywhere in the world; if it fails to fulfill the promise, it supplies the part free. Hewlett-Packard requires R&D people to make regular visits to customers to learn about their problems, talk about new product applications, and, in general, keep the company's R&D programs customer-oriented. Illustration 27 describes Nike's manufacturing policies and practices in some detail.

Well-conceived policies and procedures aid implementation; out-of-sync policies are barriers.

Wisely constructed policies and procedures help enforce strategy implementation by channeling actions, behavior, decisions, and practices in directions that improve strategy execution. When policies and practices don't support strategy, they become a barrier to the very kinds of attitudinal and behavioral changes managers are trying to promote. Often, people opposed to certain elements of the strategy or aspects of its implementation vigorously defend long-standing policies and operating procedures in an effort to stall implementation or divert the approach to implementation in a different direction. Any time a company changes its strategy, managers are well advised to review existing policies and operating procedures, proactively revising or discarding those that are now out-of-sync and formulating new ones designed to improve execution of freshly chosen strategic initiatives.

None of this is meant to suggest that an organization needs a huge manual full of policies. Too much policy can be as stifling as wrong policy or as chaotic as no policy at all. Sometimes, the best policy for implementing strategy is a willingness to empower subordinates and let them do it any way they want if it makes sense and works. A little "structured chaos" can be a good thing when individual creativity and initiative are more essential to good strategy execution than standardization and strict conformity. When Rene McPherson became CEO at Dana Corp., he dramatically threw out 22½ inches of policy manuals and replaced them with a one-page statement of philosophy focusing on "productive people."[2] Creating a strong supportive fit between strategy and policy can mean more policies, fewer policies, or different policies. It can mean policies that require things to be done a certain way or policies that give employees leeway to accomplish their jobs the way they think best.

▶ INSTITUTING BEST PRACTICES AND A COMMITMENT TO CONTINUOUS IMPROVEMENT

If value chain activities are to be performed as effectively and efficiently as possible, then each department and organizational unit needs to benchmark how it performs specific tasks and activities against best-in-industry or best-in-world performers. A strong commitment to searching out and adopting best practices, especially for those activities where the potential for better quality performance or lower costs can translate into a sizable impact on the bottom line, is integral to effective strategy implementation. Absent such a commitment, a company surrenders some of its potential for beating its toughest competitors.

Identifying and implementing best practices is a journey, not a destination; it's an exercise in doing things in a world-class manner.

The benchmarking movement to search out, study, and implement best practices has resulted in a number of spin-off efforts—reengineering (the redesign of business processes), continuous improve-

| ILLUSTRATION 27 | *Nike's Manufacturing Policies and Practices* |

When Nike decided on a strategy of outsourcing 100 percent of its athletic footwear from independent manufacturers (all of whom turned out, for reasons of low cost, to be located in Taiwan, South Korea, Thailand, Indonesia, and China), it developed a series of policies and production practices to govern its working relationships with its *production partners* (a term Nike carefully nurtured because it implied joint responsibilities):

• Nike personnel were stationed on site at all key manufacturing facilities; each Nike representative tended to stay at the same factory site for several years to get to know the partner's people and processes in detail. They functioned as a liaison with Nike headquarters, working to match Nike's R&D and new product design efforts with factory capabilities and to keep monthly orders for new production in line with the latest sales forecasts.

• Nike instituted a quality assurance program at each factory site to enforce up-to-date and effective quality management practices.

• Nike endeavored to minimize ups and downs in

monthly production orders at factory sites making Nike's premium-priced top-of-the-line models (volumes typically ran 20,000–25,000 pairs daily); the policy was to keep month-to-month variations in the order quantity under 20 percent. These factories made Nike footwear exclusively and were expected to co-develop new models and to coinvest in new technologies.

• Factory sites that made mid-priced to low-end Nike products in large quantities (usually 70,000–85,000 pairs per day), known as "volume producers," were expected to handle most ups and downs in monthly orders themselves; these factories usually produced shoes for five to eight other buyers, giving them the flexibility to juggle orders and stabilize their production.

• It was strict Nike policy to pay its production partners on time, providing them with predictable cash flows.

Source: Based on information in James Brian Quinn, *Intelligent Enterprise* (New York: Free Press, 1992), pp. 60–64.

---

ment programs, and total quality management (TQM). A 1991 survey by the Conference Board showed 93 percent of manufacturing companies and 69 percent of service companies have implemented some form of quality improvement program.[3] Another survey found that 55 percent of American executives and 70 percent of Japanese executives used quality improvement information at least monthly as part of their assessment of overall business performance.[4] Indeed, quality improvement processes have now become part of the process of implementing strategies keyed to defect-free manufacture, superior product quality, superior customer service, and total customer satisfaction.

Management interest in quality improvement programs typically originates in a company's production areas—fabrication and assembly in manufacturing enterprises, teller transactions in banks, order picking and shipping at catalog firms, or customer contact interfaces in service organizations. Other times, initial interest begins with executives who have heard TQM presentations, read about TQM, or talked to people in other companies that have benefited from total quality programs. Usually, interested managers have quality and customer satisfaction problems they are struggling to solve.

While TQM understandably concentrates on the production of quality goods and the delivery of excellent customer service, to succeed it must extend organizationwide to employee efforts in all departments—human resources, billing, R&D, engineering,

---

ILLUSTRATION 28 *Motorola's Approach to TQM and Teamwork*

Motorola is rated as one of the best companies in measuring performance against its strategic targets and in promoting total quality practices that lead to continuous improvement. Motorola was selected in 1988 as one of the first winners of the Malcolm Baldridge Quality Award, and has since improved on its own award-winning efforts. In 1993, the company estimated it was saving about $2.2 billion annually from its team-oriented approach to TQM and continuous improvement.

A central feature of Motorola's approach is a yearlong contest highlighting the successes of employee teams from around the world in improving internal company practices, making better products, saving money, pleas-

ing customers, and sharing best practices with other Motorola groups. The contest, known as the Total Customer Satisfaction Team Competition, in 1992 attracted entries from nearly 4,000 teams involving nearly 40,000 of Motorola's 107,000 employees. Preliminary judging eventually reduced the 1992 finalists to 24 teams from around the world, all of whom were invited to Chicago in January 1993 to make a 12-minute presentation to a panel of 15 senior executives, including the CEO. Twelve teams were awarded gold medals and 12 were silver medals. The gold medalists included the following:

Name of Team	Work Location	Achievement
B.E.A.P. Goes on	Florida	Removed bottleneck in testing pagers by using robots.
The Expedition	Malaysia	Designed and delivered a new chip for Apple Computer in six months.
Operation Paging Storm	Singapore	Eliminated component alignment defect in papers.
ET/EV=1	Illinois	Streamlined order process for auto electronics.
The Mission	Arizona	Developed quality system for design of iridium satellites.
Class Act	Illinois	Cut training program from five years to two with better results.
Dyna-Attackers	Dublin	Cut production time and defect rate on new battery part.
Orient Express	Malaysia	Cut response time on tooling orders from 23 days to 4.
The Dandles	Japan	Improved efficiency of boiler operations.
Cool Blue Racers	Arizona	Cut product development time in half to win IBM contract.
IO Plastics Misload	Manila	Eliminated resin seepage in modulator assembly.

Motorola does not track the costs of the contest because "the benefits are so overwhelming." It has sent hundreds of videos about the contests to other companies wanting details. However, TQM consultants are skeptical of whether other companies have progressed far enough in establishing a team-based quality culture to benefit as Motorola has from a companywide contest; the downsides to such elaborate contests, they say, are

the added costs (preparation, travel, presentation, and judging) and the risks to the morale of those who don't win.

Source: Based on information reported in Barnaby J Feder, "At Motorola, Quality Is a Team Sport," *New York Times*, January 21, 1993, pp. C1 and C6.

---

accounting and records, and information systems—that may lack less pressing customer-driven incentives to improve. This is because instituting best practices and continuous improvement programs involves reforming the whole corporate culture and shifting to a total quality/continuous improvement business philosophy that permeates every facet of the organization's work effort. TQM aims at instilling enthusiasm and commitment to doing things right from top to bottom of the organization. It entails a restless search for ways to improve, the little steps forward each day, that the Japanese

call *kaizen*. TQM is thus a journey without a finish, where the managerial objective is
to kindle an innate, burning desire in people to
use ingenuity and initiative to progressively improve
the way tasks and value chain activities are performed. TQM preaches that there's no such thing as
good enough and that everyone has a responsibility
to participate in continuous improvement—see
Illustration 28 describing Motorola's approach to involving employees in its TQM
program.

> TQM entails creating a total quality culture bent on contin-
> uously improving the performance of every task and value
> chain activity.

The efforts companies are putting into implementing best practices, reengineering,
and continuous improvement efforts like TQM all aim at improved efficiency and reduced
costs, better product quality, and greater customer satisfaction. The essential difference
between reengineering and TQM is that reengineering aims at quantum gains on the order
of 30 to 50 percent or more whereas total quality programs stress incremental progress,
striving for inch-by-inch gains again and again in a
never-ending stream. The two approaches to improved performance of value chain activities are not
mutually exclusive. It makes sense to use them in
tandem. Reengineering can be used first to produce

> Reengineering seeks one-time quantum improvement; TQM
> seeks ongoing incremental improvement.

a good basic design that yields dramatic improvements in performing a business process.
Total quality programs then follow to work out bugs, perfect the process, and gradually
improve both efficiency and effectiveness. Such a two-pronged approach to implementing
organizational change is like a marathon where you run the first four laps as fast as you
can, then gradually pick up speed the remainder of the way.

Surveys indicate that some companies have benefited from their investments of
time and money in reengineering and continuous improvement techniques and some
have not.[5] Most usually, the biggest beneficiaries have been companies that viewed
such programs not as ends in themselves but as tools for implementing and executing
company strategy more effectively. The skimpiest payoffs from best practices, TQM,
and reengineering have occurred when company
managers seized them as a quick fix or a novel
idea worth trying; in most such instances, they
resulted in strategy-blind efforts to simply manage
better. There's an important lesson here. Best
practices, TQM, and reengineering all need to be
seen and used as part of a bigger-picture effort to

> When best practices, reengineering, and TQM are not part of
> a wider-scale effort to improve strategy execution as part of
> business performance, they typically deteriorate into strat-
> egy-blind efforts to manage better.

execute strategy more proficiently. Only strategy can point to which activities matter
and what performance targets make the most strategic sense. Absent a strategic
framework, managers lack the context in which to fix things that really matter to
business unit performance and strategic success.

To make best use of benchmarking, best practices, reengineering, TQM, and related
tools for enhancing organizational competency in executing strategy, managers have to
start with a clear fix on the indicators of successful strategy execution. In other words,
managers must know what needs to be accomplished to best execute the chosen
strategy—defect-free manufacture, on-time delivery, low overall costs, exceeding

customer expectations, faster cycle time, increased product innovation. Benchmarking best-in-industry and best-in-world performance of most or all value chain activities provides a realistic basis for setting internal performance milestones and longer-range targets.

Next comes the managerial task of building a total quality culture and instilling the necessary commitment to achieve performance measures consonant with good strategy execution. The action steps managers can take include:[6]

- Visible, unequivocal, and unyielding commitment by top management to total quality and continuous improvement, including a quality vision and specific, measurable quality goals.

- Nudging people toward TQ behaviors by initiating such organizational programs as:
  –Screening job applicants rigorously and hiring only those with attitudes and aptitudes for quality-based performance.
  –Using quality training programs.
  –Using teams and team-building exercises to reinforce and nurture individual effort.
  –Recognizing and rewarding individual and team efforts regularly and systematically.
  –Putting the performance emphasis on prevention (doing it right the first time) rather than inspection (instituting procedures to correct mistakes).

- Empowering employees so that authority for delivering great service or improving products is in the hands of the doers rather than the overseers.

- Providing quick electronic information access to doers so that real-time data can drive actions and decisions to diagnose and continuously improve value chain activities.

- Preaching that performance can, and must, be improved because competitors are not resting on past laurels and customers are always looking for something better.

If the targeted performance measures are appropriate to the strategy and if all the members of the organization, from top executives to line employees, buy into the process of continuous improvement, then the work climate will become conductive to proficient strategy execution and good bottom-line business performance.

▶ INSTALLING SUPPORT SYSTEMS

Company strategies can't be implemented or executed well without a number of support systems to carry on business operations. American, United, Delta, and other major airlines cannot hope to provide world-class passenger service without a computerized reservation system, a system for accurate and expeditious handling of baggage at each airport they serve, and a strong aircraft maintenance program. Federal Express has a computerized parcel-tracking system that can instantly report where any given package is in its transit-delivery process. It has communication systems that allow it to coordinate its 21,000 vans nationwide to make an average of 720,000 stops per day to pick up customer packages, and it has leading-edge flight operations systems that allow a single controller to direct as many as 200 FedEx aircraft simultaneously, overriding their flight plans should weather or special emergencies arise. All of these systems are essential to FedEx's strategy of next-day delivery of a package that "absolutely, positively has to be there."[7]

Otis Elevator has a sophisticated support system called OtisLine to coordinate its maintenance efforts nationwide.[8] Trained operators take all trouble calls, input critical information to a computer, and dispatch people directly via a beeper system to the local trouble spot. By analyzing the trouble call data, problem patterns can be identified nationally and communicated to design and manufacturing personnel, allowing them to quickly alter design specifications or manufacturing procedures when needed to correct recurring problems. Also, much of the information needed for repairs is provided directly from faulty elevators through internally installed microcomputer monitors, further lowering outage time.

Innovative, state-of-the-art support systems can be a basis for competitive advantage if they give a firm capabilities that rivals can't match.

Procter & Gamble codes the more than 900,000 phone calls it receives annually on its toll-free 800 number to obtain early warning signals of product problems and changing consumer tastes.[9] Domino's has computerized systems at each outlet to facilitate ordering, inventory, payroll, cash flow, and work control functions. This frees managers to spend more time on supervision, customer service, and business development activities.[10] Most all telephone companies, electric utilities, and TV broadcasters have on-line monitoring systems to spot transmission problems within seconds and increase the reliability of their services. At Mrs. Fields Cookies systems can monitor sales at 15-minute intervals and suggest product mix changes, promotional tactics, or operating adjustments to improve customer response — see Illustration 29.

Well-conceived, state-of-the-art support systems not only facilitate better strategy execution, they also can strengthen organizational capabilities enough to provide a competitive edge over rivals. For example, a company with a differentiation strategy based on superior quality needs to develop systems for training personnel in quality techniques, tracking product quality at each production step, and ensuring that all goods shipped meet quality standards. A company striving to be a low-cost provider needs systems that exploit opportunities to drive costs out of its business processes. Fast-growing companies need recruiting systems to attract and hire qualified employees in large numbers. In businesses like public accounting and management consulting where large numbers of professional staffers need cutting-edge technology, companies have to install systems to train and retrain employees regularly and keep them supplied with up-to-date information. No company can hope to outexecute its competitors without ample internal support systems, many of which are state-of-the-art and technologically sophisticated. Moreover, unusually good support systems can strengthen organizational capabilities enough to provide a competitive advantage over rivals.

■ INSTITUTING FORMAL REPORTING OF STRATEGIC INFORMATION

Accurate information is an essential guide to action. Every organization needs systems for gathering and reporting information critical to strategy and for tracking key performance measures over time. Telephone companies have elaborate information systems to track signal quality, connection times, interrupts, wrong connections, billing errors, and other measures of reliability. To track and manage the quality of passenger service, airlines have information systems to monitor gate delays, on-time departures and arrivals, baggage handling times, lost baggage complaints, stockouts on meals and drinks,

---

ILLUSTRATION 29   *Operating Practices and Support Systems at Mrs. Fields Cookies, Inc.*

Mrs. Fields Cookies is one of the best known specialty foods companies in the United States with over 500 outlets in operation in malls, airports, and other high-pedestrian-traffic locations; the company also has over 250 outlets retailing other bakery and cookie products. Debbi Fields, age 37, is the company's founder and CEO. Her business concept for Mrs. Fields Cookies is "to serve absolutely fresh, warm cookies as though you'd stopped by my house and caught me just taking a batch from the oven." Cookies not sold within two hours are removed from the case and given to charity. The company's major form of advertising is sampling; store employees walk around the shopping mall giving away cookie samples. People are hired for store crews on the basis of warmth, friendliness, and the ability to have a good time giving away samples, baking fresh batches, and talking to customers during the course of a sale.

To implement its strategy, the company developed several novel practices and a customized computer support system. One key practice is giving each store an *hourly* sales quota. Another is for Fields to make unannounced visits to her stores, where she masquerades as a casual shopper to test the enthusiasm and sales techniques of store crews, sample the quality of the cookies they are baking, and observe customer reactions.

Debbi's husband Randy developed a software program that keeps headquarters and stores in close contact. Via the computer network, each store manager receives a daily sales goal (broken down by the hour) based on the store's recent performance history and on such special factors as special promotions, mall activities, weekdays versus weekends, holiday shopping patterns, and the weather forecast. With the hourly sales quotas also comes a schedule of the number of cookies to bake and when to bake them. As the day progresses, store managers type in actual hourly sales figures and customer counts. If customer counts are up but sales are lagging, the computer is programmed to recommend more aggressive sampling or more suggestive selling. If it becomes obvious the day is going to be a bust for the store, the computer automatically revises the sales projections for the day, reducing hourly quotas and instructing how much to cut back cookie baking. To facilitate crew scheduling by the store manager, sales projections are also provided for two weeks in advance. All job applicants must sit at the store's terminal and answer a computerized set of questions as part of the interview process.

In addition, the computer software contains a menu giving store staff immediate access to company personnel policies, maintenance schedules for store equipment, and repair instructions. If a store manager has a specific problem, it can be entered on the system and routed to the appropriate person. Messages can be sent directly to Debbi Fields via the computer; even if she is on a store inspection trip, her promise is to respond to all inquiries within 48 hours.

The computerized information support system serves several objectives: (1) it gives store managers more time to work with their crews and achieve sales quotas as opposed to handling administrative chores and (2) it gives headquarters instantaneous information on store performance and a means of controlling store operations. Debbi Fields sees the system as a tool for projecting her influence and enthusiasm into more stores more frequently than she could otherwise reach.

Source: Developed from information in Mike Korologos, "Debbi Fields," *Sky Magazine,* July 1988, pp. 42–50.

---

overbookings, and maintenance delays and failures. Many companies have provided customer contact personnel with instant electronic access to customer data bases so that they can respond effectively to customer inquiries and personalize customer services.

Accurate, timely information allows organizational members to monitor progress and take corrective action promptly.

To properly oversee strategy implementation, company managers need prompt, continuous feedback on implementation initiatives before they are completed in order to be able to steer them to a successful conclusion in case early steps don't produce the expected progress or things seem to be drifting off course. Monitoring the outcomes of the first round of implementation actions (1) allows early detection of the need to adjust either the strategy or how it is being implemented and (2) provides some assurance that things are moving ahead as planned.[11] Early experiences can be difficult to assess, but they provide the first hard data from the action front and should be closely scrutinized as a basis for corrective action.

Information systems need to cover four broad areas: (1) customer data, (2) operations data, (3) employee data, and (4) financial performance data. All key strategic performance indicators have to be measured as often as practical. Many retail companies generate daily sales reports for each store and maintain up-to-the-minute inventory and sales records on each item. Manufacturing plants, typically, generate daily production reports and track labor productivity on every shift. Monthly profit-and-loss statements are common, as are monthly statistical summaries.

In designing formal reports to monitor strategic progress, five guidelines should be observed:[12]

1. Information and reporting systems should involve no more data and reporting than is needed to give a reliable picture. The data gathered should emphasize strategically meaningful outcomes and potentially significant developments. Temptations to supplement what managers need to know with other interesting but marginally useful information should be avoided.

2. Reports and statistical data gathering have to be timely—not too late to take corrective action or so often as to overburden.

3. The flow of information and statistics should be kept simple. Complicated reports are likely to confound and obscure because of the attention paid to mechanics, procedures, and interpretive guidelines rather than reporting outcomes and diagnosing the variances from planned performance.

4. Information and reporting systems should aim at no surprises and generating early-warning signs rather than just producing information. It is debatable whether reports should be widely distributed (''for your information''), but they should always be provided to managers who are in a position to act when trouble signs appear.

5. Statistical reports should make it easy to flag big or unusual variances from plan, thus directing management attention to significant departures from targeted performance.

Statistical information gives the strategy implementer a feel for the numbers, reports and meetings provide information on new developments and problems, and personal contacts add a feel for the people dimension. All are good barometers of overall performance. Identifying deviations from plan and the problems areas to be addressed are prerequisites for initiating actions to either improve implementation or fine tune strategy.

▶ DESIGNING STRATEGY-SUPPORTIVE REWARD SYSTEMS

It is important for organizational subunits and individuals to be committed to implementing strategy and achieving performance targets. Company managers typically try to enlist organizationwide commitment to carrying out the strategic plan by motivating and rewarding people for good performance. The range of options includes all the standard reward-punishment techniques—inspirational challenges, the chance to be part of something exciting, greater opportunity for personal satisfaction, setting ambitious performance targets, the potential of being promoted versus being sidelined and assigned a routine or dead-end job, praise, recognition, constructive criticism, peer pressure, more (or less) responsibility, increased (or decreased) job control and decision-making autonomy, a better shot at attractive locational assignments, the bonds of group acceptance, greater job security, and the promise of sizable financial rewards. But motivational techniques and rewards have to be used *creatively* and linked tightly to the factors necessary for good strategy execution.

■ MOTIVATIONAL PRACTICES

Successful strategy implementers are good at inspiring and challenging employees to become part of a winning effort. They are skilled at getting them to buy in to the strategy and enlisting their best effort towards making it work. They allow employees to participate in making decisions about how to perform their jobs and try to make jobs interesting and satisfying—as Frederick Herzberg said, "If you want people motivated to do a good job, give them a good job to do." They structure individual efforts into teams and work groups to facilitate an exchange of ideas and a climate of support.[13] They work at devising strategy-supportive motivational approaches and using them effectively. Consider some actual examples:[14]

> One of the biggest strategy-implementing challenges is to motivate employees in a manner that fosters winning attitudes and wholehearted organizationwide commitment.

- At Mars Inc. (best known for its candy bars), every employee, including the president, gets a weekly 10 percent bonus by coming to work on time each day that week. This on-time incentive is used to minimize absenteeism and tardiness, to boost worker productivity by producing the greatest number of candy bars during each available minute of machine time.

- In a number of Japanese companies, employees meet regularly to hear inspirational speeches, sing company songs, and chant the corporate litany. In the United States, Tupperware conducts a weekly Monday night rally to honor, applaud, and fire up its salespeople who conduct Tupperware parties. Amway and Mary Kay Cosmetics hold similar inspirational get-togethers for their sales force organizations.

- A San Diego area company assembles its 2,000 employees at its six plants the first thing every workday to listen to a management talk about the state of the company. Then they engage in brisk calisthenics. This company's management believes "that by doing one thing together each day, it reinforces the unity of the company. It's also fun. It gets the blood up." Managers take turns making the presentations. Many of the speeches "are very personal and emotional, not approved beforehand or screened by anybody."

- Texas Instruments and Dana Corp. insist that teams and divisions set their own goals and have regular peer reviews.
- Procter & Gamble's brand managers are asked to compete fiercely against each other; the official policy is "a free-for-all among brands with no holds barred." P&G's system of purposeful internal competition breeds people who love to compete and excel. Those who win become corporate "heroes," and around them emerges a folklore of war stories of valiant brand managers who waged uphill struggles against great odds and made a market success out of their assigned brands.

These motivational approaches accentuate the positive; others blend positive and negative features. Consider the way Harold Geneen, former president and chief executive officer of ITT, allegedly combined the use of money, tension, and fear:

> Geneen provides his managers with enough incentives to make them tolerate the system. Salaries all the way through ITT are higher than average—Geneen reckons 10 percent higher—so that few people can leave without taking a drop. As one employee put it: "We're all paid just a bit more than we think we're worth." At the very top, where the demands are greatest, the salaries and stock options are sufficient to compensate for the rigors. As some said, "He's got them by their limousines."
>
> Having bound his men to him with chains of gold, Geneen can induce the tension that drives the machine. "The key to the system," one of his men explains, "is the profit forecast. Once the forecast has been gone over, revised, and agreed on, the managing director has a personal commitment to Geneen to carry it out. That's how he produces the tension on which the success depends." The tension goes through the company, inducing ambition, perhaps exhilaration, but always with some sense of fear: what happens if the target is missed?[14]

If a strategy implementer's motivational approach and reward structure induce too much stress, internal competitiveness, and job insecurity, the results can be counter-productive. Positive reinforcement needs to outweigh negative reinforcement for the work environment to be healthy. Yet, it is doubtful whether it is ever useful to completely eliminate constructive pressure for performance and anxiety from the strategy implementation process. There is, for example, no evidence that a no-pressure work environment leads to superior strategy execution or sustained high performance. As the CEO of a major bank put it: "There's a deliberate policy here to create a level of anxiety. Winners usually play like they're one touchdown behind."[15] High-performing organizations need a cadre of ambitious people who love a challenge, thrive in a performance-oriented environment, and find some competition and pressure useful to satisfy their own drives for personal recognition, accomplishment, and self-satisfaction. Unless meaningful incentive and career consequences are associated with successfully implementing strategic initiatives and hitting strategic performance targets, few people will attach much significance to the company's strategic plan.

Positive motivational approaches generally work better than negative ones.

■ REWARDS AND INCENTIVES

The conventional view is that a manager's push for strategy implementation should incorporate more positive than negative motivational elements. People tend to respond with more enthusiasm and more effort when their cooperation is positively enlisted and rewarded, rather than strong-armed by the boss's orders. Nevertheless, how much of which incentives to use depends on how hard the task of strategy implementation will be in light of all the obstacles to be overcome. A manager has to do more than just talk to everyone about how important new strategic practices and performance targets are to the organization's future well-being. Talk, no matter how inspiring, seldom commands people's best efforts for long. To get employees' sustained, energetic commitment, company managers have to be resourceful in designing and using motivational incentives—both monetary and nonmonetary. The more a manager understands what motivates subordinates and the more he or she relies on motivational incentives as a tool for implementing strategy, the greater will be employees' commitment to good day-in, day-out execution of their role in the company's strategic plan.

LINKING WORK ASSIGNMENTS TO PERFORMANCE TARGETS

The first step in creating a strategy-supportive system of rewards and incentives is to define jobs and assignments in terms of the *results to be accomplished,* not the duties and functions to be performed. Training the job holder's attention and energy on what to *achieve,* as opposed to what activities to perform, boosts the chances of reaching agreed-on outcomes. It is flawed thinking to stress duties and activities in job descriptions in hopes that the by-products will be the desired kinds of accomplishment. In any job,

---
Job assignments should stress the results to be achieved rather than the duties and activities to be performed.

---

performing assigned tasks is not equivalent to achieving the intended objectives. Working hard, staying busy, and diligently attending to assigned duties do not guarantee results. Stressing "what to accomplish" instead of "what to do" is an impor-

tant difference. As any student knows, just because an instructor teaches doesn't mean students are learning what is being taught. Teaching and learning are different things—the first is an activity and the second is a result.

Emphasizing what to accomplish (i.e., performance targets for individual jobs, work groups, departments, businesses, and the entire company) has the larger purpose of making the work environment results-oriented. Without target objectives, individuals and work groups can become so engrossed in the details of performing assigned functions on schedule that they lose sight of what the tasks are intended to accomplish in the first place. By regularly tracking actual outcomes versus targeted performance, managers can proactively concentrate on making the right things happen rather than closely supervising people in hopes that the right outcomes will materialize if every activity is performed according to the book. This, of course, is what results-oriented management is all about.

Creating a tight fit between work assignments and accomplishing the goals of the chosen strategy requires using the strategic and financial objectives spelled out in the strategic plan as the basis for incentive compensation. If the details of strategy have been fleshed out thoroughly from the corporate level down to the operating level, appropriate performance measures either exist or can be developed for the whole company, for each business unit, for each functional department, for each operating unit, and for each work group. These become the targets that strategy implementers aim for and the basis for deciding how many jobs and what skills, expertise, funding, and time frame it will take to achieve them.

Usually a number of performance measures are needed at each level; rarely does a single measure suffice. At the corporate and line-of-business levels, performance objectives typically revolve around profitability measures, sales and earnings growth, market share, product quality, customer satisfaction, and hard evidence that market position, overall competitiveness, and future prospects have improved. In the manufacturing area, the strategy-relevant performance measures may focus on unit manufacturing costs, employee productivity, production and shipping schedules, defect rates, or the number and extent of work stoppages due to labor disagreements and equipment breakdowns. In the marketing area, measures may include unit selling costs, dollar sales and unit volume, sales penetration of each target customer group, market share, the success of newly introduced products, the frequency of customer complaints, advertising effectiveness, the acquisition of new accounts, and customer satisfaction surveys. While most performance measures are quantitative, several may have elements of subjectivity—improvements in labor-management relations, employee morale, customer satisfaction, advertising success, and how far the firm is ahead or behind rivals on quality, service, and technological capability.

REWARDING PERFORMANCE

The most dependable way to keep people's eyes trained on the objectives laid out in the strategic plan and to make achieving them a way of life up and down the organization is to provide generous rewards to individuals and groups who achieve their assigned targets and to deny rewards to those who don't. For strategy-implementers, doing a good job needs to mean achieving the agreed-upon performance targets. Any other standard undermines implementation of the strategic plan and condones the diversion of time and energy into activities that don't matter much in accomplishing the strategic plan. The pressure to achieve the targeted strategic performance should be unrelenting. A "no excuses" standard has to prevail.[16]

> The strategy-implementer's standard for judging whether individuals and organizational units have done a good job must be whether they achieved their performance targets.

But with the pressure to perform must come deserving and meaningful rewards. Without an ample payoff, the system breaks down, and the strategy-implementer is left with the unworkable option of barking orders and pleading for compliance. Some of the most successful companies—Wal-Mart, Nucor Steel, Lincoln Electric, Electronic Data Systems, Remington Products, and Mary Kay Cosmetics—owe much of their success to having designed a set of incentives and rewards that induce people to do the very things needed to hit performance targets and execute strategy well enough to become leaders in their industries. Nucor's strategy is to be *the* low-cost producer of steel products. Because labor costs are a significant fraction of total cost in the steel business, successful implementation of Nucor's low-cost strategy requires achieving lower labor costs per ton of steel than competitors. To drive its labor costs per ton below rivals, Nucor management utilizes production incentives that give workers a bonus roughly equal to their regular wages provided their production teams meet or exceed weekly production targets; the regular wage scale is set at levels comparable to other manufacturing jobs in the local areas where Nucor has plants. Bonuses are paid every two weeks based on the prior weeks' actual production levels measured against the target. The results of Nucor's piece-rate incentive plan are impressive. Nucor's labor productivity (in output per worker) runs over 50 percent above the average of the unionized work forces of the industry's major producers; Nucor enjoys about a $50–$75 per ton cost advantage over large, integrated steel producers like U.S. Steel and Bethlehem Steel (a substantial part of which comes from its labor cost advantage); and Nucor workers are the highest paid workers in the steel industry. At Remington Products, only 65 percent of factory workers' paychecks is salary; the rest is based on piece-work incentives. The company conducts 100 percent inspections of products, and rejected items are counted against incentive pay for the responsible worker. Top-level managers earn more from bonuses than from their salaries. During the first four years of Remington's incentive program, productivity rose 17 percent.

These and other experiences demonstrate some important lessons about designing rewards and incentives:

1. *The performance payoff must be a major, not minor, piece of the total compensation package*—incentives that amount to 20 percent or more of total compensation are big attention-getters and are capable of driving individual effort.

2. *The incentive plan should extend to all managers and all workers,* not just be restricted to top management. It is a gross miscalculation to expect that lower-level managers and employees will work their tails off to hit performance targets just so a few senior executives can get lucrative rewards!

3. *The reward system must be administered with scrupulous care and fairness*—if performance standards are set unrealistically high or if individual performance evaluations are inaccurate and poorly documented, dissatisfaction and disgruntlement with the system will overcome any positive benefits.

4. *The incentives must be tightly linked to achieving only those performance targets spelled out in the strategic plan and not to any other factors.* Performance evaluation based on factors unrelated to the strategy signal that either important performance targets were left out and the strategic plan is incomplete, or management's real agenda is something other than what was stated in the strategic plan.

5. *The performance targets each individual is expected to achieve should involve outcomes that the individual can personally affect*—the role of incentives is to enhance individual commitment and channel behavior in beneficial directions. This role is not well served when the performance measures an individual is judged by are outside his or her arena of influence.

Aside from these general guidelines it is hard to prescribe what kinds of incentives and rewards to develop except to say that the payoff must be directly attached to performance measures that indicate the strategy is working and implementation is on track. If the company's strategy is to be a low-cost provider, the incentive system must reward performance that lowers costs. If the company has a differentiation strategy predicated on superior quality and service, the incentive system must reward such outcomes as zero defects, infrequent need for product repair, low numbers of customer complaints, and speedy order processing and delivery. If a company's growth is predicated on a strategy of new product innovation, incentives should be tied to factors like the percentages of revenues and profits coming from newly introduced products.

■ WHY THE PERFORMANCE–REWARD LINK IS IMPORTANT

The use of incentives and rewards is the single most powerful tool management has to win strong employee commitment to carrying out the strategic plan. Failure to use this tool wisely and powerfully weakens the entire implementation process. *Decisions on salary increases, incentive compensation, promotions, who gets which assignments, and other ways and means of awarding praise and recognition are the strategy implementer's foremost attention-getting, commitment-generating devices.* How a company's incentives are structured signals what sort of behavior and performance management wants; how managers parcel out raises, promotions, and praise says more about who is considered to be doing a good job than any other factor. Such matters seldom escape the closest employee scrutiny. A company's system of incentives and rewards thus ends up being the vehicle by which its strategy is emotionally ratified in the form of real commitment. Incentives make it in employees' self-interest to do what is needed to achieve the performance targets spelled out in the strategic plan.

The reward structure is management's most powerful strategy-implementing tool.

■ MAKING PERFORMANCE-DRIVEN COMPENSATION WORK

Creating a tight fit between strategy and the reward structure is generally best accomplished by agreeing on strategy-critical performance objectives, fixing responsibility and deadlines for achieving them, and treating their achievement as a pay-for-performance *contract*. From a strategy implementation perspective, the key is to make strategically relevant measures of performance the dominating basis for designing incentives, evaluating individual efforts, and handing out rewards. Every organizational unit, every manager, every team or work group, and ideally every employee should have clearly defined performance targets that reflect measurable progress in implementing the strategic game plan and should be held accountable for achieving them. For example, at Banc One, the fifth largest U.S. bank and the second most profitable bank in the world (based on return on assets), a high level of customer satisfaction is a key performance objective; to enhance employee commitment to the task of pleasing customers, Banc One ties the pay scales in each branch office to that branch's customer satisfaction rating—the higher the branch's ratings, the higher that branch's pay scales. By shifting from a theme of equal pay for equal work to one of equal pay for equal performance, Banc One has focused the attention of branch employees more squarely on the task of pleasing, even delighting, their customers.

To prevent undermining and undoing pay-for-performance approaches to strategy implementation, companies must be scrupulously fair and impartial in comparing actual performance against agreed-upon performance targets. Everybody needs to understand how their incentive compensation is calculated and how their performance targets contribute to the achievement of organizational performance targets. The reasons for any deviations have to be explored fully to determine whether the causes are attributable to poor individual performance or to circumstances beyond the individual's control. Skirting the system to find ways to reward nonperformers must absolutely be avoided. It is debatable whether exceptions should be made for people who've tried hard, gone the extra mile, yet still come up short of achieving their performance targets because of circumstances beyond their control—a good case can be made either way. The problem with making exceptions is that once good excuses start to creep into the rewards for nonperformers, the door is opened for all kinds of "legitimate" reasons why actual performance failed to match targeted performance. In short, people at all levels have to be held accountable for carrying out their assigned part of the strategic plan, and they have to know their rewards are based on the caliber of their strategic accomplishments.

Implementing Strategy:
Culture and Leadership

Weak leadership can wreck the soundest strategy; forceful execution of even a poor plan can often bring victory.

Sun Zi

Effective leaders do not just reward achievement, they celebrate it.

Shelley A. Kirkpatrick and Edwin A. Locke

Ethics is the moral courage to do what we know is right, and not to do what we know is wrong.

**C. J. Silas
CEO, Philips Petroleum**

A leader lives in the field with his troops.

H. Ross Perot

In the previous two chapters we examined six of the strategy implementer's tasks—building a capable organization, steering ample resources into strategy-critical activities and operating units, establishing strategy-supportive policies, instituting best practices and programs for continuous improvement, creating internal support systems to enable better execution, and employing appropriate motivational practices and compensation incentives. In this chapter we explore the two remaining implementation tasks: creating a strategy-supportive corporate culture and exerting the internal leadership needed to drive implementation forward.

► BUILDING A STRATEGY-SUPPORTIVE CORPORATE CULTURE

Every company has its own organizational culture. It has its own business philosophy and principles, its own way of approaching problems and making decisions, its own patterns of ''how we do things around here,'' its own taboos and political don'ts, and its own cache of stories that are told over and over to illustrate company values and their meaning. These ingrained beliefs, behaviors and thought patterns, business practices, and personality define an organization's culture. The bedrock of Wal-Mart's culture is dedication to customer satisfaction, zealous pursuit of low costs, hard work, Sam Walton's legendary frugality, the ritualistic Saturday morning headquarters meetings to exchange ideas and review problems, and the commitment of company executives to visit stores, talk to customers, and solicit suggestions from employees. At Frito-Lay, stories abound about potato chip route salespersons slogging through snow and mud to uphold the 99.5 percent service level to customers in which the organization takes such great pride. At McDonald's the constant message from management is the overriding importance of quality, service, cleanliness, and value; employees are drilled over and over on the need for attention to detail and perfecting every fundamental of the business.

At Nordstrom, a department store retailer noted for exceptional commitment to its customers, the motto is Respond to Unreasonable Customer Requests.[1] Living up to the company's motto is so strongly ingrained in employee behavior that they learn to relish the challenges that some customer requests pose. Usually, Nordstrom employees find that meeting customer demands in a pleasing fashion entails little more than gracious compliance and a little extra personal attention. But occasionally it means paying a customer's parking ticket when in-store gift wrapping takes longer than normal or personally delivering items purchased by phone to customers with an emergency need. At Nordstrom, each out-of-the-ordinary customer request is seen as an opportunity for a "heroic" act by an employee and a way to build the company's reputation for great service. Nordstrom encourages these acts by promoting employees noted for outstanding service, keeping scrapbooks of heroic acts, and paying its salespeople entirely on commission. (It is not unusual for good salespeople at Nordstrom to earn double what they would at other department store retailers.) For go-getters who truly enjoy retail

Corporate culture refers to a company's inner values, beliefs, rituals, operating style, and work atmosphere.

selling and pleasing customers, Nordstrom is a great company to work for. But the culture weeds out those who can't meet Nordstrom's demanding standards and rewards those who are prepared to be what Nordstrom stands for.

■ WHERE DOES CORPORATE CULTURE COME FROM?

The taproot of corporate culture is the organization's shared belief and philosophy about how its affairs ought to be conducted—the reasons why it does things the way it does. A company's culture manifests itself in the values and business principles that management preaches and practices, in its ethical standards and official policies, in its stakeholder relationships (especially its dealings with employees, unions, stockholders, vendors, and the community in which it operates), in the traditions it maintains, in its supervisory practices, in employees' attitudes and behavior, in its stories, its politics, and in the overall feel of the work environment. All these sociological forces, some of which operate quite subtly, combine to give definition to an organization's culture.

Beliefs and practices embedded in a company's culture can originate from anywhere: an influential individual, work group, department, or division, at the bottom of the organizational hierarchy or the top.[2] Often, many cultural components are associated with a founder or other early leaders who have articulated them as a vision, a set of principles which the organization should adhere to, a business strategy, or combination of these. Over time, these values and practices come to be shared by company managers and employees and then persist as new employees are encouraged to adopt and follow them.

A company's culture is thus a product of internal social forces. Moreover, the shared values and behaviors that prevail across the organization tend to be interdependent. One component relates to another. This interconnectedness makes it difficult to alter just one facet of the culture. Changing one aspect spills over to affect another aspect.

Once established, company cultures are perpetuated by continuity of leadership, selection of new group members according to how well their values and behavior fit in, systematic indoctrination of new members in the culture's fundamentals, the efforts of senior group members to reiterate core values in daily conversations and pronouncements, the telling and retelling of legendary stories, regular ceremonies honoring members that display cultural ideals, visibly rewarding those who follow cultural norms, and penalizing those who don't.[3] However, even stable cultures aren't static. Crises and new challenges evolve into new ways of doing things. New leaders and turnover of key members often spawn new or different values and practices that alter the culture. Diversification into new businesses, expansion into different geographical areas, and rapid growth that causes new employees to be hired at a fast clip can all cause a company's culture to evolve.

Although it is common to speak about corporate culture in the singular, companies typically have multiple cultures (or subcultures).[4] Values, beliefs, and practices can vary significantly by department, geographic location, division, or business unit. If recently acquired business units have not yet been assimilated or if different organizational units have conflicting managerial styles, business philosophies, and operating approaches, then a company's subcultures can clash, or at least not mesh together well.

■ THE POWER OF CULTURE

Most managers, based on their own experiences as well as on case studies reported in the business press, accept that an organization's culture is an important contributor (or obstacle) to successful strategy execution. Thomas Watson, Jr., who succeeded his father as CEO at IBM, stated the case for a culture-performance link eloquently in a 1962 speech at Columbia University:

> The basic philosophy, spirit, and desire of an organization have far more to do with its relative achievements than do technological or economic resources, organization structure, innovation, and timing. All these things weigh heavily on success. But they are, I think, transcended by how strongly the people in the organization believe in its basic precepts and how faithfully they carry them out.[5]

The beliefs, goals, and practices called for in a strategy may or may not be compatible with a firm's culture. When they are not, a company usually finds it difficult to implement the strategy successfully.[6]

— — — — — — — — — — — — — — — —
A strong culture and a tight strategy–culture fit are powerful levers for influencing people to do their jobs better.
— — — — — — — — — — — — — — — —

A close culture-strategy match that energizes people all over the firm to do their jobs in a way that supports strategy naturally is significant to successful implementation. Strong cultures promote good long-term performance when there's fit with strategy and hurt performance when there's not. When a company's culture is out of sync with what is needed for strategic success, the culture has to be changed as rapidly as can be managed; the more entrenched the culture, the greater the difficulty of implementing new or different strategies. A sizable and prolonged strategy-culture conflict weakens and may even defeat managerial efforts to make the strategy work as planned.

A tight culture-strategy alignment is a powerful lever for channeling behavior and helping employees do their jobs in a more strategy-supportive manner; this occurs in two ways:[7]

1. A work environment where the culture matches well with the conditions for good strategy execution provides a system of informal rules and peer pressure regarding

how to conduct business internally and how to go about doing one's job. Culturally approved behavior thrives, while culturally disapproved behavior gets squashed and often penalized. In a company where strategy and culture are misaligned, ingrained values and operating philosophies don't cultivate strategy-supportive work habits; often, the very kinds of behavior need to execute strategy successfully run afoul of the culture and attract negative recognition rather than praise and reward.

2. A strong strategy-supportive culture nurtures and motivates people to their best; it provides structure, standards, and a value system in which to operate; and it promotes strong company identification among employees. All this makes employees feel genuinely better about their jobs and work environment and they often end up performing closer to the best of their abilities.

This says something important about the task of leading strategy implementation: *anything so fundamental as implementing a strategic plan involves moving the organization's culture into alignment with the requirements for proficient strategy execution.* The optimal condition is a work environment that enlists and encourages people to perform activities critical to the organization's strategy in a superior fashion. As one observer noted:

> It has not been just strategy that led to big Japanese wins in the American auto market. It is a culture that enspirits workers to excel at fits and finishes, to produce moldings that match and doors that don't sag. It is a culture in which Toyota can use that most sophisticated of management tools, the suggestion box, and in two years increase the number of worker suggestions from under 10,000 to over 1 million with resultant savings of $250 million.[8]

■ STRONG VERSUS WEAK CULTURES

Company cultures vary widely in strength, that is, the degree to which they are embedded in company practices. A company's culture can be weak and fragmented in the sense that many subcultures exist, few values and behavioral norms are widely shared, and there are few strong traditions. In such cases, employees typically have no deeply felt sense of company identity, view their company as merely as place to work and their job as a way to make a living, and have divided loyalties—some to their department, some to the colleagues with whom they work closely, some to the union, and some to their boss. On the other hand, a company's culture can be strong and cohesive in the sense that the company has a clear and explicit philosophy about how its business will be conducted, management spends lots of time shaping and fine-tuning these values to its business environment and communicating them to organizational members, and values and culturally approved behavioral norms are known and shared widely across the company—by senior executives and rank-and-file employees alike.[9] Strong-culture companies typically have creeds or value statements and executives regularly and seriously encourage people to follow them. Values and behavioral norms are so deeply rooted that they don't change much when a new CEO takes over—although they can erode over time if the CEO ceases to nurture them.

Three factors contribute to the development of strong, strategy-supportive cultures: (1) a founder or strong leader who establishes values, principles, and practices that are consistent and sensible in light of customer needs, competitive conditions, and strategic requirements; (2) a sincere, longstanding commitment to operating the business according to these established traditions, thereby creating an internal environment that supports making decisions based on cultural norms; and (3) a genuine concern for the well-being of the organization's three biggest constituencies—customers, employees, and shareholders. Continuity of leadership, small group size, stable group membership, geographic concentration, and considerable success also contribute to the emergence of a strong culture.[10]

■ LOW-PERFORMANCE OR UNHEALTHY CULTURES

A number of cultural characteristics are unhealthy and tend to undermine a company's business performance.[11] One is a politicized internal environment that allows influential managers to operate their fiefdoms autonomously and resist needed change. In politically dominated cultures, many issues get resolved on the basis of turf, which options are most vocally favored or opposed by powerful executives, personal lobbying by a key executive, and coalitions among individuals or departments with vested interests in a particular outcome—what's best for the company comes second to personal aggrandizement.

A second unhealthy cultural trait is hostility to change and to people who champion new ways of doing things. When executives don't value managers who exercise initiative or lead efforts to alter the status quo, experimentation is discouraged. Avoiding risks and not screwing up become more important to a person's career advancement than entrepreneurial success and innovative accomplishments. This trait is most often found in companies with multilayered management bureaucracies that have enjoyed considerable market success and whose business environments have been slow to change. General Motors, IBM, Sears, and Eastman Kodak are classic examples; all four gradually became burdened by a stifling bureaucracy that rejected innovation. Now, they are struggling to reinvent the cultural approaches that caused them to be successful in the first place.

A strong culture is a valuable asset when it matches strategy and a dreaded liability when it doesn't.

A third characteristic, one that can eventually plague a fast-growing company, is promoting managers who understand structures, systems, budgets, and controls better than they understand vision, strategies, inspiration, and culture building. While the former are adept at solving the internal organizational challenges that accompany rapid growth, if in time they ascend to senior executive positions, the company can find itself short on the entrepreneurial skills and leadership needed to manage strategic change—a condition that erodes its capacity for sustained long-term performance.

A fourth characteristic of low performance cultures is an aversion to looking outside the company for superior practices and approaches. Sometimes a company enjoys such great market success and reigns as an industry leader for so long that its management becomes inbred and arrogant. It believes it has all the answers or can develop them on its own. Insular thinking, inward-looking solutions, and a not-invented-here syndrome are often precursors to a decline in company performance. Kotter and Heskett cite Avon, BankAmerica, Citicorp, Coors, Ford, General Motors, Kmart, Kroger, Sears, Texaco, and Xerox as examples of companies that had low-performance cultures during the late 1970s and early 1980s.[12]

Changing problem cultures is difficult because people are anchored by their values and habits, and tend to cling to the old and familiar. Sometimes executives succeed in changing the values and behaviors of small groups of managers and even whole departments or divisions, only to find the changes eroded over time by the actions of the rest of the organization. What is communicated, praised, supported, and penalized by the entrenched majority undermines the new, emergent culture and halts its progress. Executives can revamp formal organization charts, announce new strategies, bring in managers from the outside, introduce new technologies, and open new plants, yet fail at altering imbedded cultural traits and behaviors because of skepticism about the new directions and covert resistance to altering traditional approaches and ways of doing things.

■ ADAPTIVE CULTURES

In fast-changing business environments, the capacity to introduce new strategies and organizational practices is a necessity if a company is to achieve superior performance over long periods of time.[13] This requires a culture that *helps* the company adapt to environmental change rather than a culture that has to be coaxed and cajoled to change. The hallmarks of an adaptive culture are: (1) leaders who have a greater commitment to timeless business principles and to organizational stakeholders—customers, employees, shareowners, suppliers, and the communities where it operates—than to any specific business strategy or operating practice, and (2) group members who are receptive to risk-taking, experimentation, innovation, and changing strategies and practices whenever necessary to satisfy the legitimate interests of stakeholders.

In adaptive cultures, members share a feeling of confidence that the organization can handle whatever threats and opportunities arise. Hence, they willingly embrace a proactive approach to identifying issues, evaluating the implications and options, and implementing workable solutions. There's a spirit of doing what's necessary to ensure long-term organizational success *so long as core values and business principles are upheld in the process*. Managers habitually fund product development initiatives, evaluate new ideas openly, and take prudent risks to create new business positions. Entrepreneurship is encouraged and rewarded. Strategies and traditional operating practices are modified as needed to take advantage of changes in the business environment. The leaders of adaptive cultures are adept at changing the right things in the right ways, not changing for the sake of change and not compromising core values or business principles. Adaptive cultures support managers and employees alike who propose or help initiate useful change; indeed, executives consciously seek, train, and promote individuals who display these leadership traits.

One other significant defining trait of adaptive cultures is that top management genuinely cares about the well-being of all key constituencies—customers, employees, stockholders, major suppliers, and communities—and tries to satisfy their legitimate interests simultaneously. No group is ignored, and fairness to all constituencies is a standard princi-

Adaptive cultures are a strategy-implementer's best ally.

ple—a commitment often described as ''doing the right thing.''[14] In less adaptive cultures where there is resistance to change, managers often behave conservatively and politically to protect or advance their careers, their immediate work groups, or their pet projects; they avoid risk taking and prefer following to leading when it comes to technological change and new product innovation.[15]

■ CREATING THE FIT BETWEEN STRATEGY AND CULTURE

It is the *strategy-maker's* responsibility to select a strategy compatible with the sacred or unchangeable parts of prevailing corporate culture. It is the *strategy-implementer's* task, once strategy is chosen, to change whatever facets of the corporate culture hinder effective execution.

Changing a company's culture and aligning it with strategy is one of the toughest tasks managers have. It's one of those things, along with reengineering and TQM, that's easier to talk about than to do. The first step is to diagnose which facets of the present culture support strategy and which do not. Managers have to talk openly and forthrightly about those aspects of the culture that have to be changed. The talk has to be followed swiftly by visible actions to modify the culture—actions that everyone will understand are intended to establish a new culture more in tune with the strategy.

SYMBOLIC ACTIONS AND SUBSTANTIVE ACTIONS

Normally, managerial actions to tighten the culture-strategy fit need to be both symbolic and substantive. Symbolic actions are valuable for the signals they send about the kinds of behavior and performance strategy implementers wish to encourage. The most important symbolic actions are those that top executives take to serve as role models—leading cost reduction efforts by curtailing executive perks, emphasizing the importance of responding to customers' needs by requiring *all* officers and executives to spend a significant portion of each week talking with customers and understanding their requirements, and initiating efforts to alter policies and practices identified as hindrances in executing the new strategy. Another category of symbolic actions includes the events organizations hold to honor people whose actions and performance exemplify what is called for in the new culture. Many universities give outstanding teacher awards each year to symbolize their commitment to and esteem for instructors who display exceptional classroom talents. Numerous businesses have employee-of-the-month awards. The military has a long-standing custom of awarding ribbons and medals for exemplary actions. Mary Kay Cosmetics awards an array of prizes—from ribbons to pink Cadillacs—to its beauty consultants for reaching various sales plateaus.

The best companies and the best executives expertly use symbols, role models, ceremonial occasions, and group gatherings to tighten the strategy-culture fit. Low-cost leaders like Wal-Mart and Nucor are renowned for their spartan facilities, executive frugality, intolerance of waste, and zealous control of costs. Executives sensitive to their role in promoting strategy-culture fits make a habit of appearing at ceremonial functions to praise individuals and groups whose contributions are noteworthy. They honor individuals who exhibit cultural norms and reward those who achieve strategic milestones. They participate in employee training programs to stress strategic priorities, values, ethical principles, and cultural norms.

> Awards ceremonies, role models, and symbols are a fundamental part of a strategy-implementer's culture-shaping effort.

Every group gathering is seen as an opportunity to implant values, praise good deeds, reinforce cultural norms, and promote changes that assist strategy implementation. They make sure that current decisions and policy changes will be construed by organizational members as consistent with and supportive of the company's new strategic direction.[16]

In addition to being out front, personally leading the push for new behaviors and communicating the reasons for new approaches, strategy implementers have to convince all those concerned that the effort is more than cosmetic. Talk and announced plans have to be complemented by substance and real movement. The actions have to be credible, highly visible, and indicate the seriousness of management's commitment to new strategic initiatives and the associated cultural changes. There are several ways to accomplish this. One is to engineer some quick successes that highlight the benefits of strategy-culture changes, thus making enthusiasm for the changes contagious. However, instant results are usually not as important as having the will and patience to create a solid, competent team committed to pursuing the company's strategy. The strongest signs that management is truly committed to creating a new culture come from actions to replace old-culture traditionalist managers with ''new breed'' managers, to change long-standing policies and operating practices that are dysfunctional or impede new initiatives, to undertake major reorganizational moves that bring structure into better alignment with strategy, to tie compensation incentives directly to the new measures of strategic performance, and to make major budgetary reallocations that shift substantial resources from old strategy projects and programs to new strategy projects and programs.

At the same time, chief strategy implementers must be careful to *lead by example*. For instance, if the organization's strategy involves a drive to become the industry's low-cost producer, senior managers must display

---
Senior executives must personally lead efforts to align culture with strategy.
---

frugality in their own actions and decisions: spartan decorations in the executive suite, conservative expense accounts and entertainment allowances, a lean staff in the corporate office, scrutiny of budget requests, and so on. The CEO of SAS Airlines, Jan Carlzon, symbolically reinforced the primacy of quality service for business customers by flying coach instead of first class and by giving up his seat to wait-listed travelers.[17]

Implanting the needed culture-building values and behavior depends on a sincere, sustained commitment by the chief executive coupled with extraordinary persistence in reinforcing the culture at every opportunity through word and deed. Neither charisma nor personal magnetism are essential. However, personally talking to many departmental groups about the reasons for change is essential; organizational changes are seldom accomplished successfully from an office. Moreover, creating and sustaining a strategy-supportive culture is a job for the whole management team. Major cultural change requires many initiatives from many people. Senior officers, department heads, and middle managers have to reiterate values, ''walk the talk,'' and translate the organization's philosophy into everyday practice. But for the culture-building effort to be successful, strategy-implementers must enlist the support of first-line supervisors and employee opinion-leaders, convincing them of the merits of practicing and enforcing cultural norms at the lowest levels in the organization. Until a big majority of employees join the culture and share an emotional commitment to its basic values and behavioral norms, there's considerably more work to be done in both installing the culture and tightening the culture-strategy fit.

The task of making culture supportive of strategy is not a short-term exercise. It takes time for a new culture to emerge and prevail; it's unrealistic to expect an overnight transformation. The bigger the organization and the greater the cultural shift needed to produce a culture-strategy fit, the longer it takes. In large companies, changing the corporate culture in significant ways can take three to five years at minimum. In fact, it is usually tougher to reshape a deeply ingrained culture that is not strategy-supportive than it is to instill a strategy-supportive culture from scratch in a brand new organization.

■ ESTABLISHING ETHICAL STANDARDS AND VALUES

A strong corporate culture founded on ethical business principles and moral values is a vital driving force behind continued strategic success. Many executives are convinced that a company must care about *how* it does business; otherwise, a company's reputation and ultimately its performance are put at risk. Corporate ethics and values programs are not window dressing; they are undertaken to create an environment of strongly held values and convictions and to make ethical conduct a way of life. Morally upstanding values and high ethical standards nurture the corporate culture in a very positive way—they connote integrity, doing the right thing, and genuine concern for stakeholders.

> An ethical corporate culture has a positive impact on a company's long-term strategic success; an unethical culture can undermine it.

Companies establish values and ethical standards in a number of different ways.[18] Companies steeped in tradition rely on word-of-mouth indoctrination and the power of that tradition to instill values and enforce ethical conduct. But many companies today set forth their values and codes of ethics in written documents. Table 11–1 indicates the kinds of topics such statements cover. Written statements have the advantage of explicitly stating what the company intends and expects, and they serve as benchmarks for judging both company policies and actions and individual conduct. They put a stake in the ground and

TABLE 11–1   *Topics Generally Covered in Values Statements and Codes of Ethics*

Topics Covered in Values Statements	Topics Covered in Codes of Ethics
• Importance of customers and customer service.	• Honesty and observance of the law.
• Commitment to quality.	• Conflicts of interest.
• Commitment to innovation.	• Fairness in selling and marketing practices.
• Respect for the individual employee and the duty the company has to employees.	• Using inside information and securities trading.
• Importance of honesty, integrity, and ethical standards.	• Supplier relationships and purchasing practices.
• Duty to stockholders.	• Payments to obtain business/Foreign Corrupt Practices Act.
• Duty to suppliers.	• Acquiring and using information about others.
• Corporate citizenship.	• Political activities.
• Importance of protecting the environment.	• Use of company assets, resources, and property.
	• Protection of proprietary information.
	• Pricing, contracting, and billing.

ILLUSTRATION 30   *The Johnson & Johnson Credo*

- We believe our first responsibility is to the doctors, nurses and patients, to mothers and all others who use our products and services.
- In meeting their needs everything we do must be of high quality.
- We must constantly strive to reduce our costs in order to maintain reasonable prices.
- Customers' orders must be serviced promptly and accurately.
- Our suppliers and distributors must have an opportunity to make a fair profit.
- We are responsible to our employees, the men and women who work with us throughout the world.
- Everyone must be considered as an individual.
- We must respect their dignity and recognize their merit.
- They must have a sense of security in their jobs.
- Compensation must be fair and adequate, and working conditions clean, orderly, and safe.
- Employees must feel free to make suggestions and complaints.
- There must be equal opportunity for employment, development and advancement for those qualified.
- We must provide competent management, and their

actions must be just and ethical.
- We are responsible to the communities in which we live and work and to the world community as well.
- We must be good citizens—support good works and charities and bear our fair share of taxes.
- We must encourage civic improvements and better health and education.
- We must maintain in good order the property we are privileged to use, protecting the environment and natural resources.
- Our final responsibility is to our stockholders.
- Business must make a sound profit.
- We must experiment with new ideas.
- Research must be carried on, innovative programs developed and mistakes paid for.
- New equipment must be purchased, new facilities provided and new products launched.
- Reserves must be created to provide for adverse times.
- When we operate according to these principles, the stockholders should realize a fair return.

Source: 1982 annual report.

---

define the company's position. Value statements serve as a cornerstone for culture building; a code of ethics serves as a cornerstone for developing a corporate conscience. Illustration 30 presents the Johnson & Johnson credo; it is one of the most publicized and celebrated code of ethics and values among U.S. companies. J&J's CEO calls the credo "the unifying force for our corporation." Illustration 31 presents the pledge that Bristol-Myers Squibb makes to all of its stakeholders.

Once values and ethical standards have been formally set forth, they must be institutionalized and ingrained in the company's policies, practices, and actual conduct. Implementing the values and code of ethics entails several actions:

- Incorporating the statement of values and the code of ethics into employee training and educational programs.

- Giving explicit attention to values and ethics in recruiting and hiring to screen out applicants who do not exhibit compatible character traits.

Values and ethical standards must not only be explicitly stated but they must also be woven into the corporate culture.

- Communicating the values and ethics code to all employees and explaining compliance procedures.

ILLUSTRATION 31   *The Bristol-Myers Squibb Pledge*

To those who use our products . . .
We affirm Bristol-Myers Squibb's commitment to the highest standards of excellence, safety and reliability in everything we make. We pledge to offer products of the highest quality and to work diligently to keep improving them.

To our employees and those who may join us . . .
We pledge personal respect, fair compensation and equal treatment. We acknowledge our obligation to provide able and humane leadership throughout the organization, within a clean and safe working environment. To all who qualify for advancement, we will make every effort to provide opportunity.

To our suppliers and customers . . .
We pledge an open door, courteous, efficient and ethical dealing, and appreciation for their right to a fair profit.

To our shareholders . . .
We pledge a companywide dedication to continued profitable growth, sustained by strong finances, a high level of research and development, and facilities second to none.

To the communities where we have plants and offices . . .
We pledge conscientious citizenship, a helping hand for worthwhile causes, and constructive action in support of civic and environmental progress.

To the countries where we do business . . .
We pledge ourselves to be a good citizen and to show full consideration for the rights of others while reserving the right to stand up for our own.

Above all, to the world we live in . . .
We pledge Bristol-Myers Squibb to policies and practices which fully embody the responsibility, integrity and decency required of free enterprise if it is to merit and maintain the confidence of our society.

Source: 1990 Annual Report.

- Management involvement and oversight, from the CEO on down to first-line supervisors.
- Strong endorsements by the CEO.

In the case of codes of ethics, special training and attention must be given to people who work in sections of the company that are particularly sensitive and vulnerable—purchasing, sales, and political lobbying.[19] Employees who deal with external parties are in ethically sensitive positions and often are drawn into compromising situations. Gray areas need to be candidly discussed and guidelines established; when ethical issues arise, everyone needs to know whom to contact for advice and counsel. Procedures for enforcing ethical standards and handling potential violations have to be developed.

The compliance effort must permeate the company, extending into every organizational unit. The attitudes, character, and work history of prospective employees must be scrutinized. Every employee must receive adequate training. Line managers at all levels must give serious and continuous attention to the task of explaining how the values and ethical conduct apply in their areas. In addition, they must insist that company values and ethical standards become a way of life. In general, instilling values and insisting on ethical conduct must be looked on as a continuous culture-building, culture-nurturing exercise. Whether the effort succeeds or fails depends largely on how well corporate values and ethical standards are visibly integrated into company policies, managerial practices, and actions at all levels.

■ BUILDING A SPIRIT OF HIGH PERFORMANCE INTO THE CULTURE

An ability to instill strong individual commitment to strategic success and create an atmosphere where there is constructive pressure to perform is one of the most valuable strategy-implementing skills. When an organization performs consistently at or near peak capability, the outcome is not only improved strategic success but also an organizational culture permeated with a spirit of high performance. Such a spirit of performance should not be confused with whether employees are happy or satisfied or whether they get along well together. An organization with a spirit of performance emphasizes achievement and excellence. Its culture is results-oriented, and its management pursues policies and practices that inspire people to do their best.

Companies with a spirit of high performance typically are intensely people-oriented, and they reinforce their concern for individual employees at every conceivable occasion in every conceivable way to every employee. They treat employees with dignity and respect, train each employee thoroughly, encourage employees to use their own initiative and creativity in performing their work, set reasonable and clear performance expectations, utilize the full range of rewards and punishment to enforce high performance standards, hold managers at every level responsible for developing the people who report to them, and grant employees enough autonomy to stand out, excel, and contribute. To create a results-oriented organizational culture, a company needs to make champions out of the people who turn in winning performances:[20]

- At Boeing, IBM, General Electric, and 3M Corporation, top executives make a point of ceremoniously honoring individuals who believe so strongly in their ideas that they take it on themselves to hurdle the bureaucracy, maneuver their projects through the system, and turn them into improved services, new products, or even new businesses. In these companies, "product champions" are given high visibility, room to push their ideas, and strong executive support. Champions whose ideas prove out are usually handsomely rewarded; those whose ideas don't pan out still have secure jobs and are given chances to try again.

- The manager of a New York area sales office rented the Meadowlands Stadium (home field of the New York Giants) for an evening. After work, the salespeople were all assembled at the stadium and asked to run one at a time through the player's tunnel onto the field. As each one emerged, the electronic scoreboard flashed the person's name to those gathered in the stands—executives from corporate headquarters, employees from the office, family, and friends. Their role was to cheer loudly in honor of the individual's sales accomplishments. The company involved was IBM. The occasion for this action was to reaffirm IBM's commitment to satisfy an individual's need to be part of something great and to reiterate IBM's concern for championing individual accomplishment.

- Some companies upgrade the importance and status of individual employees by referring to them as Cast Members (Disney), Crew Members (McDonald's), or Associates (Wal-Mart and J. C. Penney). Companies like Mary Kay Cosmetics,

Tupperware, and McDonald's actively seek out reasons and opportunities to give pins, buttons, badges, and medals for good showings by average performers—the idea being to express appreciation and give a motivational boost to people who stand out doing ordinary jobs.

- McDonald's has a contest to determine the best hamburger cooker in its entire chain. It begins with a competition to determine the best hamburger cooker in each store. Store winners go on to compete in regional championships, and regional winners go on to the All-American contest. The winners get trophies and an All-American patch to wear on their shirts.

A results-oriented culture that inspires people to do their best is conducive to superior strategy execution.

- Milliken & Co. holds Corporate Sharing Rallies once every three months; teams come from all over the company to swap success stories and ideas. A hundred or more teams make five-minute presentations over a two-day period. Each rally has a major theme—quality, cost reduction, and so on. No criticisms and negatives are allowed, and there is no such thing as a big idea or a small one. Quantitative measures of success are used to gauge improvement. All those present vote on the best presentation and several ascending grades of awards are handed out. Everyone, however, receives a framed certificate for participating.

What makes a spirit of high performance come alive is a complex network of practices, words, symbols, styles, values, and policies complementing each other to produce extraordinary results with ordinary people. The drivers of the system are a belief in the worth of the individual, strong company commitments to job security and promotion from within, managerial practices that encourage employees to exercise individual initiative and creativity in doing their jobs, and pride in doing the "itty-bitty, teeny-tiny things" right. A company that treats its employees well generally benefits from increased teamwork, higher morale, and greater employee loyalty.

While emphasizing a spirit of high performance nearly always accentuates the positive, there are negative aspects too. Managers whose units consistently perform poorly have to be removed. Aside from the organizational benefits, weak managers should be reassigned for their own good—people who find themselves in a job they cannot handle are usually frustrated, anxiety ridden, harassed, and unhappy.[21] Moreover, subordinates have a right to be managed with competence, dedication, and achievement; unless their boss performs well, they themselves cannot perform well. In addition, poorly performing workers and people who reject the cultural emphasis on dedication and high performance have to be weeded out. Recruitment practices need to aim at selecting highly motivated, ambitious applicants whose attitudes and work habits mesh well with a results-oriented corporate culture.

▶ EXERTING STRATEGIC LEADERSHIP

The litany of good strategic management is simple: Formulate a sound strategic plan, implement it, execute it to the fullest, win! But it's easier said than done. A strategy manager has many different leadership roles to play: chief entrepreneur and strategist, chief administrator and strategy-implementer, culture-builder, supervisor, crisis solver, taskmaster, spokesperson, resource allocator, negotiator, motivator, adviser, arbitrator, consensus builder, policy-maker, policy enforcer, mentor, and head cheerleader. Sometimes it is useful to be authoritarian and hardnosed, sometimes it is best to be a perceptive listener and a compromising decision-maker, and sometimes a strongly participative, collegial approach works best. Many occasions call for a highly visible role and extensive time commitments, while others entail a brief ceremonial performance with the details being delegated to subordinates.

In general, the problem of strategic leadership is one of diagnosing the situation and choosing from any of several ways to handle it. Six leadership roles dominate the strategy implementer's action agenda:

1. Staying on top of what is happening and how well things are going.
2. Promoting a culture in which the organization is energized to accomplish strategy and perform at a high level.
3. Keeping the organization responsive to changing conditions, alert for new opportunities, and bubbling with innovative ideas.
4. Building consensus, containing power struggles, and dealing with the politics of crafting and implementing strategy.
5. Enforcing ethical standards.
6. Pushing corrective actions to improve strategy execution and overall strategic performance.

■ MANAGING BY WALKING AROUND (MBWA)

To stay on top of how well the implementation process is going, a manager needs to develop a broad network of contacts and sources of information, both formal and informal. The regular channels include talking with key subordinates, reviewing reports and the latest operating results, talking to customers, watching the competitive reactions of rival firms, tapping into the grapevine, listening to rank-and-file employees, and observing the situation firsthand. However, some information tends to be more trustworthy than other information. Written reports may represent "the truth but not the whole truth." Bad news may be covered up, minimized, or not reported at all. Sometimes subordinates delay conveying failures and problems in hopes that more time will give them room to turn things around. As information flows up an organization, there is a tendency for it to get censored and sterilized to the point that it may fail to reveal information critical to strategy. Strategy managers need to guard against major surprises by making sure that they have accurate information and a feel for the existing situation. The chief way this is done is by regular visits to the field and talking with many different people at many different levels. There are many ways to practice *managing by walking around* (MBWA):[22]

> **MBWA is one of the techniques effective leaders use.**

- At Hewlett-Packard, there are weekly beer busts in each division, attended by both executives and employees, to create a regular opportunity to keep in touch. Tidbits of information flow freely between down-the-line employees and executives—

facilitated in part because "the H-P Way" is for people at all ranks to be addressed by their first names. Bill Hewlett, one of HP's cofounders, had a companywide reputation for getting out of his office and wandering around the plant greeting people, listening to what was on their minds, and asking questions. He found this so valuable that he made MBWA a standard practice for all HP managers. Furthermore, ad hoc meetings of people from different departments spontaneously arise; they gather in rooms with blackboards and work out solutions informally.

- McDonald's founder Ray Kroc regularly visited store units and did his own personal inspection on Q.S.C.&V. (Quality, Service, Cleanliness, and Value)—the themes he preached regularly. There are stories of him pulling into a unit's parking lot, seeing litter lying on the pavement, getting out of his limousine to pick it up himself, and then lecturing the store staff at length on the subject of cleanliness.

- The CEO of a small manufacturing company spends much of his time riding around the factory in a golf cart, waving and joking with workers, listening to them, and calling all 2,000 employees by their first names. In addition, he spends a lot of time with union officials, inviting them to meetings and keeping them well informed about what is going on.

- Wal-Mart executives have had a longstanding practice of spending two to three days every week visiting Wal-Mart's stores and talking with store managers and employees. Sam Walton, Wal-Mart's founder, insisted: "The key is to get out into the store and listen to what the associates have to say. Our best ideas come from clerks and stockboys."

- When Ed Carlson became CEO at United Airlines, he traveled about 200,000 miles a year talking with United's employees. He recalled: "I wanted these people to identify me and to feel sufficiently comfortable to make suggestions or even argue with me if that's what they felt like doing. . . . Whenever I picked up some information, I would call the senior officer of the division and say that I had just gotten back from visiting Oakland, Reno, and Las Vegas, and here is what I found."

- At Marriott Corp. Bill Marriott personally inspects Marriott hotels. He also invites all Marriott guests to send him their evaluations of Marriott's facilities and services; he personally reads every customer complaint and has been known to telephone hotel managers about them.

Managers at many companies attach great importance to informal communications. They report that it is essential to have a feel for situations and to gain quick, easy access to information. When executives stay in their offices, they tend to become isolated and often surround themselves with people who are not likely to offer criticism and different perspectives; the information they get is secondhand, screened and filtered, and sometimes dated.

◼ FOSTERING A STRATEGY-SUPPORTIVE CLIMATE AND CULTURE

Strategy implementers have to be out front in promoting a strategy-supportive organizational climate and culture. When major strategic changes are being implemented, a manager's time is best spent personally leading the changes and promoting needed cultural adjustments. In general, organizational cultures need major overhaul every 5 to 25 years, depending on how fast events in the company's business environment move.[23] When only strategic fine-tuning is being implemented, it takes less time and effort to bring values and culture into alignment with strategy, but there is still a lead role for the manager to play in pushing ahead and prodding for continuous improvements. Successful strategy leaders recognize it is their responsibility to convince people that the chosen strategy is right and that implementing it to the best of the organization's ability is top priority.

The single most visible factor that distinguishes successful culture change efforts from failed attempts is competent leadership at the top. Effective management action to match culture and strategy has several attributes:[24]

- A stakeholders-are-king philosophy that links the need to change to the need to serve the long-term best interests of all key constituencies.

- An openness to new ideas.

- Challenging the status quo with very basic questions: Are we giving customers what they really need and want? How can we be more competitive on cost? Why can't design-to-market cycle time be halved? How can we grow the company instead of downsizing it? Where will the company be five years from now if it sticks with just its present business?

- Skills in persuading individuals and groups to commit themselves to the new direction and to energize individuals and departments sufficiently to make it happen, despite the obstacles.

- Repeating the new messages again and again, explaining the rationale for change, and convincing skeptics that all is not well.

- Recognizing and generously rewarding those who exhibit new cultural norms and who lead successful change efforts—this helps cultivate expansion of the coalition for change.

- Creating events where everyone in management is forced to listen to angry customers, dissatisfied stockholders, and alienated employees to keep them informed and to help them realistically assess organizational strengths and weaknesses.

Great power is needed to force major cultural change—to overcome the change-back resistance of entrenched cultures. Such power normally resides only at the top. Moreover, the interdependence of values, strategies, practices, and behaviors inside organizations makes it difficult to change anything fundamental without simultaneously undertaking wider-scale changes. Usually the people with the power to effect change of that scope are those at the top.

> Only top management has the power to bring about major cultural change.

Both words and deeds play a part in strategic leadership. Words inspire people, infuse spirit and drive, define strategy-supportive cultural norms and values, articulate the reasons for strategic and organizational change, legitimize new viewpoints and new priorities, urge and reinforce commitment, and arouse confidence in the new strategy.

Deeds bring credibility to the words, create strategy-supportive symbols, and teach the organization by example what sort of behavior is needed and expected.

Highly visible symbols and imagery are needed to complement substantive actions. One General Motors manager explained how symbolism and managerial style accounted for the striking difference in performance between two large plants:[25]

> At the poorly performing plant, the plant manager probably ventured out on the floor once a week, always in a suit. His comments were distant and perfunctory. At South Gate, the better plant, the plant manager was on the floor all the time. He wore a baseball cap and a UAW jacket. By the way, whose plant do you think was spotless? Whose looked like a junkyard?

As a rule, the greater the degree of strategic change being implemented and/or the greater the shift in cultural norms needed to accommodate a new strategy, the more visible and unequivocal the strategy implementer's words and deeds need to be. Lessons from well-managed companies show that what the strategy leader says and does has a significant bearing on down-the-line strategy implementation and execution.[26] According to one view: "It is not so much the articulation . . . about what an [organization] should be doing that creates new practice. It's the imagery that creates the understanding, the compelling moral necessity that the new way is right."[27] Moreover, the actions and images, both substantive and symbolic, have to be consistent and constant, not just restricted to ceremonial speeches and special occasions. This is where a high profile and MBWA can be so important. As a Hewlett-Packard official expresses it in the company publication *The HP Way:*

> Once a division or department has developed a plan of its own—a set of working objectives—it's important for managers and supervisors to keep it in operating condition. This is where observation, measurement, feedback, and guidance come in. It's our "management by wandering around." That's how you find out whether you're on track and heading at the right speed and in the right direction. If you don't constantly monitor how people are operating, not only will they tend to wander off track but also they will begin to believe you weren't serious about the plan in the first place. It has the extra benefit of getting you off your chair and moving around your area. By wandering around, I literally mean moving around and talking to people. It's all done on a very informal and spontaneous basis, but it's important in the course of time to cover the whole territory. You start out by being accessible and approachable, but the main thing is to realize you're there to listen. The second reason for MBWA is that it is vital to keep people informed about what's going on in the company, especially those things that are important to them. The third reason for doing this is because it is just plain fun.

Such contacts give the manager a feel for how things are progressing, and they provide an opportunity to encourage employees, lift spirits, shift attention from the old to the new priorities, generate some excitement, and project an atmosphere of informality and fun—all of which drive implementation in a positive fashion and intensify the organizational energy behind strategy execution. Jack Welch of General Electric sums up the hands-on role and motivational approach well: "I'm here every day, or out into a factory, smelling it, feeling it, touching it, challenging the people."[28]

The vast majority of companies probably don't have strong, adaptive cultures capable of producing excellent long-term performance in a fast-paced market and competitive environment. In such companies, managers have to do more than show incremental progress. Conservative incrementalism seldom leads to major cultural adaptations; more usually, gradualism is defeated by the resilience of entrenched cultures and the ability of vested interests to thwart or minimize the impact of piecemeal change. Only bold leadership and concerted action on many fronts make a company succeed in tackling so large and difficult a task as major cultural change.

■ KEEPING THE INTERNAL ORGANIZATION RESPONSIVE AND INNOVATIVE

While formulating and implementing strategy is a manager's responsibility, the task of generating fresh ideas, identifying new opportunities, and being responsive to changing conditions cannot be accomplished by a single person. It is a task for the entire organization, particularly in large corporations. One of the toughest parts of exerting strategic leadership is generating a dependable supply of fresh ideas from the rank and file, managers and employees alike, and promoting an entrepreneurial, opportunistic spirit that permits continuous adaptation to changing conditions. A flexible, responsive, innovative internal environment is critical in fast-moving high-technology industries, in businesses where products have short life cycles and growth depends on new product innovation, in companies with widely diversified business portfolios (where opportunities are varied and scattered), in markets where successful product differentiation depends on out innovating the competition, and in situations where low-cost leadership hinges on continuous improvement and new ways to drive costs out of the business. Managers cannot mandate such an environment by simply exhorting people to be creative.

One useful leadership approach is to take special pains to foster, nourish, and support people who are willing to champion new ideas, better services, new products and product applications and are eager for a chance to try turning their ideas into new divisions, new businesses, and even new industries. When Texas Instruments reviewed 50 or so successful and unsuccessful new product introductions, one factor marked every failure: "Without exception we found we hadn't had a volunteer champion. There was someone we had cajoled into taking on the task."[29] The rule seems to be that the idea of something new or something better either finds a champion or it dies. And the champion is usually persistent, competitive, tenacious, committed, and fanatic about the idea and seeing it through to success.

High-performance cultures make champions out of people who excel.

EMPOWERING CHAMPIONS

In order to promote an organizational climate where champion innovators can blossom and thrive, strategy managers need to do several things. First, individuals and groups have to be encouraged to bring their ideas forward, be creative, and exercise initiative. The culture has to nurture, even celebrate, experimentation and innovation. Everybody must be expected to contribute ideas and seek out continuous improvement. The trick is to keep a sense of urgency alive in the business so that people see change and innovation as a necessity. Second, the champion's maverick style has to be tolerated and given room to operate. People's imaginations need to be encouraged to "fly in all directions." Freedom to experiment and informal brainstorming sessions need to become habitual. Above all, people with creative ideas must not be looked on as disruptive or troublesome. Third, managers have to induce and promote lots of "tries" and be willing to tolerate mistakes and failures. Most ideas don't pan out, but the organization learns from a good attempt even when it fails. Fourth, strategy managers should be willing to use all kinds of ad hoc organizational forms to support ideas and experimentation—venture teams, task forces, "performance shootouts" among different groups working on competing approaches, informal "bootlegged" projects composed of volunteers, and so on. Fifth, strategy managers have to see that the rewards for successful champions are large and visible and that people who champion an unsuccessful idea are encouraged to try again rather than punished or sidelined. In effect, the leadership task is to create an adaptive, innovative culture that embraces organizational responses to changing conditions, rather than fearing or seeking to minimize them. Companies with conspicuously innovative cultures include Wal-Mart, Sony, 3M, Levi Strauss, Microsoft, and Motorola—all inspire their employees with strategic vision to excel and be world-class at what they do.

> The faster a company's business environment changes, the more attention managers must pay to keeping the organization innovative and responsive.

■ DEALING WITH COMPANY POLITICS

A manager can't effectively formulate and implement strategy without being perceptive about company politics and being adept at political maneuvering.[30] Politics virtually always comes into play in formulating a strategic plan. Inevitably, key individuals and groups form coalitions, and each group presses the benefits and potential of its own ideas and vested interests. Political considerations enter into which objectives take precedence and which lines of business in the corporate portfolio have top priority in resource allocation. Internal politics is a factor in building a consensus for one strategic option over another.

As a rule, there is even more politics in implementing strategy. Typically, internal political considerations affect whose areas of responsibility get reorganized, who reports to whom, who has how much authority over subunits, which individuals should fill key positions and head strategy-critical activities, and which organizational units will get the biggest budget increases. As a case in point, Quinn cites a situation where three strong managers who fought each other constantly formed a potent coalition to resist a reorganization scheme that would have coordinated the very things that caused their friction.[31]

> Company politics presents strategy leaders with the challenge of building consensus for the strategy and its implementation.

In short, political considerations and the forming of individual and group alliances are integral parts of building organizationwide support for the strategic plan and gaining consensus on its implementation. Political skills are a necessary asset for managers in orchestrating the whole strategic process successfully.

A strategy manager must understand how an organization's power structure works, who wields influence in the executive ranks, which groups and individuals are activists and which are defenders of the status quo, who can be helpful in a showdown on key decisions, and which way the political winds are blowing on a given issue. When major decisions have to be made, strategy managers need to be especially sensitive to the politics of managing coalitions and reaching consensus. As the chairman of a major British corporation expressed it:

> I've never taken a major decision without consulting my colleagues. It would be unimaginable to me, unimaginable. First, they help me make a better decision in most cases. Second, if they know about it and agree with it, they'll back it. Otherwise, they might challenge it, not openly, but subconsciously.[32]

The politics of strategy centers chiefly around stimulating options, nurturing support for strong proposals and killing weak ones, guiding the formation of coalitions on particular issues, and achieving consensus and commitment. A recent study of strategy management in nine large corporations showed that successful executives relied upon the following political tactics:[33]

- Letting weakly supported ideas and proposals die through inaction.
- Establishing additional hurdles or tests for strongly supported ideas that the manager views as unacceptable but that are best not opposed openly.
- Keeping a low political profile on unacceptable proposals by getting subordinate managers to say no.
- Letting most negative decisions come from a group consensus that the manager merely confirms, thereby reserving personal veto for big issues and crucial moments.
- Leading the strategy but not dictating it—giving few orders, announcing few decisions, depending heavily on informal questioning and seeking to probe and clarify until a consensus emerges.
- Staying alert to the symbolic impact of one's actions and statements lest a false signal stimulate proposals and movements in unwanted directions.
- Ensuring that all major power bases within the organization have representation in or access to top management.
- Injecting new faces and new views into considerations of major changes to prevent those involved from coming to see the world in the same way and then acting as systematic screens against other views.
- Minimizing political exposure on issues that are highly controversial and in circumstances where opposition from major power centers can trigger a "shootout."

The politics of strategy implementation is especially critical in attempting to introduce a new strategy against the support enjoyed by the old strategy. Except for crises where the old strategy is plainly revealed as out-of-date, it is usually bad politics to push the new strategy with attacks on the old one.[34] Bad-mouthing old strategy can easily be interpreted as an attack on those who formulated it and those who supported it. The former strategy and the judgments behind it may have been well suited to the organization's earlier circumstances, and the people who made these judgments may still be influential.

In addition, the new strategy and/or the plans for implementing it may not have been the first choices of others and lingering doubts may remain. Good arguments may exist for pursuing other actions. Consequently, in trying to surmount resistance, nothing is gained by knocking the arguments for alternative approaches. Such attacks often alienate instead of encouraging cooperation.

In short, to bring the full force of an organization behind a strategic plan, the strategy manager must assess and deal with the most important centers of potential support and opposition to new strategic thrusts.[35] He or she needs to secure the support of key people, co-opt or neutralize serious opposition and resistance when and where necessary, learn where the zones of indifference are, and build as much consensus as possible.

■ ENFORCING ETHICAL BEHAVIOR

For an organization to display consistently high ethical standards, the CEO and those around the CEO must be openly and unequivocally committed to ethical and moral conduct.[36] In companies that strive to make high ethical standards a reality, top management communicates its commitment in a code of ethics, in speeches and company publications, in policies concerning the consequences of unethical behavior, in the deeds of senior executives, and in the actions taken to ensure compliance. Senior management stresses to employees that it is their *duty* not only to observe ethical codes but also to report ethical violations. While such companies have provisions for disciplining violators, the main purpose of enforcement is to encourage compliance, rather than administer punishment. Although the CEO leads the enforcement process, all managers are expected to make a personal contribution by emphasizing the importance of ethical conduct with their subordinates and by involving themselves in the process of monitoring compliance with the code of ethics. Gray areas must be identified and openly discussed with employees, and procedures created for offering guidance when issues arise, investigating possible violations, and reaching resolution of individual cases. The lesson from these companies is that it is never enough to assume activities are being conducted ethically, nor can it be assumed that employees understand they are expected to act with integrity.

> Ethical standards cannot be enforced without the open and unequivocal commitment of the chief executive.

Managers can take several concrete actions to exercise ethics leadership.[37] First and foremost, they must set an excellent ethical example in their own behavior and establish a tradition of integrity. Company decisions have to be seen as ethical—actions always speak louder than words in such matters. Second, managers and employees have to be educated about what is ethical and what is not; ethics training programs may have to be established and gray areas explored and debated. Everyone must be encouraged to raise issues with ethical dimensions, and such discussions should be treated as a legitimate topic. Third, top management should regularly reiterate its unequivocal support of the company's ethical code and take a strong stand on ethical issues. Fourth, top management must be prepared to act as the final arbiter on hard calls; this means removing people from a key position or terminating them when they are guilty of a violation. It also means reprimanding those who have been lax in monitoring and enforcing ethical compliance. Failure to act swiftly and decisively in pursuing ethical misconduct is interpreted as a lack of real commitment.

A well-developed program to ensure compliance with ethical standards typically includes: (1) an oversight committee of the board of directors, usually made up of outside directors; (2) a committee of senior managers to direct ongoing training, implementation, and compliance; (3) an annual audit of each manager's efforts to uphold ethical standards and formal reports on the actions taken by managers to remedy deficient conduct; and (4) periodically requiring people to sign documents certifying compliance with ethical standards.[38]

■ LEADING THE PROCESS OF MAKING CORRECTIVE ADJUSTMENTS

No strategic plan and no scheme for strategy implementation can foresee all the events and problems that will arise. Making adjustments and midcourse corrections is normal and a necessary part of strategic management.

Corrective adjustments in the company's approach to strategy implementation should be made on an as-needed basis.

When responding to new conditions involving either the strategy or its implementation, prompt action is often needed. In a crisis, the typical approach is to push key subordinates to gather information and formulate recommendations, personally preside over extended discussions of the proposed responses, and quickly try to build a consensus among members of the executive inner circle. If no consensus emerges or if several key subordinates remain divided, the burden falls on the strategy manager to choose the response and urge its support.

When time permits a full-fledged evaluation, strategy managers seem to prefer a process of incrementally solidifying commitment to a response.[39] The approach involves:

1. Staying flexible and keeping a number of options open.

2. Asking a lot of questions.

3. Gaining in-depth information from specialists.

4. Encouraging subordinates to participate in developing alternatives and proposing solutions.

5. Getting the reactions of many different people to proposed solutions to test their potential and political acceptability.

6. Seeking to build commitment to a response by gradually moving toward a consensus solution.

The governing principle seems to be to make a final decision as late as possible (1) to bring as much information to bear as needed, (2) to let the situation clarify enough to know what to do, and (3) to allow the various political constituencies and power bases within the organization to move toward a consensus on a solution. Executives are often wary of committing themselves to a major change too quickly because it limits the time for further fact-finding and analysis, discourages others from asking questions that need to be raised, and precludes thorough airing of all the options.

Corrective adjustments to strategy need not be just reactive, however. Proactive adjustments can improve the strategy or its implementation. The distinctive feature of a proactive adjustment is that it arises from management initiatives rather than forced reactions. Successful strategy managers employ a variety of proactive tactics:[40]

Strategy leaders should be proactive as well as reactive in reshaping strategy and its implementation.

---

1. Commissioning studies to explore and amplify areas where they have a gut feeling that a need exists.

2. Shopping ideas among trusted colleagues and putting forth trial concepts.

3. Teaming people with different skills, interests, and experiences and letting them push and tug on interesting ideas to expand the variety of approaches considered.

4. Contacting a variety of people inside and outside the organization to sample viewpoints, probe, and listen, thereby trying to get early warning signals of impending problems/issues and deliberating short-circuiting all the careful screens of information flowing up from below.

5. Stimulating proposals for improvement from lower levels, encouraging the development of competing ideas and approaches, and letting the momentum for change come from below, with final choices postponed until it is apparent which option best matches the organization's situation.

6. Seeking options and solutions that go beyond extrapolations from the status quo.

7. Accepting and committing to partial steps forward as a way of building comfort levels before proceeding.

8. Managing the politics of change to promote managerial consensus and solidify management's commitment to whatever course of action is chosen.

The process leaders use to choose adjusting actions is essentially the same for proactive changes as for reactive changes; they sense needs, gather information, amplify understanding and awareness, put forth trial concepts, develop options, explore the pros and cons, test proposals, generate partial solutions, empower champions, build a managerial consensus, and formally adopt an agreed-on course of action.[41] The ultimate managerial prescription may have been given by Rene McPherson, former CEO at Dana Corporation. Speaking to a class of students at Stanford, he said: "You just keep pushing. You just keep pushing. I made every mistake that could be made. But I just kept pushing."[42]

All this, once again, highlights the fundamental nature of strategic management: The job of formulating and implementing strategy is not one of steering a clear-cut, linear course where the original strategy is implemented intact according to some preconceived and highly detailed plan. Rather, the job of formulating and implementing strategy requires (1) creatively adapting and reshaping strategy to unfolding events and (2) creatively applying whatever managerial techniques are needed to align internal activities and attitudes with the strategy. The process is interactive, with much looping and recycling to fine-tune and adjust visions, objectives, strategies, and implementation approaches in a continuously evolving process where the conceptually separate acts of crafting and implementating strategy blur and join together.

The action menu for implementing strategy is thus expansive, sweeping broadly across virtually every aspect of administrative and managerial work. Because each instance of strategy implementation occurs under different organizational circumstances, a strategy-implementer's action agenda must always be situation-specific—there is no neat, generic procedure to follow. Moreover, as we said at the beginning, implementing strategy is an action-oriented, make-things-happen task that tests a manager's ability to lead and direct organizational change, create or reinvent business processes, manage people, and achieve performance targets. If you now better understand the nature of the challenge, the range of available approaches, and the matters that need to be considered, then we will look upon our discussion in these last three chapters as a success.

Notes

CHAPTER 2

1. Derek F Abell, *Defining the Business: The Starting Point of Strategic Planning* (Englewood Cliffs, NJ: Prentice Hall, 1980), p. 169.

2. Coca-Cola's foray into wines was not viewed as successful enough to warrant continuation; the division was sold about five years after initial acquisition.

3. Tom Peters, *Thriving on Chaos,* (New York: Harper & Row, Perennial Library Edition, 1988), pp. 486–87.

4. The literature of management is filled with references to *goals* and *objectives*. These terms are used in a variety of ways, many of them conflicting. Some writers use the term *goals* to refer to the long-run results an organization seeks to achieve, and *objectives* to refer to immediate, short-run performance targets. Some writers reverse the usage, others use the terms interchangeably, and still others use the term *goals* to refer to broad organizationwide performance targets and *objectives* to designate specific targets set by subordinate managers in response to the broader, more inclusive goals of the whole organization. In our view, little is gained from semantic distinctions between *goals* and *objectives;* the important thing is to recognize that the results an enterprise seeks to attain vary both in scope and in time perspective. Nearly always, organizations need to have broad and narrow performance targets for both the near-term and long-term. It is inconsequential which targets are called goals and which are called objectives. To avoid a semantic jungle, we will use the single term *objectives* to refer to the performance targets and results an organization seeks to attain. We will use the adjectives *long-range* (or *long-run*) and *short-range* (or *short-run*) to identify the relevant time frame, and we will try to describe objectives in words that indicate their intended scope and level in the organization.

5. The concept of strategic intent is described in more detail in Gary Hamel and C K Pralahad, "Strategic Intent," *Harvard Business Review* 89, no. 3 (May–June 1989), pp. 63–76. This section draws upon their pioneering discussion.

6. Peter F Drucker, *Management: Tasks, Responsibilities, Practices* (New York: Harper & Row, 1974), p. 100. See also Charles H Granger, "The Hierarchy of Objectives," *Harvard Business Review* 42, no. 3 (May–June 1963), pp. 63–74.

7. Henry Mintzberg, "The Strategy Concept II: Another Look at Why Organizations Need Strategies," *California Management Review* 30, no. 1 (Fall 1987), pp. 25–32.

8. Functional managers can sometimes be more interested in doing what is best for their own areas, in building their own empire, and in consolidating their personal power and organizational influence than in cooperating with other functional managers to unify behind the overall business strategy. Consequently, it is easy for functional area support strategies to get at cross purposes, thereby forcing the business-level general manager to expend time and energy refereeing functional strategy conflicts and building support for a more unified approach.

9. David T Kollat, Roger D Blackwell, and James F Robeson, *Strategic Marketing* (New York: Holt, Rinehart & Winston, 1972), p. 24.

10. See, for instance, William D Guth and Renato Tagiuri, "Personal Values and Corporate Strategy," *Harvard Business Review* 43, no. 5 (September–October 1965), pp. 123–32; Kenneth R Andrews, *The Concept of Corporate Strategy,* 3rd ed (Homewood, IL: Richard D. Irwin, 1987), chap. 4; and Richard F Vancil, "Strategy Formulation in Complex Organizations," *Sloan Management Review* 17, no. 2 (Winter 1986), pp. 4–5.

11. Andrews, *The Concept of Corporate Strategy,* p. 63.

12. Sam Walton with John Huey, *Sam Walton: Made in America* (New York: Doubleday, 1992), and John P Kotter and James L Heskett, *Corporate Culture and Performance* (New York: The Free Press, 1992), pp. 17 and 36.

13. Kotter and Heskett, *Corporate Culture and Performance,* pp. 60–61.

14. For another example of the impact of values and beliefs, see Richard T Pascale, "Perspectives on Strategy: The Real Story behind Honda's Success," in Glenn Carroll and David Vogel, eds., *Strategy and Organization: A West Coast Perspective* (Marshfield, MA: Pitman Publishing, 1984), p. 60.

15. Harry Downs, "Business Ethics: The Stewardship of Power," working paper provided to authors.

16. Ibid.

17. Ibid.

18. This discussion is based on David R Brodwin and L J Bourgeois, "Five Steps to Strategic Action," in Glenn Carroll and David Vogel, eds., *Strategy and Organization: A West Coast Perspective* (Marshfield, MA: Pitman Publishing, 1984) pp. 168–78.

CHAPTER 3

1. For a thoroughgoing treatment of the five-forces model by its originator, see Michael E Porter, *Competitive Strategy: Techniques for Analyzing Industries and Competitors* (New York: Free Press, 1980), chap. 1.

2. These indicators of what to look for in evaluating the intensity of intercompany rivalry are based on Porter, *Competitive Strategy,* pp. 17–21.

3. Michael E Porter, "How Competitive Forces Shape Strategy," *Harvard Business Review* 57, no. 2 (March–April 1979) p. 138.

4. Porter, *Competitive Strategy,* pp. 7–17.

5. Porter, "How Competitive Forces Shape Strategy," p. 140, and Porter, *Competitive Strategy,* pp. 14–15.

6. Porter, "How Competitive Forces Shape Strategy," p. 142, and Porter, *Competitive Strategy,* pp. 23–24.

7. Porter, *Competitive Strategy,* p. 10.

8. Ibid., pp. 27–28.

9. Ibid., pp. 24–27.

10. For a more extended discussion of the problems with the life cycle hypothesis, see Porter, *Competitive Strategy,* pp. 157–62.

11. Ibid., p. 162.

12. What follows draws on the discussion in Porter, *Competitive Strategy,* pp. 164–183.

13. For further discussion of the nature and use of environmental scanning, see Roy Amara and Andrew J Lipinski, *Business Planning for an Uncertain Future: Scenarios and Strategies* (New York: Pergamon Press, 1983); Harold E Klein and Robert U Linneman, "Environmental Assessment: An International Study of Corporate Practice," *Journal of Business Strategy* 5, no. 1 (Summer 1984), pp. 55–75; and Arnoldo C Hax and Nicolas S Majluf, *The Strategy Concept and Process* (Englewood Cliffs, NJ: Prentice Hall, 1991), chaps. 5 and 8.

14. Porter, *Competitive Strategy,* chap. 7.

15. Ibid., pp. 129–30.

16. Ibid., pp. 152–54.

17. Ibid., pp. 130, 132–38, and 154–55.

CHAPTER 4

1. For a fuller discussion of the core competence concept, see C K Prahalad and Gary Hamel, "The Core Competence of the Corporation," *Harvard Business Review* 90, no. 3 (May–June 1990), pp. 79–93.

2. Value chains and strategic cost analysis are described at greater length in Michael E Porter, *Competitive Advantage* (New York: Free Press, 1985), chaps. 2 and 3; Robin Cooper and Robert S Kaplan, "Measure Costs Right: Make the Right Decisions, *Harvard Business Review* 66, no. 5 (September–October 1988), pp. 96–103; and John K Shank and Vijay Govindarajan, *Strategic Cost Management* (New York: The Free Press, 1993), especially chaps 2–6 and 10.

3. M Hegert and D Morris, "Accounting Data for Value Chain Analysis," *Strategic Management Journal* 10 (1989), p. 183.

4. Porter, *Competitive Advantage,* p. 34.

5. Hegert and Morris, "Accounting Data for Value Chain Analysis," p. 180.

6. For discussions of the accounting challenges in calculating the costs of value chain activities, see Shank and Govindarajan, *Strategic Cost Management,* pp. 62–72, and chap. 5, and M Hegert and D Morris, "Accounting Data for Value Chain Analysis," pp. 175–88.

7. Porter, *Competitive Advantage,* p. 45.

8. For a discussion of activity-based cost accounting, see Cooper and Kaplan, "Measure Costs Right: Make the Right Decisions," pp. 96–103; Shank and Govindarajan, *Strategic Cost Management,* chap. 11; and Terence P Paré, "A New Tool for Managing Costs," *Fortune,* June 14, 1993, pp. 124–29.

9. Shank and Govindarajan, *Strategic Cost Management,* p. 62.

10. Benchmarking involves more than just comparing companies' costs of performing an activity, however; the ultimate objective is to understand what the best practices in performing an activity are, to learn how lower costs are actually achieved, and to take action to improve a company's cost competitiveness whenever benchmarking reveals that the costs of performing an activity are out of line with what other companies (competitors or noncompetitors) have been able to achieve successfully. See Gregory H. Watson, *Strategic Benchmarking* (New York: John Wiley, 1993). See also Alexandra Biesada, "Strategic Benchmarking," *Financial World,*

September 29, 1992, pp. 30–38.

11. Jeremy Main, "How to Steal the Best Ideas Around," *Fortune,* October 19, 1992, pp. 102–3.

12. Main, "How to Steal the Best Ideas Around," p. 104, and Biesada, "Strategic Benchmarking," p. 34.

13. Shank and Govindarajan, *Strategic Cost Management,* p. 50.

14. Porter, *Competitive Advantage,* chap. 3.

15. Ibid.

16. Ibid.

17. James Brian Quinn, *Intelligent Enterprise* (New York: The Free Press, 1993), p. 54.

18. Quinn, *Intelligent Enterprise,* p. 34.

CHAPTER 5

1. The definitive work on this subject is Michael E Porter, *Competitive Advantage* (New York: Free Press, 1985). The treatment in this chapter draws heavily on Porter's pioneering contribution.

2. The classification scheme is an adaptation of one presented in Michael E Porter, *Competitive Strategy: Techniques for Analyzing Industries and Competitors* (New York: Free Press, 1980), chap. 2 and especially pp. 35–39 and 44–46.

3. Porter, *Competitive Advantage,* p. 97.

4. This listing and explanation is condensed from Porter, *Competitive Advantage,* pp. 70–107.

5. A firm can improve its capacity utilization by *(a)* serving a mix of accounts having peak volumes spread throughout the year, *(b)* finding off-season uses for its products, *(c)* serving private-label customers that can intermittently use the excess capacity, *(d)* selecting buyers with stable demands or demands that are counter to the normal peak/valley cycle, *(e)* letting competitors serve the buyer segments whose demands fluctuate the most, and *(f)* sharing capacity with sister units having a different pattern of needs.

6. Porter, *Competitive Advantage,* p. 124.

7. This discussion draws from Porter, *Competitive Advantage,* pp. 138–42. Porter's insights here are particularly important to formulating differentiating strategies because they highlight the relevance of intangibles and signals.

8. Porter, *Competitive Advantage,* pp. 160–62.

9. Ian C MacMillan, "How Long Can You Sustain a Competitive Advantage," reprinted in Liam Fahey, *The Strategic Planning Management Reader* (Englewood Cliffs, NJ: Prentice Hall, 1989), pp. 23–24.

10. Ian C. MacMillan, "Controlling Competitive Dynamics by Taking Strategic Initiative," *The Academy of Management Executive* 2, no. 2 (May 1988), p. 111.

11. Philip Kotler and Ravi Singh, "Marketing Warfare in the 1980's," *Journal of Business Strategy* 1, no. 3 (Winter 1981), pp. 30–41; Philip Kotler, *Marketing Management,* 5th ed. (Englewood Cliffs, NJ: Prentice Hall, 1984), pp. 401–6; and Ian MacMillan, "Preemptive Strategies," *Journal of Business Strategy* 14, no. 2 (Fall 1983), pp. 16–26.

12. Kotler, *Marketing Management,* p. 402.

13. Kotler, *Marketing Management,* p. 403.

14. For a discussion of the use of surprise, see William E Rothschild, "Surprise and the Competitive Advantage," *Journal of Business Strategy* 4, no. 3 (Winter 1984), pp. 10–18.

15. As cited in Kotler, *Marketing Management,* p. 404.

16. For more details, see MacMillan, "How Business Strategists Can Use Guerrilla Warfare Tactics," pp. 63–65; Kathryn R Harrigan, *Strategic Flexibility* (Lexington, MA: Lexington Books, 1985), pp. 30–45; and Liam Fahey, "Guerrlla Strategy: The Hit-and-Run Attack," in Fahey, *The Strategic Management Planning Reader;* pp. 194–97.

17. The use of preemptive moves is treated comprehensively in MacMillan, "Preemptive Strategies," pp. 16–26. What follows in this section is based on MacMillan's article.

18. Kotler, *Marketing Management,* p. 400.

19. Porter, *Competitive Advantage,* p. 518.

20. Ibid., pp. 520–22.

21. For more details, see MacMillan, "Controlling Competitive Dynamics," pp. 112–16.

22. Porter, *Competitive Advantage,* pp. 489–494.

23. Ibid., pp. 495–97. The listing here is selective; Porter offers a greater number of options.

24. See Kathryn R Harrigan, "Matching Vertical Integration Strategies to Competitive Conditions," *Strategic Management Journal* 7 no. 6 (November–December 1986), pp. 535–56; for a fuller discussion of the advantages and disadvantages of vertical integration, see Kathryn R Harrigan, *Strategic Flexibility* (Lexington, MA: Lexington Books, 1985), p. 162.

25. Porter, *Competitive Strategy,* pp. 232–33.

CHAPTER 6

1. *Michael E Porter, *Competitive Strategy,* (New York: Free Press, 1980), pp. 216–23.

2. Charles W Hofer and Dan Schendel, *Strategy Formulation: Analytical Concepts* (St. Paul, MN: West Publishing, 1978), pp. 164–65.

3. Phillip Kotler, *Marketing Management,* 5th ed. (Englewood Cliffs, NJ: Prentice Hall, 1984) p. 366, and Porter, *Competitive Strategy,* chap. 10.

4. Hofer and Schendel, *Strategy Formulation,* pp. 164–65.

5. Porter, *Competitive Strategy,* pp. 238–240.

6. The following discussion draws on Porter, *Competitive Strategy,* pp. 241–46.

7. R G Hamermesh and S B Silk, "How to Compete in Stagnant Industries," *Harvard Business Review* 57, no. 5 (September–October 1979), p. 161.

8. Ibid., p. 162.

9. Ibid., p. 165.

10. This section is adapted from Porter, *Competitive Strategy,* chap. 9.

11. C K Prahalad and Yves L Doz, *The Multinational Mission,* (New York: Free Press, 1987), p. 60.

12. Michael E Porter, *The Competitive Advantage of Nations* (New York: Free Press, 1990), pp. 53–54.

13. Porter, *The Competitive Advantage of Nations,* p. 61.

14. Porter, *The Competitive Advantage of Nations,* p. 54.

15. Porter, *The Competitive Advantage of Nations,* p. 57.

16. Porter, *The Competitive Advantage of Nations,* p. 65. Also see Kenichi Ohmae, "The Global Logic of Strategic Alliances," *Harvard Business Review* 89, no. 2 (March–April 1989), pp. 143–54.

17. Porter, *The Competitive Advantage of Nations,* p. 66; also see Jeremy Main, "Making Global Alliances Work," *Fortune,* December 17, 1990, pp. 121–26.

18. Jeremy Main, "Making Global Alliances Work," p. 125.

19. Ibid.

20. Prahalad and Doz, *The Multinational Mission,* p. 52.

21. Prahalad and Doz, *The Multinational Mission,* p. 61.

22. Kotler, *Marketing Management,* chap. 23; Michael E Porter, *Competitive Advantage,* (New York: Free Press, 1985), chap. 14; and Ian C. MacMillan, "Seizing Competitive Initiative," *The Journal of Business Strategy* 2, no. 4 (Spring 1982), pp. 43–57.

23. Porter, *Competitive Advantage,* p. 514.

24. For more details, see Kotler, *Marketing Management,* pp. 397–412; RG Hamermesh, MJ Anderson, Jr., and JE Harris, "Strategies for Low Market Share Businesses," *Harvard Business Review* 56, no. 3 (May–June 1978), pp. 95–102; and Porter, *Competitive Advantage,* chap. 15.

25. Hamermesh, Anderson, and Harris, "Strategies for Low Market Share Businesses," p. 102.

26. Phillip Kotler, "Harvesting Strategies for Weak Products," *Business Horizons* 21, no. 5 (August 1978), pp. 17–18.

27. William K Hall, "Survival Strategies in a Hostile Environment," *Harvard Business Review* 58, no. 5, (September–October 1980), pp. 75–85.

CHAPTER 7

1. C Roland Christensen, Norman A Berg, and Malcolm S Salter, *Policy Formulation and Administration,* 7th ed. (Homewood, IL: Richard D. Irwin, 1976), pp. 16–18.

2. Michael E Porter, "From Competitive Advantage to Corporate Strategy," *Harvard Business Review* 45, no. 3 (May–June 1987), pp. 46–49.

3. Michael E Porter, *Competitive Strategy: Techniques for Analyzing Industries and Competitors* (New York: Free Press, 1980), p. 354–55.

4. Porter, *Competitive Strategy,* pp. 344–45.

5. Peter Drucker, *Management: Tasks, Responsibilities, Practices* (New York: Harper & Row, 1974), pp. 720–24. Strategic alliances offer much the same benefits as joint ventures, but represent a weaker commitment to entering a new business.

6. Porter, *Competitive Strategy,* p. 340.

7. Michael E Porter, *Competitive Advantage* (New York: Free Press, 1985), pp. 318–19 and pp. 337–53; Kenichi Ohmae, *The Mind of the Strategist* (New York: Penguin Books, 1983), pp. 121–24; and Porter, "From Competitive Advantage to Corporate Strategy," pp. 53–57.

8. Carter F Bales, "Strategic Control: The President's Paradox," *Business Horizons* 20, no. 4 (August 1977), p. 17.

9. Of course, management may be willing to assume the risk that trouble will not strike before it has had time to learn the business well enough to bail it out of almost any difficulty. See Drucker, *Management,* p. 709.

10. Drucker, *Management,* p. 767. Research studies in the interval since 1974, when Drucker made his observation, uphold his conclu-

sion—on the whole, broadly diversified firms do not outperform less-diversified firms over the course of the business cycle.

11. Drucker, *Management*, pp. 692–693.

12. Drucker, *Management*, p. 709.

13. Drucker, *Management*, p. 94.

14. Ibid., p. 719.

15. CK Prahalad and Yves L Doz, *The Multinational Mission* (New York: Free Press, 1987), p. 2.

16. Ibid., p. 15.

17. Yves L Doz, *Strategic Management in Multinational Companies* (New York: Pergamon Press, 1985), p. 1.

18. Ibid., pp. 2–3.

19. Pralahad and Doz, *The Multinational Mission*, pp. 62–63.

20. Ibid.

21. Ibid. p. 64.

22. Ibid.

CHAPTER 8

1. For the original presentation, see Bruce D Henderson, "The Experience Curve—Reviewed. IV. The Growth Share Matrix of the Product Portfolio," Perspectives No. 135, The Boston Consulting Group, Boston, MA, 1973. For an excellent chapter-length treatment of the use of the BCG growth-share matrix in strategic portfolio analysis, see Arnoldo C Hax and Nicolas S Majluf, *Strategic Management: An Integrative Perspective* (Englewood Cliffs, NJ: Prentice Hall, 1984), chap. 7.

2. For two discussions of the strategic importance of the experience curve, see Pankoy Ghemawat, "Building Strategy on the Experience Curve," *Harvard Business Review* 64, no. 2 (March–April 1985), pp. 143–49, and Bruce D Henderson, "The Application and Misapplication of the Experience Curve,"

Journal of Business Strategy 4, no. 3 (Winter 1984), pp. 3–9.

3. Derek F Abell and John S Hammond, *Strategic Market Planning* (Englewood Cliffs, NJ: Prentice Hall, 1979), p. 212.

4. For an expanded treatment, see Michael G Allen, "Diagramming GE's Planning for What's WATT," in *Corporate Planning: Techniques and Applications*, ed. Robert J. Allio and Malcolm W Pennington (New York: AMACOM, 1979), and Hax and Majluf, *Strategic Management*, chap. 8.

5. Essentially the same procedure is used in company situation analysis to do a competitive strength assessment (see Table 4–3 in Chapter 4). The only difference is that in the GE methodology the same set of competitive strength factors are used for every industry to provide a common benchmark for making comparisons across industries. In strategic analysis at the business level, the strength measures are *always* industry-specific, never generic generalizations.

6. At General Electric, each business actually ended up in one of five types of categories: (1) *High-growth potential* businesses deserving top investment priority, (2) *Stable base* businesses deserving steady reinvestment to maintain position, (3) *Support* businesses deserving periodic investment funding, (4) *Selective pruning or rejuvenation* businesses deserving reduced investment funding, and (5) *Venture* businesses deserving heavy R&D investment.

7. Charles W Hofer and Dan Schendel, *Strategy Formulation: Analytical Concepts* (St. Paul, MN: West Publishing, 1978), p. 33.

8. Ibid., p. 34. This approach to business portfolio analysis was reportedly first used in actual practice

by consultants at Arthur D Little, Inc. For a full-scale review of this portfolio matrix approach, see Hax and Majluf, *Strategic Management*, chap. 9.

9. Hofer and Schendel, *Strategy Formulation*, p. 80.

10. Michael E Porter, *Competitive Advantage* (New York: Free Press, 1985), chap. 9.

11. Barry Hedley, "Strategy and the Business Portfolio," *Long Range Planning* 10, no. 1 (February 1977), p. 13; and Hofer and Schendel, *Strategy Formulation*, pp. 82–86.

12. Hofer and Schendel, *Strategy Formulation*, pp. 93–100.

13. For an excellent discussion of the benefits of alliances among competitors in global industries, see Kenichi Ohmae, "The Global Logic of Strategic Alliances," *Harvard Business Review* 67, no. 2 (March–April 1989), pp. 143–54.

14. Porter, *Competitive Advantage*, pp. 370–71.

15. Ibid., p. 371.

16. Ibid., pp. 58 and 196.

CHAPTER 9

2. For an analytical framework in top management team analysis, see Donald C Hambrick, "The Top Management Team: Key to Strategic Success," *California Management Review* 30, no. 1 (Fall 1987), pp. 88–108.

3. James Brian Quinn, *Intelligent Enterprise* (New York: Free Press, 1992), p. 76.

4. Ibid.

5. Ibid., pp. 52–53, 55, 73, and 76.

6. Ibid., p. 73.

7. Ibid.

8. Ibid., pp. 73–74.

9. Peter F Drucker, *Management: Tasks, Responsibilities, Practices*

(New York: Harper & Row, 1974), pp. 530, 535.

10. Michael Hammer and James Champy, *Reengineering the Corporation* (New York: Harper Business, 1993), pp. 26–27.

11. Ibid., p. 26–27.

12. Ibid.

13. Quinn, *Intelligent Enterprise*, p. 32.

14. Ibid., p. 37.

15. Ibid., pp. 33 and 89.

16. Ibid., pp. 39–40.

17. Ibid., p. 43.

18. Ibid., p. 47.

19. Alfred Chandler, *Strategy and Structure* (Cambridge, MA: MIT Press, 1962). Although the stress here is on matching structure to strategy, it is worth noting that structure can and does influence the choice of strategy. A good strategy must be doable. When an organization's present structure is so far out of line with the requirements of a particular strategy that the organization would have to be turned upside down to implement it, the strategy may not be doable and should not be given further consideration. In such cases, structure shapes the choice of strategy. The point here, however, is that once strategy is chosen, structure must be modified to fit the strategy if, in fact, an approximate fit does not already exist. Any influences of structures on strategy should, logically, come before the point of strategy selection, rather than after it.

20. Hammer and Champy, *Reengineering the Corporation,* p. 28.

21. Ibid., p. 66.

22. Ibid., pp. 66–67.

23. Raymond Corey and Steven H Star, *Organization Strategy, A Marketing Approach* (Boston: Harvard Business School, 1971) pp. 23–24.

24. William K Hall, "SBUs: Hot, New Topic in the Management of Diversification," *Business Horizons* 21, no. 1 (February 1978), p. 19. For an excellent discussion of the problems of implementing the SBU concept at 13 companies, see Richard A Bettis and William K Hall, "The Business Portfolio Approach—Where It Falls Down in Practice," *Long Range Planning* 16, no. 2 (April 1983), pp. 95–104.

25. For two excellent critiques of matrix organizations, see Stanley M Davis and Paul R Lawrence, "Problems of Matrix Organizations," *Harvard Business Review* 56, no. 3 (May–June 1978), pp. 131–42, and Erik W Larson and David H Gobeli, "Matrix Management: Contradictions and Insights," *California Management Review* 29, no. 4 (Summer 1987), pp. 126–38.

26. Ibid., p. 132.

27. Thomas J Peters and Robert H Waterman, Jr., *In Search of Excellence* (New York: Harper & Row, 1982), pp. 306–7.

28. Peters and Waterman, *In Search of Excellence,* pp. 127–32.

29. Quinn, *Intelligent Enterprise*, p. 163.

30. "Can Jack Smith Fix GM?" *Business Week,* November 1, 1993, pp. 130–31.

31. Hammer and Champy, *Reengineering the Corporation,* pp. 62–63.

32. Drucker *Management,* pp. 601–2.

33. Evidence is contained in the scores of examples reported in Tom Peters, *Liberation Management* (New York: Knopf, 1992), Quinn, *Intelligent Enterprise,* and Hammer and Champy, *Reengineering the Corporation.*

34. Quinn, *Intelligent Enterprise,* p. 162.

35. T Stuart, "GE Keeps Those Ideas Coming," *Fortune,* August 12, 1991. For other examples, see Gene Hall, Jim Rosenthal, and Judy Wade, "How to Make Reengineering Really Work," *Harvard Business Review* 71, no. 6 (November–December 1993), pp. 119–31.

CHAPTER 10

1. Thomas Peters and Robert Waterman, *In Search of Excellence* (New York: Harper & Row, Publisher, 1980), p. 125.

2. Peters and Waterman, *In Search of Excellence,* p. 65.

3. Judy D Olian and Sara L Rynes, "Making Total Quality Work: Aligning Organizational Processes, Performance Measures, and Stakeholders," *Human Resource Management* 30, no. 3 (Fall 1991), p. 303.

4. Ibid.

5. See, for example, Gene Hall, Jim Rosenthal, and Judy Wade, "How to Make Reengineering Really Work," *Harvard Business Review* 71, no. 6 (November–December 1993), pp. 119–31.

6. Olian and Rynes, "Making Total Quality Work," pp. 305–6 and 310–11.

7. James Brian Quinn, *Intelligent Enterprise* (New York: Free Press, 1992) pp. 114–15.

8. Ibid., p. 181.

9. Ibid., p. 186.

10. Ibid., p. 111.

11. Boris Yavitz and William H Newman, *Strategy in Action* (New York: Free Press, 1982), p. 209–10.

12. Drucker, *Management,* pp. 498–504; Harold Koontz, "Management Control: A Suggested Formulation of Principles," *California Management Review* 2, no. 2 (Winter 1959), pp. 50–55; and William H Sihler, "Toward Better Management Control Systems," *California*

Management Review 14, no. 2 (Winter 1971), pp. 33–39.

13. Alfie Kohn, ''Rethinking Rewards,'' *Harvard Business Review* 71, no. 6 (November–December 1993), p. 49.

14. Anthony Sampson, *The Sovereign State of ITT* (New York: Stein and Day, 1973), p. 132.

15. Quoted in John P Kotter and James L Heskett, *Corporate Culture and Performance* (New York: Free Press, 1992), p. 91.

16. Tom Peters and Nancy Austin, *A Passion for Excellence* (New York: Random House, 1985), p. xix.

CHAPTER 11

1. Tracy Goss, Richard Pascale, and Anthony Athos, ''Risking the Present for a Powerful Future,'' *Harvard Business Review* 71, no. 6 (November–December 1993), pp. 101–2.

2. John P Kotter and James L Heskett, *Corporate Culture and Performance* (New York: Free Press, 1992), p. 7.

3. Ibid., pp. 7–8.

4. Ibid., p. 5.

5. ''A Business and Its Beliefs,'' McKinsey Foundation Lecture, cited in Kotter and Heskett, *Corporate Culture and Performance*, p. 17.

6. Kotter and Heskett, *Corporate Culture and Performance*, p. 5.

7. Ibid., pp. 15–16.

8. Robert H Waterman, Jr., ''The Seven Elements of Strategic Fit,'' *Journal of Business Strategy* 2, no. 3 (Winter 1982), p. 70.

9. Terrence E Deal and Allen A Kennedy, *Corporate Cultures* (Reading, MA: Addison-Wesley, 1982), p. 22.

10. Vijay Sathe, *Culture and Related Corporate Realities* (Homewood, IL: Richard D. Irwin, 1985).

11. Kotter and Heskett, *Corporate Culture and Performance*, chap. 6.

12. Ibid., p. 68.

13. This section draws heavily from Kotter and Heskett, *Corporate Culture and Performance*, chap. 4.

14. Ibid., p. 52.

15. Ibid., p. 50.

16. Judy D Olian and Sara L Rynes, ''Making Total Quality Work: Aligning Organizational Processes, Performance Measures, and Stakeholders,'' *Human Resource Management* 30, no. 3 (Fall 1991), p. 324.

17. Ibid.

18. The Business Roundtable, *Corporate Ethics: A Prime Asset*, February 1988, pp. 4–10.

19. Ibid., p. 7.

20. Peters and Waterman, *In Search of Excellence*, pp. xviii, 240, and 269, and Peters and Austin, *A Passion for Excellence*, pp. 304–7.

21. Peter Drucker, *Management: Tasks, Responsibilities, Practices* (New York: Harper & Row, 1974), p. 457.

22. Ibid., pp. xx, 15, 120–23, 191, 242–43, 246–47, 287–90. For an extensive report on the benefits of MBWA, see Thomas J Peters and Nancy Austin, *A Passion for Excellence* (New York: Random House, 1985), chaps. 2, 3, and 19.

23. Kotter and Heskett, *Corporate Culture and Performance*, p. 91.

24. Ibid., pp. 84, 144, and 148.

25. As quoted in Peters and Waterman, *In Search of Excellence*, p. 262.

26. Peters and Waterman, *In Search of Excellence*, chap. 9.

27. Warren Bennis, *The Unconscious Conspiracy: Why Leaders Can't Lead* (New York: AMACOM, 1987), p. 93.

28. Cited in Ann M Morrison, ''Trying to Bring GE to Life,'' *Fortune*, January 25, 1982, p. 52.

29. Cited in Peters and Waterman, *In Search of Excellence*, pp. 203–4.

30. For further discussion of this point see Abraham Zaleznik, ''Power and Politics in Organizational Life,'' *Harvard Business Review* 48, no. 3 (May–June 1970), pp. 47–60; R M Cyert, H A Simon, and D B Trow, ''Observation of a Business Decision,'' *Journal of Business*, October 1956, pp. 237–48; and James Brian Quinn, *Strategies for Change: Logical Incrementalism* (Homewood, IL: Richard D. Irwin, 1980).

31. Quinn, *Strategies for Change*, p. 68.

32. Sir Alastair Pilkington, Chairman, Pilkington Brothers, Ltd., cited in Quinn, *Strategies for Change*, p. 65.

33. Quinn, *Strategies for Change*, pp. 128–45.

34. Ibid., pp. 118–19.

35. Ibid., p. 205.

36. The Business Roundtable, *Corporate Ethics*, pp. 4–10.

37. Ibid.

38. Ibid.

39. Quinn, *Strategies for Change*, pp. 20–22.

40. Ibid., chap. 4.

41. Ibid., p. 146.

42. Cited in Peters and Waterman, *In Search of Excellence*, p. 319.

Index